"*The Whole Internet Catalog & User's Guide* will probably become the Internet user's bible because it provides comprehensive, easy instructions for those who want to get the most from this valuable electronic tool."

—*David J. Buerger, Editor, Communications week*

"*The Whole Internet User's Guide & Catalog* is currently THE definitive user guide to the Internet, and it frankly has no rivals. A simple recommendation—if you are interested in the Internet, buy it."

—*Jack Rickard, Editor, Boardwatch Magazine*

"*The Whole Internet User's Guide & Catalog* is the single best book on what's out there in the global electronic village. It does for the free Internet what Alfred Glossbrenner's books did for fee-based online databases. It's the first compendium on the world's largest computer network."

—*Greg Goode, Syndicated News Service*

"I recommend *The Whole Internet User's Guide & Catalog* very highly. Although there are many other competing works out there, this one covers almost everything anyone could want to know, is well written for both the novice and the experienced user, and is available now at a very reasonable price. All who are reading this review should have a copy on their desk, and a copy in their public, academic, or special library for reference by other potential users."

—*Dan Lester, Associate University Librarian, Boise State University*

"This is the kind of book that you get several extra copies of to give away when someone asks you 'What's Internet?' or to staff or colleagues when you want to give them the hint that they could be more effective in their work if they used Internet."

—*Anthony M. Rutkowski, SprintLink*

"In a word, it is a *must* for all Internet sites as a complement to much of the resource material and guides you would already have accumulated."

—*Dr. Ian Hoyle, Senior Research Scientist, BHP Research-Melbourne Laboratories*

"There is a new book out called *The Whole Internet* by Ed Krol. I highly recommend this book to anyone interested in learning more about the Internet, and be sure to look or me on page 325!!:):)"

—*Scott Yanoff, the "Yanoff list", Inet Services*

"I wasn't sure that an 'old hand' like me would learn much from an overview guidebook targeted at mere users, but there are whole chapters in here on subjects I've been meaning to find out about, such as gopher, wais, and www."

—*Steve Summit, Grizzled Internet Vet*

"Krol's style throughout the book is a breezy conversational style that is designed to not intimidate users but rather, make them feel at ease as they explore a potentially complex area."

—*Naor Wallach Newsbytes News Network*

"*The Whole Internet User's Guide & Catalog*, published by O'Reilly & Associates an prepared by Ed Krol, covers the basic utilities used to access the network and then guides the reader through Internet's 'databases of databases'. The book also covers how to find software and how to deal with network problems and other troublesome issues."

—*UNIX Review, October 1992*

"You can imagine that on Friday (the day I received *The Whole Internet*), the moment I laid it down, someone else was snapping it up. I had to guard it with my life! I think that pretty much speaks for itself."

—*Phil Draughon, Sr. Analyst, Distributed Systems, ACNS Networking*

THE WHOLE INTERNET

USER'S GUIDE & CATALOG

ED KROL

O'REILLY & ASSOCIATES, INC.
103 MORRIS STREET, SUITE A
SEBASTOPOL CA 95472
(800) 998-9938 • (707) 829-0515
EMAIL: *nuts@ora.com* OR *uunet!ora!nuts*

The Whole Internet User's Guide & Catalog
by Ed Krol

Editor: Mike Loukides

Printing History:

September 1992:	First Edition.
November 1992:	Minor corrections.
February 1993:	Minor corrections.

ISBN: 1-56592-025-2

TABLE OF CONTENTS

CHAPTER THREE

HOW THE INTERNET WORKS

CHAPTER FOUR

WHAT'S ALLOWED ON THE INTERNET?

CHAPTER SEVEN

ELECTRONIC MAIL   91

CHAPTER TWELVE

SEARCHING INDEXED DATABASES: WAIS   211

CHAPTER THIRTEEN

HYPERTEXT SPANNING THE INTERNET: WWW   227

CHAPTER FOURTEEN

OTHER APPLICATIONS_____243

CHAPTER FIFTEEN

DEALING WITH PROBLEMS _____261

FIGURES

TABLES

PREFACE

This is a book about the Internet, the world's largest computer network. It's aimed at the "garden variety" computer user: not the expert or the computer afficionado, just someone who has a job to get done. To those of us who have been using the Internet for a long time, a lot of what we discuss has become commonplace. But to get a sense for what the Internet is, and why this book is important, we need to take a few steps back.

Ten or twelve years ago, a minor revolution occurred when personal computers became common. Within a few years everyone had a computer at home, or in the office. And, to be honest, most people thought that was adequate: a little help doing budget planning, a nice word processor for writing letters, and we were satisfied. Some visionaries talked about computers as "information appliances": you could use your home or office computer to connect to the national news services, get stock reports, do library searches, even read professional journals or literary classics—but, at the time, these were far-reaching ideas.

Well, time has passed since computers first moved from behind the "glass wall" into our offices and homes. In those dozen or so years, another revolution, arguably more important than the first, has taken place. And that revolution was computer networking. Personal computers are great, but computers become something special when they're connected to each other.

With the Internet, networking has "come of age." The information resources that visionaries talked about in the early 80's are not just "research realities" that a few advanced thinkers can play with in some lab—they're "real life" realities that you can tap into from your home. Once you're connected to the Internet, you have instant access to an almost indescribable wealth of information. You have to pay for some of it, sure—but most of it is available for free. Through electronic mail and bulletin boards (called "news groups" in Internet-lingo), you can use a different kind of resource: a worldwide supply of knowledgeable people, some of whom are certain to share your interests, no matter how obscure. It's easy to find a discussion group on almost any topic, or to find some people interested in forming a new discussion group. While free advice is often worth what you pay for it, there are also lots of well-informed experts who are more than willing to be helpful.

Well, then, where do you start? Getting a handle on the Internet is a lot like grabbing a handful of Jello—the more firm you think your grasp is, the more oozes down your arm. You don't need to deal with Jello in this manner to eat it, you just need the right tool: a spoon. And you need to dig in and start eating. The same is true of the Internet. You don't need to be an expert in telephone lines, data communications, and network protocols for it to be useful. And no amount of gushing about the Net's limitless resources will make the Internet useful. You just need to know how to use some tools, and to start working with them.

As for uses, we've got millions of them. They range from the scholarly (you can read works analyzing Dante's *Divine Comedy*); to the useful (you can look at agricultural market reports); to the recreational (you can get ski reports for Aspen); to the humorous ("How do I cook Jello?"). It is also an amazing tool for collaboration: working with other people on your own "magnum opus."

In a sense, the existence of this book is a tribute to the power and usefulness of the Internet. Mike Loukides, the editor, and I met via electronic mail. Network users were clamoring to get me to update a help guide I wrote a long time ago, "The Hitchikers Guide to the Internet." I was about to volunteer when Mike sent me an electronic mail message and asked "How about doing it as a book?" This spurred a number of messages about outlines and time frames until both were finalized. The legalities and contracts were handled by the Postal Service; electronic contracts were too commercial for the Internet at the time, and are still too high-tech for courts to deal with. And we were on our way.

Shortly thereafter, I was shipped macro libraries to use in production, and began shipping chapters to Mike, all by e-mail. He would annotate, change and ship them back to me by the same means. Occasionally, we would trade file directories, screen images, and illustrations. Except for the final review copies and illustrations, everything was handled via the Internet. The whole process was accomplished with less than ten telephone calls.

Think for a minute about what this means. Traditional Post Office service between Illinois (where I live) and Connecticut (where Mike lives) takes three days. If you want to pay extra, you can use a courier service and cut the time down to one day. But I can ship the entire book to Mike over the Internet in a few minutes.

I also gathered the information in the *Resource Catalog* without having to leave home. I watched news groups, followed e-mail discussions, and used various tools to acquire the information for the catalog, all of which are explained in the book.

Before including any of the resources, I verified that they really existed by reaching out across the network and touching them.

Now, a year after it all began, there is this book. I still have not met anyone who works for O'Reilly and Associates, in person. I'd certainly like to some day—they are an amazingly professional group helping me through my first book.

Audience

This book is intended for anyone who wants access to the Internet's tremendous resources. It's a book for professionals, certainly, but not computer professionals. It's designed for those who want to use the network, but who don't want to become a professional networker in order to use it. If you're a biologist, or a librarian, or a lawyer, or a clergyman, or a high school teacher, or _____ (fill in your profession here), there's a lot of material and data available that will help you do your job. At the same time, you'll probably find recent Supreme Court opinions or chromosome maps much more interesting than the network itself. You want to use the network as a tool; you don't want to make the network your life. If this description fits you, you need this book. It will get you started and point you towards some interesting resources. If, after this, you find that networking becomes your life—well, that's your decision. The Internet has a way of becoming habit forming.

Although I've based our examples on UNIX, this book does not assume that you're a UNIX user. We had to choose some common ground; UNIX systems are prevalent on the Internet, so it was a logical choice. However, the same utilities are available for virtually any operating system; and, with minor variations, you'll find that they work the same way. If you're using DOS, a Macintosh, VAX/VMS, or some other kind of computer, please pardon the UNIX bias—but you really shouldn't find it a problem.

Very specifically: while writing this book, my model audience was a new graduate student in some non-technical discipline (i.e., not computer science or any form of engineering) who needed to use the Internet to do research. Of course, this presumes an audience ranging from Italian scholars to sociologists to physicists, with a correspondingly wide range of computer experience. I do assume that you're computer literate—if you weren't you probably wouldn't even be looking at this book—and that you are familiar with *some* computer and its operating system, but not necessarily UNIX.

This book is also intended for the experienced network administrator: the guy whose job it is to keep a company's or campus's networks working reasonably well. No, you're not supposed to read it; you probably know everything in here already. (Maybe not, though. Check out the chapters on WAIS, **gopher**, and the World-Wide Web, three of the newest services.) If you have this job, you probably spend most of your time answering the same fifty questions. When a new crop of students or employees arrives, you might not get any work done for weeks. With any luck, this book answers most of their questions. From the beginning, we were trying to write a book that would answer as many questions as possible. If you are a network administrator, this book is intended for you—so you can give it away, or post a note on your door saying, "go to the bookstore, buy this book, and read it before bugging me!"

As with all Nutshell handbooks, O'Reilly and Associates is interested in hearing from readers. If you have any comments or suggestions, please send them to **nuts@ora.com**. (If you don't know what this means, read Chapter 7, *Electronic Mail.*)

Approaching This Book

Of course, there are many ways to approach the Internet; likewise, there are many ways to read this book. Here are a few suggestions. If you:

Are completely new to the Internet
> Start at the beginning and read to the end. You might want to pay particular attention to the *Resource Catalog*, which tells you what you'll find, and Appendix A, *Getting Connected to the Internet*, which tells you how to get connected. But, basically, you ought to read the entire book. If you want, you can skim Chapters 3 and 4, which explain how the Internet works, and what's allowed; but please revisit these later.

Are familiar with the Internet, but not a user
> Skip to Chapter 5; in this chapter, we start discussing the basic utilities that you use on the Internet.

Are an experienced Internet user
> Skip to Chapter 9. Chapters 9 through 13 discuss the newest tools to come on the scene: Archie, some newer "white pages" services, Gopher, WAIS, and the World-Wide Web. Even if you've been around for a while, you may want to brush up on these. If you're not familiar with these tools, you really should be.

Have used the Internet casually
> Read the first four chapters to get the background you may have missed; and then scan the Table of Contents for chapters whose topics are unfamiliar to you. If you do this, read the chapters in order because many of the newer facilities (Chapter 9 and above), build on each other.

Want to get connected to the Internet
> Look at Appendix A, which discusses various ways of getting a connection.

Want to know what's available before committing yourself
> Look at the *Resource Catalog.*

Are only interested in electronic mail and network news
> Read Chapters 7 and 8, which discuss the e-mail and news services. But—please, read the rest of the book, too. You don't know what you're missing.

Conventions

In this book, we use the following conventions:

- Command names are printed in **bold**; for example, **telnet** or **archie**.
- Names of services or protocols are printed in uppercase or with the initial letter capitalized; for example, TELNET or Archie.
- Input typed literally by the user is printed in **bold**; for example, **get host-table.txt**.
- Internet names and addresses are printed in **bold**; for example, **ora.com**.
- Filenames are printed in *italic*; for example, */etc/hosts*.
- Names of USENET news groups are printed in *italic*; for example, *rec.music.folk*.
- "Variables"—placeholders that the reader will replace with an actual value—are printed in *italic*. For example, in the command **ftp** *hostname*, you must substitute *hostname* for the name of some computer on the Internet.
- Within examples, output from the computer is printed in `constant width` type.
- Within examples, text typed literally by the user is printed in **`constant bold`** type.
- Within examples, variables are printed in `constant italic` type.
- Within examples, explanatory comments are often placed in *italic* type.

Acknowledgements

A whole host of people helped with this book. First and foremost is my wife Margaret. Without her support and help, it never would have come to pass. She read and corrected most of it, searched Gopher for resources, and tried things to see if my explanations really were sufficient for a computer professional to use the Internet. Also, she took over enough of the running of our home to give me time to devote to the project.

Next comes my daughter Molly, who did without me in many ways for the better part of a year while I was writing. (This is Molly's second experience with computing fame—she was the toddler with a penchant for emergency-off switches, after whom "Molly-guards" are named in the "Hackers Dictionary.")

Then there is Mike Loukides, the editor, project leader, confidence builder and cheerleader, who dragged me, sometimes kicking and screaming, to the finish line. In the beginning, Mike helped me to think through just what the book needed to contain, and then made sure that everything made it in. Near the end, when Tim O'Reilly asked us to beef up the coverage of a couple of topics, Mike did most of the restructuring and wrote a significant part of the new material.

Next are all the people at the University of Illinois who helped. George Badger, the head of the Computing and Communications Service Office, for the support I needed with the project. Beth Scheid for picking up some pieces of my real job while I was preoccupied with book-related problems. The real technical people, who answered some bizarre questions and made some of the examples possible: Charley Kline, Paul Pomes, Greg German, Lynn Ward, Albert Cheng, Sandy Seehusen, Bob Booth, Randy Cotton, Allan Tuchman, Bob Foertsch, and Ed Kubaitis. The faculty of the Graduate School of Library Science was also involved, especially Greg Newby, who had a number of suggestions about how to approach the searching tools of the Internet.

Two people were my test audience: Lisa German, a recent library science graduate, and Pat King, a then-neophyte system administrator. They knew little about the Internet when they began reading the book as it was written, chapter by chapter. They pointed out all the things that were used before explained or were just plain explained too technically. Lisa also spent many hours visiting most of the notable anonymous FTP servers on the Internet searching for resources. It's pretty amazing what someone with a knowledge of common cataloging words and phrases can do with Archie,* but I guess that's what librarians are trained to do.

A large group of people read the book checking for technical errors, inconsistencies, and "useful stuff that I left out." These included Eric Pearce, Robin Peek, Jerry Peek, Mitch Wright, Rick Adams, Tim Berners-Lee, Martyne Hallgren, and Jim Williams. The book would not be anywhere near as useful without their help.

The interior design of the book, which is a departure from O'Reilly & Associates' previous books, was sparked by a comment of Dale Dougherty's. He thought it a shame that the standard dry "technical book" interior didn't live up to the whimsical promise of Edie Freedman's cover. Tim O'Reilly picked up on that comment, and insisted on a redesign to make the book and catalog more accessible to a non-technical audience. Edie actually developed the design (with her usual flair) and selected all of the illustrations for both the chapter dividers and the catalog. Her design work was not just something that happened after the book was done, but an integral part of how it turned out. The design was then implemented in **troff** by Lenny Muellner, something no sane person should be asked to do. It included the illustrations of Chris Reilley and the text copy-edited by Rosanne Wagger, who corrected more typos than I thought existed. Together this crew turned a rough manuscript into a work of art.

Finally, I'd like to thank Karen Kolling for permission to reprint her recipe for Loubia (posted on the Net) in the *Resource Catalog*.

---

*A file search tool explained in Chapter 9, *Finding Software*.

## CHAPTER ONE

WHAT IS THIS BOOK ABOUT?

Something for Everyone
What You Will Learn
What You Need
What an Internet Connection Means
How This Book Is Organized

In the early 1900's, if you wanted to tinker with horseless carriages, you fell in with other tinkerers and learned by doing. There were no books about automobiles, no schools for would-be mechanics, no James Martin courses. The market was too small for these training aids. In addition, there were good reasons to fall in with a group of experts: early cars were so unreliable that they could hardly be called transportation. When your car broke down, you needed to fix it yourself, or have some good friends who could come to the rescue. You fiddled and asked questions of others. Soon you could answer questions for a novice. Eventually, you might become a highly regarded mechanic (in computing referred to as a "guru"). When you got to this level, your car might actually be useful transportation, not just an expensive hobby.

Seven years ago, the Internet was in much the same state. The network only had a few thousand users. All of its users either had ready access to experts, or were experts themselves. And they needed expertise—the network was slow and unreliable. Its major purpose was not to do anything useful, but to help people learn how to build and use networks.

In the past seven years, the number of Internet users has increased a thousand-fold. These people use the network for their daily work and play. They demand reliability, and don't want to be mechanics. They want to be chemists, librarians, meteorologists, kindergarten teachers . . . , who happen to use the network. So now they demand documentation. Something to read on the train to work to improve their job skills. They are computer-literate, but not network-literate. This book is about network literacy.

Something for Everyone

The usefulness of the Internet parallels the history of computing with a lag of about ten years. About ten years ago, personal computers brought computing from the realm of technical gurus to the general public: "the rest of us," as Apple said in their advertisements. The Internet is currently making the same transition.

As with personal computers (or, for that matter, automobiles), the Internet made the transition from an expert's plaything to an everyday tool through a "feedback loop." The network started to become easier to use—in part because the tools were better, in part because it was faster and more reliable. Of the people who were previously scared away from the Internet, the more venturesome started to use it. These new users created a demand for new resources and better tools. The old tools were improved, and new tools were developed to access new resources, making the network easier to use. Now another group of people starts finding the Internet useful. The process repeats itself; and it's still repeating itself.

Whatever their sophistication, Internet users are, as a whole, looking for one thing: information. They find information from two general classes of sources: people and computers. It's easy to forget about the Internet's "people" resources, but they're just as important (if not more so) as the computers that are available. Far from being a machine-dominated wasteland, where antisocial misfits sporting pocket protectors flail away at keyboards, the Internet is a friendly place to meet people just like yourself. You're a potential network user if you are:

- A science teacher in an area who needs to remain current and develop curricula

- A Unitarian-Universalist minister in a town of fundamentalists, looking for some spiritual comraderie

- A criminal lawyer who needs to discuss a case with someone who has a particular kind of legal expertise

- An eighth grader looking for others whose parents don't understand real music

And so on. For all of these people, the Internet provides a way of meeting others in the same boat. It's possible—in fact, it's usually easy—to find an electronic discussion group on almost any topic, or to start a new discussion group if one doesn't already exist.

The Internet also provides these people with access to computer resources. The science teacher can access a NASA-funded computer that provides information, past, present, and future, about space science and the space program. The minister can find the Bible, the Koran, and the Torah, waiting to be searched for selected passages. The lawyer can find timely transcriptions of U.S. Supreme Court opinions in Project Hermes.* The eighth grader can discuss musical lyrics with other eighth graders, or can appear to be an expert among adults. After all, he is the only one who understands the lyrics.

---

*Mead Data's Lexis is being 'test marketed' to law schools across the Internet.

This is just the beginning. Sure, you will still find a lot of things about computer internals and the network itself, but this is quickly being eclipsed by information about non-computer related fields. A large part of this book is a catalog of information sources you can access through the Internet. In creating this catalog, we picked as broad a range of sources as possible, to show that the Net really does have something for everyone. If we cataloged every resource on the Internet, the book would be huge—and most of it would be telling you about different software repositories. While we cover our share of software repositories, anyone can find software (if you can't this book will show you how). What's harder is finding the other gems half-buried in the muck. Since one person's gem is another's muck, we grouped the catalog by subject.

The nice thing about all this is that you play on your terms. When trying something new in person, you're likely to be plagued by doubts. You hear about a bridge gathering at the community center, and think "Am I good enough?", "Am I too good?", "Will my ex-wife be there?" On the network, you can:

- Devote as much or as little time as you like

- Become casual acquaintances or fast friends with someone

- Observe discussions or take part

- Walk away from anything you find objectionable, or fight every wrong

If you'd like, you could make your collected works of poetry available to anyone who would like to read them. There is very little risk, so you might as well try.

What You Will Learn

Just as there is no one use for the network, there is no one way to use the network. If you learn everything in this book, you will become a competent network user. You will know how to access every common thing on the network, and you'll know how to get the software needed to do the uncommon things. But it will still be only one way. There are different software packages and philosophies of use which you may like better—there is nothing wrong with them.

Many people view the Internet as the Interstate Highway System for information. You can drive cross-country in a Porsche, a pick-up truck, or a Yugo—they all get you there. (Well, maybe not the Yugo.) This book takes you on a tour in a 1985 Chevy Impala. A Chevy may not be as sexy or fast as a Porsche, but it does offer you a comfortable ride to your destination. Also, you won't get stuck in Outback, Montana because the one mechanic in town has never seen a metric wrench.

In particular, here's what we will cover:

- How to log on to other computers on the Internet (**telnet**). Many computers are "publicly available" for various kinds of work. Some of these computers allow anyone to use them; for some, you have to arrange for an account in advance. Some of these computers can be used for "general purpose" work; others provide some special service, like access to a library catalog or a database.

- How to move files from one computer to another (**ftp**). There are many public archives scattered around the network, providing files that are free for the taking. Many of these archives provide source code for various computer programs, but other archives hold recipes, short stories, demographic information, and so on. You name it, you can probably find it (or something reasonably close).

- How to send electronic mail to other people who use the Internet. The Internet provides worldwide electronic mail delivery.

- How to read and participate in group discussions (USENET news). There are discussion groups for topics ranging from the obscure to the bizarre to the practical.

- How to find where various network resources, ranging from people to software to general databases, are located ("white pages," **archie**, **gopher**, WAIS, World-Wide Web). One of the Internet's problems is that it's too rich; there are so many resources available, it's hard to find what you want, or to remember where what you want is located. A few years ago, the network was like a library without a catalog. The "cataloging" tools are just now being put into place. We'll tell you how to use some new and exciting tools (and some older, less-exciting tools) to locate almost anything you might possibly want, ranging from people and software to sociological abstracts and fruit-fly stocks.

With these tools, you'll have the network at your fingertips. There is one problem, though. There are many different versions of all of these tools. I had to pick one configuration to discuss in this book. I typically chose basic software, on which you type commands to make it do your bidding, running on UNIX for the examples. I did this for a couple of reasons. First, people who are going to have the most trouble dealing with the network probably have the least sophisticated computer setup. They are more likely to have a PC with two floppy drives than a high-end computer with a graphics monitor and a mouse. With the software I'm discussing, a lower-end computer will work fine. Second, when you start using the Internet, you may not be connected to it directly. You may access the network by using a modem to "dial-up" a computer that is connected. Most of the time, that computer will be running UNIX; it's a fact of Internet life. Well, under those conditions you either are using a real terminal (like a Digital Equipment VT100) or some emulation program, like Procomm, Versaterm, or Kermit, that makes the fanciest computer act like a VT100 terminal. In either case you are stuck with characters and commands.

For the most part, what you can do on the Internet is defined by the network itself, not by the software you run on your computer to gain access. Using a mouse and pull-down menus may make the network easier to use, but it really doesn't let you do anything you couldn't do with a character-oriented display and keyboard. So, by making this choice, we're not limiting what you can do. Nor are we limiting the book. If you go out and buy some mouse-based software, you'll find that all the concepts in this book are still applicable. You'll just be pushing buttons rather than typing commands.

What If I Don't Know UNIX?

It doesn't matter if you don't know UNIX. The Internet is not UNIX. There are two parts to using the network: running programs on your computer to access the Internet, and using those programs to do things across the network. For a PC/DOS user the program that lets you connect to another system for an interactive terminal session is no different from any other PC/DOS program. The program's name is **telnet**, so you type:

```
A: telnet
```

This looks just like starting WordPerfect or Lotus. The same is true for any other brand of computer.

For your edification, let me show you the comparable UNIX command:

```
% telnet
```

Still think you need to know UNIX?

Once you get the program running, it will look just like every other program you run on your computer: if you normally use commands, it will have commands; if you use pull-down menus, it will have menus. Regardless of how you do things, the things you can do will be the same. Think about how the network works (a subject we'll discuss more in Chapter 3). Cooperating computers send precisely defined messages back and forth. These messages only allow certain things to happen. If those messages allow something to happen, it can. If they don't, it can't. It doesn't matter whether your computer is a PC, a Macintosh, a VAX, or a UNIX workstation;* the messages it sends to other Internet computers are the same.

So, the examples in this book were all done on UNIX systems—it shouldn't matter. The commands you use may be slightly different, to make them more like a "normal" command on your computer system, but when and why you use which command will remain the same. If an example shows that you start the **ftp** program (you use this to move files), connect to a file archive on some computer, and retrieve a certain file; then on an PC/DOS computer, you would need to do those same steps in the same order. If you know how to run standard software on a computer and read this book, you should be able to use the Internet.

At times, you may find that this discussion briefly descends into UNIX details, like "uses the PAGER environment variable." I tried to be very explicit in explaining examples, and this is the price I paid. If you're not interested in UNIX, skip the details, but look at the explanation of what's going on. If the UNIX version of the program has to deal with some condition, like the screen filling up, the PC/DOS or Macintosh program will have to do it, too. They will do it in a manner that is

---

*This is not strictly true. The programs may be limited by what a particular computer's operating system may allow. Or the software for your computer may be an older (or newer) version than the corresponding program on another computer.

"normal": i.e., the way PC/DOS or a Macintosh handles similar events in other programs. So, you might even be able to guess what you should do in an emergency.

What You Need

You need three things to explore and use the Internet: a desire for information, the ability to use a computer, and access to the Internet. Desire for information is the most important. That's what the Internet offers: the information you want, when you want it—not "details at noon, six and ten, stay tuned." Without that desire, this book's contents won't impress you. If I say, "let's check the agricultural markets, the special nutritional requirements of AIDS sufferers, ski conditions, and home beer recipes," and you reply, "so what?" then you're not ready. If your response was, "Wow," then the Internet is for you.

You use the Internet with a computer. You don't have to be a computer scientist to use it. You do need to be able to operate one, run existing programs, and understand what files are. Some computer jargon might help, but mostly you need a couple of very basic buzzwords:

bit   The smallest unit of information. A bit can have the value 1 or the value 0. Everything in computing is based on collecting hunks of bits together, manipulating them, and moving them from place to place. For example, it takes eight bits to represent a standard alphabetic character.

K   A suffix meaning "about 1000," derived from the Greek kilo. For example, 8.6K characters meaning 8600 characters. In computing, K may refer to 1000 or 1024 depending on the context, but who cares? For our purposes, "about 1000" is good enough.

click   A verb meaning "to select something with a mouse." I did have to talk about one interface which required a mouse. Sliding a mouse around on the desk moves an arrow on the screen. Programs that use a mouse frequently display simulated "push-buttons" on the screen. You activate those buttons by positioning the arrow on the button you want to push, and pressing the button on the mouse. This is commonly called "clicking" on that button.

If I did my job in writing this book, you will learn what you need to know along the way. How's that for going out on a limb?

Finally, you need an Internet connection. This book is oriented towards someone who has a connection and needs to know how to use it. That connection can take a variety of flavors, ranging from a full connection via a local area network (*LAN*), to limited dial-up connections using a terminal emulation package. If you already have a connection, you can skip the next section. If you don't have a connection, Appendix A discusses how to get one.

What an Internet Connection Means

If you ask someone, "Are you connected to the Internet?" you might get some strange answers. The question has a good, precise answer, but that's not what many people think about. For many people, the question, "Are you connected" is similar to the question "Do you shop at Sears?"* Shopping at Sears means different things to different people. To some, Sears is a store at the mall; to others, it is a catalog. Whether the answer to the question is "yes" or "no" probably depends on whether the respondent has been able to get what he or she wanted at Sears, not the means by which the purchases were made. The same is true of Internet connections. If I ask, "Are you connected?", the question you will likely hear is, "Can I do the Internet things I want to do from my terminal?" For example, many people who only use electronic mail think they are connected to the Internet when, in fact, they aren't. Before you get started, it's important to know what a connection means. Once you know what a connection means, you can figure out whether or not you already have one; if you don't have one, you can determine what kind of connection service you want to buy and how much you should pay.

The Internet offers a wide range of services. We've already seen a partial list of these services: electronic mail, bulletin boards, file transfer, remote login, index programs, and so on. To get the complete set of services, you must have a TCP/IP style connection (treat this as a buzzword right now—we'll get to what it means in a while). A TCP/IP connection to the Internet is like a Vulcan mind meld on *Star Trek*. Your computer is part of the network: your computer knows how to contact every computer service on the Internet, though it may need some special software to use some of them. Anything which can happen between networked computers can occur. For example, if you want a file, you can move it directly to your workstation as in Figure 1-1.

If you are only interested in some limited services, you don't necessarily need a full connection to the Internet. That is: you can beg, borrow, or buy an account on a computer that is connected to the Internet. Then you can use some terminal emulator to dial in from your computer to the Internet machine; log in; read mail, fetch files, and do whatever you want (Figure 1-2). In this situation it's fair to say, "I have access to the Internet" or, "I have an Internet connection" because you can do anything the Internet will allow you to do—on the remote machine.†

But you can't say, "My home computer is connected to the Internet," because it isn't. What's the difference? Well, once you've dialed in to your remote system, you can read and write electronic mail. But you can't send or receive electronic mail from your home system directly; you have to log in to some remote access point first. If you want to save an important mail message, you can save it on the remote system. But you can't save it on your own computer's disk directly; you'll have to first save

---

*Sears is, by the way, connected to the Internet.

†Of course, the remote (Internet) computer might not have some useful program installed. You'll have to talk that system's manager into finding it and installing it. Installing it on your home PC won't do any good.

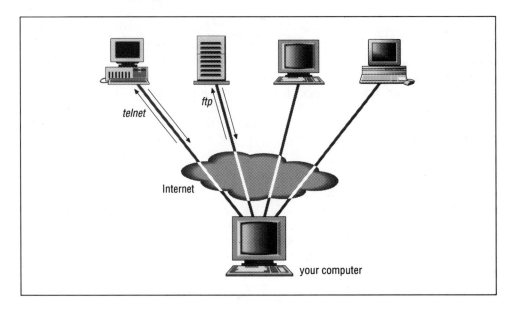

Figure 1-1: A true Internet connection

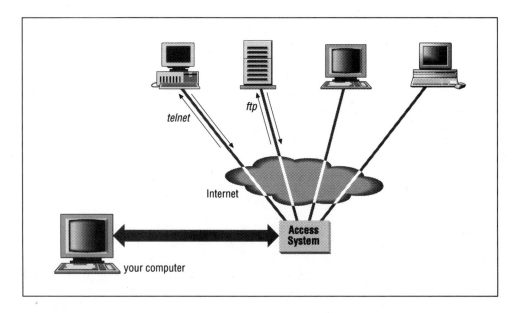

Figure 1-2: A dial-up Internet connection

the file on the remote system's disk then use your communications program to move files from the remote system back to your desktop computer. Likewise, you can fetch a file from any of the Internet's public archives; but you still need to go through an extra step of moving that file from the access computer to your personal computer.

One step further away, you can get a kind of limited access to the Internet. If you're a Compuserve or Bitnet user, you can send mail to the Internet, and (with the right software) read Internet bulletin boards (known as *news*). A UNIX user who uses UUCP* for electronic mail and news is in the same boat. Although it's common for people in this situation to say that they're "connected to the Internet," they aren't in any real sense. With this kind of connection, you can use a few popular Internet services—but you can't use most of them. The fact that I can send a postcard to my friends in Paris doesn't make me a citizen of France.

Getting Connected?

Here's the big surprise: You may already have an Internet connection and not know it. Most Internet users have a connection through work or school: their corporation or university is connected to the Internet, and they use it for work or for pleasure. If your company has an Internet connection, and you have a computer in your office, getting on the Net should be simple. Ask a system administrator whether or not the company is on the Internet, and (if so) how you can get your office system hooked up. If you're lucky, you may not have to do anything at all—you might be able to sit down, type **telnet**, and go to work. Don't think this is unrealistic: there are *a lot* of people who are this lucky. If you're unlucky and the administrator says that your company or school is not on the Internet, ask the obvious question: "why not?" For a small company, some relatively inexpensive Internet connections can give you the kind of worldwide corporate network that, previously, only companies like EXXON or IBM could afford.

If you're not already connected, there are many ways to get connected. These range from large, fairly expensive solutions that are appropriate for large corporations or universities to relatively low-cost solutions that are appropriate for very small businesses or home use. No matter what level you're at, Internet access always comes via an "access provider": an organization whose job it is to sell Internet access. There are access providers for every level of service: from expensive dedicated Internet connections, to inexpensive dial-up connections for home users. Appendix A, *Getting Connected to the Internet*, lists many (though not all) access providers and the types of service they provide. It also gives you some hints as to how an individual may be able to get connected for little personal cost.

---

*UUCP is an ancient way of configuring a UNIX computer to automatically dial-up another UNIX computer and transfer files. This is the basis for a very popular mail service.

How This Book Is Organized

This book is organized like a class in high school woodshop. First, you talk about the history and theory of carpentry. You then discuss tool use and safety, one tool at a time. On the last day of class, you go on a field trip to the lumber yard to get a feel for what you have to work with.

In Chapters 2 through 4, we'll start with some history and theory. We'll keep the background material to a minimum—just enough so you can understand why the Internet is like it is. We'll discuss a little bit about how the Internet works: not a lot of "this bit moves here," but mostly handwaving and conceptual explanations. This isn't really required reading, and can usually be skipped over safely. It's fairly short, and I think it's important. If you get into a bind, and have to guess at what is going on, or what to do next, nothing helps more than a feel for how things work. If you would like to know more about the history of the Internet or its technology, there are other books which go into a lot more detail.*

Most of the book (Chapters 5 to 15) discusses how to use the tools that allow your computer to do things on the Internet. I've tried to focus on what you're likely to do, and why: not just which knob to turn and which button to push, but why you need them. A lot of attention is paid to some relatively "fuzzy," but ultimately practical, issues: what's allowed and what isn't? What's polite and what isn't? What's the best way to find the kind of information you want?

The final large section of this book is a *Resource Catalog*: a list of things we (I had some helpers) found on the Internet. It's organized by subject, so you shouldn't have trouble finding topics that interest you. We found these resources by using the tools explained in this book, and just looking around. The list is not complete, but no list is. Pere Marquette didn't throw a dart at a map of the world and decide to look for Indians to convert where the dart landed. He started in a place where he knew there were Indians and began walking from there. This is your place to start. Start at some place interesting and begin to look and wander. It's amazing what you will find.

If you still think this thing called the Internet is for you, press on and you can find out what it is.

---

*The best of these is probably Douglas Comer's book, *Internetworking with TCP/IP: Principles, Protocols, and Architectures* (Prentice-Hall). Technically, it's quite advanced, but it's the standard work on the topic.

CHAPTER TWO

WHAT IS THE INTERNET?

What Makes Up the Internet?
Who Governs the Internet?
Who Pays for It?
What Does This Mean for Me?
What Does the Future Hold?

The Internet was born about 20 years ago, as a U.S. Defense Department network called the ARPAnet. The ARPAnet was an experimental network designed to support military research—in particular, research about how to build networks that could withstand partial outages (like bomb attacks) and still function. (Think about this when I describe how the network works; it may give you some insight into the design of the Internet.) In the ARPAnet model, communication always occurs between a source and a destination computer. The network itself is assumed to be unreliable; any portion of the network could disappear at any moment (pick your favorite catastrophe—these days backhoes cutting cables are more of a threat than bombs). It was designed to require the minimum of information from the computer clients. To send a message on the network, a computer only had to put its data in an envelope, called an Internet Protocol (IP) packet, and "address" the packets correctly. The communicating computers—not the network itself—were also given the responsibility to ensure that the communication was accomplished. The philosophy was that every computer on the network could talk, as a peer, with any other computer.

These decisions may sound odd, like the assumption of an "unreliable" network, but history has proven that most of them were reasonably correct. Although the Organization for International Standardization (ISO) was spending years designing the ultimate standard for computer networking, people could not wait. Internet developers, responding to market pressures, began to put their IP software on every conceivable type of computer. It became the only practical method for computers from different manufacturers to communicate. This was attractive to the government and universities, which didn't have policies saying that all computers must be bought from the same vendor. Everyone bought whichever computer they liked, and expected the computers to work together over the network.

About ten years later, Ethernet local area networks (*LAN*) and workstations came on the scene. Most of these workstations came with Berkeley UNIX, which came with IP networking. This created a new demand: rather than connecting to a single large timesharing computer per site, organizations wanted to connect the ARPAnet to their entire local network. This would allow all the computers on that LAN to access ARPAnet facilities. About the same time, other organizations started building their own networks using the same communications protocols as the ARPAnet: namely, IP and its relatives. It became obvious that if these networks could talk together, users on one network could communicate with those on another; everyone would benefit.

One of the most important of these newer networks was the NSFNET, run by the National Science Foundation (NSF), an agency of the U.S. Government. In the late 80's the NSF created five supercomputer centers. Up to this point, the world's fastest computers had only been available to weapons developers and a few researchers from very large corporations. By creating supercomputer centers, the NSF was making these resources available for any scholarly research. Only five centers were created because they were so expensive—so they had to be shared. This created a communications problem: they needed a way to connect their centers together and to allow the clients of these centers to access them. At first, the NSF tried to use the ARPAnet for communications, but this strategy failed because of bureaucracy and staffing problems.

In response, NSF decided to build its own network, based on the ARPAnet's IP technology. It connected the centers with 56,000 bit per second* (56k bps) telephone lines. It was obvious, however, that if they tried to connect every university directly to a supercomputing center, they would go broke. You pay for these telephone lines by the mile. One line per campus with a supercomputing center at the hub, like spokes on a bike wheel, adds up to lots of miles of phone lines. Therefore, they decided to create regional networks. In each area of the country, schools would be connected to their nearest neighbor. Each chain was connected to a supercomputer center at one point, and the centers were connected together. With this configuration, any computer could eventually communicate with any other by forwarding the conversation through its neighbors.

This solution was successful—and, like any successful solution, a time came when it no longer worked. Sharing supercomputers also allowed the connected sites to share a lot of other things not related to the centers. Suddenly these schools had a world of data and collaborators at their fingertips. The network's traffic increased until, eventually, the computers controlling the network and the telephone lines connecting them were overloaded. In 1987, a contract to manage and upgrade the network was awarded to Merit Network Inc., which ran Michigan's educational network, in partnership with IBM and MCI. The old network was replaced with faster telephone lines (by a factor of 20), and with faster computers to control it.

---

*This is roughly the ability to transfer two full typewritten pages per second. That's slow by modern standards, but it was reasonably fast in the mid 80's.

The process of running out of horsepower and getting bigger engines and better roads continues to this day. Unlike changes to the highway system, however, most of these changes aren't noticed by the people trying to use the Internet to do real work. You won't go to your office, log in to your computer, and find a message saying that the Internet will be inaccessible for the next six months because of improvements. Perhaps even more important: the process of running out of capacity and improving the network has created a technology that's extremely mature and practical. The ideas have been tested; problems have appeared, and problems have been solved.

For our purposes, the most important aspect of the NSF's networking effort is that it allowed everyone to access the network. Up to that point, Internet access had been available only to researchers in computer science, government employees, and government contractors. The NSF promoted universal educational access by funding campus connections only if the campus had a plan to spread the access around. So everyone attending a four-year college could become an Internet user.

The demand keeps growing. Now that most four-year colleges are connected, people are trying to get secondary and primary schools connected. People who have graduated from college know what the Internet is good for, and talk their employers into connecting corporations. All this activity points to continued growth, networking problems to solve, evolving technologies, and job security for networkers.

What Makes Up the Internet?

What comprises the Internet is a difficult question; the answer changes over time. Five years ago the answer would have been easy: "All the networks, using the IP protocol, that cooperate to form a seamless network for their collective users." This would include various federal networks, a set of regional networks, campus networks, and some foreign networks.

More recently, some non-IP-based networks saw that the Internet was good. They wanted to provide its services to their clientele. So they developed methods of connecting these "strange" networks (e.g., Bitnet, DECnets, etc.) to the Internet. At first these connections, called *gateways*, merely served to transfer electronic mail between the two networks. Some, however, have grown to full service translators between the networks. Are they part of the Internet? Maybe yes and maybe no. It depends on whether, in their hearts, they want to be. If this sounds strange, read on—it gets stranger.

Who Governs the Internet?

In many ways the Internet is like a church: it has its council of elders, every member has an opinion about how things should work, and you can either take part or not. It's your choice. The Internet has no president, chief operating officer, or Pope. The constituent networks may have presidents and CEOs, but that's a different issue; there's no single authority figure for the Internet as a whole.

The ultimate authority for where the Internet is going rests with the Internet Society, or ISOC. ISOC is a voluntary membership organization whose purpose is to promote global information exchange through Internet technology.* It appoints a council of elders, which has responsibility for the technical management and direction of the Internet.

The council of elders is a group of invited volunteers called the *Internet Architecture Board*, or the IAB. The IAB meets regularly to "bless" standards and allocate resources, like addresses. The Internet works because there are standard ways for computers and software applications to talk to each other. This allows computers from different vendors to communicate without problems. It's not an IBM-only or Sun-only or Macintosh-only network. The IAB is responsible for these standards; it decides when a standard is necessary, and what the standard should be. When a standard is required, it considers the problem, adopts a standard, and announces it via the network. (You were expecting stone tablets?) The IAB also keeps track of various numbers (and other things) that must remain unique. For example, each computer on the Internet has a unique 32-bit address; no other computer has the same address. How does this address get assigned? The IAB worries about these kinds of problems. It doesn't actually assign the addresses, but it makes the rules about how to assign addresses.

As in a church, everyone has an opinion how things ought to run. Internet users express their opinions through meetings of the Internet Engineering Task Force (IETF). The IETF is another volunteer organization; it meets regularly to discuss operational and near-term technical problems of the Internet. When it considers a problem important enough to merit concern, the IETF sets up a "working group" for further investigation. (In practice, "important enough" usually means that there are enough people to volunteer for the working group.) Anyone can attend IETF meetings and be on working groups; the important thing is that they work. Working groups have many different functions, ranging from producing documentation, to deciding how networks should cooperate when problems occur, to changing the meaning of the bits in some kind of packet. A working group usually produces a report. Depending on the kind of recommendation, it could just be documentation and made available to anyone wanting it, it could be accepted voluntarily as a good idea which people follow, or it could be sent to the IAB to be declared a standard.

If you go to a church and accept its teachings and philosophy, you are accepted by it, and receive the benefits. If you don't like it, you can leave. The church is still there, and you get none of the benefits. Such is the Internet. If a network accepts the teachings of the Internet, is connected to it, and considers itself part of it, then it is part of the Internet. It will find things it doesn't like and can address those concerns through the IETF. Some concerns may be considered valid and the Internet may change accordingly. Some of the changes may run counter to the religion, and be rejected. If the network does something that causes damage to the Internet, it could be excommunicated until it mends its evil ways.

---

*If you'd like more information, or if you would like to join, see "Network Organizations" in the *Resource Catalog*.

Who Pays for It?

The old rule for when things are confusing is "follow the money." Well, this won't help you to understand the Internet. No one pays for "it"; there is no Internet, Inc. that collects fees from all Internet networks or users. Instead, everyone pays for their part. The NSF pays for NSFNET. NASA pays for the NASA Science Internet. Networks get together and decide how to connect themselves together and fund these interconnections. A college or corporation pays for their connection to some regional network, which in turn pays a national provider for its access.

What Does This Mean for Me?

The concept that the Internet is not a network, but a collection of networks, means little to the end user. You want to do something useful: run a program, or access some unique data. You shouldn't have to worry about how it's all stuck together. Consider the telephone system—it's an internet, too. Pacific Bell, AT&T, MCI, British Telecom, Telefonos de Mexico, and so on, are all separate corporations that run pieces of the telephone system. They worry about how to make it all work together; all you have to do is dial. If you ignore cost and commercials, you shouldn't care if you are dealing with MCI, AT&T, or Sprint. Dial the number and it works.

You only care who carries your calls when a problem occurs. If something goes out of service, only one of those companies can fix it. They talk to each other about problems, but each phone carrier is responsible for fixing problems on its own part of the system. The same is true on the Internet. Each network has its own network operations center (NOC). The operations centers talk to each other and know how to resolve problems. Your site has a contract with one of the Internet's constituent networks, and its job is to keep your site happy. So if something goes wrong, they are the ones to gripe at. If it's not their problem, they'll pass it along.

What Does the Future Hold?

Finally, a question I can answer. It's not that I have a crystal ball (if I did I'd spend my time on Wall Street instead of writing a book). Rather, these are the things that the IAB and the IETF discuss at their meetings. Most people don't care about the long discussions; they only want to know how they'll be affected. So, here are highlights of the networking future.

New Standard Protocols

When I was talking about how the Internet started, I mentioned the Organization for International Standardization (ISO) and their set of protocol standards. Well, they finally finished designing it. Now it is an international standard, typically referred to as the ISO or OSI (Open Systems Interconnect) protocol suite. Many of the Internet's component networks use OSI today. There isn't much demand, yet. The U.S. Government has taken a position that government computers should be able to speak these protocols. Many have the software; few are using it now.

It's really unclear how much demand there will be for OSI, notwithstanding the government backing. Many people feel that the current approach isn't broke, so why fix it? They are just becoming comfortable with what they have, why should they have to learn a new set of commands and terminology just because it is the standard?

Currently there are no real advantages to moving to OSI. It is more complex and less mature than IP, and hence doesn't work as efficiently. OSI does offer hope of some additional features, but it also suffers from some of the same problems which will plague IP as the network gets much bigger and faster. It's clear that some sites will convert to the OSI protocols over the next few years. The question is: how many?

International Connections

The Internet has been an international network for a long time, but it only extended to the United States' allies and overseas military bases. Now, with the less paranoid world environment, the Internet is spreading everywhere. It's currently in over 40 countries, and the number is rapidly increasing. Eastern European countries longing for Western scientific ties have wanted to participate for a long time, but were excluded by government regulation. This ban has been relaxed. Third world countries that formerly didn't have the means to participate now view the Internet as a way to raise their education and technology levels.

The ability of the Internet to speak OSI protocols should help the Internet to expand into more countries. Except for the Scandinavian countries, which embraced the Internet protocols long ago and are already well-connected, most of Europe regards IP as a cultural threat akin to EuroDisney. Networks based on the OSI protocols are much more palatable for them. If the two protocols could co-exist, everyone would be happy.

At present, the Internet's international expansion is hampered by the lack of a good supporting infrastructure, namely a decent telephone system. In both Eastern Europe and the third world, a state-of-the-art phone system is nonexistent. Even in major cities, connections are limited to the speeds available to the average home anywhere in the U.S., 9600 bits/second. Typically, even if one of these countries is "on the Internet," only a few sites are accessible. Usually, this is the major technical university for that country. However, as phone systems improve, you can expect this to change too; more and more, you'll see smaller sites (even individual home systems) connecting to the Internet.

Commercialization

Many big corporations have been on the Internet for years. For the most part, their participation has been limited to their research and engineering departments. The same corporations used some other network (usually a private network) for their business communications. After all, this IP stuff was only an academic toy. The IBM mainframes that handled their commercial data processing did the "real" networking using a protocol suite called System Network Architecture (SNA).

Businesses are now discovering that running multiple networks is expensive. Some are beginning to look to the Internet for "one-stop" network shopping. They were scared away in the past by policies which excluded or restricted commercial use. Many of these policies are under review and will change. As these restrictions drop, commercial use of the Internet will become progressively more common.

This should be especially good for small businesses. Motorola or Standard Oil can afford to run nationwide networks connecting their sites, but Joe's Custom Software couldn't. If Joe's has a San Jose office and a Washington office, all it needs is an Internet connection on each end. For all practical purposes, they have a nationwide corporate network, just like the big boys.

Privatization

Right behind commercialization comes privatization. For years, the networking community has wanted the telephone companies and other for-profit ventures to provide "off the shelf" IP connections. That is, you could order an Internet connection just like you order a telephone jack for your house. You order, the telephone installer leaves, and you plug your computer into the Internet. Except for Bolt, Beranek and Newman, the company that ran the ARPAnet, there weren't any takers. The telephone companies have historically said, "We'll sell you phone lines, and you can do whatever you like with them." By default, the Federal government stayed in the networking business.

Now that large corporations have become interested in the Internet, the phone companies have started to change their attitude. Now they and other profit-oriented network purveyors complain that the government ought to get out of the network business. After all, who best can provide network services but the "phone companies"? They've got the ear of a lot of political people, to whom it appears to be a reasonable thing. If you talk to phone company personnel, many of them still don't really understand what the Internet is about. They ain't got religion, but they are studying the Bible furiously.*

Although most people in the networking community think that privatization is a good idea, there are some obstacles in the way. Most revolve around the funding for the connections that are already in place. Many schools are connected because the government pays part of the bill. If they had to pay their own way, some schools would probably decide to spend their money elsewhere. Major research institutions would certainly stay on the Net; but some smaller colleges might not, and the costs would probably be prohibitive for most secondary schools (let alone grade schools). What if the school could afford either an Internet connection or a science lab? It's unclear which one would get funded. The Internet has not yet become a "necessity" in many people's minds. When it does, expect privatization to come quickly.

---

*Apologies to those telephone company employees who saw the light years ago and have been trying to drag their employers into church.

Well, enough questions about the history of the information highway system. It's time to walk to the edge of the road, try and hitch a ride, and be on your way.

## CHAPTER THREE

HOW THE INTERNET WORKS

Moving Bits from One Place to Another
Making the Network Friendly

It's nice to know a bit about how things work. It allows you to make sense out of some of the hints you will see in this book. They will make sense, rather than seeming like capricious rules to be learned by rote. Lest you be scared away, we will explore this with a maximum amount of handwaving. We'll never say "this field is 3 bits long . . ."; we won't even think about it! If you want to know more, several books on the Internet's implementation are available.*

In this chapter, we will look at packet switching networks and how, by putting TCP/IP on top of such a network, something useful happens. We will talk about the basic protocols that govern how the Internet communicates: TCP and its poor cousin, UDP. These are the network's building blocks. At this point the Internet is fairly boring (frustrating and hard to use). When you put the Domain Name System and a few applications on top of it, it becomes something useful.

If you decide this isn't your cup of tea, feel free to skip the beginning of this chapter. Do read the section on the Domain Name System. It is something that you will be using indirectly for your entire Internet career.

Moving Bits from One Place to Another

Modern networking is built around the concept of "layers of service." You start out trying to move bits from here to there, losing some along the way. This level consists of wires and hardware, and not necessarily very good wires. Then you add a layer of basic software to shield yourself from the problems of hardware. You add another layer of software to give the basic software some desirable features. You continue to add functionality and smarts to the network, one layer at a time, until

---

*Comer, Douglas, *Internetworking with TCP/IP: Principles, Protocols, and Architecture*, Volumes I and II (Prentice Hall).

you have something that's friendly and useful. Well, let's start at the bottom and work our way up.

Packet Switch Networks

When you try to imagine what the Internet is and how it operates, it is natural to think of the telephone system. After all, they are both electronic, they both let you open a connection and transfer information, and the Internet is primarily composed of dedicated telephone lines. Unfortunately, this is the wrong picture, and causes many misunderstandings about how the Internet operates. The telephone network is what is known as a *circuit switched* network. When you make a call, you get a piece of the network dedicated to you. Even if you aren't using it (for example, if you are put on hold), your piece of the network is unavailable to others wishing to do real work. This leads to underutilization of a very expensive resource, the network.

A better model for the Internet, which may not instill confidence in you, is the U.S. Postal Service. The Postal Service is a *packet switched* network. You have no dedicated piece of the network. What you want to send is mixed together with everyone else's stuff, put in a pipe, transferred to another Post Office, and sorted out again. Although the technologies are completely different, the Postal Service is a surprisingly accurate analogy; we'll continue to use it throughout this chapter.

The Internet Protocol (IP)

A wire can get data from one place to another. However, you already know that the Internet can get data to many different places, distributed all over the world. How does that happen?

The different pieces of the Internet are connected by a set of computers called *routers*, which connect networks together. These networks are sometimes Ethernets, sometimes token rings, and sometimes telephone lines, as shown in Figure 3-1.

The telephone lines and Ethernets are equivalent to the trucks and planes of the Postal Service. They are means by which mail is moved from place to place. The routers are postal substations; they make decisions about how to route data ("packets"), just like a postal substation decides how to "route" envelopes containing mail. Each substation or router does not have a connection to every other one. If you put an envelope in the mail in Dixville Notch, New Hampshire, addressed to Boonville, California, the Post Office doesn't reserve a plane from New Hampshire to California to carry it. The local Post Office sends it to a substation; the substation sends it to another substation; and so on, until it reaches the destination. That is, each sub-station only needs to know what connections are available, and what is the best "next hop" to get a packet closer to its destination. Similarly, with the Internet: a router looks at where your data is going and decides where to send it next. It just decides which pipe is best and uses it.

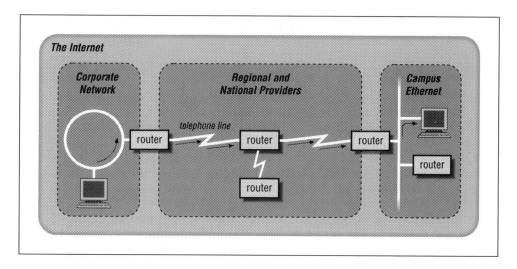

Figure 3-1: Internet hardware

How does the Net know where your data is going? If you want to send a letter, you can't just drop the typed letter into the mailbox and expect delivery. You need to put the paper in an envelope, write an address on it, and stick a stamp on it. Just as the Post Office has rules about how to use its network, the Internet has rules about how to use it. The rules are called *protocols*. The Internet Protocol (IP) takes care of addressing, or making sure that the routers know what to do with your data when it arrives. Sticking with our Post Office analogy, the Internet Protocol works just like an envelope (Figure 3-2).

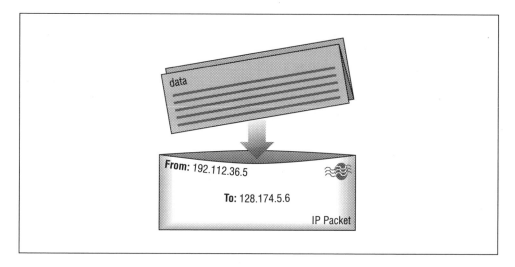

Figure 3-2: IP envelopes

Some addressing information goes at the beginning of your message; this information gives the network enough information to deliver the *packet* of data.

Internet addresses consist of four numbers each less than 256. When written out, the numbers are separated by periods like this:

```
192.112.36.5
128.174.5.6
```

(Don't worry; you don't need to remember numbers like these to use the network.) The address is actually made up of multiple parts. Since the Internet is a network of networks, the beginning of the address tells the Internet routers what network you are part of. The right end of the address tells that network which computer or *host* should receive the packet.* Every computer on the Internet has a unique address under this scheme. Again, the Postal Service provides a good analogy. Consider the address "50 Kelly Rd., Hamden, CT." The "Hamden, CT" portion is like a network address; it gets the envelope to the right local Post Office, the Post Office that knows about streets in a certain area. "50 Kelly Rd." is like the host address; it identifies a particular mailbox within the Post Office's service area. The Postal Service has done its job when it has delivered the mail to the right local office, and when that local office has put it into the right mailbox. Similarly, the Internet has done its job when its routers have gotten data to the right network, and when that local network has given the data to the right computer, or host, on the network.

For a lot of practical reasons (notably hardware limitations), information sent across IP networks is broken up into bite-sized pieces, called *packets*. The information within a packet is usually between 1 and about 1500 characters long. This prevents any one user of the network from monopolizing the network and allows everyone to get a fair shot. It also means that if the network isn't fast enough, as more people try to use it, it gets slower for everyone.

One of the amazing things about the Internet is that, on a basic level, IP is all you need to participate. It wouldn't be very friendly but, if you were clever enough, you could get some work done. As long as your data is put in an IP envelope, the network has all the information it needs to get your packet from your computer to its destination. Now, however, we need to deal with several problems:

- Most information transfers are longer than 1500 characters. You would be disappointed, indeed, if the Post Office would only carry postcards, but refused anything larger.

- Things can go wrong. The Post Office occasionally loses a letter; networks sometimes lose packets, or damage them in transit. Unlike the Post Office, we'll see that the Internet can deal with these problems successfully.

---

*Where the network portion ends and the host portion begins is a bit complicated. It varies from address to address based on an agreement between adjacent routers. Fortunately, as a user you'll never need to worry about this; it only makes a difference when you're setting up a network.

- Packets may arrive out of sequence. If you mail two letters to the same place on successive days, there's no guarantee that they will take the same route or arrive in order. The same is true of the Internet.

So, the next layer of the network will give us a way to transfer bigger chunks of information, and will take care of the many "distortions" that can creep in because of the network.

The Transmission Control Protocol (TCP)

TCP is the protocol, frequently mentioned in the same breath as IP, that is used to get around these problems. What would happen if you wanted to send a book to someone, but the Post Office only accepted letters? What could you do? You could rip each page out of the book, put it in a separate envelope, and dump them all in a mailbox. The recipient would then have to make sure the pages all arrived and paste them together in the right order. This is what TCP does.

TCP takes the information you want to transmit and breaks it into pieces. It numbers each piece so receipt can be verified and the data can be put back in the proper order. In order to pass this sequence number across the network, it has an envelope of its own which has the information it requires "written on it" (Figure 3-3). A piece of your data is placed in a TCP envelope. The TCP envelope is, in turn, placed inside an IP envelope and given to the network. Once you have something in an IP envelope, the network can carry it.

On the receiving side, a TCP software package collects the envelopes, extracts the data, and puts it in the proper order. If some are missing, it asks the sender to retransmit them. Once it has all the information in the proper order, it passes the data to whatever application program is using its services.

This is actually a slightly utopian view of TCP. In the real world not only do packets get lost, they can also be changed by glitches on telephone lines in transit. TCP also handles this problem. As it puts your data into an envelope, it calculates something called a *checksum*. A checksum is a number that allows the receiving TCP to detect errors in the packet.* When the packet arrives at its destination, the receiving TCP calculates what the checksum should be and compares it to the one sent by transmitter. If they don't match, an error has occurred in the packet. The receiving TCP throws that packet away and requests a retransmission.

---

*Here's a simple example, if you're interested. Let's assume that you're transmitting raw computer data in 8-bit chunks, or bytes. A very simple checksum would be to add all of these bytes together. Then stick an extra byte onto the end of your data that contains the sum. (Or, at least, as much of the sum as fits into 8 bits.) The receiver makes the same calculation. If any byte was changed during transmission, the checksums will disagree, and you'll know there was an error. Of course, if there were two errors, they might cancel each other out. But more complicated computations can handle multiple errors.

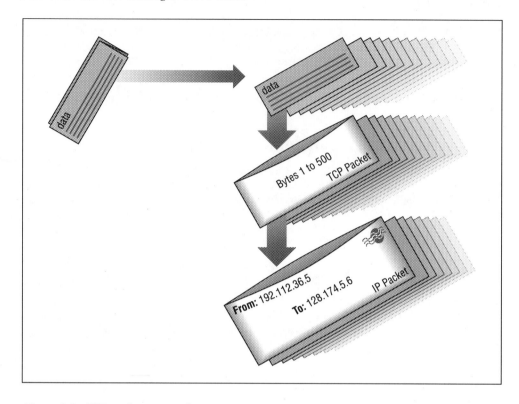

Figure 3-3: TCP packet encapsulation

Other Transmission Protocols

TCP creates the appearance of a dedicated wire between the two applications, guaranteeing that what goes in one side comes out the other. You don't have a dedicated link between the sender and receiver (other people can use the same routers and network wires in the gaps between your packets); but, for all practical purposes, it looks like you do.

Ideal as this may sound, it is not the best approach for every program to use. Setting up a TCP connection requires a fair amount of overhead and delay; if this machinery isn't needed, it's better not to use it. If all the data you want to send will fit in one packet and you don't particularly care to guarantee delivery, TCP may be overkill.

It turns out that there is another standard protocol that does away with this overhead. This protocol is called the *user datagram protocol* or *UDP*. It is used instead of TCP in some applications; that is, instead of wrapping your data in a TCP envelope and putting that inside an IP envelope, the application puts your data into a UDP envelope, which goes in the IP envelope.

UDP is a lot simpler than TCP because it doesn't worry about missing packets, keeping data in the right order, or any of those niceties. UDP is used for programs that only send short messages, and can just resend the message if a response does not come in a short time. For example, assume that you're writing a program that looks up phone numbers in a database somewhere else on the network. There is no reason to set up a TCP connection to transmit 20 or so characters in each direction. You can just put the name into one UDP packet, stick that into an IP packet, and send it. The other side of the application gets the packet, reads the name, looks up the phone number, puts that into another UDP packet, and sends it back. What happens if the packet gets lost along the way? Your program has to handle that: if it waits too long without getting a response, it justs sends another request.

Making the Network Friendly

Now that we have the ability to transfer information between places on the network, we can start working on making the Internet more friendly. This is done by having software tailored to the task at hand, and using names rather than addresses to refer to computers.

Applications

Most people don't get really excited about having a guaranteed bit stream between machines, no matter how fast the lines or exotic the technology that creates it. They want to use that bit stream to do something useful, whether that is to move a file, access some data, or play a game. Applications are pieces of software that allow this to happen easily. They are yet another "layer" of software, built on top of the TCP or UDP services. Applications give you, the user, a way to do the task at hand.

What an application is varies greatly. Applications can range from home-grown programs to proprietary programs supplied by a vendor. There are three "standard" Internet applications: remote login, file transfer, and electronic mail, as well as other commonly used but not standardized applications. Chapters 5 through 14 of this book describe how to use most of the common Internet applications.

One problem with talking about applications is that the application's appearance to you is determined by your local system. The commands, messages, prompts, etc., may be slightly different on your screen than in the book or on someone else's screen. So, don't worry because the book says the message is "connection refused" and the error message you receive is "Unable to connect to remote host: refused"; they are the same. Try and distill the essence of the message, rather than matching the exact wording. And don't worry if some of the commands are named slightly differently; most of the applications have reasonable "help" facilities that will let you figure out the right command.

The Domain Name System

Fairly early on, people realized that addresses were fine for machines communicating with machines, but humans preferred names. It is hard to talk using addresses (who would say, "I was connected to 192.112.36.5 yesterday and . . . "?), and even harder to remember them. Therefore, computers on the Internet were given names for the convenience of their human users. The preceding conversation becomes "I was connected to the NIC* yesterday and...". All of the Internet applications let you use system names, rather than host addresses.

Of course, naming introduces problems of its own. For one thing, you have to make sure that no two computers that are connected to the Internet have the same name. You also have to provide a way to convert names into numeric addresses. After all, names are just fine for people; but the computers really prefer numbers, thank you. You can give a program a name, but it needs some way to look that name up and convert it into an address. (You do the same thing whenever you look someone up in the phone book.)

In the beginning, when the Internet was a small folksy place, dealing with names was easy. The NIC (*Network Information Center*) set up a registry. You would send in a form, electronically of course, and they would maintain a file of names and addresses. This file, called the *hosts* file, was distributed regularly to every machine on the network. The names were simple words, every one chosen to be unique. If you used a name, your computer would look it up in the file and substitute the address. It was good.

Unfortunately, when the Internet went forth and multiplied, so did the size of the file. There were significant delays in getting a name registered, and it became difficult to find names that weren't already used. Also, too much network time was spent distributing this large file to every machine contained in it. It was obvious that a distributed, online system was required to cope with the rate of change. This system is called the *Domain Name System* or *DNS*.

The Domain System Structure

The Domain Name System is a method to administer names by giving different groups responsibility for subsets of the names. Each level in this system is called a *domain*. The domains are separated by periods:

```
ux.cso.uiuc.edu
nic.ddn.mil
yoyodyne.com
```

There can be a variable number of domains within the name but practically there are usually five or less. As you proceed left to right through the domains, the number of names contained in the group gets bigger.

In the first line above (**ux.cso.uiuc.edu**), **ux** is the name of a host, a real computer with an IP address (Figure 3-4). The name for that computer is created and maintained by the **cso** group, which happens to be the department where the computer resides. The department **cso** is a part of the University of Illinois at Urbana Champaign (**uiuc**). **uiuc** is a portion of the national group of educational institutions (**edu**). So the zone **edu** contains all computers in all U.S. educational institutions; the zone **uiuc.edu** contains all computers at the University of Illinois; and so on.

---

*A Network Information Center is a repository for information about a network.

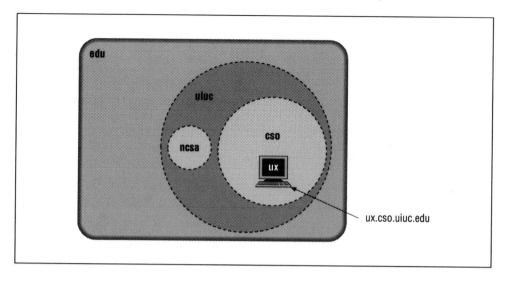

Figure 3-4: Domain authority

Each group can create or change whatever lies within it. If **uiuc** decided to create another group called **ncsa**, it could do so without asking anyone's permission. All it has to do is add the new names to its part of the worldwide database, and sooner or later everyone who needs to know will find out about the new name. Similarly, **cso** can buy a new computer, assign it a name, and add it to the network without asking anyone's permission. If every group from **edu** on down plays by the rules and makes sure that the names it assigns are unique, then no two systems anywhere on the Internet will have the same name. You could have two machines named **fred**, but only if they are in different domains (for example, **fred.cso.uiuc.edu** and **fred.ora.com**).

In practice, being the name administrator for a group requires certain skills, and is not fun. Therefore, at some level around the enterprise level (**uiuc**) or one level below it, there is a person who is responsible for maintaining all lower levels. There is some locally defined procedure for requesting that a name get created or changed.

It's easy to see where domains and names come from within an organization like a university or a business. However, where do the "top level" domains like **edu** come from? They were created by *fiat* when the domain system was invented. Originally, there were six highest level domains (see Table 3-1).

Table 3-1: Original High-level Domains

Domain	Usage
com	For commercial organizations (i.e., businesses)
edu	Educational organizations (universities, secondary schools, etc.)
gov	Governmental organizations, non-military
mil	Military (army, navy, etc.)
org	Other organizations
net	Network resources

As the Internet was a worldwide network, there needed to be a way to give foreign countries responsibility for their own names. To this end, there are a set of two letter domains which correspond to the highest level domains for countries. Since **ca** is the country code for Canada, a Canadian computer might be named:

```
hockey.guelph.ca
```

There are almost 300 country codes, about 100 of which have some kind of computer networking. There is a list of the country codes in Appendix B, *International Network Connectivity*, in case you want to see where mail you received came from.

It's worth noting that the U.S. has its own country code, although it isn't used too often; in the U.S., most network sites use the "organizational" domains (like **edu**), rather than the "geographical" domains (like **va.us**—Virginia). However, you will see both kinds of names. One computer may even have both kinds of names just for completeness. There's no way to "convert" between organizational names and geographical names. For example, even though **uxc.cso.uiuc.edu** happens to be in Urbana, Illinois, U.S.A., there is *not* necessarily a name **uxc.urbana.il.us**. Even if there is, they aren't necessarily the same computer.

Domain Name Lookup

Now you know how domains relate to each other and how a name gets created. Now you might just wonder how to use this marvelous system. You use it automatically, whenever you use a name on a computer that knows about it. You never need to look a name up "by hand," or give some special command to find out about some name, although you can if you want. All computers on the Internet can use the domain system, and most do.

When you use a name like **ux.cso.uiuc.edu**, the computer needs to turn it into an address. To do so, it starts asking DNS servers for help, starting at the right end and working left. First, it asks the local DNS servers to look up the address. At this point, there are three possibilities:

- The local server knows the address, because the address is in the local server's part of the worldwide database. For example, if you're in the computer science department of the University of Illinois, your local server probably has information about the computers in your department.

- The local server knows the address because someone else has asked for the same address recently. Whenever you ask for an address, the DNS server keeps it on hand for a while, just in case someone else wants the same address later; this makes the system a lot more efficient.

- The local server doesn't know the address, but it knows how to find out.

How does the local server find out? Its software knows how to contact a *root* server. This is the server that knows the addresses of name servers for the highest level (rightmost) zone (**edu**). It asks the root server for the address of the computer responsible for the **edu** zone. Having that information, it contacts that server and asks that server for the address of the **uiuc** server. Your software then contacts that computer and asks for the address of the server for **cso**. Finally, it contacts that machine and gets the address of **ux**, the host that was the target of the application.

A few computers are still configured to use the old-style *hosts* file. If you find yourself on one of these, you may have to ask its administrator to look up the address you need by hand (or look it up yourself); then the administrator will have to add the machine you want to contact to the local *hosts* file. While you're doing this, you can hint that the administrator *really ought to install* the DNS software so you won't have to do this again.

Domain Name System Hints

There are a few common misconceptions that you may encounter dealing with names. Here are a few we can dispel now:

- The pieces of a domain-style name tell you who is responsible for maintaining the name. It may not tell you anything about who maintains the computer corresponding to that IP address, or even (despite the country codes) where that machine is located. It would be perfectly legal for me to have the name **oz.cso.uiuc.edu** (part of the University of Illinois' name space) point to a machine in Australia. It isn't normally done, but it could be.

- The pieces of a domain name don't even necessarily tell you what network a computer is located on. Domain names and networking often overlap, but there's no necessary connection between them; two machines in the same domain may not be on the same network. For example, the systems **uxc.cso.uiuc.edu** and **ux1.cso.uiuc.edu** may be on different networks. Once again, domain names only tell you who is responsible for the domain.

- A machine can have multiple names. This is especially true of machines that offer services, where the service may be moved to a different computer in the future. My Sun workstation may be known by **ek.cso.uiuc.edu**. It also might be the computer where you can go to get publicly available files at the University of Illinois. So it might also have the name **ftp.uiuc.edu** (**ftp** being the name of the file moving program). Some time in the future, this service might be moved to some other computer. When this happens, the name **ftp.uiuc.edu** would move along with the service (my computer gets to keep its old name **ek.cso.uiuc.edu**). People wanting the particular service use the same name regardless of which computer is providing the service. Names that symbolically refer to a service are called "canonical names" or *cnames*. You will see them frequently as you wander about the Internet.

- Names aren't necessary for communication. Unless the error message you receive is "host unknown," the name worked fine. A message like "host unknown" means your system could not translate the name you gave into an address. Once your system has the address in hand, it never uses the name again.

- It is better to remember names than addresses. Some people feel that the name system is "just one more thing to go wrong." The problem is that an address is tied to a network. If the computer providing a service is moved from one building to another, its network and hence its address will likely change. The name needn't change. When the administrator assigns the new address, he only needs to update the name record so that the name points to the new address. Since the name still works, you don't particularly care if the computer or function has changed locations.

The Domain Name System may sound complicated, but it's one of the things that make the Internet a comfortable place to live. If you don't like the periods wandering around, forget about what they mean: they're just names. However, pretty soon you'll start realizing, "yes, this resource is at the University of Virginia; this person works for IBM in Germany; this is the address for reporting bugs in Nutshell Handbooks (**nuts@ora.com**)" and so on. The real advantage of the domain system is that it breaks the gigantic worldwide Internet into a bunch of manageable pieces. Although hundreds of thousands of computers are "on the Net," they're all named; and the names are organized in a convenient, perhaps even rational way, making it easier for you to remember the ones you need.

## CHAPTER FOUR

WHAT'S ALLOWED ON THE INTERNET?

Legal Implications
Politics and the Internet
Network Ethics
Security Consciousness

I n earlier chapters, I told you very generally what the Internet is good for, where it came from, and how it works. Now it's time to get to the real nitty-gritty. We will talk about what you are allowed to do on the network; in the next chapter, we will start discussing "how to do it."

What you are allowed to do is a very complex issue. It is influenced by law, ethics, and politics. How these inter-relate and which is paramount vary from place to place. The Internet isn't a network—it's a network of networks—and each network may have its own policies and rules. Lest you should give up before starting, the rules are reasonably uniform, and you'll be safe if you keep a few guidelines in mind. Fortunately, these guidelines aren't terribly restrictive. As long as you stay within those guidelines, you can do whatever you want. If you feel yourself getting near the edges, contact your network provider to determine exactly what is allowed and what isn't. It may be possible to do what you want, but it's your responsibility to find out. Let's look at the issues so you can see where the borders are.

Legal Implications

Three areas of the law affect the Internet:

- Federal subsidies pay for large sections of the Internet. These subsidies exclude purely commercial use.

- The Internet is not just a nationwide network, but a true global network. When shipping anything across a national boundary, including bits, export laws come into effect and local laws change.

- Whenever you are shipping software (or, for that matter, ideas) from one place to another, you must consider intellectual property and license issues.

First, let's deal with the federal dollars.

Research, Education, and the Federal Dollar

Many of the networks in the Internet are sponsored by federal agencies. Under federal law, an agency may only spend its budget on things that it is charged to do. For example, the Air Force can't secretly increase its budget by ordering rockets through NASA. These same laws apply to the network—if NASA funds a network, it must be used for space science. As a user, you may have no idea which networks your packets are traversing, but they better fall within the scope of each network's funding agency. If they don't, it's off to Leavenworth.

Actually, it is not as bad as it sounds. A couple of years ago, the folks in Washington realized that multiple parallel IP networks (NSFNET, NASA Science Internet, etc.—one network per federal agency) was a waste of money (a radical idea). Legislation was passed to create the National Research and Education Network, or *NREN*. This was to be a portion of the Internet dedicated to supporting research and education that was common to all federal agencies. This means that you can use the NREN* to do basic research and education, or in support of research and education.

The importance of the clause "in support of research or education" cannot be over-emphasized. This provision legitimizes important ways to use the network that don't, at first glance, seem appropriate. For example, if a vendor distributes software that is used in research or education, it can distribute updates and answer questions through electronic mail. This usage is considered "in support of research or education" (RE). The vendor can't use the NREN for business functions, like marketing, billing, or accounting. For this, it must use a commercial part of the Internet.†

Commercial Use

When your site arranged for its Internet connection, someone needed to tell the network provider whether the connection would be used for research and education, or for commercial purposes. If your site decided it was "RE," your network traffic is routed to prefer subsidized NREN routes. If you are a commercial site, your traffic is routed over private routes. As you'd expect, your site's network access fees depend on these decisions; "commercial" use is generally more expensive than "RE" because it isn't subsidized. Only someone in your network administration can tell you whether commercial dealings are allowed over your connection. Check before you do.

Of course, many corporations join the Internet as "research and education" sites—and this is appropriate, since the motivation for joining the Internet is often research. For example, a seed company may wish to do joint soybean research with a university. Yet many corporate legal departments decide to declare their

---

*Actually, the NREN is a real network that hasn't yet been built. The bill also authorizes this traffic on existing federal networks. The correct term for what we have now is the Interim Interagency NREN.

†A copy of the official NSFNET acceptable use policy is included in Appendix C, *Acceptable Use*. It is one of the most restrictive with regard to commercial use. If your usage is acceptable to NSFNET, it is likely acceptable to the other networks as well.

connections commercial. This ensures there will not be a legal liability in the future, when some uninformed employee uses the research connection for commercial work. To many businesses, the added fees are well worth the comfort.

There are a number of commercial Internet providers: Advanced Networking Services (ANS), Performance Systems International (PSI), and UUnet are a few of them. Each of these companies has its own market niche and its own national network to provide commercial Internet services. In addition, state and regional networks carry commercial traffic for their members. There are connections between each of these and the federally supported networks. Using these connections and some nifty accounting agreements, all of these networks inter-operate legally.

Export Laws

Whether you know it or not, exporting bits falls under the auspices of the Department of Commerce export restrictions.* The Internet, being a virtually seamless global network, makes it very easy to export things without your knowledge. Because I'm not a lawyer I won't get very technical, but I will try to sketch what is required to stay legal. If you think you might run afoul of the law after reading this, seek competent legal help.

Export law is based on two points:

1. Exporting anything requires a license.
2. Exporting a service is roughly equivalent to exporting the pieces necessary to provide that service.

The first point is fairly obvious: if you ship, carry, transfer a file, or electronically mail anything out of the country it needs to be covered by an export license. Luckily, there is a loophole called a *general license* that covers most things. The general license allows you to export anything that is not explicitly restricted, and is readily available in public forums in the United States. So anything you can learn from walking into a conference or classroom that does not have security restrictions is probably covered by the general license.

However, the list of restricted items has a lot of surprises, and does cover things that you can learn as a student in any university. Networking code and encryption code might be restricted, based upon their capabilities. Many times, one little item is of concern, but by the time the regulations are written, they cover a much wider area. For example, during the Persian Gulf War, it was a lot harder to knock out Iraq's command and control network than anticipated. It turned out they were using commercial IP routers which were very good at finding alternative routes quickly. Suddenly, exporting any router that could find alternate routes was restricted.

The second point is even simpler. If exporting some hardware, say a supercomputer, is not allowed, then remote access to that hardware within this country is prohibited as well. So, be careful about granting access to "special" resources (like

---

*This is a strictly U.S.-centric discussion. Other laws apply to servers in other countries.

supercomputers) to people in foreign countries. The exact nature of these restrictions depends, of course, on the foreign country and (as you can probably imagine, given the events of the last few years) can change quickly.

When investigating their potential for legal liability, the consortium that runs the Bitnet (CREN) came to the following conclusions:* A network operator is responsible for illegal export only if the operator was aware of the violation and failed to inform proper authorities; the network operator isn't responsible for monitoring your usage and determining whether or not it's within the law. So network personnel nationwide probably aren't snooping through your packets to see what you are shipping overseas (although who knows what the National Security Agency looks at). However, if a network technician sees your packets, and if the packets are obviously in violation of some regulation, then the technician is obliged to inform the government.

Property Rights

Property rights can also become an issue when you ship something to someone else. The problem gets even more confusing when the communication is across national borders. Copyright and patent laws vary greatly from country to country. You might find on the network a curious volume of forgotten lore whose copyright has expired in the U.S. Shipping these files to England might place you in violation of British law. Know who has the rights to anything you give away across the network. If it is not yours, make sure you have permission before giving something away.

The law surrounding electronic communication has not kept pace with the technology. If you have a book, journal, or personal letter, you can ask almost any lawyer or librarian if you can copy or use it in a particular manner. They can tell you if you can, or whose permission you need to obtain. Ask the same question regarding a network bulletin board posting, an electronic mail message, or a report in a file available on the network, and they will throw up their hands. Even if you knew whose permission to obtain, and obtained that permission via electronic mail, it's not clear whether an e-mail message offers any useful protection. Just be aware that this is a murky part of law which will likely be hammered out in the next decade.

Please note that property rights can be a problem even when using publicly available files. Some software available for public retrieval through the Internet must be licensed from the vendor. For example, a workstation vendor might make updates to its operating system software available via anonymous FTP. So you can easily get the software, but in order to use it legally you must hold a valid software maintenance license. Just because a file is there for the taking doesn't mean that taking it is legal.

---

*The actual legal opinions are available on the network; see the *Resource Catalog* Law - Legal Opinions on International Networking.

Politics and the Internet

Many network users view the political process as both a blessing and a curse. The blessing is money. Subsidies provide many people a utility they could not afford otherwise. The curse is that their individual actions are under constant scrutiny. Someone in Washington may decide, after the fact, that something you have done can be exploited for political gain. The digitized centerfold you had on your machine can suddenly become the center of an editorial entitled "Tax Dollars Fund Pornography Distribution."* This causes everyone responsible for the Internet's funding no end of grief.

It's important to realize that the Internet has many political supporters, including congressmen, presidential advisors, educational leaders, and federal agency heads. They support the Internet because it benefits the country: it increases the U.S.'s ability to compete in international research and trade. Speeding communications allows the research and educational process to speed up; because of the Net, our researchers and their students can develop better solutions to technical problems.

As is typical in the political world, there are also those people who see these benefits as drivel. The millions of dollars spent on the network could be better spent buying pork barrels in their own congressional district.

The bottom line in the politics of networking is that political support for the network is broad, but relatively thin. Any act that can cause political waves might radically change it, probably for the worse.

Network Ethics

For the novice network user, the apparent lack of ethics on the network is fairly disquieting. In actuality, the network is a very ethical place; the ethics are just a bit different than normal. To understand this, consider the term "frontier justice." When the West was young, there was a set of laws for the United States, but they were applied differently west of the Mississippi river. Well, the network is on the frontier of technology, so frontier justice applies here, too. You can delve here safely, provided you know what to expect.

The two overriding premises of network ethics are:

- Individualism is honored and fostered.

- The network is good and must be protected.

Notice these are very close to the frontier ethics of the West, where individualism and preservation of lifestyle were paramount. Let's look a bit more at how these points play off each other on the network.

---

*Something like this actually happened. The files were slightly more explicit than centerfolds, and it did jeopardize the funding of the entire NSFNET.

Individualism

In normal society, everyone may claim to be an individual, but many times their individualism is compromised by the need for a sufficiently large group that shares their concerns. This is called "critical mass." You may love medieval French poetry, but try starting a local group to discuss it. It is not convenient. You probably won't be able to find enough people who are interested and willing to meet often enough to support a chain of discussions. In order to at least get some interaction for your love, you join a poetry society with more general interests—perhaps one on medieval poetry in general. Maybe there's only one poetry society in town, and it spends most of its time discussing bad pseudo-religious verse. That's the problem with "critical mass." If you can't assemble enough people to form a group, you suffer. You may join a larger group out of necessity, but it may not be what you want.

On the network, critical mass is two. You interact when you want and how you want—it's always convenient, no driving is required. Geography doesn't matter. The other person can be anywhere on the network (virtually anywhere in the world). Therefore, a group, no matter how specific, is possible. Even competing groups are likely to form. Some groups may choose to "meet" by electronic mail, some on bulletin boards, some by making files publicly available, and some by other means. People are free to operate in the manner they like. Since no one needs to join a large group to enjoy critical mass, everyone is part of some minority group. Everyone is equally at risk of being singled out for persecution. Because of this, no one wants to say "this topic should not be discussed on the network." If I said that about French poets, you could attack my favorite group, cross-dressing male adventurers. People understand that others couldn't care less about the information they live and die for. Many Internet users are nervous (justifiably) that support for outside censorship could arise and, eventually, succeed in making the Net less useful.

Of course, individualism is a two-edged sword. It makes the network a nice place for finding diverse information and people, but it may tax your liberality. People have many differing opinions about acceptable behavior. Since a lot of the behavior on the network is between you and a computer somewhere, most people will not be aware of anything you are doing. Those who might, may or may not care. If you put your machine on the network, you should realize that many users feel that any files that they can get to are fair game to retrieve. After all, if you didn't intend to make them available, you shouldn't have put them there. This view, of course, has no basis in law, but a lot of things on the frontier don't either.

Protecting the Internet

Frequent users find the Internet extremely valuable for both work and play. Since the Internet access usually requires no personal expense (or very little), they view this valuable resource as something that must be protected. The threats to the Internet come in two areas:

- Excessive unintended use
- Political pressures

The NREN is being built with a purpose. A company's commercial connection to the Internet has a purpose. No one may prosecute a person who uses these connections for unintended purposes, but it is still discouraged by other means. If you use an employer's computer for a bit of personal use, like balancing your checkbook, it will probably be ignored. Likewise, small amounts of network time used for unintended purposes will likely be ignored. (In fact, many seemingly unintended uses, say a high school student playing a game across the network, might actually qualify as "intended." She must have learned a lot about computing and networking to get that far.) It is only when someone does something unignorable, perhaps organizing a nationwide multi-user dungeon game day on the network, that problems occur.

Unintended use does not only come in the form of games or recreational activities. It can also come in the form of ill-conceived types of supported usage. The network was not built to be a substitute for inadequate local facilities. For example, using an exported disk system half-way across the world because your employer wouldn't buy a $300 disk for your workstation is unacceptable. You may need the disk to do valuable research, but the cost of providing that storage across the network is outrageous. The network was designed to allow easy access to unique resources, not gratuitous access to common ones.

Heavy network users and network providers are not stodgy. They enjoy a game as well as the next guy. They are also not stupid. They read news. They work on the network regularly. If performance goes bad for no apparent reason, they investigate. If they find that the traffic in a particular area has gone up a hundredfold, they will want to know why. If you are the "why" and the use is unacceptable, you will probably get a polite electronic mail message asking you to stop. After that, you may get some less polite messages; finally, someone will contact your local network provider. You may end up losing your network access entirely, or your employer or campus may have to pay higher access fees (which, I assume, they will not be happy about).

Self-regulation is important because of the politics that surround the network. No reasonable person could expect the network to exist without occasional abuses and problems. However, if these problems aren't resolved within the network community, but are thrown into newspapers and Congress, everyone loses. To summarize, here are some areas that are considered "politically damaging" to the network and should be avoided:

- Excessive game playing

- Excessive ill-conceived use

- Hateful, harassing, or other antisocial behavior

- Intentional damage or interference with others (e.g., the Internet Worm*)

- Publicly accessible obscene files

---

*The Internet Worm was a program which used the Internet to attack certain types of computers on the network. It would gain unauthorized access and then use those computers to try to break into others. It was a lot like a personal computer "virus," but technically it is called a worm because it did not cause intentional damage to its hosts. For a good description, see *Computer Security Basics* (Russell and Gangemi), O'Reilly and Associates, page 3.

It is difficult to justify the NREN's budget to Congress if "Sixty Minutes" is doing a feature on network abuse the Sunday before the budget hearings.

Security Consciousness

A computer connected to the Internet is not, in itself, a much bigger security problem than a machine you can dial-up with a modem. The problems are the same; it's the magnitude of the problem that can be different. If you have a dial-up modem, anyone can dial the number and try to break in. There are three mitigating factors: the computer's phone number probably isn't widely known; if the intruder is outside your local calling area, he has to pay for the experience (or have stolen something else to get there); and there is only one interface which can be attacked.

If you are on the Internet, the mitigating factors are gone. The general address of your network is easily found, and it is easy to try a few host numbers before stumbling onto an active one. In principle, this is still no worse than computer services that provide dial-in access to their machines through toll-free "800 numbers." The problem is that those services have staff who worry about security and there is still only one point to break in from: the ASCII terminal port. On the Internet, someone could try to break in through the interactive terminal port, the file transfer port, the e-mail port, etc. It's easy for someone to pull a workstation out of the box and put it on the Internet without thinking about security at all. He or she plugs the machine in, turns it on, and it works. The job is done, until someone breaks in and does something bad. As hard as it is to understand, it is less time consuming to put a little thought into security beforehand than to deal with it after the fact.

You can start by having the right attitude towards security. Believe that it is your workstation's responsibility to protect itself, and not the network's job to protect it. A network provider can restrict who may talk over your connection. However, that probably isn't what you want, because it strips away much of the Internet's value. Most of this book describes how to reach out to random places and find good things. A network conversation is a two-way pipe. If a remote machine can't talk to you, you can't talk to it either. And if that computer has some resource that you might find useful next month, it's your loss. In order to take advantage of the Internet, you must be a part of it. This puts your computer at risk, so you need to protect it.

Security on the Internet is really a group effort by the whole community. One technique that break-in artists use is to break into a chain of computers (e.g., break into A, use A to break into B, B to break into C, etc.). This allows them to cover their tracks more completely. If you think your lil' ole machine won't be a target because it is so small, dream on. Even if there's nothing of use on your computer, it's a worthwhile intermediate for someone who wants to break into an important system. And some people are out to accumulate notches on their keyboard, counting how many machines they have broken into. Size does not matter.

Discussing security and rumors of security problems is a bit of a problem. Can you imagine the following news story:

> At a news conference today officials of the ACME Safe and Vault Company announced that their locks will unlock with any combination . . . .

There needed to be a way to investigate a purported problem, find a solution, and inform people without making the problem worse. To solve this problem, the government has funded an organization named CERT: the Computer Emergency Response Team.

CERT does a number of things. It investigates security problems, works with manufacturers to solve them, and announces the solutions. It also produces a number of aids to allow people to assess how secure their computers are. They prefer to work with site security personnel but will, in an emergency, field questions from anyone. If you feel you are out in the woods alone and must talk to someone about security, you can contact them via electronic mail at:

```
cert@cert.sei.cmu.edu
```

There are four ways in which network machines become compromised. In decreasing order of likelihood, these are:*

1. Choosing bad passwords

2. Importing corrupt software by valid users

3. Entering through misconfigured software

4. Entering through an operating system security flaw

You can draw one very important conclusion from this list. It is well within your ability to protect your system. Let's look at what you can do to stay out of trouble.

Passwords

Most people choose passwords for their convenience. Unfortunately, what is convenient for you is also convenient for the hacker. CERT believes that 80% of computer break-ins are caused by poor password choice. Remember, when it comes to passwords, computers break in, not people. Some program spends all day trying out passwords; it's not going to get tired when the first three passwords don't work. But you can easily make it very hard to guess the right password. Most password crackers don't pick random letters; they pick common words from the dictionary and simple names. So, pick a good password which:

- Is at least six characters long

- Has a mixture of uppercase, lowercase, and numbers

---

*A good place if you want to learn more about security issues is RFC1244 and the CERT server machine (see the *Resource Catalog* under "Security"). Also, see *Computer Security Basics* (Russell and Gangemi) for a general discussion of security issues, and *Practical UNIX Security* (Garfinkel and Spafford) for UNIX-related system administration issues. Both are published by O'Reilly and Associates.

- Is not a word

- Is not a set of adjacent keyboard keys (e.g., QWERTY)

It is hard for many people to conceive of a password that will meet all the above criteria and will still be easy to remember. One common thing to do is pick the first letters of a favorite phrase, like FmdIdgad (Frankly my dear, I don't give a damn).

When you install a workstation, make sure that you assign passwords to *root*, *system*, *maint*, and any login names that have special powers. Change these passwords regularly. Some machines come out of the box with standard passwords on their system. If you don't change them, everyone who bought the same type of workstation knows your password.

Finally, be careful about techniques to bypass password requirements. There are two common ones: the UNIX *rhosts* facility and *anonymous FTP*. **rhosts** lets you declare "equivalent" login names on multiple machines. You list explicit machine names and logins in a file named *.rhosts*. For example, the *rhosts* entry:

```
uxh.cso.uiuc.edu krol
```

tells the computer on which this file resides to bypass password requirements when it sees someone trying to log in from the login name **krol** on the machine **uxh.cso.uiuc.edu**. When it sees this login name and this host, the computer will assume the login is valid. Obviously, this means that anyone who manages to break into **krol**'s account on **uxh.cso.uiuc.edu** can also break into this machine.

Anonymous FTP (discussed in Chapter 6, *Moving Files: FTP*) is a facility to allow easy retrieval of selected files without requiring a password. It is beyond the scope of this book to tell you how to set up an anonymous FTP server.* However, we will note that it's easy to make more things available through the service than you really want. Make sure you know what you are doing before you turn this facility on. (Note, though: merely using anonymous FTP to retrieve files does not place you at risk.)

Importing Software

The following story illustrates the second most common source of security problems:†

> Two Cornell University undergraduates were arrested for computer tampering. They tampered with a Tetris-style game on a public server at the school. When played, the game would appear to work normally but cause damage to the machine running it. It was spread throughout the world by computer networks. The FBI is investigating and expects further charges to be filed . . .

---

*This is covered in the Nutshell handbook *TCP/IP Network Administration*, by Craig Hunt (O'Reilly and Associates, 1992).

†This story is a paraphrase of an article in the news group *clari.biz.courts*, February 26, 1992.

This is a classic "trojan horse" program: something threatening hidden in a gift.

Whenever you put software on your machine you place it at risk. Sharing software can be a great benefit. Only you can decide whether the risk is worth it. Buying commercial software entails minimal risk, especially if you buy from reputable vendors. On the network there are no assurances. You find a computer that has good stuff on it. You want it. You take it and compile it. What can you do to make using it as safe as possible? Here are some rules of thumb:

- Try and use "official" sources. If you are after a bug fix to Sun Workstation software, it's safer to get the code from a machine whose name ends with **sun.com** than **hacker.hoople.usnd.edu**.

- Get source code if possible. Once you get the source code, read it before you install it. Make sure it isn't doing anything strange. This also applies to "shar" archives, "make" files, etc. I know this may be a daunting task (or impossible for some), but if you want to be safe this is what you need to do. Even common "public domain" or "free" software can be risky.* You have to decide how much risk you are willing to live with.

- Before installing the software on an important, heavily-used system, run it for a while on a less critical computer. If you have one machine on which you do your life's work and another which is only used occasionally, put the new software on the second machine. See if anything bad happens.

- Do a complete backup of your files before using the software.

Remember: only files that are executed can cause damage. Binary files are the most dangerous; source code is much safer. Data files are never a threat to a computer—though you should be aware that data files may be inaccurate.

Misconfigured Software

This is where it becomes difficult to talk about security. I can't really talk about the problem in concrete terms because it would turn into a hacker's guide to break-in techniques. A more general discussion will have to suffice.

Some system codes have debugging options which can be turned on or off at installation or startup time. These options are occasionally left enabled on "production" systems—either inadvertently, or so the developers can get in at a later time (for example, if you start having problems) and see what's going on. However, any hole that's large enough to let a legitimate software developer in can also let a cracker in. Some break-ins (including the Internet Worm) have occurred through these means. Make sure that, unless needed, debugging options are turned off on system software.

---

*We do not, of course, mean software produced by the Free Software Foundation. That software is trustworthy—at least in its original state. We'll repeat the first point: it's worth making sure you get an "official" copy of the sources.

In fact, unless a facility is needed on your system, why turn it on at all? Most vendors configure their operating systems to run everything right out of the box. This makes it easier to install; if all the options are turned on automatically, you don't have to run around figuring out which are needed. Unfortunately, this practice also makes it easier for someone to break in. If you don't plan to let people use a program like **tftp**, why run a server for it?

System Software Flaws

Operating system flaws are either found and fixed, or workaround procedures are developed quickly. A computer manufacturer doesn't want his product to get a reputation as an "easy mark" for break-ins. The bigger problem comes after the manufacturer takes corrective action. You need to get the update and install it before it will protect anything. You can only install software updates if you know that they exist. Therefore, you need to keep up with the current state and release of your operating system. The easiest way to do this is to maintain a dialog with your campus, corporate, or vendor software support staff. For some obvious reasons, vendors don't make public announcements like, "Listen, everyone, Release 7.4.3.2 has this terrible security problem."

What If My Computer Is Violated?

The first question to ask is really, "How will I know if my computer is violated?" Someone who breaks in tries to be as discrete as possible, covering his tracks as he goes. Once you discover him, you should take corrective action. So, how do you discover a break-in? Most people don't take advantage of security information provided regularly by their computer. Let's say that your machine tells you, "Last login 06:31 26 Jan 1992." Can you remember when you last logged in? Probably not exactly. But you might notice that a login at 6:30 A.M. was strange, given your usual work habits. This is how many break-ins are discovered. The process often starts when someone simply "feels" that something is wrong. For example:

- I don't think I logged in then.
- The machine feels slow today.
- I don't remember deleting or changing that file.

If something like this happens, don't just say, "Oh well" and move on. Investigate further.

If you suspect that you have been broken into, there are a few things you should look into:

- Examine the password file (on UNIX, */etc/passwd*) and look for unusual entries, typically with lots of permissions.
- List all the tasks (on BSD-based UNIX versions, **ps aux**; on System V versions, **ps –el**) and see if there are any unusual system tasks running.
- Get an extended directory listing (like UNIX **ls –la**) of your normal working directory and any other directory which appears "too big" or to have changed unusually. Look for unfamiliar files or strange modification dates.

However, before you can investigate, you must know what the password file, the active process list, etc., normally look like. If you don't know what "normal" is, you're certainly in no position to decide whether or not something is abnormal! Therefore, you should check the password files, your working directory, and so on, *now* and continue to do so regularly. If you perform these checks periodically, you'll make sure that nothing suspicious is going on, and you'll stay familiar with your system.

If you see anything that looks suspicious, get help from either your campus or corporate security departments. If you don't have one, ask your vendor. Act quickly to get help; try not to proceed on your own. Don't destroy anything before you get help. Don't do another disk dump on a standard tape or diskette backup set; the backup tape you are overwriting may be the last uncorrupted one around. Don't assume that closing one hole fixes the problem. When a break-in artist gains access, the first thing he will do is cover his tracks. Next, he'll create more holes to maintain access to your system.

All of this may sound frightening, but don't let fear paralyze you. After all the cautions I've given, paralysis might sound like a good option. However, the non-networked world is full of dangers; if you become overzealous about eliminating danger, you'll spend the rest of your life in a concrete-lined underground shelter (oops, can't do that, radon). Most people structure their lives to keep danger to a manageable level. This is a safe, healthy response: healthy adults don't intentionally subject themselves to dangers that they could easily minimize, and try to live with the dangers that they can't minimize. They wear seat belts; they don't stop traveling. In the network's world, you need to do the same thing. Make sure your password is good, be careful about installing public domain software, watch your system so that you'll be aware of a break-in if one happens, and get help if you need it.

CHAPTER FIVE

REMOTE LOGIN

Simple Telnet
What's Really Going On
Telnet Command Mode
Non-standard Telnet Servers
Telnetting to IBM Mainframes

W e've been through a lot of background information. We've talked generally about what the Internet can do for you, what you're allowed to do,
how the Internet works, how it developed, and so on. We haven't yet said
anything concrete about *how* to get anything done; at this point, the Net is still a
vague, magical entity. A medieval carpenter might be amazed by a modern
woodshop, but it would be useless to him unless he knew what the tools were and
how to use them.

Now we're going to get real. In the next few chapters, we'll discuss the basic tools
for working on the Internet. We mentioned these tools briefly in the first chapter. In
case you've forgotten, though, here's a recap:

telnet   Is used for logging into other computers on the Internet. It's used to
access lots of public services, including library card catalogs and other
kinds of databases.

ftp   Moves files back and forth. It's most useful for retrieving files from public archives that are scattered around the Internet. This is called "anonymous FTP," because you don't need an account on the computer you're
accessing. Anonymous FTP is covered in Chapter 6, *Moving Files: FTP.*

Electronic mail
Lets you send messages. You probably know about electronic mail and
how useful it can be already. The Internet's slant on e-mail is discussed
in Chapter 7, *Electronic Mail.*

USENET News
Lets you read (and post) messages that have been sent to public "news
groups." This may sound obscure, but it's really what everyone else calls
"bulletin boards" or discussion groups. USENET is the world's largest bulletin board service. We discuss it in Chapter 8, *Network News.*

These are the Internet's basic services. After Chapter 8, we discuss a different kind of service: how to find all the "good stuff" that's available. The problem with the Internet is that it's messy and poorly coordinated. There are incredible resources, but there's no central coordination to help you find what you want. In the last few years, developers have made tremendous progress in sorting out the mess, and providing tools to help you find what's interesting. Chapters 9 through 14 discuss these new tools. If Chapters 5 through 8 discuss the Skil saws and drill presses of the Internet's tool shop, 9 through 14 discuss the computer-controlled lathes and milling machines.

That's enough introduction. It's time to get started with TELNET. Our goal is to get you familiar with TELNET and its use. We will look at a simple TELNET session, talk a bit about what is happening behind the scenes, and then look at some more esoteric uses.

Simple Telnet

As we've said, **telnet** is the Internet's remote login application. It lets you sit at a keyboard connected to one computer and log on to a remote computer across the network. The connection can be to a machine in the same room, on the same campus, or a computer in a distant corner of the world. When you are connected, it is as if your keyboard is connected directly to that remote computer. You can access whatever services that remote machine provides to its local terminals. You can run a normal interactive session (logging in, executing commands), or you can access many special services: you can look at library catalogs, find out what's playing in Peoria, access the text of the *USA Today*, and take advantage of the many other services that are provided by different hosts on the network.

The simplest way to use **telnet** is to type:

```
% telnet remote-computer-name
```

at command level. We're using a UNIX system's C shell, so the command prompt is the percent sign (%). If you're using some other computer system (like DOS, VAX/VMS, or a Macintosh), the command would be fundamentally the same, though the details might be slightly different. Here's a very basic example:

```
% telnet sonne.uiuc.edu
Trying...
Connected to sonne.uiuc.edu.
Escape character is '^]'.

SunOS UNIX (sonne)

login: krol                          logging in to remote system
Password:                            password not echoed by the system
Last login: Sat Sep  7 17:16:35 from ux1.uiuc.edu
SunOS Release 4.1(GENERIC) #1:Tue Mar 6 17:27:17 PST 1990
sonne% ls                            command executed by remote system
Mail          News          development          project1
sonne% pwd                           command executed by remote system
```

```
/home/sonne/krol
sonne% logout                          logout from remote system
%                                      back to local system
```

We told TELNET to find a remote computer called **sonne.uiuc.edu**. After finding the
computer, it started a terminal session. Once this session starts, the dialog appears
to be the same as if you were at a terminal connected to that host.* In particular,
you must login and logout just as if you were directly attached to that computer.
After you have logged in, you can give any commands that are appropriate for the
remote system; because **sonne.uiuc.edu** happens to be a UNIX system, all of the
standard UNIX commands (like **ls** and **pwd**) are available. When you log out from
the remote system, **telnet** quits. Any further commands will be executed by your
local system.

That's really all that TELNET is: it's a tool that lets you log in to remote computers. In
the course of this chapter, we'll discuss a number of fancy **telnet** commands and
options, and we'll see that you can use it to access some special-purpose "servers"
with their own behavior. But the simple **telnet** command above (plus an account
on the remote computer) is all you need to get started.

What's Really Going On

Let's take a deeper look at what happens when you start a TELNET session. An
application consists of two pieces of software that cooperate: the *client*, which runs
on the computer that is requesting the service, and the *server*, which runs on the
computer providing the service. The network, using either TCP or UDP services, is
the medium by which the two communicate.

The client, which is the program that began running when you typed in the **telnet**
command, must:

- Create a TCP network connection with a server
- Accept input from you in a convenient manner
- Reformat input to some standard format and send it to a server
- Accept output from a server in some standard format
- Reformat that output for display to you

The server software runs on the machine delivering the service; if the server isn't
running, the service isn't available. On UNIX systems, servers are often referred to as
daemons, system jobs which run in the background all the time. These "silent

---

*TELNET may not communicate your exact terminal specification to the remote host. This is especially
true if you start from some strange sized terminal like an X terminal (more on these later). You might
have to do something to set the terminal specifications after you log in. On BSD UNIX you would do this
with **setenv TERM** and **stty** (to specify the number of rows and columns on your screen).

helpers" wait for their services to be required and when they are, spring into action. When a typical server is ready to accept requests it:

- Informs the networking software that it is ready to accept connections

- Waits for a request in a standard format to occur

- Services the request

- Sends the results back to the client in a standard format

- Waits again

A server must be able to handle a variety of clients, some running on the same kind of computer, and some running on IBM/PCs, Macintoshes, Amigas—whatever happens to be out there. In order to do this, there is a set of rules for communicating with the server. This set of rules is generally called a *protocol*. In this case, since it is a protocol used between pieces of an application, it is called an *application protocol*. Anyone can write a client on any type of computer. As long as that client can communicate across the network to the server and can speak the protocol properly, it can access the service. In practice, this means that your Macintosh (or IBM PC, etc.) can use TELNET and the other Internet tools to do work on an incredible number of different systems, ranging from UNIX workstations to IBM mainframes.

An application protocol usually allows the client and server to differentiate between data destined for the user, and messages the client and server use to communicate with each other. This is frequently done by adding a few characters of text onto the beginning of each line. For example, if the server sends the client a line which begins with the characters "TXT," then the rest of the line is data to be passed on to the screen. If the line begins with "CMD," it is a message from the server software to the client software. Of course, you never see any of this; by the time the message gets to you, the control information is stripped off. So let's get back to looking at how all this relates to TELNET.

Telnet Command Mode

TELNET has more features than our first example would lead you to believe. The clue to this was the "Escape character is ' ^] '" message. TELNET sends any character you type to the remote host, with one exception: the *escape character*. If you type the escape character, your **telnet** client enters a special command mode. By default, the escape character is usually **CTRL-]**. Don't confuse this with the ESC key on the keyboard! The escape character to TELNET can be any character that you will never want to send to the remote system. The ESC key on the keyboard is a special nonprintable character which you frequently need to send to remote systems to flag commands. Also, remember that there are exceptions: the escape character isn't always **CTRL-]**. **telnet** clients that run on machines with slick interfaces generally use menus or function keys instead of an obscure escape character.

You can also enter the command mode by typing **telnet** alone, with no machine name following it. When you're in command mode (no matter how you got there), you will see the prompt telnet>; this means that TELNET is waiting for you to type a command. Once you're in command mode, typing a question mark (?) will get you a list of the commands available:

```
telnet> ?
Commands may be abbreviated.  Commands are:

close         close current connection
display       display operating parameters
mode          try to enter line-by-line or character-at-a-time mode
open          connect to a site
quit          exit telnet
send          transmit special characters ('send ?' for more)
set           set operating parameters ('set ?' for more)
status        print status information
toggle        toggle operating parameters ('toggle ?' for more)
z             suspend telnet
?             print help information
```

Although there are a number of commands, and even more subcommands (try a **set ?** sometime), only a few are generally used:

close   Terminates the connection which is currently made or in the process of being made. It automatically disconnects you from the remote system; it may also quit from TELNET if you specified a hostname with the **telnet** command. This command is useful if you get into a bind across the network and want to get out.

open *name*   Attempts to create a connection to the named machine. The name or address of the target machine is required. Most TELNETs will prompt for a machine name if it is not specified. Note that you must **close** any existing connection before opening a new one.

set echo   Turns local echoing on or off. "Echoing" is the process by which the characters you type appear on your screen. Usually, the remote computer is responsible for sending the character back to your terminal after it receives it. This is called "remote echoing," and is generally considered more reliable, because you know that the remote system is receiving your keystrokes correctly. "Local echoing" means that the local computer (in this case, the **telnet** client) sends the characters you type back to the display screen. Because remote echoing is more reliable, TELNET usually starts with echoing turned "off." To turn it "on," enter command mode and type the **set echo** command. To turn it off again, just type **set echo** again. (This command is like a light switch: giving the command repeatedly turns echoing on or off.) It has the same effect as the half/full duplex switch on modems and computer terminals, if you have any experience with them.

How do you know whether local echoing should be on or off? If local echoing is turned off and it should be on, any characters you type won't be echoed; you won't see the commands you send to the remote system, but you will see the output from these commands. If local echoing is turned on and it should be off, you'll see every character you type twice. In either case, the solution is the same: enter command mode and type **set echo**.

set escape *char*

Sets the escape character to the specified character. You will usually want to use some kind of control character, which you can either type "as is" (for example, if you want to use **CTRL-b**, just type **b** while holding down the CTRL key), or by typing a caret (^) followed by the letter (for example, **^b**). It is important that your escape character be a character that you'll never need to type while doing your normal work. This can be a problem—many programs (the *emacs* editor in particular) assign meanings to virtually every key on the keyboard.

The ability to change the escape character is really useful if you are running daisy-chained applications. For example, you **telnet** from system A to system B, log in and then **telnet** to system C. If what you are doing on system C goes bad, and if the escape characters are the same, there is no way to break the B-to-C connection; typing the escape character will always put you into command mode on system A. If you use a different escape character for each TELNET session, then you can choose which one to put into command mode by typing the appropriate character. This also applies to other applications like terminal emulators (e.g., **kermit**).

quit

Gets you out of the **telnet** program gracefully.

z

Temporarily suspends the TELNET session to allow other commands to be executed on the local system. Connections and other options remain set when the session is resumed. The session is resumed by normal operating system means, which on BSD UNIX is usually an **fg** command. System V UNIX places you in a subshell to do other commands. To return to your TELNET session you exit the shell. (This facility depends on operating system support, so it may not be available on all systems.)

Carriage Return

Without issuing a command (a blank line in command mode) will return you to your connection to the remote machine from command mode. In addition, many of the other commands implicitly take you out of command mode.

Here's a sample session in which we log in to **sonne.uiuc.edu**, go into command mode for a few commands, and then return to **sonne**:

```
% telnet sonne.uiuc.edu
Trying...
Connected to sonne.uiuc.edu.
Escape character is '^]'.

SunOS UNIX (sonne)

login: krol                             logging in to remote system
Password:
Last login: Sat Sep  7 17:16:35 from ux1.uiuc.edu
SunOS Release 4.1(GENERIC) #1:Tue Mar 6 17:27:17 PST 1990
sonne% ls
Mail         News          development        project1
sonne% pwd
/home/sonne/krol
sonne% CTRL-]                           enter telnet command mode
telnet> ?                               print help message
Commands may be abbreviated.  Commands are:

close           close current connection
display         display operating parameters
...                                     several commands omitted
z               suspend telnet
?               print help information
telnet> set escape ^b                   change escape character
escape character is '^B'
sonne% pwd                              back to sonne; give a command
/home/sonne/krol
sonne% logout                           and quit
%                                       back to local system
```

Note that the **set** command implicitly takes you out of command mode. If it didn't, of course, you could just enter a blank line to get back to **sonne**.

Non-standard Telnet Servers

I have implied that there is a one-to-one correspondence between servers and clients. That is, if you have a **telnet** client, it must always access a TELNET server. Or, in other words, that TELNET is only useful for logging on to other computers. This is not strictly the case. If I were writing an application and would be happy with TELNET's user interface (typically a VT100-like terminal), why not use **telnet** as the client and write a server that does what I want it to do? All I have to do is make the server talk the TELNET applications protocol. On the positive side, it saves me the trouble of distributing a special client program to everyone who is going to use my application. It also gives the users an interface with which they are already familiar: anything that works with TELNET will work with the new application. On the negative side, it means that the server machine is virtually dedicated to the single application: anyone who **telnet**s to it, by default, will end up in my application.

To you, it also means that when you connect to a computer using TELNET, you won't get the normal login prompt, which I hope you are familiar with by now.* You get whatever the writer of the service wanted to give you. So, you need to approach these services with a bit more caution. Here are a few notes which you might keep in mind when dealing with one of these beasties:

- Almost every server is different. Some have good user interfaces; some have horrible user interfaces. What you get is what you get. Most have help facilities (some useful, some not so useful).

- Most servers will ask for a terminal type of some sort when you enter. "VT100" is probably the most common choice—many terminal emulators, and most window systems deal with it. If you don't know what kind of terminal to ask for, if your terminal isn't represented, or "VT100" does strange things, then fall back to "hardcopy" or "dumb."

- On their first screen, most servers will tell you how to log out, or terminate your session. Look for this information when you start a session; that will keep you from getting stuck. Of course, you can always use TELNET's escape character to get out of a session. (Make sure you know what it is.)

Telnet to Non-standard Ports

Requiring that you dedicate a computer to a non-standard service limits non-standard servers to applications where user friendliness is paramount. However, there's another solution to this problem which strikes a compromise between friendliness and capital investment. What you really want to do is use the user's existing **telnet** client program, but write a special application server without preventing the serving machine from offering normal TELNET services. This can be done, but to understand how you need to know a bit more about how the Internet works. Since most computers provide many different servers (for **telnet** and other applications), there needs to be a way for the software communicating with the network to decide which server is to handle a request. This is accomplished by assigning each server a specific *port* number as identification. When the server starts running, it tells the network software which port it is responsible for servicing.† When a client program wants to connect to some service, it must specify both the address (to get to a particular machine) and a port number (to get to a particular service on that machine). Frequently-used applications have standard port numbers assigned to them; TELNET is assigned to port 23, for example.‡

---

*There's one variation of a "non-standard" server that's worth knowing about. Sometimes you get a standard login prompt; then you use a special login name (like "library") to start a special application program. You're still using the standard TELNET server.

†These are "virtual" ports that are used by software to differentiate between various communications streams. Don't confuse them with terminal ports, SCSI ports, etc., which are actual hardware plugs.

‡On BSD UNIX systems, the standard port numbers can be found in the file */etc/services*. Standard port number assignments are documented in an RFC titled "Assigned Numbers." At the time of this printing, this number is RFC1340, but it gets updated periodically; newer versions will have a different number.

Now we can see how to use a standard client for another application—all we need is some way to make use of another port number. Private applications have to use an unassigned port that the client and server agree upon. If we write our non-standard server and tell it to listen to some other port (say, for example, port 10001), and if we can tell users to "connect" their **telnet** client to port 10001 on our machine, we're home free.

In fact, there are many such applications scattered around the Internet. When applications are provided over non-standard ports, the documentation about the service (or the person telling you to use it) must tell you which port to use. For example, let's try to use the LCSgated service, which provides access to the University of Illinois's library card catalog. If this service were in the *Resource Catalog* in the back of this book, you'd see an entry:

```
Access:  telnet garcon.cso.uiuc.edu port 620
```

This tells you to "connect to **garcon.cso.uiuc.edu** using **telnet**, but don't use the default port (23); use port 620 instead." Frequently, this is done by adding the target port number after the machine name. For example:

```
% telnet remote-machine-name port#
```

Here is the actual session accessing that service:

```
% telnet garcon.cso.uiuc.edu 620
Trying 128.174.5.58...
Connected to garcon.cso.uiuc.edu.
Escape character is '^]'.
Connected to LCSgated..

   You are connected to LCSgated, a network interface
to Illinet Online, the library system at the
University of Illinois at Urbana-Champaign.  This
interface has special commands in addition to supporting
LCS and FBR commands to help you find the books you want.

Type "?" for a list of commands.

For instructions, type 'help'.  To exit, type 'exit'.

Mail questions or comments to gibbs@garcon.cso.uiuc.edu .
logged in.

LCSgated> exit

Connection from LCSgated closed.
Connection closed by foreign host.
%
```

There are two things worth noting about this session. First, rather than receiving the usual login prompt, you ended up right in the middle of an application. If you type **help**, you'll see a list of commands that are valid for this particular server. Every non-standard server has its own set of commands. To find out how to use the server, you'll have to rely on its "help" facility. Most servers tell you how to get help when you establish a connection.

Second, because you never saw a login prompt, you never had to log in—you didn't even need an account on **garcon.cso.uiuc.edu** to use the service. Of course, the non-standard server can have its own login procedure; you may need to register with some authority to use the service, and that authority may want to bill you for your usage. But many services are free and "open to the public."

In this example, we used TELNET to connect to a non-standard port, and thus accessed a special service. In practice, you will see both solutions: non-standard TELNET servers that use the standard port (port 23), that are therefore dedicated to a particular task; and non-standard servers that use a non-standard port. Our *Resource Catalog*, and other databases of network resources, tell you when a non-standard port is necessary.

Mimicking Alternate Clients

Another use for **telnet**ting to a different port is to masquerade as a different client. This technique is used primarily to debug the client-server relationships when developing applications. If I were having trouble with my network news reading program (more on net news later) and didn't know whether the problem lay with the client or with the server, I could bypass the client on my machine by using the command:

```
% telnet sonne.uiuc.edu 119
```

This command connects me directly to the news server on **sonne** rather than the TELNET server; 119 happens to be the port that the news server uses. At this point, I could type in NNTP (the news distribution protocol) commands to exercise the server and see if it is acting as expected.

Telnetting to IBM Mainframes

If you've used computers for very long, you've probably come to expect IBM mainframes to exhibit their own behaviors, just to confuse the rest of the world. TELNET is no exception. As far as TELNET is concerned, we can divide IBM applications into two classes: "line-mode" applications and "3270" (or "full-screen") applications. We'll consider each of them separately.

First, line-mode applications. These are more-or-less what you're used to. Line-mode means that the terminal sends characters to the computer a line at a time. This is the way most common terminals behave, and it's the way TELNET normally behaves. So line-mode applications don't present a problem. You might have to issue the **set echo** command to **telnet**, since line-mode applications sometimes don't echo the characters you type. But with this warning, you're all set. You can **telnet** to an IBM system, start your application (giving the **set echo** command if the characters you type don't appear on your screen), and everything will work normally.

Now for 3270 applications, which are (unfortunately) nowhere near as simple. First, what does "3270" mean? For a long time, IBM computers have used a proprietary full-screen terminal known as a 3270. The 3270 was designed to make data entry (filling in forms, etc.) easier for the user and less of a load on the system. Therefore, they have many features that you won't find on garden-variety terminals: protected fields, numeric fields, alphabetic fields, etc. There are also several special purpose keys, notably *programmed function* ("PF keys"), which may have special commands tied to them. The terminal operates on block transfers, which means that it doesn't send anything to the host until you press the ENTER key or a PF key; when you do, it sends a compressed image of the screen changes since the last transmission. Obviously, then, a 3270 application is going to require some special handling. It is usually possible to use a 3270 application in line mode, but it will be pretty unpleasant.

To use a 3270 application on its own terms, you really need a "terminal emulator" that can make your system act like a 3270 terminal. In many cases, the IBM mainframe that you're connected to will provide the terminal emulation itself. In this case, you can use the garden-variety TELNET to "connect" to the computer. When TELNET connects, the mainframe will ask you what kind of terminal you are using. After you tell the system your terminal type, you're ready to go. You don't need to do anything special, but you do need to know what the special keys are on your terminal, so read on.

If the host you contact does not provide some kind of 3270 emulation, you need to use a special version of TELNET that has an emulator built-in. This version is called **tn3270**. First, how do you know when you need **tn3270**? If you **telnet** to some system and see a message like this:

```
% telnet vmd.cso.uiuc.edu
Trying 128.174.5.98...
Connected to vmd.cso.uiuc.edu.
Escape character is '^]'.
VM/XA SP ONLINE-PRESS ENTER KEY TO BEGIN SESSION .
```

you know you're talking to an IBM mainframe. Two flags should give you a clue to this. One is the string "VM" or "MVS" in the message; these are the names of IBM operating systems. The other clue is that the message is entirely in capital letters, which is fairly common in IBM land. (Of course, there are other operating systems that do all their work with uppercase letters.) In this case, you should be able to use the computer system with regular TELNET, but it will be cumbersome; **tn3270** will probably work better. Definitely try **tn3270** if you run into trouble.

You should also try **tn3270** if something funny happens to your session:

```
% telnet lib.cc.purdue.edu
Trying 128.210.9.8...
Connected to lib.cc.purdue.edu.
Escape character is '^]'.
 Connection closed by foreign host.
```

TELNET managed to connect to the remote system, but something went wrong, and the remote system gave up. In this example, the remote system is so entrenched in the 3270's features that it quit and closed the connection when it found you were not using them. (Note: many things can cause a connection to close immediately; this is only one of them.)

In this case, using **tn3270** gives you completely different results. Here's how you start:

```
% tn3270 lib.cc.purdue.edu
Trying...
Connected to lib.cc.purdue.edu.
```

Then the screen clears and you see:

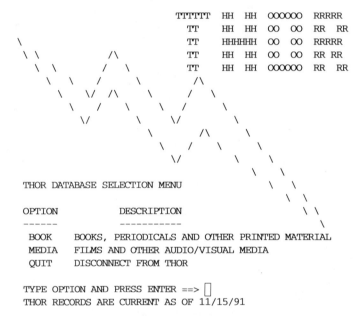

```
                                TTTTT  HH  HH  OOOOOO  RRRRR
                                 TT    HH  HH  OO  OO  RR  RR
\                                TT    HHHHHH  OO  OO  RRRRR
 \ \             /\              TT    HH  HH  OO  OO  RR RR
  \ \       /  \                 TT    HH  HH  OOOOOO  RR  RR
   \  \  /      \       /\
    \  \/  /\    \     /  \
     \  /  \  \   \   /     \
      \/       \  \/         \
        \         /\          \
         \   /   /  \          \
          \/        \           \
                     \  \
   THOR DATABASE SELECTION MENU   \  \
                                   \  \
   OPTION          DESCRIPTION      \  \
   ------          -----------       \
     BOOK    BOOKS, PERIODICALS AND OTHER PRINTED MATERIAL
     MEDIA   FILMS AND OTHER AUDIO/VISUAL MEDIA
     QUIT    DISCONNECT FROM THOR

   TYPE OPTION AND PRESS ENTER ==> []
   THOR RECORDS ARE CURRENT AS OF 11/15/91
```

This is more like what the designer of the THOR system wanted.

Using a system in 3270 mode usually involves "filling in the blanks" and hitting PF keys or ENTER to get work done. You get to the blanks you want to fill in by moving the cursor to them and typing. When you want to send the completed form to the computer, you hit ENTER. Optional commands can be executed by hitting PF keys rather than ENTER. The bottom of the screen frequently lists the functions that are available through the PF keys; they often vary, depending on what you are doing. If the screen gets too full, or if the system prints an "important" message, the keyboard will lock until the screen is cleared using the CLEAR key. Clearly, this is not your run-of-the-mill terminal.

tn3270 is the only practical way to use some machines on the network, but it is confusing. The first problem is finding the program. Sometimes it is a funny mode of TELNET; if your **telnet** client detects it is talking to an IBM system, it may start talking **tn3270** automatically. With some versions of TELNET, you may find a **tn3270** option in the command menu. Most of the time, however, **tn3270** is a stand-alone program. If you need it, try typing **tn3270** and see if it starts. **tn3270** is currently part of the normal distribution of BSD 4.3 UNIX, but some older systems may not have it. It comes with most TCP/IP products for microcomputers. You can use Archie to locate a free copy of the software (for UNIX or any other system). See Chapter 9, *Finding Software*, for information about how to use the Archie service.

Once you've found **tn3270**—or even if the mainframe is taking care of 3270 emulation for you—you need to figure out how the 3270's special keys have been mapped onto your keyboard. There is no agreement on how to do this; it differs from system to system. That is, some implementations think that the PF keys should be mapped onto the numeric keypad that's to the right of the keyboard (PF1 being 1, PF2 being 2, and so on); other emulators think that the key sequence **ESC 1** should stand for PF1; some use the special function keys that are often placed above the keyboard; etc. In this book, we can't describe the different variations that you might encounter, because it is determined by the person who installed the emulator or **tn3270** you are using. However, we can tell you what you need to know and how to "feel" your way around. You need to know the keys for moving the cursor, clearing the screen, PF, and "reset."* In addition, make sure you know how to escape to command mode, so you can "close" the connection if things go wrong. This should be similar to the regular **telnet** program's "escape" command.

If you are lucky, the program's documentation or the person who installed the program might be able to provide a key map. If not, here are some hints to help you:

- Make sure that you identify your terminal correctly. (If you are using an ADM 3A terminal and the computer thinks you are using a VT100, things will be really confused.)

- To position the cursor, first try arrow keys, if they exist on your keyboard. If there are no arrow keys, or if you try the arrow keys and the cursor doesn't move, try the h, j, k, l keys (just like the UNIX text editor *vi*, if you are familiar with that). Failing that, the TAB key almost always works. It takes you to the next field you can type into. By using TAB repeatedly you can move the cursor around, albeit inconveniently.

- ENTER is usually the carriage return or the ENTER key near the numeric keypad.

- To find the function keys: First try any keys marked F1, F2, etc., or PF1, PF2, etc. You are looking for the screen to change, or for a message like "PF4 Undefined" to appear. (This message means that you have successfully sent a PF key, but no command has been assigned to it.) If that doesn't work, try the numeric keypad, or the sequence "ESC-number;" e.g., try typing **ESC 1** to send PF1. If you still have no luck, you need to search for the key map (as described below).

---

*Reset unlocks the terminal after you have typed something illegal. Some implementations don't support reset.

- To clear the screen, try **CTRL-z**, **CTRL-l** (lowercase L, not the digit one), or **CTRL-home**. One of these should work.

- Implementations running on menu-driven workstations sometimes use menu items to send special keys.

If these hints didn't help, and you are using regular TELNET to contact the host (i.e., if the terminal emulator is running on the remote system, not your local system), you're out of luck. Try to contact the help desk for the remote computer and asking for a copy of their key mappings. If you are using **tn3270**, there is one more thing you try: look around for a file named *map3270* (or something similar), either in same directory as the program, the system area or folder, or in the */etc* directory. It should contain a list of terminal types and, for each terminal type, the key sequences which do good things. Unfortunately, its form is fairly unreadable. This is a portion of the entry for VT100-type terminals from the standard BSD UNIX distribution:

```
vt100 | vt100nam | pt100 | vt125 | vt102 |          the list of terminals
   direct831 | tek4125 | pcplot |  microvax{        this map describes
enter = '^m';
clear = '^z' | '\EOM';                              the clear key is
...                                                 control-z or ESC O M
# pf keys
pfk1 = '\EOq' | '\E1'; pfk2 = '\EOr' | ...          PF1 is either ESC O q
...                                                 or ESC 1; PF2 is ...
# local control keys

escape = '^c';  # escape to telnet command mode
master_reset = '^g';
...
}     # end of vt100, etc.
```

This particular key mapping is the basis for many **tn3270** implementations. There may be a guide for reading it at the beginning of the file to help you along, but the two major notational hints you need are: a **\E** stands for the ESC key on the keyboard, and the **^** stands for the control version of the following letter. That is, **^c** stands for hitting the c key while holding down the CTRL key.

A final word of caution. There are many **tn3270** programs that don't work well in more specialized IBM applications. You may find that your version of **tn3270** works just fine doing mundane things on an IBM system (e.g., electronic mail, editing files, etc.), but as soon as you start the big software package you really wanted to use, it dies with a message:

```
Unexpected command sequence - program terminated
```

This is because the original **tn3270** program, which is the basis for a lot of implementations, could not handle certain correct, but infrequent, 3270 control codes. Therefore, **tn3270** will work correctly until you try to run a program that uses one of the codes that it can't handle. There is only one solution to this problem: try to get a better, usually newer, version of **tn3270**.

CHAPTER SIX

MOVING FILES: FTP

Getting Started with FTP
Anonymous FTP
Handling Large Files and Groups of Files
Special Notes on Various Systems
Last Words: Some Practical Advice

Often, you will find information on the Internet which you don't want to examine on a remote system: you want to have a copy for yourself. You've found, for example, the text of a recent Supreme Court opinion, and you want to include pieces of it in a brief you are writing. Or you found a recipe that looks good, and you want to print a copy to take to the kitchen. Or you found some free software that just might solve all your problems, and you want to try it. In each case, you need to move a copy of the file to your local system so you can manipulate it there. The tool for doing this is **ftp**.

ftp is named after the application protocol it uses: the "File Transfer Protocol (FTP)." As the name implies, the protocol's job is to move files from one computer to another. It doesn't matter where the two computers are located, how they are connected, or even whether or not they use the same operating system. Provided that both computers can "talk" the FTP protocol and have access to the Internet, you can use the **ftp** command to transfer files. Some of the nuances of its use do change with each operating system, but the basic command structure is the same from machine to machine.

Like **telnet**, **ftp** has spawned a broad range of databases and services. You can, indeed, find anything from legal opinions to recipes to free software (and many others) in any number of publicly available online databases, or archives, that can be accessed through **ftp**. For a sampling of the archives that you can access with **ftp**, look at the *Resource Catalog* in this book. If you're a serious researcher, you will find **ftp** invaluable; it is the common "language" for sharing data.

ftp is a complex program because there are many different ways to manipulate files and file structures. Different ways of storing files (binary or ASCII, compressed or uncompressed, etc.) introduce some complications, and may require some additional thought to get things right. First, we will look at how to transfer files between two computers on which you have an account (a login name and, if needed, a

59

password). Next, we'll discuss "anonymous FTP," which is a special service that lets you access public databases without obtaining an account. Most public archives provide anonymous FTP access, which means that you can get gigabytes of information for free—without even requiring that you have a login name. Finally, we'll discuss some common cases (accessing VMS, VM, DOS, or Macintosh systems) which require some special handling. Unfortunately, there are a number of partial implementations of **ftp**, so all facilities may not be available on your system.

Getting Started with FTP

First, we'll consider how to move files between two computers on which you already have accounts. Like **telnet**, **ftp** requires you to specify the machine with which you would like to exchange files. This can be done with the command:

```
% ftp remote-machine-name
```

This starts the **ftp** program and connects to the named machine.

When **ftp** makes the connection with the remote computer, you will be asked to identify yourself with a login name and password:

```
% ftp sonne.uiuc.edu
Connected to sonne.uiuc.edu.
220 sonne FTP server (SunOS 4.1) ready.
Name (ux.uiuc.edu:krol): krol          send login name krol
331 Password required for krol.
Password:                              type the password; it isn't echoed
230 User krol logged in.
```

With some operating systems, like DOS and the Macintosh system, **ftp** may not ask for a password; it may only demand a login name, since there is no password security on the system. On these machines, protection from unwanted access is usually handled by disabling the FTP server software.

If you respond to the "name" prompt with a carriage return, many versions of **ftp** will send the login name that you are using on the local system. In the above example, the name of the local system and the default login name are shown in parentheses (**ux.uiuc.edu:krol**). Therefore, as a shortcut we could have typed a carriage return instead of the full login name. The login name you use will determine which remote files you can access, just as if you logged into it locally. However, remember that you have to use a login name and password that are appropriate for the remote system.

After the remote system has accepted your login name and password, you are ready to start transferring files. **ftp** prints ftp> to prompt you for further commands. **ftp** can transfer files in two directions. It can take a file on the local machine (the one initiating the transfer) and **put** it on the remote machine; or it can **get** a file from the remote machine and place it on the local machine. The **get** and **put** commands have the syntax:

```
ftp> get source-file destination-file
ftp> put source-file destination-file
```

The *source-file* is the name of the existing file (the file that you want to copy); *destination-file* is the name of the newly created copy. The *destination-file* name is optional; if it is omitted, the copy is given the same name as the source file. In the following example, we start by logging into machine **ux.uiuc.edu** under the name **edk**. We transfer the file *comments* from the machine **sonne.uiuc.edu** under login name **krol**'s default directory to the originating machine. Then we transfer the file *newversion* to **sonne.uiuc.edu**, renaming the new copy to *readthis*:

```
ux login:    edk                      send login name edk to ux
password:                             type the password; it isn't echoed


    Welcome to ux.uiuc.edu

ux% ftp sonne.uiuc.edu
Connected to sonne.uiuc.edu.
220 sonne FTP server (SunOS 4.1) ready.
Name (ux.uiuc.edu:edk): krol          send login name krol
331 Password required for krol.
Password:                             type the password; it isn't echoed
230 User krol logged in.
ftp> get comments                     request copy of file comments
200 PORT command successful.          be moved from sonne to ux
150 ASCII data connection for comments (128.174.5.55,3516) (1588 bytes).
226 ASCII Transfer complete.
1634 bytes received in 0.052 seconds (30 Kbytes/s)
ftp> put newversion readthis          copy newversion to sonne
200 PORT command successful.          from ux; rename it as readthis
150 ASCII data connection for readthis (128.174.5.55,3518)
226 ASCII Transfer complete.
62757 bytes sent in 0.22 seconds (2.8e+02 Kbytes/s)
ftp> quit                             end this session
221 Goodbye.
ux%
```

There are a few things worth mentioning about the example. First, knowing how to quit from any program is as important as knowing how to start it. When we finished transferring the files, we gave the **quit** command to terminate the **ftp** program. The command **bye** does the same thing; depending on your background, you may find **bye** easier to remember.

Notice that we did not show you how to look around and figure out which files you actually wanted; we just "knew" that there would be a file named *comments* in our home directory on **sonne**. Don't be afraid; omniscience isn't required. **ftp** has commands to list and change directories; we'll explain them a little later in this chapter. But if you already know what you're looking for, **put** and **get** are all you need.

ftp is fairly verbose; it gives you a lot of information about what it's doing. Unfortunately, the messages are rather arcane and inconsistent; **ftp** was designed before "user-friendliness" was invented. All of the messages begin with a "message number," which is eminently ignorable. However, the message texts (arcane though they may be) are worth scanning.

Finally, after each transfer, the program tells you what it transferred, how big it was, and the average transfer rate. The transfer rate will vary, depending on the load on the end machines and what network route the packets are taking. You might find this information interesting but, if not, you can ignore it.

Common Problems

In the previous example, we typed the password and login name correctly. However, you won't always be so lucky. If you make a mistake, you'll get a "Login incorrect" message. There are two ways to handle this. You can exit **ftp** and try again; or you can give the **user** command, followed by your login name, to restart the login process. You'll be prompted again for your password, and can continue from there:

```
ux% ftp sonne.uiuc.edu
Connected to sonne.uiuc.edu.
220 sonne FTP server (SunOS 4.1) ready.
Name (ux.uiuc.edu:edk): krol          login name krol
331 Password required for krol.
Password:                             type the password incorrectly
530 Login incorrect.
Login failed.
ftp> user krol                        start again with the login name
331 Password required for krol
Password:                             this time, get the password right
230 User krol logged in.
ftp>
```

It's a bit confusing because if your first attempt to log in fails, you get an `ftp>` prompt, but you can't do anything with it. You have to complete the login process before proceeding.

There are, of course, other things that can go wrong. You can misspell the name of the computer you're trying to reach; this will probably earn you the message "unknown host" (or something of that sort). Check the spelling of the hostname. If the host you're trying to access has crashed, or is unreachable for some other reason, you'll see the message "host not responding," "host unreachable," "connection timed out," or something along those lines. In this case, your only solution is to wait and try again later. If the situation persists for a long time, try contacting whoever is responsible for the remote system. (More help on how to deal with problems in Chapter 15, *Dealing with Problems*).

If you misspell the name of the file you're trying to transfer, you'll see a message saying "no such file or directory," or the equivalent. Make sure you typed the name correctly, and make sure that the file you want to copy actually exists; we'll show you how to do that in the next section.

Finally, remember that some files you may find on the Net are huge (all right, pretty big—over a million characters). Some systems place file size limits on their customers, or your diskette may not have room for large files. Make sure you have room for the file before you start to transfer it. In the next section we'll see how to find out just how big a file is.

Browsing on a Remote Machine

When you are using **ftp**, you frequently don't know exactly what files you want and where they are located; you usually need to browse around to figure out what you really want to transfer. There are a few useful commands and techniques to allow this. The basic commands to list directory information on the remote machine are **dir** and **ls**. The two commands have the same format:

```
ftp> dir directory-name local-file-name
ftp> ls directory-name local-file-name
```

Both commands list the files in the given directory on the remote machine, putting their output into a local file. Both arguments are optional. The second argument (the *local-file-name*) tells **ftp** to put the listing into the given filename on the local system. If you want the listing to appear on your terminal rather than saving it in a file, just omit this argument. Since you usually want the listing to appear on the terminal, the *local-file-name* argument is rarely used.

The first argument, *directory-name*, gives the name of the directories or files that you want listed. If it is omitted, **ftp** lists the current remote directory. The first argument may contain "wildcard" characters, which are useful if you want to list something like "all files ending in the extension *.txt.*" However, there are no easy rules for wildcards; the wildcards are interpreted by the remote system. Therefore, their meaning will differ somewhat depending on what kind of computer you are trying to browse. Luckily, on *most* computer systems, the asterisk (*) is a wildcard that matches any group of characters. For example, on many machines the command:

```
ftp> dir test*
```

lists only files whose names begin with "*test.*" The biggest difference between systems is whether or not a wildcard can match a period.* On computers running the UNIX operating system, it can; so *test** would match filenames like *test.c* and *test.sh*, in addition to filenames like *test1* and *test*. On computers running the VAX/VMS or MS-DOS operating system, the "filename" and "extension" are considered different entities, so *test** only matches files with no extension (like *test1* and *testout*). In these systems, to match a name like *test1.txt*, you'd need a name like *test*.*.*

Now, back to the basic listing commands, **ls** and **dir**. Their output should be quite different. The **ls** command, by default, gives you a simplified listing of filenames

---

*This is, admittedly, a UNIX user's way of looking at the world. To do justice to VMS and DOS, we'll say it more precisely. Filenames have two fields, a "name" and an "extension," separated by a period. A wildcard can appear in either field (or both). But, since the name and extension are different entities, a wildcard in the name can't match any characters in the extension, and vice-versa. Under UNIX, there is no formal difference between a "name" and the "extension." Many (probably most) filenames have extensions, but there's nothing special about the extension; it's just part of the name.

with no additional information. It is designed primarily for making a list of files that can be easily used as input to another program. It should look something like this:

```
ftp> ls
150 Opening ASCII mode data connection for file list.
nsfnet
CIC
campus
scott
```

The **dir** command produces more complete information:

```
ftp> dir
150 Opening ASCII mode data connection for /bin/ls.
total 2529
-rw-------  1 krol    cso      110 Oct 31 08:18 .Xauthority
-rw-r--r--  1 krol    cso      821 Nov 21 15:11 .cshrc
-rw-------  1 krol    cso       68 Mar  4  1989 .exrc
```

The output of this command looks just like a full directory listing on the remote system. So, if you are connected to a computer running the VMS operating system, it will look like a VMS **direct** command. If you are connected to a UNIX machine, it will look like a Berkeley UNIX **ls –lga** command was issued. This is because the client tells the server to send the directory information; the server executes an appropriate command, and then sends the listing back to the client untouched. There are some sloppy **ftp** implementations for which the **dir** and **ls** commands are synonyms.

The ultimate in directory commands, which only works if the remote system is running UNIX, is **ls –lR**. This is a "recursive" listing; it lists all files in the current directory and, if there are subdirectories, lists those files too, continuing until it exhausts the subdirectories of subdirectories. This lists just about every file which you can get to with **ftp**. Output from this command looks like:

```
ftp> ls -lR
200 PORT command successful.
150 Opening ASCII mode data connection for /bin/ls.
total 2529
-rw-------  1 krol    cso      110 Oct 31 08:18 .Xauthority
-rw-r--r--  1 krol    cso      821 Nov 21 15:11 .cshrc
drwx------  3 krol    cso      512 Oct  3  1989 iab
-rw-r--r--  1 krol    cso     2289 Jan  5 12:34 index

iab:                     contents of iab directory above
total 51
-rw-r--r--  1 krol    cso    25164 Sep  1  1989 crucible
-rw-r--r--  1 krol    cso    14045 Oct  3  1989 iab
drwx------  3 krol    cso     1024 Jan  3  1990 ietf
-rw-------  1 krol    cso    10565 May 15  1989 inarc

iab/ietf:                contents of subdirectory ietf of iab
total 416
-rw-r--r--  1 krol    cso    24663 Jan 17  1990 agenda
drwxr-xr-x  2 krol    cso      512 Jul 13  1989 reports
```

```
iab/ietf/reports:
total 329
-rw-r--r--  1 krol    cso   46652 Jul 13  1989 jun89
-rw-r--r--  1 krol    cso   53905 May 11  1989 mar89
-rw-r--r--  1 krol    cso   53769 Jun 15  1989 may89
-rw-------  1 krol    cso   47429 Dec 15  1988 nov88

226 Transfer complete.
```

Be careful: it may produce large amounts of output. It is often a good idea to save the results of **ls –lR** in a file with the command:

```
ftp>ls -lR filename
```

So you do a few **dir** commands and see a few files which are likely candidates to **get**, but you're still not sure exactly which file you want. You could **get** the file, **quit** or suspend the FTP program, list the file, restart **ftp** if you find out that the file isn't what you want, and so on, but it would be a pain. What you would really like to do is list the file on your terminal to see if it is the right one. Many **ftp** implementations provide this facility; to invoke it, use a minus sign (–) instead of a destination filename:

```
ftp> get source-file -
```

For example:

```
ftp> get index -
200 PORT command successful.
150 Opening ASCII mode connection for index (2289 bytes).
The following archives are available at this site:

activism   Files related to activism in general, NOT to any
           particular "cause."


226 Transfer complete.
2289 bytes received in 0.41 seconds (5.5 Kbytes/s)
```

The problem with this technique is that the entire file is transferred to your terminal; this can be more than you want to see. One solution in this situation is to try to suspend the output with CTRL-S. (And, start it again when you have finished reading with a CTRL-Q). These are fairly standard suspend characters and may work on your computer.

A slightly more drastic approach is to send an interrupt to the server telling it to stop sending. (On UNIX, this is a CTRL-C character). This cancels the current transfer. Unfortunately, this will not stop the output immediately. The CTRL-C has to traverse the network to the sender and tell it to stop. While this is occurring, the server continues merrily pumping the file towards your terminal, so your system is still queuing data for your terminal because it is slower than the network. All of this means that you've got a lot more to look at before the interrupt takes effect.

On some systems, **ftp** allows you to pass the output of the listing into another program, which may treat it more rationally. Two obvious candidates in a UNIX environment are **more** and **grep**.* For example:

```
ftp> get source-file "|more"
```

lists a screen worth of data and waits for you to tell it to send more. And:

```
ftp> get source-file "|grep RFC"
```

scans the file as it is sent and only prints the lines which have the characters "RFC" in them.†

Neither command diminishes the network load very much. The sender doesn't know that the receiver is handling the output in a special way, so it still tries to send the file as quickly as possible. In the first case, congestion at the receiving end forces your system to tell the sender to stop sending temporarily. In the second case, the entire file is sent even though only pieces of it are typed. If you are likely to scan the file repeatedly for different strings, it is more efficient to get it once and process it locally on your system than to send it repeatedly across the network.

Directories in FTP

There are a number of commands in **ftp** to deal with filesystem directories—probably more commands than you'd want to have. There are so many commands because two sets of directories are involved during an **ftp** session: the working directory on the machine you are logged into (the local directory) and the directory on the machine you have asked **ftp** to contact (the remote directory). Moving around the local directory is easy:

```
ftp> lcd directory
```

where the usage rules are the same as for the UNIX **cd** command. These can be summarized as follows:

- If no directory is given, **lcd** sets your position back to the default directory for your account.

- If the directory starts with a slash (/), it moves you to the directory given regardless of your current position (absolute positioning).

- If the directory is . ., it moves you up one level from the directory at which you are currently positioned.

- If the directory starts with an alphanumeric character, it looks for the directory as a subdirectory of the current one.

****more** prints a file a screen at a time. **grep** prints only lines which contain a specified character or string.

†We won't describe the intricacies of **more**, **grep**, and pipes. If you're a UNIX user, you should know about them. If you don't, we strongly recommend that you look them up—but until you've figured them out, you can treat the "**|more**" and "**|grep** *string*" notations as "magic cookies": type them as-is, and they'll work. If you're not using UNIX, your system may provide some other way to handle this problem; check your documentation.

Manipulating the remote directory is a bit more restrictive,* and is done using the **cd** command:

```
ftp> cd directory
```

When you create a connection to a remote computer using **ftp**, you are initially placed in the same directory you would have had if you logged into that machine directly. You are also governed by the file and directory access permissions of the login name you are using on that computer. That is, you can't do anything you couldn't do if you were using that computer interactively, using either **telnet** or a terminal connected directly to it.

The format of the directory specification is the same as for the **lcd** command, except there is often no easy way to return to your default directory. If you were logged in directly, a UNIX **cd** command with no argument would return you to your default directory. **ftp** requires an argument to its **cd** command, and most implementations will prompt you for it if you omit it.

One way to get around this problem is to know the full directory path you are using on the remote computer. If you know it, whenever you get lost you can just specify the whole thing to **ftp** and be back on familiar turf. If you get lost, you can use the **pwd** command to find out where you are. **pwd** returns the path of the current working directory:

```
ftp> pwd
/mnt/staff/krol
```

You are then home free with **cd /mnt/staff/krol**.

ASCII and Binary Transfers

Now that you can move around and find files, let's think a bit more about how to transfer data. **ftp** has two commonly used ways ("modes") of transferring data, called "binary" and "ASCII." In a binary transfer, the bit sequence of the file is preserved so that the original and the copy are bit-by-bit identical, even if a file containing that bit sequence is meaningless on the destination machine. For example, if a Macintosh transferred an executable file to an IBM VM system in binary, the file could not be executed on that system. (It could, however, be copied from that VM system to another Macintosh in binary and be executed there.)

ASCII mode is really a misnomer: it should be called "text" mode. In ASCII mode, transfers are treated as sets of characters; the client and server try to ensure that the characters they transfer have the same meaning on the target computer as they did on the source computer. Again, think of a Macintosh file being transferred to an IBM VM system. If the file contains textual data, the file would be meaningless on the IBM VM machine because the codes used to represent characters on the Macintosh are different than those used on the IBM. That is, the bit patterns used to represent

---

*This is especially true if you are using the guest account, *anonymous*. We'll discuss this extensively later in this chapter.

an "A" on the Mac is not the same bit pattern as used on the VM system. In ASCII mode, **ftp** automatically translates the file from a Mac text file to an IBM VM text file: hence the file would be readable on the IBM machine.

If you are confused by this, think of giving someone a journal article published in German. Binary mode would be equivalent to photocopying the article, in which case it is useless unless the recipient understands German. (But if the recipient photocopies the article again and gives it to another German, it is useful even if the original recipient didn't understand it.) ASCII mode is equivalent to translating the article before giving it to the other person. In this case, it becomes useful to the person who doesn't understand German, but probably loses some detail in the translation process.

In the previous example, some of the messages made a big point of saying that this was an ASCII transfer. This is appropriate because the two files we were transferring were both text files. We don't know what kind of machine we're taking them from, and don't care; we just want to make sure that we can read the files on our machine. To make sure that **ftp** is in ASCII mode, enter the command **ascii**. To put **ftp** into binary mode, enter the command **binary**. The command **image** is a synonym for **binary**; you'll find that a lot of **ftp** messages use the phrase "image mode," or "I mode" when they mean "binary." For example:

```
ftp> binary            now we're ready to transfer a binary file
200 Type set to I.     I stands for "image," or "binary"
ftp> put a.out         transfer a UNIX executable (binary)
ftp> ascii             now we're ready to transfer a text file
200 Type set to A.     A stands for "ASCII," or "text"
ftp> get help.txt      retrieve a text (ASCII) file
```

Even if you are transferring files between identical machines, you need to be aware of the proper mode for what you are transferring. The **ftp** software doesn't know the machines are identical. So, if you transfer a binary file in ASCII mode, the translation will still take place, even though it isn't needed. This may slow the transfer down slightly, which probably isn't a big deal; but it may also damage the data, perhaps making the file unusable. (On most computers, ASCII mode usually assumes that the most significant bit of each character is meaningless, since the ASCII character set doesn't use it. If you're transferring a binary file, all the bits are important.) If you know that both machines are identical, binary mode will work for both text files and data files.

This means that it is important to know what kind of data you want to transfer. Table 6-1 gives you hints for some common file types:

Table 6-1: Common File Types and Modes

File	Mode
Text file	ASCII, by definition
Spreadsheet	Probably binary
Database file	Probably binary, possibly ASCII
Word processor file	Probably binary, possibly ASCII
Program source code	ASCII
Electronic mail messages	ASCII
UNIX "shell archive"	ASCII
UNIX "tar file"	Binary
Backup file	Binary
"Compressed file"	Binary
"Uuencoded"* file	ASCII
Executable file	Binary, but see below
"Postscript" (laser printer) file	ASCII

Many database programs use a "binary" format to store their data, even if the data is inherently textual. Therefore, unless you know what your software does, we recommend trying binary mode first for database files. Then see whether or not the file you have transferred works correctly. If not, try the other mode. For word processing programs, you can get a few additional clues. The so-called "WYSYWIG" word processors (word processors that produce typeset output on a laser printer, and have an elaborate display that matches the actual output very closely) usually store documents in a binary format. Some of these programs have a special command for writing text (i.e., ASCII) files that can be transferred in ASCII mode, but you may lose some formatting information. The simpler (and older) word processors that prepare text for a daisy-wheel or dot-matrix printer typically store data in an ASCII format.

"Executable" files are generally binary files; however, there are exceptions. Programs that are compiled and executed directly by the processor are always binary. However, most operating systems provide at least one "scripting" language that allows you to write sequences of commands that are then interpreted by some other program. UNIX provides several scripting languages, including the "shell" itself; it is very common to write programs from basic UNIX commands. With some operating systems, scripts are called "command files." Scripts are always text files.

On UNIX, you can use the **file** command to figure out the type of any file. This utility wasn't written with **ftp** in mind, so it gives you a lot more information than you really need. Here are some examples, taken from a SunOS system:

```
% file /bin/spell
/bin/spell:     executable shell script
% file /bin/ls
```

---

*__uuencode__ is a UNIX utility that we will mention in Chapter 7, *Electronic Mail*. The UNIX UUCP utilities use it to encode binary files in an all-ASCII representation, which makes them easier to transfer correctly.

```
/bin/ls          mc68020 pure dynamically linked executable
% file outline.txt
outline.txt      ascii text
% file telnet.ms
telnet.ms:       [nt]roff, tbl, or eqn input text
```

These commands tell you that the file */bin/spell* is an executable shell script, which you'd transfer using ASCII mode. This might surprise you; most people assume that any file in the UNIX */bin* directory is a binary executable. That's not true. The file */bin/ls* is a true binary executable (as you would expect), so you would transfer it in "binary" mode. *outline.txt* and *telnet.ms* are text files that you'd transfer in ASCII mode. *telnet.ms* happens to be input for the **troff** typesetting program. If you don't know what mode to use, binary is probably the best bet. Non-ASCII computers are becoming less common, so the translation step often isn't needed.

There are actually more modes available in many FTP implementations (e.g., **tenex**, an obsolete operating system format; **jis78kj**, a *kanji* character set for Japanese), but they are not commonly used.

Transferring Multiple Files

The **get** and **put** commands that we discussed earlier can only transfer one file at a time. On occasion, you want to transfer groups of files at a time. To do so, you can use the **mput** and **mget** commands. They have the syntax:

```
ftp> mput list of source files
ftp> mget list of source files
```

The **mput** command takes the files in the list and moves them to the remote system. The **mget** command moves files from the remote system to the local system. In both cases, the filenames will be the same on both the local and remote systems. The list of files can be arbitrarily long, and can include wildcards.

The actual rules for how wildcards are expanded are more complicated than the **ftp** documentation lets on. You can usually use an asterisk (*) to match zero or more characters and forget about the complexities. On UNIX systems, you can use a question mark (?) to match any single character. On other systems, you'll have to do some experimentation or some careful reading of the documentation to see what's legitimate.* Here's a typical session using **mget** and **mput**:

```
ftp> cd work                      change the remote directory
250 CWD command successful.
ftp> ls b*                        see what files are there
200 PORT command successful.
150 ASCII data connection for /bin/ls (127.0.0.1,1129) (0 bytes).
```

---

*The actual rules go something like this: When you're using **mput**, you're moving files from your local system to the remote system. The wildcards are expanded by your local system, and use the local system's wildcard rules. When you're using **mget**, you need to locate files on the remote system. In this case, **ftp** uses the remote system to see what, if anything, matches the wildcards. Therefore, the wildcard rules that **mput** and **mget** obey may differ, and **mget**'s rules depend on the remote system.

```
b.tst
bash.help
bsdman.sh
226 ASCII Transfer complete.
remote: b*
29 bytes received in 0.03 seconds (0.94 Kbytes/s)
ftp> mget b*                              try to transfer the files
mget b.tst? yes                           first file: do I really want it?
200 PORT command successful.
150 ASCII data connection for b.tst (127.0.0.1,1133) (68112 bytes).
226 ASCII Transfer complete.
local: b.tst remote: b.tst
81927 bytes received in 0.41 seconds (2e+02 Kbytes/s)
mget bash.help? no                        second file; do I really want it?
mget bsdman.sh? no                        third file; do I really want it?
```

Now let's try to "put" a group of files. This time, we'll explicitly put two filenames on the command, just to show you that it can be done.

```
ftp> mput login tblsz.c                   now try to put some files
mput login? yes                           first file: do I really want it?
200 PORT command successful.
150 ASCII data connection for login (127.0.0.1,1139).
226 Transfer complete.
local: login remote: login
2785 bytes sent in 0.03 seconds (91 Kbytes/s)
mput tblsz.c? y                           second file: do I really want it?
200 PORT command successful.
150 ASCII data connection for tblsz.c (127.0.0.1,1141).
226 Transfer complete.
local: tblsz.c remote: tblsz.c
975 bytes sent in 0.04 seconds (24 Kbytes/s)
ftp>
```

Note that the command we just gave, **mput login tblsz.c**, does *not* mean "put *login* on the remote system with the filename *tblsz.c*," as it would if it were a simple *put* command. It means "copy all the files on the command line to the remote system, in the current remote directory, without changing their names."

ftp normally asks you whether or not you want to transfer each file; you have to type **y** (or **yes**) to transfer the file.

Typing **n** (or **no**)* cancels the transfer. Being prompted for each file is annoying (particularly if you're transferring a large group of files), but it helps prevent mistakes. If you really dislike being prompted, or need to transfer a huge group of files, give the command **prompt**; that disables prompting. The whole group of files will be transferred without further intervention. Giving the **prompt** command again re-enables prompting.

---

*Actually, anything that begins with the letter **n** will do. In some implementations anything that does *not* begin with the letter **n** is taken as a "yes," so be careful!

There are a few things to watch out for:

- Remember that you don't get to specify the name for the destination file. All the names on the command line are interpreted as source files. It's particularly tempting to try to copy a group of files into a directory; watch out for this! You cannot use a command like the following:

```
ftp> mput ch*.txt book
```

where *book* is the name of a remote directory. Instead, you must use **cd** to change the remote directory.

```
ftp> cd book
...
ftp> mput ch*.txt
```

The same goes for **mget** commands.

- You cannot use **mput** or **mget** (or, for that matter, the regular **get** and **put**) commands to copy a directory. You can only use them to copy groups of plain files. Copying a directory yields unpredictable results. If you need to transfer a directory, create an archive of some sort and transfer the archive. We'll discuss how to do this later in the chapter.

- I have noticed that the **mget**, with wildcards, doesn't always work properly; it appears to depend on whether or not the **ls** command is implemented correctly by the remote FTP server. *Caveat emptor.*

FTP Command Summary

The following table summarizes **ftp**'s most useful commands. It includes all of the commands that we have discussed so far. These commands are available on most, if not all, **ftp** clients. **ftp** will show you the commands that are available on your particular client if you type **help**.

account *info*	Supplies additional accounting or security information which must sometimes be given within a session. Later, we'll see a situation in which the **account** command is needed for accessing IBM mainframes.
ascii	Enters ASCII mode, for transferring text files.
binary	Enters binary mode, for transferring binary files.
cd *remote-directory*	Changes the working directory on the remote machine.
close	Ends the **ftp** session with a particular machine and returns to **ftp** command mode. After a **close**, you can **open** a connection to a new system, or **quit** from **ftp**.
delete *filename*	Deletes the named file on the remote system.
dir *file destination*	Gives a full directory listing on the remote machine. *File* and *destination* are both optional. *File* can either be a single file

or a wildcard construction with a question mark (?) and an asterisk (*). The listing will show all filenames that match the specification. If *file* is omitted, the listing will show all files in the current remote directory. The *destination* is where the output should be put. It can either be a file on the local machine or a command which should filter the file. If omitted, the listing appears on the terminal.

hash

Tells **ftp** to print a pound sign (#) every time a block of data is transferred by a **get** or **put** command. Useful if you are not certain the network is working; it gives you a visual signal that data is actually moving. It is also lets you know that something's happening when you're transferring a very long file. If **ftp** is already printing hashes, the **hash** command tells it to stop.

help *command*

Prints a short bit of documentation about the command.

lcd *directory*

Changes the default directory on your local machine to named directory.

ls *file destination*

Gives a short directory listing on the remote machine. The arguments are the same as for **dir**.

mget *file-list*

Gets multiple files from the remote machine. The file list could be either a list of filenames separated by a space or a wildcard type construction usually with a "*" meaning any file and a "?" meaning anything at this position.

mput *file-list*

Puts multiple files onto the remote machine. The file list could be either a list of filenames separated by a space or a wildcard construction using "*" and "?".

open *machine-name*

Connects to the named machine. This is useful if you want to **connect** to a new system after transferring files from some other system. You must **close** your old connection first.

prompt

With **mget** or **mput**, the **prompt** command tells **ftp** to prompt you for confirmation before transferring each file. This is useful if you want to make sure you're not needlessly transferring files or (worse) overwriting files that already exist. If prompting is already enabled when you give the **prompt** command, **ftp** turns prompting off; it transfers all the files without asking any questions.

pwd

Prints the name of the current remote directory.

quit

Closes any connections that are currently open, and exits **ftp**.

user *user-name*   Sends the username to the remote machine to log in. This is useful if you type your username or password incorrectly. Rather than closing the connection and opening a new one, you can try again by issuing a **user** command.

Most **ftp** implementations actually have 70 or 80 commands, so this is obviously a shortened list. However, most of the commands are really only needed for esoteric purposes; unless you have very special needs, the commands we listed above will suffice.

Anonymous FTP

So far, the facilities we've discussed make it difficult to make a file available for everyone to use. For example, if I wanted to distribute a software package, I'd have to put it on the system and then pass out login/password combinations to everyone who wanted to get the software. This would be a burden, particularly for the administrator, but also for the user.

Anonymous FTP bypasses this limitation. It allows users who don't have a login name or a password to access certain files on a machine. Of course, there are strong restrictions: anonymous users can normally only **get** files (i.e., copy them); they can't install new files or modify files that already exist.* And there are strict limits to the files that they can copy.

When anonymous FTP is enabled, there is a special login name called *anonymous*. If you start **ftp**, connect to some remote computer, and give *anonymous* as your login name, **ftp** will accept any string as your password. It is generally considered good form to use your electronic mail address as the password, so the managers of the server have some idea of who is using it and can easily contact you if needed. (In fact, some systems are starting to demand you use a valid e-mail address before they will let you in.) After signing in as *anonymous*, you are allowed to **get** those files which are expressly permitted to the anonymous FTPers.

These additional restrictions on the files which you can access with anonymous FTP are enforced by changing the **cd** command. When you enter a system anonymously, you are placed at a particular place in the file directory system. That initial starting point is the starting point for all anonymous FTP access. From there, you can only move to subdirectories by giving the name of the subdirectory, or move back from a subdirectory to its "parent" by using the **..** argument. Positioning yourself absolutely, by using a directory beginning with a slash (/), is usually not allowed. Technically, it is legal; but **cd /pub** has been redefined to mean "move to the *pub* subdirectory of the initial anonymous FTP directory." You can use this if you get lost in an anonymous FTP session and need to get back to where you began. Your other

---

*There is a way to create directories which can be written by anonymous FTP users. This is frequently used for allowing people to submit articles or software for inclusion in an archive. If it is implemented it will work just like any other **ftp put**.

option is to use **cd ..** repeatedly to move up to where you started. The command **cdup** is a synonym for cd . . . .

Remember, when you are using anonymous FTP, you are a guest on some foreign system. Sometimes there will be usage restrictions posted:

```
230-Available for anonymous ftp only between 5 pm EST
230-and 8 am EST.
```

These are displayed when you first log in. Please observe them—if you don't the server might become disabled for us all.

Well, I guess it's time for an example. You were browsing through the *Resource Catalog*, and ran across a document called "Not Just Cows", a directory of useful agriculture oriented Internet resources. The entry for this document gave access information:

ftp ftp.sura.net; login **anonymous**; cd **pub/nic**;
get agriculture.list

This tells you to get a copy of the document via anonymous FTP from **nic.sura.net**. Your dialog with **ftp** to get this resource would look like this:

```
% ftp ftp.sura.net                      start up ftp to the server
Connected to nic.sura.net.
220 nic.sura.net FTP server (Version 6.9 Sep 30 1991) ready.
Name (ftp.sura.net:krol): anonymous    anonymous login
331 Guest login ok, send e-mail address as password.
Password: krol@ux1.cso.uiuc.edu        password doesn't really echo
230 Guest login ok, access restrictions apply.
ftp> cd pub/nic                         move to the directory
250-######WELCOME TO THE SURANET NETWORK INFORMATION CENTER##########
250-SURAnet                            info@sura.net
250-8400 Baltimore Blvd.               301-982-4600(voice)
250-College Park, Maryland  USA 20740-2498    FAX 301-982-4605
250-    Many of the documents available in this ftp archive are geared
250-towards the new user of the Internet. SURAnet has provided several
250-"How To" guides for network navigation tools such as, telnet, ftp,
250-and e-mail. These "How To" guides are available in the directory
250 CWD command successful.
ftp> dir                                list files
200 PORT command successful.
150 Opening ASCII mode data connection for /bin/ls.
total 4096
-rw-rw-r--   1 mtaranto 120       1226 Jun  4 17:39 .message
-rw-rw-r--   1 mtaranto 120       7545 Jul 15 18:30 00-README.FIRST
-rw-rw-r--   1 mtaranto 120      47592 Mar  5 17:04 BIG-LAN-FAQ
-rw-rw-r--   1 root     120     216594 Jan  3  1992 Internet-Tour.txt
drwxr-sr-x   2 mtaranto 120        512 Jul 22 13:37 NREN
-rw-r--r--   1 mtaranto 120       1657 Jul 10 20:17 NSFNET.policy.statement
drwxr-sr-x   2 mtaranto 120        512 Jun 29 13:17 ZEN
-rw-rw-r--   2 root     120       2555 Jan  3  1992 acceptable.use.policy
-rw-rw-r--   1 mtaranto 120      85677 May 11 17:29 agricultural.list
-rw-rw-r--   1 mtaranto 120      27840 Apr 17 14:10 archie.manual
        <remainder of list deleted for space>
```

```
226 Transfer complete.
1752 bytes received in 1.2 seconds (1.4 Kbytes/s)
ftp> get agricultural.list NJC          move the file
200 PORT command successful.
150 Opening ASCII mode data connection for agricultural.list (85677 bytes).
226 Transfer complete.
local: NJC remote: agricultural.list
88383 bytes received in 2.8 seconds (31 Kbytes/s)
ftp> quit
221 Goodbye.
%
```

Let's examine the preceding example and see what happened. Once you were connected to **ftp.sura.net**, which was specified on the **ftp** command, you used *anonymous* as the login name. As a password, you sent your e-mail address—it didn't print when you typed it. Next you issued the **cd pub/nic** to move to the directory specified in the *Resource Catalog* entry. The server responded with a message (all the lines beginning 250). Some newer FTP servers automatically display a file on your terminal whenever you enter a directory. You are likely to see this more and more. This feature is very helpful because it saves you having to look for files like *README* to find out what's in the directory. After listing the files to see if there is anything else you might want, you get around to copying the file you wanted named *agricultural.list* on the remote computer to *NJC* on your home computer.

That's all there is to it. Anonymous FTP is just like regular FTP, except that you don't need a password. The *Resource Catalog* in this book lists many other FTP archives that you can access; the "Archie" service can give you more information about what is available, and where to find it.

Handling Large Files and Groups of Files

Network users often need to transfer extremely large files, or large batches of files, across the network. You may need a large database, an archive of a discussion group, a set of reports, or the complete source code to BSD UNIX. All of these tend to be large. In this section, we'll discuss techniques for handling large files ("compression") and ways to accumulate large groups of files into a single archive to make them easier to transfer. Because most anonymous FTP sites already store files as compressed archives, we'll also discuss how to "unpack" such a file once you've transferred it to your system.

Compressed Files

To reduce the cost of storage and transmission across the network, large files are sometimes stored in *compressed format*. There are many techniques for data compression, and consequently a number of different compression programs that can be used. Text files run through a good data compression program can be reduced anywhere from 30% to 70% in size.

Compressed files are not really a problem to move across the network. They should always be treated as *binary* files for the transfer. The problem with them is that getting the file to the target system is only half the battle. After it is there, you must uncompress it before it is usable. This may or may not be easy, since there is no one standard for compression utilities.

Compressed files are usually flagged by an unusual suffix or extension on the filename. The most common compression utilities are:

Compression Program	Decompression Program	File Suffix	Typical Filename
compress	uncompress	.Z	*rfc1118.txt.Z*
pack	unpack	.z	*textfile.z*
Stuffit	unsit	Sit	*program.Sit*
PackIt	unpit	.pit	*report.pit*
PKZIP	unzip41	.ZIP	*package.ZIP*
zoo210	zoo210	.zoo	*picture.zoo*

If you are looking at the files available on a remote system and see these suffixes, that's a hint that the files are probably compressed. The suffix gives you a hint about what utility should be used to uncompress it. The program you need to uncompress the file will vary depending on what kind of computer you are using and what kind of compression was used. This is only the tip of the iceberg; there are about as many compression programs as there are types of computers. A very useful chart is available via **ftp** (see, I told you **ftp** was useful); after you finish the chapter you can get it yourself. See the *Resource Catalog* section for Computing - Compression and Archival Software Summary.

On UNIX, compression and decompression are usually done using the **compress** and **uncompress** utilities. Let's take the file we just retrieved, *NJC*, check its size, and compress it:

```
% ls -l NJC*                      list all files starting with NJC
-rw-r--r--  1 krol        61411 Dec 20 14:46 NJC
% compress -v NJC                 -v says tell me how much compression
NJC: Compression: 57% - replaced with NJC.Z
% ls -l NJC*                      now I have a .Z file only
-rw-r--r--  1 krol        26230 Dec 20 14:46 NJC.Z
```

Now we have a file called *NJC.Z*. The original file was 61411 characters long; the compressed file is only 26230 characters long, for a savings of roughly 57%. This means that the compressed file will take less than half as much storage, and half as much time to transfer from one computer to another. For a relatively small file (and 60 KB is not terribly large), the savings may not be important; but if you're storing many megabytes of data, and have a slow communications line, a 57% savings is very significant.

Let's decompress *NJC.Z*, to make the original file again:

```
% uncompress NJC.Z
% ls -l NJC*
-rw-r--r--  1 krol        61411 Dec 20 14:46 NJC.txt
```

We have the same useful file back. Note that its size hasn't changed; the uncompressed file is still 61411 bytes, just like the original. This is a quick, unreliable, and (frankly) unnecessary check that the file was decoded correctly.

Moving a Whole Directory

When you're using **ftp**, you often want to receive a whole file structure: a directory or collection of directories, not just a single file. **ftp** really isn't designed to do this effectively; it's not convenient to move 50 or 100 files at a time, and there are no commands for moving entire directories.

While this situation comes up all the time, it is particularly common when you want to get a set of files from some remote FTP archive. For example, someone who distributes a free software package by putting it in an FTP package usually needs to make dozens (maybe even hundreds) of files available. Rather than telling users to "ftp these 50 files," he or she usually uses a backup utility to aggregate all of these files into a single file (shown in Figure 6-1).

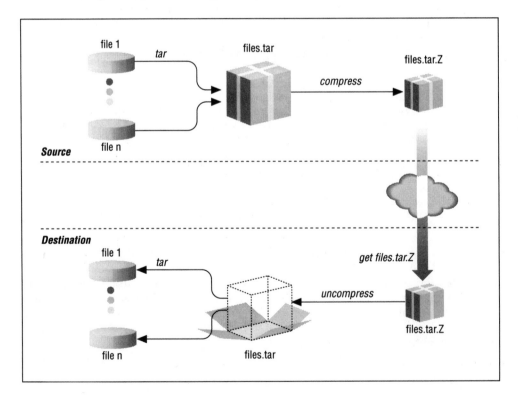

Figure 6-1: Moving many files

On the source computer containing the files to be distributed, the person responsible must copy all the files into one package. When someone gets the package, he or she must open it up to get the group of files that are contained. On a UNIX system, this single file is typically created using **tar**, as follows:

```
% cd book                              let's see what's in the directory
% ls                                   we plan to dump
README        ftp.2        news            tmac.Seffnuts
applications  ftp.bak      nut.guide       tmac.Sioc
% cd ..                                move to parent directory
% tar -cf book.tar book                dump directory book into book.tar
% ls -l book.tar                       how big is book.tar
-rw-r--r-- 1 krol        802816 Dec 21 06:35 book.tar
```

The directory to be packaged is called *book* and can be seen to contain a number of files. From the parent directory of *book*, the **tar** command is used to create a file named *book.tar* which contains all the data to be distributed. The file is quite large and is of no benefit to the owner anymore (he has the directory already). So, it makes sense to compress it as follows:

```
% compress -v book.tar
book.tar: Compression: 60.13% -- replaced with book.tar.Z
% ls -l book.tar*
-rw-r--r-- 1 krol        321717 Dec 21 06:35 book.tar.Z
```

That's better, only 40% as much disk space. The friendly system administrator now puts this file into the anonymous FTP directory, where it can be fetched by anyone in the world.

Some time later, you decide you want to pick up the "book" package and install it on your computer. You begin by using anonymous FTP to contact the server and retrieve *book.tar.Z*:

```
% ftp ux1.cso.uiuc.edu                 start an ftp to the server
Connected to ux1.cso.uiuc.edu.
220 ux1.cso.uiuc.edu FTP server (Version 5.60) awaits your command
Name (ux1.cso.uiuc.edu:): anonymous   log in as appropriate
331 Guest login ok, send ident as password.
Password:
230 Guest login ok, access restrictions apply.
Remote system type is UNIX.
Using binary mode to transfer files.  note binary mode
ftp> get book.tar.Z                    get the aggregate dump file
200 PORT command successful.
150 Opening BINARY mode data connection for book.tar.Z (321717 bytes).
226 Transfer complete.
321717 bytes received in 2.4 seconds (1.3e+02 Kbytes/s)
ftp> quit                              quit ftp
221 Goodbye.
```

You now have the compressed **tar** file; you only need to undo all the operations done to it to make it usable. Sometimes people are confused by the order of doing these multiple operations. You must undo them in exactly the opposite order they were performed to create the file. The rule of thumb is to do whatever it takes to handle the filename extensions right to left. So, with a file like *book.tar.Z*, you must first get rid of the *Z*:

```
% uncompress book.tar.Z          file is unusable until uncompressed
% ls -l book*                    now one file book.tar
-rw-r--r--  1 krol        802816 Dec 21 07:00 book.tar
```

Now you have an uncompressed **tar** file, *book.tar*. Get rid of the **tar** and you are done:

```
% tar -xf book.tar               extract all files in book.tar
% ls -l book*                    same file as before
-rw-r--r--  1 krol        802816 Dec 21 07:00 book.tar

book:                            and a whole new directory
total 792
-rw-r--r--  1 krol          4630 Sep  3 10:43 README
-rw-r--r--  1 krol         14461 Nov 11 15:18 applications
    <remainder deleted for space considerations>
```

You will find the command **tar –tf** *filename* useful, too. This lists the files that are present in the **tar** file; by looking at the list, you can figure out whether or not you got the right file.

From time to time, you will see some other complications. At some sites, extremely large archives are cut into many smaller pieces (usually 100 KB or so). Each piece is typically assigned a two-digit decimal number, which is the last part of the filename. For example, you might see files named *book.tar.Z.01*, *book.tar.Z.02*, etc. Transfer all of these files to your system. (Yes, this is a pain; yes, we did tell you that archive managers use **tar** to avoid large collections of files. If it's any consolation, remember that something large enough to require this treatment probably includes several hundred files. This is why **mget** exists.) Then assemble them in order; usually, a command like the following will work correctly:

```
% cat book.tar.Z.* > book.tar.Z
```

This assumes that the administrator has named each "chunk" of the archive so that **cat book.tar.Z.*** will produce the files in the right order. That's usually the case. Then proceed as normal; use **uncompress** to get a "tar" file, and **tar** to extract the source files from the archive:

```
% uncompress book.tar.Z
% tar xf book.tar
```

Some hints:

- Before you unpack a **tar** file, it's a good idea to give the command **tar –tf book.tar** to find out what files are contained. Make sure that unpacking the archive won't overwrite any files that you want. One misfeature of **tar** is that it can't rename files as it unpacks them; the names you see are the names you'll get.

- You can combine the "uncompress" and "unpack" steps into one command with **zcat book.tar.Z | tar –xf –**. This way, you don't leave an extra temporary file lying around.

Shell Archives

If you're using a UNIX system, you will also see *shell archives* from time to time. A shell archive is simply a composite file that is a Bourne shell script, or command file. Executing this shell script extracts the files. For example, say that you retrieve a file called *goodies.shar* from your favorite anonymous FTP site. To unpack this, just give the command:

```
% sh goodies.shar
```

It is very common to see shell archives that have been compressed, cut into chunks, or both. You should already know how to handle these special cases: reassemble the chunks, do whatever's necessary to decompress the file, and then use **sh** to unpack the archive.

When you're unpacking a shell archive, you're executing a program that someone else gave you. As we all know by now, it's unwise to place much trust in programs someone else wrote. There have been reports of malicious shell archives that delete all your files and take other hostile actions. Therefore, two warnings:

- *Always* look at the archive's contents before unpacking it. Make sure it doesn't do anything unreasonable. You'll have to learn a little shell programming (though not much) to do this.

- *Never* unpack a shell archive when you are logged in as "root." Should the archive do something hostile, you won't have any protection.

While there are many programs for creating a shell archive, and therefore many slightly different formats, don't worry: any properly constructed shell archive can be unpacked by any UNIX Bourne or Korn shell. If you want to create a shell archive, any number of **shar** programs are available from the Internet.

Other Archival Utilities

In my experience, **tar** archives are by far the most important, with "shell archives" a close second. There are a few other archive types you may see from time to time. You will occasionally see archives created by the UNIX **cpio** utility. You may see archives created by various programs on DOS systems (FASTBACK, ZIP, PCBACKUP, etc.) or the BACKUP utility on VMS operating systems. Unfortunately, most archival tools are specific to one operating system—if you're using a Macintosh, you probably don't have a **tar** command, let alone a VMS BACKUP command. Likewise, if you're using a UNIX system, you probably don't have a DOS FASTBACK program lying around. As a rule, therefore, an archive is only useful if you're unpacking it on the same kind of computer that created it. (The archive might be stored on another kind of computer, which is not important—as long as it is treated as a binary file.)

However, all is not lost. If the Internet presents some problems, it also gives you a way to resolve these problems. If you have the time and energy to poke through the acres of free software that's available on the Net, you *may* be able to find a program that will unpack some strange archive format on your system. There are definitely UNIX implementations of VMS BACKUP floating around; if you look hard enough, you might be able to find equivalent utilities for other operating systems. There is even some commercial software for this purpose; it costs money, but then you don't have to debug it yourself. (The chapter on Archie will tell you how to locate software.)

Special Notes on Various Systems

ftp's biggest virtue is that it lets you move files between computers regardless of their type. In many cases, you don't need to know anything about the remote systems. However, this isn't completely true; in practice, whenever you have two systems, you usually end up needing to know something (certainly not much, but something) about the remote system.

The problems are relatively minor, and typically have to do with the way the remote system specifies filenames. As much as possible, **ftp** uses a uniform, UNIX-like notation for filenames and addresses. However, this can be confusing, since **ftp** doesn't try to interpret **dir** listings and other output generated by the remote system: it just sends it back to you verbatim. Deciphering the output from **ls**, **dir**, or any other command usually isn't too difficult. It's fairly easy to find the filename, the file's size, and the last modification date, and that's usually all the information you care about. But you do need to know how to convert remote filenames into a form that **ftp** understands.

Here are a number of examples using **ftp** to access various kinds of systems that you will find as servers on the Internet. Remember that these are examples. There are many vendors of TCP/IP software for the Macintosh, Digital Equipment, and IBM computers. The server you are contacting might look a bit different from the examples we show here. Also, in most of the examples the remote system tells you what kind of computer it is. This is not always the case. If you don't know what kind of system you're using, your best bet is to look for *README* files; there's often one that explains what archive you're looking at, what kind of a system you're using, and so on. If this doesn't work, do a **dir** and try matching the format to the examples.

Target: Digital Equipment VMS Systems

VMS systems have a fairly feature-rich file structure. Logging into one presents no particular problems:

```
% ftp vaxb.cs.usnd.edu
Connected to vaxb.cs.usnd.edu.
220 FTP Service Ready
Name (vaxb.cs.unsd.edu:krol): anonymous        anonymous ftp
331 ANONYMOUS user ok, send real identity as password.
```

```
Password:
230 ANONYMOUS logged in, directory HSC1$DUA1:[ANON], restrictions apply.
Remote system type is VMS.
```

ftp was nice enough to tell you that it's talking to a VMS system, so you know what to expect. The complexity surrounding VMS lies in its file structure. We have been placed in a directory containing files accessible via anonymous FTP; the complete name of this directory is *HSC1$DUA1:[ANON]*. This name consists of two parts: *HSC1$DUA1* is the name of a disk; and *[ANON]* is a directory on that disk.*

Now that we have logged in, let's try a **dir** command to see what's available:

```
ftp> dir
200 PORT Command OK.
125 File transfer started correctly
Directory HSC1$DUA1:[ANON]

AAAREADME.TXT;9    2-MAY-1991 15:45:51    730/2    (RWED,RE,,R)
ARTICLES.DIR;1    28-MAY-1990 10:20:14   1536/3    (RWE,RE,RE,R)
LIBRARY.DIR;1     30-APR-1991 11:13:06   1536/3    (RWE,RE,RE,RE)
WAIS.DIR;1         1-OCT-1991 10:21:16    512/1    (RWE,RE,RE,RE)

Total of 4 files, 1448 blocks.

226 File transfer completed ok
```

Each file consists of a name (e.g., *AAAREADME*), an extension (e.g., *TXT*), and a version number (e.g., *9*). Ignore the version number;† you will almost always want the most recent version of a file, which is what you'll get if you pretend the version number doesn't exist. The extension tells you something about the file. *TXT* is the extension for text files, so these files may be read directly. Files with the extension *DIR* are directories. There are a number of other standard extensions, like *FOR* for FORTRAN files, *EXE* for executable files, *COM* for command files.

We see that the default directory for anonymous FTP has three subdirectories. Let's use **cd** to look at the subdirectory *wais.dir*. When you use **cd** to change directories, you use the directory name without the extension:

```
ftp> cd wais
200 Working directory changed to "HSC1$DUA1:[ANON.WAIS]"
```

Now our working directory is *HSC1$DUA1:[ANON.WAIS]*. Notice that VMS specifies a subdirectory by listing each subdirectory after a period within the brackets. So this subdirectory is roughly equivalent to the UNIX path *HSC1$DUA1/ANON/WAIS*. Likewise, it's equivalent to the DOS path *\ANON\WAIS*, on a disk named *HSC1$DUA1:*.

---

*If we had been using regular **ftp**, rather than anonymous FTP, we probably would have been placed in a "default directory," which is similar to the UNIX "home directory." The home directory name would probably be *HSC$1DUA1:[KROL]*.

†All right, we'll explain it. VMS has the peculiarity that it tries to keep around old versions of your files, until you explicitly tell it to delete them. This can waste tremendous amounts of disk space, but it does make it easy to undo your mistakes.

Unfortunately, the people who sell TCP/IP software for VAX/VMS systems don't agree about how the **cd** command should work, particularly when you want to move through multiple levels of directories. With some VMS FTP servers, you have to use a VMS-style directory specification, like this:

```
cd [x.y.z]
```

If the FTP server you're using expects this syntax, then to move up a level, you must use the command **cdup**; the UNIX-style **cd ..** will not work.

Other implementations expect you to specify multiple directories using the UNIX "slash" notation:

```
cd x/y/z
```

Which do you use? As I said, it depends on the software the FTP server is running. The easiest way to find out which syntax to use is to try one approach; if it doesn't work, try the other. No harm will be done if it doesn't work. If you want to be safe, you can move through one directory level at a time:

```
cd x
cd y
cd z
```

This strategy works in either case. And, once again, you must omit the *.dir* extension from the directory's name whenever you use it in a **cd** command.

get and **put** work in the usual way. You must specify the extension as part of the filename. You can include the version number, but it's easier to omit it (unless you want an old version for some special reason).* In this example, we will move two levels "down" the directory tree, and retrieve the file *waissearch.hlp* from there:

```
ftp> cd wais/doc          change to directory anon/wais/doc
200 Working directory changed to "HSC1$DUA1:[ANON.WAIS.DOC]"
ftp> get waissearch.hlp     get the file waissearch.hlp
200 PORT Command OK.
125 ASCII transfer started for
    HSC1$DUA1:[ANON.WAIS.DOC]WAISSEARCH.HLP; (1076 bytes)
226 File transfer completed ok
1076 bytes received in 0.35 seconds (3 Kbytes/s)
ftp>
```

As long as you aren't confused by the VMS-style file specifications, you should have no problems dealing with VAX/VMS systems.

---

*If you specify an old file version be sure to specify a local filename. If you don't you will probably end up with a filename that has a semicolon in it.

Target: IBM/PC DOS Systems

MSDOS systems look very much like other network servers. You log in using the normal manner:

```
% ftp server.uiuc.edu
Connected to server.uiuc.edu.
220-server.uiuc.edu PC/TCP 2.0 FTP Server by FTP Software ready
220 Connection is automatically closed if idle for 5 minutes
Name (server.uiuc.edu:): krol
331 User OK, send password
Password:
230 krol logged in
Remote system type is MSDOS.
```

Note that the remote system tells you that you are connected to a system running DOS.

It's also fairly obvious how to interpret the output of the **dir** command:

```
ftp> dir
200 Port OK
150 Opening data connection
        336             FS.BAT    Tue Dec 17 21:36:56 1991
          0             MBOX      Thu Nov 07 14:46:30 1991
        123             NS.BAT    Tue Jan 08 22:34:44 1991
<dir>             NETWIRE    Tue Jun 11 02:37:34 1991
<dir>             INCOMING.FTP    Tue Dec 17 21:42:24 1991
226 Transfer successful. Closing data connection
```

Filenames on a DOS computer consist of a filename (e.g., *FS*) and a three character extension (e.g., *BAT*). Subdirectories are flagged with the character string **<dir>** on the beginning of their line.

When you're dealing with a DOS server, you may be confused by the way that it handles directories. First, directories are disk-specific; you sometimes need to specify the disk on which the directory resides. Disks are identified by a single letter followed by a colon (:). The following **cd** command changed the "working disk" to the **h** disk:

```
ftp> cd h:
200 OK
```

If you now do another directory command, you will see a different set of files:

```
ftp> dir
200 Port OK
150 Opening data connection
<dir>             SYSTEM    Wed Dec 31 00:00:00 1980
<dir>             PUBLIC    Wed Dec 31 00:00:00 1980
226 Transfer successful. Closing data connection
```

Changing directories within a disk is done with a "normal" **cd** command:

```
ftp> cd public
200 OK
```

which changes to the subdirectory *public*. You can also move down multiple direc-tories at once with a command:

```
ftp> cd h:public/ibm_pc/msdos
200 OK
```

The trick is that DOS uses backslashes (\) to separate directory levels. However, when you access a DOS server with **ftp**, the server will try to be Internet-compat-ible and accept the slash rather than the backslash. If you use a backslash (as an experienced DOS user would expect), you'll get an error message:

```
ftp> cd h:public\ibm_pc\msdos
550 can't CWD: Error 2: No such file or directory
```

To add to the confusion, when you check the current directory, **ftp** will print the name using backslashes:

```
ftp> pwd
250 Current working directory is H:\PUBLIC\IBM_PC\MSDOS
```

Once you are positioned in the directory where the file you want lives, moving it works as expected:

```
ftp> get config.bak
200 Port OK
150 Opening data connection
226 Transfer successful. Closing data connection
99 bytes received in 0.12 seconds (0.82 Kbytes/s)
```

The moral of the story is very simple. When you're accessing a MS-DOS system using **ftp**, use slashes instead of backslashes. With this in mind, you won't be con-fused.

Target: IBM/VM Systems

IBM VM systems require a little more special handling. Most of the special handling is needed because VM doesn't have a hierarchical filesystem. On VM you have disks; each disk can have multiple passwords (one for read-only access and one for read/write access); and filenames are short but have two parts. When you **ftp** to a VM system and log in it looks like this:

```
% ftp vmd.cso.uiuc.edu
Connected to vmd.cso.uiuc.edu.
220-FTPSERVE at vmd.cso.uiuc.edu, 14:46:14 CST MONDAY 12/16/91
220 Connection will close if idle for more than 5 minutes.
Name (vmd.cso.uiuc.edu:krol):          took the default name: krol
331 Send password please.
Password:
230 KROL logged in; no working directory defined. Remote system type is VM.
```

Once again, **ftp** was nice enough to inform you that the remote system is VM. It also tells you that, even though you are logged in, you can't get at the files you want. The message "no working directory defined," which you see when **ftp** confirms that you are logged in, tells you that you aren't ready to transfer files yet.

When you do a **cd** command on a VM system, you are really asking to get at another disk. Disks are functions of a login name and an address. So, to cram this into a **cd** command you need to say:

```
ftp> cd login-name.disk-address
```

For example, the command:

```
ftp> cd krol.191
```

starts the connection to the disk addressed 191 of user krol. (You can find the name and addresses of the disks you normally use when logged in to a VM system by doing a **q disk** command while you are logged in.) A disk password is usually required; to supply the password, use the **account** command immediately *after* the **cd** command. Continuing the previous example:

```
ftp> cd krol.191
550 Permission denied to LINK to KROL 191; still no working directory
ftp> account j9876hoh
230 Working directory is KROL 191
```

Note that message 550 implies your **cd** command failed, even though it looked correct at the time. The **account** command, which you must give next, "fixes" the original **cd** command, so you can access files. Also, since your local system does not really know what the **account** command does on the remote computer, it makes no attempt to hide your password. Take precautions to make sure that others don't find out your password.

Now you have established a directory to work in. The output from a **dir** command looks like this:

```
ftp> dir
200 Port request OK.
125 List started OK
ACCNT    LEDGER   V    80     59      5 12/20/90  9:04:24 LEN
AGENDA   MEETING  V    73     34      2  9/24/91 10:23:01 LEN
ALL      NOTEBOOK V    80   5174    233 12/10/91 15:17:11 LEN
```

Each filename on an IBM VM system consists of two character strings. Each string has at most eight characters. The first string is called the "filename" and the second is call the "file type." Above, the filenames are in the first column (e.g., **ALL**), while the second column shows the file type (e.g., **NOTEBOOK**).

If **dir** doesn't show you all the files you expect to see, it's because there is also a file mode (1 or 0) associated with a file. A file with the mode 0 is considered "private" and cannot be seen with the "read" password. If you give the "write" password, you can see all the files. Again, the "read" and "write" passwords are set by the owner of the disk.

The filename and file type both must be specified if you try to move a file. Since both are variable length, you use a period (.) to separate the two. So:

```
ftp> get all.notebook mbox
```

transfers the file *all* of type *notebook* to the file *mbox* on the local machine.

If you're doing anonymous FTP and the remote host is a VM system, you still have to give a **cd** command before you can access any files. You don't have to give a second password with the **account** command. When you actually **get** files, you must (as you'd expect) give a complete, two-part filename.

Target: Macintosh

Using **ftp** to access a Macintosh server is fairly straight-forward, once you get connected. Getting connected might be a problem if the Mac is on a network that dynamically assigns addresses. Older Macs could not be connected directly to an IP network. They were frequently connected to a proprietary Apple network called *Localtalk*. Localtalk networks are connected with a gateway to the Internet. Some gateways would assign Internet addresses to computers as they are turned on, taking addresses from a pool reserved for the Localtalk net. This means that the address or name of a machine might change from day to day; the address that works today might not work tomorrow. This isn't usually a problem with public archives; anyone who configures their Macintosh as a public server usually takes steps to prevent this from happening. You are most likely to run into this problem when someone tells you to "grab this file from my workstation" on the spur of the moment. The remote system's owner tells you the IP number and you can grab the file, provided that the owner doesn't turn the system off first. Newer Macintoshes usually don't have this problem because they can handle Ethernet cards and be connected directly to the Internet.

When you get connected to a Macintosh, **ftp** will ask you for a name, but no password:

```
% ftp 128.174.33.56                    used an IP address this time
Connected to 128.174.33.56.            rather than a name
220 Macintosh Resident FTP server, ready
Name (128.174.33.56:krol):             send default name
230 User logged in
```

Doing a **dir** command will get a listing which looks like this:

```
ftp> dir
Accelerator
Administration/
Applications Combined
Article T3 connections
```

There are two things to note about this listing. One is that subdirectories, which in the Mac world are called *folders*, are flagged by the trailing slash (/). The second is that filenames can have spaces in them, which requires special handling. If a filename contains spaces, you must put the entire name within quotes. For example:

```
ftp> get "Applications Combined" applications
```

This gets the file *Applications Combined*, putting it into the file *applications* on the local machine. Aside from the Macintosh, most systems cannot handle names with spaces properly. Therefore, in the previous command we made a point of specifying a local filename without a space.

Changing directories is handled in the usual way. The command:

```
ftp> cd Administration
```

changes the current directory to *Administration*. If I wanted to move through multiple folders and subfolders, I would list the whole path separated with slashes:

```
ftp> cd Administration/Personnel
```

Last Words: Some Practical Advice

Because using **ftp** is fairly straight-forward, it is easy to get enthralled with the power it puts at your fingers and lose sight of its limitations. Here are a couple of hints that you may find useful:

- **ftp** allows you to create, delete, and rename files and directories on a remote system. Treat this ability as a convenience to use occasionally, rather than a technique to use all the time. If you are making a lot of changes to a remote system instead of moving files, it is probably easier to use **telnet** and do your changes as a timesharing session.

- Directions about anonymous FTP are frequently sketchy. Someone will tell you, "Anonymous FTP to **server.public.com** and get the Whizbang editor, it's really neat." Servers designed for these type of distributions frequently have a lot of things in them stashed in various directories. If you can't find what you are after, try looking for files in the default directory named *README*, *index*, *ls-lR*, or something like that for instructions to find your way around.

- On UNIX, **ftp** allows you do make some convenient things happen by putting instructions in the *.netrc* file of your home directory. This feature is usually used to create procedures of files manipulation commands and give instructions for automatically logging into a remote computer. You shouldn't setup automatic logins for computers needing a private login name and password (because you should never put your password in a file). But if you use one anonymous FTP server frequently, say **ftp.sura.net**, you could bypass the log in step by putting something like this in *.netrc*:

```
machine ftp.sura.net
login anonymous
password krol@ux1.cso.uiuc.edu
```

More information about this facility can be found in your FTP documentation.

- When you copy a file with FTP the file gets created with the standard access permissions that are used for any new file you create. If the file has special permissions on its originating system, they will not be preserved. In particular, if you transfer a file that requires execute permission (like *plan* or *.Xsession*), you'll have to give a **chmod +x** command before you'll be able to use it.

- Some **ftp** servers allow you to put "extensions" on filenames that are really file reformatting commands to the server. The two most common ones are **.tar** and **.Z**. For example, if a file named *program* exists and you issue the command **get program.Z**, the server will automatically compress the file before the transfer. With the **.tar** ending (e.g., **get pub.tar**), the file or directory is converted to a UNIX **tar** archive before transmittal. This makes it possible to transfer an entire directory tree with a single command. As you might expect, the server does nothing special if a file with the suffix already exists: for example, if *program.Z* already exists, the server will give it to you as is, without trying to compress it.

These are extensions to the normal FTP service which will probably become more widespread in the future. Right now, they may work and may not. If you use a server regularly, you might give them a try to see if they work.

ELECTRONIC MAIL

Most network users get their start by using electronic mail (*e-mail* for short). After sending a few hesitant messages (frequently followed up by a telephone call to ask if the mail arrived), most e-mail users quickly become comfortable with the system. Your confidence, too, will grow after you've gotten past the first few awkward messages; you'll be using mail frequently and with authority, customizing the system to meet your own needs and establishing your own mailing lists. Soon you will find that e-mail means much more than faster letters and memos. You can take part in electronic conversations about mystery writers, the stock market, or just about anything else you'd like. You might even decide that your telephone is superfluous.

How quickly you become comfortable with electronic mail has a lot to do with your knowledge of the medium and some basic technical decisions you make in choosing and using your e-mail system. There are any number of electronic mail programs for each kind of computer. To get enough background to talk about what good e-mail software is, we will start out discussing general facilities of electronic mail, mail addressing, and how electronic mail works. After that, using UNIX **mail** as an example, we will look at what features exist in e-mail packages. Finally, we will talk about how to use those features in concert to move files, take part in discussions, and deal with problems that you might run across.

When Is Electronic Mail Useful?

Like any other tool, electronic mail has its strengths and weaknesses. On the surface, it appears to be just a faster way of delivering letters, or their equivalent. To know when electronic mail is appropriate, think about how it differs from other communications media. In some ways, e-mail is very similar to the telephone; in other ways, it's similar to traditional postal mail. Table 7-1 makes a quick comparison.

Table 7-1: Comparison of Communication Techniques

	Telephone	**E-mail**	**Post**
Speed	High	Moderate	Low
Synchronized	Yes	No	No
Formality	Varies	Moderate	Varies
Accountability	Low	Moderate	High
Conferencing	Small group	Any to all	One way only
Security	Moderate	Low	High

First, let's think about how quickly each medium gets a message from one point to another. The telephone offers immediate delivery and works at a fairly high communication speed (although it is still far less than 64K bits per second). The time it takes to deliver electronic mail ranges from seconds to a day; and, as I'm sure you know, postal delivery can be overnight in the best case, but often takes several days. The price you pay for the quick communication of telephony is that the caller and the sender must be synchronized: that is, they must both be on the phone at the same time. E-mail and postal mail are both asynchronous: the sender sends when the time is ripe, and you read it at your leisure. This comes in handy if you are trying to communicate a long distance (e.g., over many time zones) when daily schedules are quite different.

The delivery time for e-mail consists of two parts: the time it takes the network to deliver the message to your mail computer, and the delay in your reading it once it gets there. The first part is a function of how your mail machine is connected to the network; it can only be changed with an influx of money. The second part is under your control. If you don't check your e-mail regularly, then quick delivery is meaningless. Your messages just sit there waiting for you to come look at them. Electronic mail becomes more useful as the delay in machine-to-human delivery is reduced. Try and keep it under a few hours. When electronic mail is delivered (and read) quickly, it can become almost as convenient and fluent as a personal conversation.

Formality and accountability are closely related. On the telephone, formality varies: with some people you are very formal; with others, very casual. The same is true of postal mail. You have a lot of time to construct messages and multiple formats to choose from (handwritten notes, typed business letters, etc.). These formats and other cues (e.g., a perfumed envelope) give signals, both to yourself and your reader, to the purpose of the note. E-mail is always typed, and there is no chapter in any high school typing book on the format of an e-mail letter. Also, individuals are somewhat hidden in e-mail (i.e., the big boss's e-mail address looks just like everyone else's). Since e-mail often flies between parties at a rate approaching a conversation, and since most people are more comfortable being friendly than combative, many people tend to drift into informality in their electronic messaging. This can be a problem when it comes to accountability: the necessity of writers to take responsibility for their messages.

Written media tend to hold writers more accountable for their actions than spoken media. If you are having a telephone conversation and make some comments you wish you hadn't, you can later claim that you didn't say them or that the hearer misunderstood (or take comfort knowing that only one person heard them). If you try and do this with e-mail, someone will have saved a copy of the message in a file and will trot it out to be rehashed. The only factor that reduces e-mail accountability is that the sender's identity can be easily spoofed. I could send you an e-mail with the return address "**bush@whitehouse.gov**," offering you a seat on the Supreme Court. It is also possible to forge paper mail, but it is a lot more difficult: I would have to mimic stationary, postmarks, signatures, etc.

Next, we need to examine group communications. The telephone is a fine medium, but only for small groups. Conference calls allow groups to talk with each other, but as the group gets larger, scheduling and setup get prohibitively difficult. On the other end of the spectrum, bulk mail is easy to use and can reach millions with little difficulty. The problem with junk mail (aside from being a nuisance) is that all messages originate from one point and go to the whole group. Communications from any point (i.e., any member of the group) cannot easily be sent to the whole group. Electronic mail allows you to set up arbitrarily large groups, and any member of the group can communicate with the whole at any time. This makes it very useful both to disseminate information and to query a group for answers to questions.

Finally, the security of electronic mail is usually low, compared to the other media. If I am careful with the post, a letter could remain within locked boxes or the Postal Service until it gets into the recipient's hands. If it is opened along the way, damage to the envelope normally makes the intrusion obvious. Telephone tapping by normal folks requires access to the facilities at one end or the other to intercept a conversation. Once a conversation makes it outside your building and into the telephone network, it is technically difficult for anyone to intrude without the phone company's help. E-mail, however, takes a fairly predictable route through computers, some of whose security may be questionable. Also, there are error modes where a message might be undeliverable and a computer, not knowing what else to do, delivers it to a mail administrator. "Privacy enhanced mailers" try to encrypt the message to combat these security deficiencies, but they are not in general use. As a general rule, you can't trust e-mail's security, and therefore you shouldn't use it when security is an issue.

Hints for Writing Electronic Mail

If you read much e-mail, you'll see a lot of messages that should never have been sent—and that the sender probably wishes he or she hadn't sent. To prevent making such mistakes yourself, you should develop some electronic mail "etiquette."

Creating good habits while you're beginning can prevent big embarrassments later on. Here is some advice:

- Never commit anything to e-mail that you wouldn't want to become public knowledge. As was discussed previously, you never really know who may end up reading your e-mail message. This may be on purpose (e.g., if a co-worker covers someone's e-mail while he's on vacation), or by mistake, either yours or a misbehaving computer's. The threat does not end when the mail is deleted from the mail system. E-mail messages are frequently caught in system backups and sit on tapes in machine rooms for years. With enough effort, an old message might be found and resurrected. (This was how much of Oliver North's connection to the Iran-Contra affair was documented.)

- Don't send abusive, harassing or bigoted messages. While abuse, harassment, and even bigotry are hard to define, there's one good rule of thumb: if a message's recipient complains, stop. E-mail can usually be traced to its originating machine, and systems on the Internet are "liable" for the misdeeds of their users. You don't want your system administrator (or the system administrator of your electronic mail link) to receive complaints about your activity. It could come back to haunt you.

- Writers frequently approach electronic mail as a friendly conversation, but recipients frequently view e-mail as a cast-in-stone business letter. You might have had a wry smile on your face when you wrote the note, but that wry smile doesn't cross the network. You also can't control when the message will be read, so it might be received at the worst possible moment. Consider sitting around after work having a drink with a co-worker and saying "You really blew that sale." You could judge his frame of mind before speaking so you're sure he will take it jokingly. That same thing in e-mail, which he reads after just being chewed out by the boss, comes off as "YOU REALLY BLEW THAT SALE!!!"

- Be very careful with sarcasm. Consider this exchange with the big boss (a real "hands-on" manager):

  > You worked with Sam a while ago. What would you think of promoting him to regional sales manager?

  To which you respond:

  > He's a real winner!

  Does he get the promotion? The answer could either mean that he won the last three "salesperson of the year" awards, or that he hasn't sold anything for the past three years. There is no body language, nor perhaps any personal knowledge on the recipient's side (e.g., she may not know that you are quite the wise-cracker). Some help is available for these situations. For example, inserting a smiley face into a message denotes "said with a cynical smile." So:

  > He's a real winner! :-)

  means he couldn't sell his way out of a paper bag. Another symbol is the wink meaning "it's better left unsaid but catch my drift." Like:

Sam and Bertha spent a long time in her room last night working on the presentation. ;-)

A sentence whose meaning is left to the reader. ;-)

There are many others which are used less frequently. In general, their meanings are pretty discernible, so you'll have to figure them out for yourself. :-(

Aside from basic mail etiquette, there are a couple of style guidelines that, if followed, make e-mail easier to read and understand:

- Keep the line length reasonable (less than 60 characters). You want it to display on just about any terminal. If the note gets forwarded it might be indented by a tab character (usually 8 columns). Messages that consist of a single extremely long line are particularly obnoxious. You have a RETURN key; use it!

- Use mixed case. Even though some operating systems don't understand lowercase letters, virtually all modern terminals can generate them. All uppercase sounds harsh, like shouting. UPPERCASE CAN BE USED FOR EMPHASIS!

- Don't use exotic features of your terminal (bold, italics, etc.). These frequently send a string of control characters which wreak havoc on some types of terminals.

- Read your message before you send it and decide if you'll regret it in the morning. On most systems, once you send it you are committed to it.

How Electronic Mail Works

Electronic mail differs from the other applications we are looking at because it is not an "end to end" service: the sending and receiving machine need not be able to communicate directly with each other to make it work. It is known as a "store and forward" service. Mail is passed from one machine to another until it finally arrives. This is completely analogous to the way the U.S. Postal Service delivers mail; if we examine that, we can draw some interesting conclusions.

The U.S. Postal Service operates a "store and forward" network. You address a message and put it into a post box. The message is picked up by a truck and sent to another place and stored there. It is sorted and forwarded to another place. This step is repeated until it arrives at the recipient's mailbox. If the recipient's mailbox happens to be in a place where the U.S. Postal Service cannot deliver directly (e.g., another country) you can still send the message; the U.S. Post will pass the message to the Postal Service of that country for delivery.

We can infer a couple of things from this analogy. First, if you correctly address a message, the network will take it from there. You needn't know much about what's going on. We can also infer that messages can be moved between the Internet and other mail networks. This is true, but the address required may be more complex in order to get to and through the foreign network.

Just as in the Postal Service, if the destination and source are not on the same network, there needs to be a place where the e-mail from one network is handed to the e-mail service of another. Points of connection between e-mail networks are computers called "application gateways." They are called "gateways" because they can be viewed as magic doors between worlds; they are "application gateways" because they know enough about the e-mail applications on both sides to reformat messages so they are legal on the new network. To send mail through a gateway, you frequently have to give an address which contains both information about how to get to the gateway, and information about how to deliver the mail on the other side. We'll discuss addressing further below.

Finally, before you can put a postal letter into a mailbox, you put it in an envelope. The same happens to e-mail, except that the "envelope" is called a *mail header*. The header is the **To:**, **From:**, **Subject:** stuff on the front of the message. Just as an envelope may get changed enroute (e.g., a hand scribbled "not at this address" here, a yellow sticker with a forwarding address there, etc.), the mail header gets stuff stuck into it while the message is traveling to help you figure out what route it took, just in case it doesn't get through.

It's All in the Address

Whether or not your e-mail gets to its destination depends almost solely on whether or not the address is constructed correctly. (E-mail sometimes fails because machines or pieces of the network are unavailable, but usually the network tries to send mail for days before giving up.) Unfortunately, e-mail addresses are a bit more complex than the simple host addresses we've seen so far.* They are more complex for several reasons:

- The world of e-mail is bigger than the Internet.

- E-mail needs to be addressed to a person, not just a machine.

- Personal names are sometimes included as comments in e-mail addresses.

Let's start with the Internet's addressing rules. On the Internet, the basis for all mail is the domain name of the machine which is acting as a mail agent (say **ux1.cso.uiuc.edu**). In fact, this is all that the network, per se, worries about. Once it has delivered a message to the named machine, the network's task is over. It's up to that computer to deliver it the rest of the way, but the machine requires more information about further routing: at the minimum, the name of a user, but possibly extended information for routing the mail to another kind of network. To form an e-mail address, we use this additional information as a prefix to the destination system's domain name. In order to tell where one ends and the other starts, they are separated by an "at" sign (@). So the form of an e-mail address is:

```
login-name@machine-name
```

---

*An authoritative work on e-mail addressing is, *@#!%, The Directory of Electronic Mail and Addresses*, O'Reilly and Associates.

For example, the e-mail address:

```
krol@ux1.cso.uiuc.edu
```

sends mail to someone whose login name is **krol** on a machine named **ux1.cso.uiuc.edu**. If you are lucky, regardless of where the person is in the world, all you need to do is specify that person's e-mail address as the recipient of your message.

Whether or not you are lucky depends on how smart the first few machines that handle your mail are. The domain name system will also work for some non-Internet addresses. These names usually have a network flag as their highest level domains, rather than an organization type or a country; for example:

```
uiucvmd.bitnet
hacker.uucp
collision.hepnet
```

While these may look like Internet addresses, they aren't. Instead of returning the address of the named computer, the domain name system returns the name of a computer that knows how to handle this kind of mail. Enough machines understand these conventions so that these addresses will usually work. If your mail message encounters a machine that understands how to route this type of mail before some stupid machine gives up on it, then the mail will go through with no additional effort. There is only one way to find out: *TRY IT*. If it doesn't work, you'll find out fairly quickly and it won't hurt anything.

If your e-mail machine is not smart enough to deal with these addresses on its own, or if the address you have doesn't remotely look like an Internet address, you will have to intervene manually. Here are some hints that might help you to succeed:

Bitnet   Bitnet addresses normally have the form *name@host. bitnet*. Change this address to something like *name%host*, and use that for the login name part of the address. Use the address of a Bitnet-Internet gateway for the machine name side (for example, **cunyvm.cuny.edu**). If you are going to do this regularly, find out the best gateway for you to use from someone local. Separate the two with an "at" (@) sign. For example, rewrite the address **krol@uiucvmd.bitnet** as **krol%uiucvmd@cunyvm.cuny.edu**.*

Compuserve   Compuserve addresses consist of two numbers separated by a comma. Change the comma to a period and use that on the left-hand side of the address. To the right of the @ use **compuserve.com**. So, a Compuserve address of 76543,123 would be addressed **76543.123@compuserve.com**.

---

*This is a non-standard format for an address, known as the "BBN hack", but it is in common use, is easy for people to understand, and it works. The standard way of doing this would be **@cunyvm.cuny.edu:krol@uiucvmd**.

Fidonet   Fidonet addresses consist of a first and last name, and a set of numbers of the form a:b/c.d. Separate the first and last names with a period (.) and send to **p***d***.fc.n***b***.z***a***.fidonet.org**. For example, send mail to Willie Martin at 1:5/2.3 by using the address **willie. martin@p3.f2.n5.z1.fidonet.org**. Some machines still may have trouble with an address like this. If yours does, try sending the above address to the gateway machine: **willie. martin%p3.f2.n5.z1.fidonet.org@zeus.ieee.org**.

Sprintmail   Complete Sprintmail addresses look like "John Bigboote" /YOYODYNE/TELEMAIL/US. If the address is used within Sprintmail, it can be abbreviated to John Bigboote/ YOYODYNE. These first two parameters are the person and an organization. When someone gives you a Sprintmail address, this is all they will provide. The positional parameters need to be plugged into a command like the following:

/**PN**=*John.Bigboote*/**O**=*YOYODYNE*/**ADMD=TELEMAIL/C=US/@sprint.com**.

Even if the person only gives you the first two parts of the address, the complete address should be used when sending it to **sprint.com**.

MCImail   There are multiple ways of addressing MCImail. MCI mail-boxes have both an address and a person's name associated with them. The address looks a lot like a phone number. If that's what you have, then use that number on the left side of the @, and use the gateway name **mcimail.com** on the right side. For example: **1234567@mcimail.com**. If you are given the name of a person on MCImail, you can send mail by addressing it to **firstname_lastname@mcimail.com**, like: **John_ Bigboote@mcimail.com**.

UUCP   Change the UUCP address, which looks like **name@host.uucp**, to *name%host*. Use that for the login name portion of the address. Use the address of a UUNET-Internet gateway as the machine name. Internet service providers provide these gateways for these constituents. Of course, separate the two with an "at" sign. For example, a user receiving mail via uucp from PSI, Inc. should be sent mail through **uu.psi.com**, like **john_w%yoyo-dyne@uu.psi.com**. You can ask your e-mail or system adminis-trator for a good gateway for you to use.

Many people also give UUCP addresses in the form: **...!uunet!host!name**. This is a UUCP "path"; it means "you fig-ure out how to get the mail to the system named **uunet**, and then **uunet** will send it to **host**, which will deliver it." Convert this to: *name%host@gatewaymachine*. You pick the proper gateway by examining the UUCP path address. If it has **uunet** as part of the address you could use **uunet.uu.net**, if it has **uupsi** as part of the address you could use **uu.psi.com**, etc. On very rare occasions, you may see gateway names other than **uunet** or **uupsi** in the path; you will have to figure out the Internet address of the gateway. Giving addresses as "paths" is, fortunately, becoming less common. If you are forced to use a UUCP path address, be careful. When you're using the UNIX C shell, you must "quote" the exclamation points with a backslash (\), like **mail \!uunet\!host\!name**. If you give the address inside the **mail** program, you don't need to do this.

Acquiring Electronic Mail Addresses

Once you decide to jump into the e-mail world, you'll have to start collecting e-mail addresses. There is no national registry of e-mail addresses. There are a few specialized servers that one can peruse to try and find someone's address. These servers are known as *white pages* servers because they provide the electronic equivalent to the white pages telephone book. (Chapter 10, *Finding Someone*, tells you how to use the common ones.) But the easiest and best way of acquiring these addresses is via information sent directly to you, be it a business card, a phone call, a postal letter, an e-mail message, or a news group posting.

This method of acquiring e-mail addresses has two advantages over all others:

- You are fairly sure it is an e-mail address which is current and checked regularly. An address found in some index might be an old e-mail address used at a previous employer, or on a machine which no longer exists.

- If there are typically problems getting to the person's e-mail address, the address he gives out will probably reflect the best way to get to his machine from a common point (like the Internet). For example, if Joe's business card gives his e-mail address as **joe%bizarrenet@bizarregate.com**, very likely that will work and should be tried first.

Sometimes when you try to glean e-mail addresses from mail you receive, you will see an address which looks like:

```
John Bigboote<johnb@yoyodyne.com>
```

This address is in a slightly more elaborate format, with the general form:

```
comments<email-address>
```

Adding "comments" to the e-mail address is a really nice thing to do. As in the example above, the comment is usually the addressee's name. Putting the name in a comment makes it a little more obvious to other recipients who also got the message. This is especially true if the person's e-mail address is computer generated, like **ajzxmvk@uicvmc.bitnet**. Wouldn't you like to know who reads that mail! If you get a message as part of a mail distribution list, and if the list's manager has included comments, you can look at the **To:** field and easily see who else got the message—even if the e-mail addresses themselves are not recognizable. (You might want to squirrel away some of those addresses in case you want to send one of them a message later.)

Choosing a System

Electronic mail systems evolved in two separate environments: on wide area networks, where the goal was to provide a "least common denominator" service to everyone in the world, and on local area networks (*LANs*) where feature-rich service to a work group in a small area was the target. As a result, people on wide area nets were frustrated because e-mail was hard to use, but they could send e-mail to anyone. People on LANs were frustrated because they could easily send e-mail to virtually no one. As e-mail evolved, the wide area network mailers added nicer user interfaces and features, while the LAN products added the ability to send over wide area networks. We have reached the point where most e-mail systems can exchange basic e-mail with any other e-mail system. This means that when you decide how you want to use e-mail, if you have a choice, the choice will be made on the basis of extended features and comfort, not connectivity.*

When you decide how to approach e-mail, a number of questions will affect the decision:

- Who are you going to be exchanging mail with?
- How closely are you "tied" to them?
- What do you like in a user interface?
- How much do you travel?

Many facilities are common to all mailers. Other features (like digitized pictures and voice) can only be used when the sender and recipient both use the same mail software and operating system. If your goal is to transfer all kinds of files between a small circle of friends with as little trouble as possible, then you and your friends should agree on a single mail system and use it. If that is not a big concern, then you should pick the e-mail software that you find the easiest to use and with which you can feel at home. That is, if you like Macintoshes, you should pick something that works, looks, and feels like a Macintosh. Don't pick something else just because all your friends are doing it.

If you are a frequent traveler, you should investigate systems that allow you to connect a portable computer to the network (even by dial-up) and download mail. You can then read your mail and queue new messages while disconnected from the network. The next time you connect to the Net, the queued mail gets sent. So you could dial-up in Chicago, download 20 messages, read and respond to them at 30,000 feet over Cleveland, queue your responses and, finally, send the queued mail and pick up a new batch when you arrive in Washington D.C. These systems are

---

*That is not to say that some decisions will not cost more than others. Connecting a LAN-based mail system to the Internet may require a dedicated PC and some fairly expensive software.

based on the Post Office protocol or *POP*, which allows remote interaction between a workstation and a mail repository.

So, pick your mail system to suit your needs. If your needs are not that great and you are mainly concerned with basic messaging, then pick something that is free and that other people are using.

The UNIX Mail Program

The UNIX **mail** program is the Chevy Impala of electronic mail packages. It doesn't make anyone ecstatic about using it, but it gets the job done. That's why I chose it. With a few commands, you can use all of its basic features. While you may never use the **mail** program, it provides a good basis for discussing how to use a mail system.*

To start the **mail** program, give the command:†

```
% mail address-string
```

The *address-string* is optional. If it is there, the command sends a message to those people listed in the address string. You can usually use either spaces or commas to separate different addressees in the list. If the address string is absent, **mail** enters command mode. One of the things you do in command mode is read your incoming messages.

Reading Your Mail

To read your mail, enter command mode. If you don't have any mail to read, the program tells you:

```
% mail
No mail for krol
```

If you have messages waiting, **mail** will list the first 20 new message headers:

```
% mail
"/usr/spool/mail/krol": 5 messages 1 new
    1 LISTSERV@bitni Fri Nov  8 16:02 128/6172 "File: "LISTSERV FILELI"
    2 LISTSERV@bitni Fri Nov  8 16:08 164/9834 "File: "BITNODE FILELIS"
 U  3 daemon@pit-man Sat Nov  9 09:26  72/2817 "Reply from mserv re: s"
 U  4 akida          Sat Dec 28 05:53  12/298  "Overthruster found"
>N  5 buckaroo       Thu Jan  2 19:15  11/305  "Aliens in Grovers Mill"
 &
```

---

*If you think I have an oversimplified view of e-mail, look into **mh** and the whole book dedicated to its use. (*MH and xmh: E-mail for Users and Programmers*, O'Reilly and Associates.) For yet another approach to UNIX mail, consider Z-mail, which was known as **mush** in an earlier incarnation (discussed in *The Z-mail Handbook*, O'Reilly and Associates).

†Unfortunately, some UNIX systems have two different mail programs with almost the same name. The proper command may be **mailx**.

Each message has a status and a number. The status is flagged by the letter (or the lack of a letter) at the beginning of each line. These letters might be:

N   New messages received since the last time you entered mail in command mode to read messages.

P   Signifies preserved messages, those which you have read and decided to put back in your "in-basket" within this invocation of the *mail* program.

U   Unread messages. New messages turn into unread messages if you exit mail without reading them.

no letter   The message was read and preserved in a previous mail session.

The message number is used in various commands to refer to that particular message (more on this when we talk about commands). Finally, notice one message has a greater than sign (>) pointing to it. This is the current message. If you give any commands without specifying a message number, the command applies to the current message.

The & that follows the message list is **mail**'s command prompt, telling you that it's waiting for you to type a command. You only need to know about four commands to read e-mail for fun and profit. Commands are usually single letters, but there are a couple which are longer to remove ambiguity. To read messages, use the **p**rint command, which has the general format:

> & **p** *messages*

The *messages* parameter is optional. If you leave it off, the current message is displayed on the screen. The parameter can take one of the following forms:

> & **p** 3   *display message #3*
> & **p** 3-5   *display message #3 through #5*
> & **p** $ *display the last message*
> & **p** 3-$ *display message #3 through the last message*

All commands that allow a message number as a parameter operate in this same fashion. Remember that you can use **$** to indicate the last message.

The print command is also the default command. So the following commands are the same:

> & 3
> & **p** 3

Therefore, a carriage return with no command just prints the current message.

The **f**ast print command gives you an in-basket "table of contents," just like the menu you receive when you start up **mail**. The initial list tries to give you 20 new messages, starting with the oldest new message. Should you have more, you can move around in the menu by issuing successive **f** commands:

```
& f 1-20        display sender & subject 1 to 20
& f 21-$        display sender & subject 21 to the end
```

Another way to do this is with the **z** command. **z** prints the fast print description for the next screen full of messages. If you want to move backwards in the list you can use **z-**.

Unless you do something special, any messages you read while you are in a mail session get moved from your in-basket into the file *mbox* when you quit. The usual commands to change this action are:

d *messages* Delete the messages specified (or the current one if not specified). This deletes the message number from the menu and deletes the message at the end of the mail session.

pre *messages* Preserve the specified messages (or the current one if none are specified). That is, keep them in your in-basket where they may be viewed in future sessions.

q Exit the mail program.

Sending Messages

In this section, we'll tell you how to originate a new e-mail message. You can also respond to a message that someone sent you; we'll cover that later.

To send a message, either give the UNIX **mail** command, followed by a list of addresses, or by giving the **mail** command within the **mail** program (i.e., after the & prompt). Both commands have the same syntax:

```
% mail address-list   --or--
& mail address-list
```

The address list can be one or more addresses separated by commas. If the addresses are not full domain names like **krol@ux1.cso.uiuc.edu**, then the mail program usually completes the address by adding the domain of the machine it is running on. So, if **krol** has a mailbox on **ux1.cso.uiuc.edu**, **mail krol** works fine on the computer **ux1.cso.uiuc.edu**. If you execute it on the computer **yoyodyne.com**, it will fail because on that computer **mail krol** means **mail krol@yoyodyne.com**.

After getting the destination address straightened out, you get prompted for a subject:

```
% mail johnb@yoyodyne.com
Subject: Do you have the Overthruster
```

Enter a meaningful synopsis for the message as a subject. That and your name will be all the recipient has to decide on the priority to give this message.* After the subject, you get no prompt, but it is time to type the text of the message. The completed message we started above is:

```
% mail johnb@yoyodyne.com
Subject: Do you have the Overthruster
John Warfin was wondering if you had acquired the
overthruster yet?  He is pretty excitable.
.
```

Notice the period in column one. A period on a line by itself signifies the end of the message to the UNIX **mail** program. When the message is completed, you return to whatever you were doing before issuing the command. That is, you return to the UNIX prompt if you sent your message from the UNIX command line; you return to **mail**'s command mode if you sent your message from command mode.

Typing the message like this is very inconvenient, particularly if the message is long. It's hard to correct mistakes, particularly if you don't notice them until you're already typing the next line. You can use the **vi** editor to compose your message by giving the command **~v**, putting the **~** in the first column on the screen. This starts the **vi** editor; if you've already typed part of the message, you should see it within **vi**. Use **vi**'s commands to edit your message; then, when you're ready, save the message and quit. You'll be back within **mail**; type a period in the first column to complete the message and send it.

If you don't like **vi**, quit **mail** and give the UNIX command:

```
% setenv EDITOR my-favorite-editor
```

where *my-favorite-editor* is the name of an editor you'd rather use. For example, if you like the **emacs** editor, give the command **setenv EDITOR emacs**; then, use the **~e** command while composing a message. **mail** will start **emacs** for you. These two commands do very similar things. **~v** starts the "visual" editor **vi**. **~e** starts the editor specified by the environment variable; if you haven't set one, it starts the **ex** editor. (You don't want to use **ex**!)

The **~e** command belongs to a large set of commands called *tilde escapes*. Tilde escapes are commands issued while typing in the message body. They are flagged by a tilde in column one of a line. You'll see several more tilde escape commands as we work through common **mail** features. (If you want to see which ones are available try **~?**.)

---

*Not all **mail** programs prompt for the subject by default. Sometimes, you have to put a line reading `set ask` (or, for some versions, `set asksub`) into the file *.mailrc* in your home directory. We strongly recommend that you *always* put a subject on your message. That makes it much easier for the recipient (who may get hundreds of messages a day) to handle.

A Shopping List of Features

I wish I could give you the definitive list of e-mail packages and tell you which one to get, but there are at least five for UNIX systems, three for IBM VM systems, five for PCs, and three for Apple machines. They all have some common features which can be used when sending mail to any other mailer, some features which look similar but are implemented differently and therefore can't be used with other kinds of mailers (they don't *interoperate* in the vernacular), and some features which are unique. So here are some common features of mail systems, what they do, and how much interoperability you can expect.

Universally Supported Features

Aside from the basic ability to send mail, almost any e-mail facility gives you the following features, which can work with other mail systems.

Aliasing

Aliasing is the ability to define nicknames for people. If you don't like typing complete Internet addresses (and who does?), you can decide that **edk** is shorthand for **krol@ux1.cso.uiuc.edu**; if you then use **edk** as the recipient of a message, your system will substitute the complete address for you. Don't decide on aliases arbitrarily: pick some convention and stick to it. Having an alias doesn't do you any good if you can't remember or guess it. You may need to remember an alias even though you haven't used it for a long time. It is common to use a first name, followed by the last initial, as an alias. It is also common to have nicknames that are tied to "functions," rather than a specific person (e.g., secretary or sweetie); over time, the person may change, but the function will remain the same.

With UNIX **mail**, you can put alias definitions in the file *.mailrc*. The *.mailrc* file is a general place for personal mail configuration commands. To define aliases, add lines to the file of the form:

```
alias nickname actual-address
```

So, the following line would define the **edk** alias that we discussed above:

```
alias edk "Ed Krol<krol@ux1.cso.uiuc.edu>"
```

This example includes a "comments" field in the address, a practice we recommended earlier. After you have defined an alias, it may be used anywhere you would normally use an address. So, the following commands are synonymous:

```
% mail krol@ux1.cso.uiuc.edu
% mail edk
```

Caution: if a nickname is the same as a login name on your machine, its definition will be used in preference to the login name. That is, if I have an alias defined as:

```
alias krol "Karen Rolex<karen@blitzos.com>"
```

then the command:

```
% mail krol
```

sends a message to Karen Rolex (whose address is **karen@blitzos.com**), not the local user **krol**.

Folders

Folders let you save messages in an organized way. For example, you could have a folder for each project you're involved with, and one called "personal." As mail arrives, you can file it in the appropriate folder for future reference. These can usually be examined from within the **mail** reading program, using the same facilities you would normally use to read incoming mail. You merely tell **mail** to read the mail in a folder instead of the incoming mail.

In UNIX, a folder is a file that contains messages stored in a format the **mail** program can understand. The file *mbox*, where **mail** stores the message that you don't delete, preserve, or file elsewhere, is really just the default folder. To create another folder or append to an existing one, use the **s** command. It has the format:

```
& s folder-name
```

This command saves the current message in the named folder. The following command stores the current message in a folder named **ietf**:

```
& s ietf
```

Switching to a different folder is accomplished with the **folder** command, with one of the following forms:

```
& folder name          switch to the named folder
& folder #             switch back to the previous folder
& folder %             switch to your in-basket
```

When you switch folders, **mail** lists the contents of the new folder. This list looks just like the list that **mail** gives when you start the **mail** program. For example:

```
% mail "/usr/spool/mail/krol": 1 message 1 new
>N 1 johnb@yoyodyne.cso   Fri Jan  3 13:27  11/307   "junk"
& folder mbox
Held 1 message in /usr/spool/mail/krol
"mbox": 2 messages
   1 quayle@lawyersRus. Fri Nov 15 19:48  46/1852 "More stupid remarks"
>  2 Kennedy@senate.gov Thu Nov 21 10:09  52/2352 "Candidate wanted"
&
```

Once you are in a folder you can use all of the normal commands (**print**, **delete**, etc.) to manipulate or read your archived messages.

Forwarding

Within UNIX mail, "forwarding" has two slightly different meanings. First, forwarding means automatically sending all mail received by a particular login on one computer to another. This is particularly useful if you have accounts on several different computers. So that you don't have to check mail on different computers constantly, you may want any mail sent to any of your accounts to be forwarded to the one where you normally read mail.

UNIX uses the file *.forward* to accomplish this. You create this in your home directory on each system from which you want mail forwarded. In the file, you place the mail address to which you want the mail to be sent. For example, the *.forward* file is taken from the home directory for **johnb** at **yoyodyne.com**; it contains a single line:

```
krol@ux1.cso.uiuc.edu
```

This file causes any mail sent to **johnb@yoyodyne.com** to be forwarded to **krol@ux1.cso.uiuc.edu**.

Forwarding also means taking a message you have received and sending it on to someone else who might be interested. This can usually be done either in its entirety, or as a part of a message which you compose. (This is another big boss tool: she forwards you the original message adding something like, "Take care of this, Sam." Suddenly, it's your problem.)

With UNIX **mail**, this is not as convenient as it should be. In **mail**, you must start a new message to the person to whom you want to forward the message. Then you insert the old message into the new message with the **~m** or **~f** commands. The **~m** and **~f** both take an optional parameter, which is the message number to be inserted. If it is not given, the current message is inserted. The difference between **~m** and **~f** is that **~m** adds a tab character at the beginning of each line of the old message. This is useful when you want to insert text into the old message—for example, to respond to a previous message point by point. The lines that are indented by tabs belong to the original message; the lines that aren't indented are your additions. Alternatively, **~f** inserts the old message exactly as received. This is useful either when the message contains something to be processed by a computer (in which case, the format is critical), or when you expect the new recipient to respond point by point. Let's peek at the big boss' **mail** session while she forwards a complaint to Sam:

```
% mail
"/usr/spool/mail/krol": 2 messages 2 new
>N  1 pking@ux1.cso.uiuc.e  Fri Jan  3 13:48  16/621  "ctp-100 price"
 N  2 whiner@bigaccount.com Fri Jan  3 14:00  13/559  "Bad service"
& mail sam
 Subject: complaint from Mr. Whiner
See if you can make him happy:
~m 2
Interpolating: 2
(continue)
.
```

When Sam checks his mail, he receives a message like this:

```
/cso/staff/sam-6>mail
"/usr/spool/mail/sam": 1 message 1 new
>N  1 Bertha the Boss Fri Jan  3 14:12  23/718  "complaint from Mr. Whi"
& 1
From bertha Fri Jan  3 14:12:56 1992
Date: Fri, 3 Jan 1992 14:12:55 -0600
From: Bertha the Boss<bertha@fledgling.com>
To: sam@fledgling.com
Subject: complaint from Mr. Whiner

See if you can make him happy

        From whiner Fri Jan  3 14:12:06 1992
        Received: by fledgling.com id AA09908
          (5.65d/IDA-1.4.4 for bertha); Fri, 3 Jan 1992 14:12:05 -0600
          Date: Fri, 3 Jan 1992 14:12:05 -0600
        From: whiner@bigaccount.com
        Message-Id: <199201032012.AA09908@fledgling.com>
        To: bertha@fledgling.com
        Subject: Bad Service

        I got bad service from your office...
```

Inclusion of Text Files

You often want to send someone a text file via electronic mail. You would like to keep the file intact and insert a copy of it into the message being sent. That way, the file will be immediately useful to the recipient, who doesn't have to use **ftp** to get the file. You can also insert an explanation into the message, telling the recipient what to do with the file.

An example may make this clearer:

```
% mail johnb                          start a normal message
Subject: Check this out
Here is the draft proposal.  Make changes and get
back to me ASAP.
~r draft                              include file draft
"draft" 300/13427                     300 lines 13427 chars long
.
```

In this example, you built a mail message by typing some introductory text, and then inserting a copy of your file called *draft*. To insert the file, you used the ~**r** command. The general format of this command is:

```
~r filename
```

You can give this command at any place in the text of the message, provided that the ~ is in column one, and provided that you're not using an editor to construct the message.* The named file is unchanged by the command.

---

*That is, you can't type ~**r** while you're using **vi** or some other editor. Any reasonable text editor has its own commands for inserting files—use them instead.

Mailing Lists

With electronic mail, it is just as easy to send a message to a group of people as it is to send a message to a single person. The facility that makes this possible is called a "mailing list." It allows an alias or nickname to stand for a group of recipients; for example, the alias **staff** can be defined as "all employees." When you send mail to the name **staff**, the mail is actually delivered to everyone in the group.

With many mailers, including UNIX **mail**, this is a simple extension of the **alias** command we discussed earlier. Instead of listing one recipient after the alias name, you can list many. If all the names won't fit on one line, you can put multiple alias lines in succession:

```
alias staff tommy@banzai.edu, pecos@banzai.edu
alias staff akida@banzai.edu, newjersey@banzai.edu
alias staff buckaroo@banzai.edu, rawhide@banzai.edu
```

With these entries in your *.mailrc* file, you could send mail to them all by typing:

```
% mail staff
Subject: Staff Meeting at 9am
To discuss the 8th dimension
.
```

Your mailer expands the mailing list name to a set of normal e-mail addresses. This means that the recipients' e-mail addresses will be listed in the **To:** part of the header.

Reply

Replying is a shorthand for telling your mailer that you want to send a response back to the person who sent you some particular message. It saves you the trouble of typing in the e-mail address. Your mailer typically copies the **From:** (or **Reply-To:**) field from the original message to create the **To:** line of a new message; to create the new **Subject:** line, your mailer just copies the original.

Replies can be tricky. Your mailer may not be able to convert the original **From:** field into something reasonable. Whether or not a reply will work correctly depends on whether the sender's return address is complete and acceptable to your mailer. If it doesn't work, you might need to look at the **From:** address and modify it, based on your experience (see the section, "Acquiring E-mail Addresses," earlier in this chapter).

Like most mailers, UNIX **mail** has two commands to support this feature:

```
& r message#
& R message#
```

The **r** command sends a message back to the original sender and all of the original recipients. **R** only sends the reply back to the original sender. The *message#* is optional. If it is not given, the current message is used. Which form of the "reply" command you choose obviously depends on the nature of your message. If you're taking part in a discussion, you probably want all of the recipients to receive your response (**r**). If you're just providing some information (like "yes, I can make it to the company picnic"), you can assume that the other recipients probably don't need to get your reply (so you would use **R**).

Let's let Sam respond to the complaint from Mr. Whiner he was sent earlier:

```
& 1
>From bertha Fri Jan  3 14:12:56 1992
Date: Fri, 3 Jan 1992 14:12:55 -0600
From: Bertha the Boss<bertha@fledgling.com>
To: sam@fledgling.com
Subject: complaint from Mr. Whiner

See if you can make him happy

        From whiner Fri Jan  3 14:12:06 1992
        Received: by fledgling.com id AA09908
          (5.65d/IDA-1.4.4 for bertha); Fri, 3 Jan 1992 14:12:05 -0600
          Date: Fri, 3 Jan 1992 14:12:05 -0600
        From: whiner@bigaccount.com
        Message-Id: <199201032012.AA09908@fledgling.com>
        To: bertha@fledgling.com
        Subject: Bad Service

        I got bad service from your office...
& R
To: bertha@fledgling.com
Subject: complaint from Mr. Whiner
I took care of it.
.
```

mail doesn't automatically insert the message that you're replying to into the body of the reply (many mailers do). If you want it, you must insert it with the ~**m** or ~**f** command, just like in any other message.

Locally Supported Features

There are several common features that are supported by some local mail programs, but not all of them. If your mailer supports any of these features, then you can use them when sending messages to any other mailer—regardless of its type.

Carbon Copies

All mailers let you put several addresses in the **To:** field of the header. It is frequently useful to differentiate between those to whom the message is primarily directed, and those who receive it for their information. To do so, the mail forwarding software recognizes a line beginning with **Cc:** containing a list of addresses; anyone listed on the **Cc:** line will also receive a copy, just as if he or she were listed on the **To:** line. Thus, the **Cc:** field has the same meaning as the old "cc:" line on a business letter. Many mailers have some facility for creating a **Cc:** line automatically. If the mailer allows you to edit the header, you can create a **Cc:** line manually.

UNIX **mail** gives you two ways to generate a **Cc:** line. First, you can use the tilde escape **~c** anywhere in the text of the message:

```
~c johnb@yoyodyne.com          ~ must be in column 1
```

You can also add the line **set askcc** to your *.mailrc* file. This tells the mailer that whenever you end a message, it should ask you who should get "carbon copies." When **askcc** is set, a typical **mail** session might look like this:

```
& mail johnb
Subject: Can you make the meeting
remember the meeting at 0900.  Can you make it?
.
Cc: secretary
&
```

Some UNIX systems have this facility turned on as an installation option. Your mail package may ask for a carbon copy list, even if you don't set the **askcc** variable.

Blind Carbon Copies

Blind carbon copies are copies sent to a list of readers, just like carbon copies. However, the header line that lists the recipients is automatically deleted from the outgoing mail. Therefore, none of the other recipients will know who (if anyone) received "blind carbon copies." Since there is no record in the received message that these copies were ever sent, later actions which use data in the header (for example, replies to the message) will not include these recipients in their action.

Blind cc's in UNIX **mail** are available through the tilde escape **~b**. The facility works just like the **~c**. There is no switch to prompt for blind carbons. If the mailer allows you to edit the header, you can create a **BCC:** line manually.

Signature Files

Signature files are a way to append additional information to outgoing mail messages. They are often used to include information about who you are and how you can be contacted. So, if you don't think:

```
From: johnb@yoyodyne.com
```

conveys a lot of information about yourself, you could set up a file which gives your name, postal address, phone number, FAX number, other e-mail addresses, etc. For example, such a file might look like:

```
_____
John Bigboote        | Yoyodyne Industries
johnb@yoyodyne.com   |
(212)333-4444        | "The Future Begins Tomorrow"
-------------------------------------------------------
```

Remember, if the recipient cannot get e-mail back to you, what's in your signature file might be the only means at his disposal to get in touch with you.

Keep it short and useful, however. It is really pushing it (and irritating) when you get to dog's and kid's names, pictures of your favorite cult icons, and it begins to take up 15 to 20 lines.

There is no signature file facility in UNIX **mail**. The best you can do is make a file and then do a ˜**r** at the end of each message to include it.

Unusual and Non-standard Features

The following features are found in some electronic mail packages, but aren't widely available, and they aren't yet defined by any "standards." Whoever wrote your mailer got to decide how (and if) these features should work. As a result, you probably can't use these features unless the recipient's mailer is identical to yours. None of these features are available in UNIX **mail**.

Attaching Documents

Some electronic mail systems allow you to mail files as separate entities along with a message. That is, when you send a message to someone you can say: "send this file, too." When the message is read, the receiving mailer asks the person reading the message where the file should be stored. These files can be either binary or ASCII, and system information about the file is preserved in the move. For example, you could send a message which says, "Take a look at the spreadsheet I've enclosed and get back to me" and you could attach an Excel spreadsheet from a Macintosh. When the recipient reads the message and accepts the attachment, his Mac automatically creates an Excel spreadsheet file on his machine.

A facility called "multi-media mail" is related to attached documents. This extension allows you to send digitized voice and pictures as part of a message. It is really neat, but few systems can do it. Also, digitized sound and video take a lot of time to transmit and a lot of disk space to store.

Notification of Receipt

Notification of receipt automatically sends you a message when the mail you've sent is placed in the recipient's electronic "in-basket." This prevents someone from saying "Well, I never got the message"; just as with the Post Office, a "return receipt" proves that the mail was delivered.

Notification of Reading

This feature automatically sends you a message when the mail you've sent is displayed by the recipient. It doesn't mean that he actually read or understood it. It does mean that he is not being truthful when the excuse is: "I just read it this morning." You know it was displayed two days ago!

Message Cancel

Message cancel allows you to take back a message after you have sent it. This can be handy if you often write cantankerous messages, and then wish (later) that you hadn't sent them. Obviously, there's a limited window during which you can cancel any message. The length of this time window varies with the message's destination (where the mail is going) and how the mailers are connected. If the message is sent to another user within the same mail system, it can usually be cancelled until it is read. If it is destined to an in-basket on another mail system, it usually cannot be retrieved after it has passed from the sender's system to the recipient's.

Sending Binary Data as ASCII

At times, you want to send a binary file (for example, files from WordPerfect, disk dumps, etc.) through electronic mail. **ftp**, which is designed for transferring files, may not be possible or practical. E-mail can reach many places that **ftp** can't: it can traverse networks which are not directly connected to the Internet, or networks which provide only mail service. In addition, **ftp** can't send a file to many recipients; you may want to post an executable of your new NEWS reader to a large mailing list, in which case **ftp** will be impractical.

So electronic mail looks like what you need. Unfortunately, it is a text-only medium. That is, it only deals with messages that are constructed from characters. As we said a few pages ago, any mailer will let you insert a text file into a message. However, relatively few mailers allow you to send binary (i.e., non-text) files directly, and (as we said) those that do probably aren't compatible with each other.

But, with a little additional work, it's possible for any mailer to transmit a binary file, provided that both the sending and receiving computers have a utility to convert binary files into some ASCII representation. All UNIX systems have such utilities; one is called **uuencode**, and we'll use it as an example below. Many other systems have an equivalent utility; if you're a programmer, it's not difficult to write your own, and give it to your friends.

Of course, the ability to transfer a binary file doesn't mean that the binary file will be *useful* at the destination. You may be able to mail a **tar** dump of a directory to someone; but that **tar** dump is only useful if the recipient has a utility capable of reading **tar** files. If those files are executable files, they will only work if the computer hardware is the same as that of the creating computer. However, whether or not the binary data you send is *useful* is a different problem that has nothing to do with electronic mail.

At any rate, if we have the same utilities available on the systems at each end, we are home free. You need to find a program that converts a binary file into a printable character representation of the binary data. You could do this yourself, if you wanted, by taking each byte, turning it into a number between 0 and 255, and storing this sequence of three-digit numbers in another file. You would have to write the inverse program at the other end to convert this representation back into binary. But why bother? As we said, most systems have this kind of utility available. **uuencode** comes with UNIX; **btoa** is available on many UNIX systems; and both are available in the public domain for PCs. **BinHex** performs a similar function in the Macintosh world. With these utilities, you can encode the file, turning the binary file into a textual representation. Once you have a textual representation, you can send it through electronic mail. The recipient takes the message, edits off the headers (sometimes this is not necessary), decodes it, and has the original binary file.

Maybe an example is in order:

```
% uuencode overthruster < a.out > temp
% mail john@yoyodyne.com
Subject: Program
Here is the program you wanted (you need to uudecode it):
~r temp
"temp" 7216/447224
.
Cc:
%
```

The first line (**uuencode**) takes the file *a.out* and encodes it as printable text. It puts the output into the file *temp* (making it about a third bigger as well). In the process, it flags the file internally with the name *overthruster* (more on this later). Next, we begin an e-mail message to **john@yoyodyne.com**, and give him a little hint about what to do with it (always a good idea). The **~r** line is this mailer's command for copying a file into a message; here, we copy the *temp* file that we created earlier. The next line informs us that the file *temp* was inserted, and it is 7216 lines and 447224 characters long.* Typing a period (.) in column one says "end of message"; a return in response to the **Cc:** prompt says, "no carbon copies to anyone."

Some time later John logs in to check his mail. He'll see:

```
% mail
"/usr/spool/mail/john": 1 message 1 unread
>N 1 krol           Sat Nov 2 19:57 7245/448458 "Program"
& 1
Received: from uxh.cso.uiuc.edu by uxc.cso.uiuc.edu with...
   (5.65c/IDA-1.4.4 for <john@yoyodyne.com>);
   Sat, 2 Nov 1991 19:56:31 -0600
Received: by uxh.cso.uiuc.edu id AA22546
   (5.65c/IDA-1.4.4 for john@yoyodyne.com);
   Sat, 2 Nov 1991 19:56:16 -0600
Date: Sat, 2 Nov 1991 19:56:16 -0600
From: Ed Krol <krol@uxh.cso.uiuc.edu>
Message-Id: <199111030156.AA22546@uxh.cso.uiuc.edu>
To: john@yoyodyne.com
Subject: Program

Here is the program you wanted (you need to uudecode it):
begin 755 overthruster
```

---

*Some e-mail systems have limits on the size of any one message, like 1000 lines or 50,000 characters. If you run into one of these limits you can use the UNIX **split** utility to break up a file into multiple pieces and mail them separately.

```
M'''!@0D''''I$U;Q''''!0''''''''''!<''''''''''''''!,J<'''''''''*4H'
M'''''''''''''''''''''''''''''''''!*'''''#C0'''''"''!'P@''''''''
Interrupt
& s encodedprog
"encodedprog" [New file] 7244/448458
& q
% uudecode encodedprog
```

He sees one message from "krol," and it's huge (7244 lines). In response to the & prompt, he enters a **1**, meaning "read message 1." It starts like a normal, everyday message until the line starting with **begin**; this is the start of an encoded binary file. After seeing a few lines, he interrupts the listing (in this case by pressing CTRL-C) and issues the command **s encodedprog**. This command saves the current message in a new file named *encodedprog*. He then runs **uudecode** on the new file. It ignores any text before the "begin" line, and decodes the ASCII garbage that follows. In doing so, it creates a new binary file that matches the original. It gives the binary file the name you called it on the **uuencode** command (**overthruster**), which was recorded on the "begin" line. In the end, John has the **overthruster** program.

When Electronic Mail Gets Returned

When electronic mail cannot be delivered, you normally get a message telling you why. This takes the format of a really ugly, strange message in your in-basket:

```
% mail
"/usr/spool/mail/krol": 1 message 1 unread
>N 1 MAILER-DAEMON@uxc.cs Sun Nov 3 09:03 29/1233 "Returned mail: Host un"
&
```

At this point, all you know is that your mail didn't go through; you have no idea why. To find out, you have to wade through the cryptic message that got returned.

There are three common reasons for electronic mail to fail:

- The mail system can't find the recipient's machine.
- The recipient is unknown at that machine.
- The mail can find the machine but still can't deliver it.

Let's investigate these causes one at a time.

Unknown Hosts

When you send a message to someone, the network tries to make some sense out of the stuff to the right of the @. If it can't make sense of it, or if it can't look up the address of the named machine, the mailer that gives up sends you a message saying that the host is unknown. Look at the previous example, in which we encoded a binary program and sent it to **john@yoyodyne.com**. Assume that the Net was unable to recognize the system **yoyodyne.com**. Eventually, you'll get a returned message like this:

```
& 1
From MAILER-DAEMON@uxc.cso.uiuc.edu Sun Nov  3 09:03:18 1991
Date: Sun, 3 Nov 1991 09:02:57 -0600
From: Mail Delivery Subsystem <MAILER-DAEMON@uxc.cso.uiuc.edu>
To: krol@ux1.cso.uiuc.edu
Subject: Returned mail: Host unknown

    ----- Transcript of session follows -----
550 yoyodyne.com (TCP)... 550 Host unknown

    ----- Unsent message follows -----
Received: from ux1.cso.uiuc.edu by uxc.cso.uiuc.edu with SMTP id AA17283
   (5.65c/IDA-1.4.4 for <john@yoyodyne.com>); Sun, 3 Nov 1991 09:02:57 -0600
Received: by ux1.cso.uiuc.edu id AA17906
   (5.65c/IDA-1.4.4 for john@yoyodyne.com); Sun, 3 Nov 1991 06:22:30 -0600
Date: Sun, 3 Nov 1991 06:22:30 -0600
From: Ed Krol <krol@ux1.cso.uiuc.edu>
Message-Id: <199111031222.AA17906@uxh.cso.uiuc.edu>
To: john@yoyodyne.com
Subject: The program you wanted.
```

In response to the & prompt, you entered the message number that you wanted to read (just like any other message). You see a message from the MAILER-DAEMON on a machine named **uxc.cso.uiuc.edu**. **uxc.cso.uiuc.edu** is an intermediate mail handler. Your message was sent to this system enroute to **yoyodyne.com**; this is where it ran into trouble. Past the header for the returned message, in a section marked "Transcript of session," it tells you that the host **yoyodyne.com** is "unknown" to the network. After these messages, you will usually find the unsent message itself. This saves you the trouble of re-entering it. However, you have to delete the junk from the front before using the message again.

What should you do when something like this happens? First, check the address: is the name **yoyodyne.com** spelled correctly? Second, check whether the address is complete. When presented with an incomplete name like **yoyodyne**, many machines add a domain suffix automatically; they assume that the suffix should be the same as their own. So, on a machine named **ux1.cso.uiuc.edu**, the address **yoyodyne** will be expanded to **yoyodyne.cso.uiuc.edu**. This is a nice shorthand because most mail is directed within the same organization. However, you must be careful to provide the proper domain when sending mail to someone outside your organization.

A variant of this problem occurs when people give out partial addresses, assuming that you'll be able to figure out the rest. For example, someone might give you an address like **joe@turing.cs**. He is assuming that you know he's in the CS department of the University of Illinois (Urbana-Champaign), which is the domain **uiuc.edu**, and that his complete address is therefore **joe@turing.cs.uiuc.edu**. If you don't realize this, and simply use the address **joe@turing.cs**, mail forwarding software will get confused—in this case, really confused. To a computer, **turing.cs** looks exactly like the complete name of **turing** in Czechoslovakia (**.cs** is

Czechoslovakia's country code). If you're lucky, **turing.cs** doesn't exist, and you'll get an "unknown host" message. If you're unlucky, **turing.cs** does exist, and you'll be even more confused. (If you're really unlucky, **joe@turing.cs** will even exist, and he'll get your mail.) The moral of the story is two-fold. First, you may need to finish the address yourself from your own knowledge of where the guy really resides. Second, when you give your address to someone, always give a complete address; don't assume that your correspondents will be smart enough to figure out the rest.

One last warning. You might find a returned message where the unknown host has multiple highest level domains:

```
yoyodyne.com.cso.uiuc.edu
```

If you run across something like this, you have run into a misconfigured mailer. **yoyodyne.com** was a perfectly fine address. Some mailer along the way decided it wasn't and tried to complete it by tacking on its own domain **.cso.uiuc.edu**, really screwing things up. In this case, there is nothing you can do. Find someone who knows about mailers and ask for help.

What was wrong with the particular message we have been discussing? Let's assume that John gave you the address **yoyodyne.com**, and that you spelled it correctly. Since the domain **.com** is a valid highest-level domain, name completion shouldn't be a problem. So, it looks like nothing is wrong from the network's standpoint. At this point I would assume that the computer **yoyodyne.com** does not exist. Either John gave it to you in error, or it passed out of existence over the course of time.

It's also possible that your computer just doesn't "know about" the system you're trying to send to. Some mailers have lists of valid hostnames which are not updated continuously. The target machine may just not be in the list. If you think this may be the problem, talk to whoever manages the mail system you are using.

Similar errors may occur when you reply to someone's message. Some mailers fail to fill out their full name in the **From:** section of the header. Let's assume that **john@yoyodyne.com** uses one of these mailers; he sends you a message, for which the **From:** field simply says **john@yoyodyne**. Since the **From:** field has nothing to do with delivering the message, you receive the message just fine. The **From:** field gets copied to the **To:** field when you do a reply. You then have exactly the same situation as above. Your mail is addressed to **john@yoyodyne**. Your computer will complete the name, but probably won't complete the name correctly. In this situation, if your mailer allows you to edit the header, you can do a reply and then fix the address. If you aren't allowed to do this, you have no recourse other than to skip **reply** and start a new message.

If none of these hints apply, you have no recourse other than calling the person to see if some other address might work better.

Unknown Recipients

Now, let's assume that your mail made its way to the correct host. Eventually, a machine forwarding your mail makes contact with the destination machine and tells it the recipient's name. What happens if the destination machine hasn't heard of the message's addressee? In this case, the returned mail header looks something like:

```
>From daemon Mon Nov  4 14:44:31 1991
Received: by uxh.cso.uiuc.edu id AA08280
  (5.65c/IDA-1.4.4 for krol); Mon, 4 Nov 1991 14:44:26
Date: Mon, 4 Nov 1991 14:44:26 -0600
From: Mail Delivery Subsystem <MAILER-DAEMON>
Message-Id: <199111042044.AA08280@uxh.cso.uiuc.edu>
To: krol
Subject: Returned mail: User unknown Status: RO

    ----- Transcript of session follows -----
While talking to yoyodyne.com:
>>> RCPT To:<johm@yoyodyne.com>
<<< 550 <johm@yoyodyne.com>... User unknown
550 johm@yoyodyne.com... User unknown
```

This failure is frequently caused by mistyping the username in the address. (That's what happened above, I mistyped joh**n**.) It is also possible that the username is correct, and the hostname is incorrect, but legal. For example, if you address a message to **john@ux2** rather than **john@ux1**, you may get a "User Unknown" message. The machine **ux2** exists, but there is no user **john** on it. (In the worst case, this may lead to the wrong person receiving your mail: some "john" that you've never met, but who happens to have an account on **ux2**.)

Mail Can't Be Delivered

The previous examples show the most frequent ways of failing, but if you're clever you may find others. You may see the message:

```
    ----- Transcript of session follows -----
    554 <john@yoyodyne.com>... Service unavailable
```

This message tells us that, although the machine was located and in communication, it wasn't accepting electronic mail at this time. In this case, your best bet is to wait a while and try again, perhaps during normal working hours. (Or, if you tried during working hours, try again during off-hours.) Some machines are set up so that they won't accept mail on weekends or some other arbitrary time.

In the previous cases, you would receive notification of the problem almost immediately. For example, if the destination host is unknown to the network, you will receive notification as soon as some system that's handling the mail tries to look up the destination and fails. This should happen in minutes or, at most, a few hours. There is an additional common failure mode in which the problem might not be known for days: the machine is known to the network, but unreachable. In these cases, the sending machine may try and send the mail for two or three days (or more) before it gives up and tells you about it. This looks like:

```
From: Mail Delivery Subsystem <MAILER-DAEMON@ux1.cso.uiuc.edu>
Message-Id: <199111091804.AA27807@ux1.cso.uiuc.edu>
To: e-krol@uiuc.edu
Subject: Returned mail: Cannot send message for 2 days
Status: RO


    ----- Transcript of session follows -----
421 deadhost.cso.uiuc.edu (TCP)... Deferred:
    Connection timed out during user open
    with deadhost.cso.uiuc.edu


    ----- Unsent message follows -----
```

This message can mean several different things:

- The network may be faulty, making it impossible to contact the remote system.

- The remote system may be dead; for example, it may be having severe hardware problems.

- The remote system may be misconfigured; it isn't uncommon for someone to change the configuration of their system and forget to "tell" the network.

Note that the message does not imply that the host was completely unreachable for the entire two days. After a few failures, the sending machine might only try to send the message every few hours or so. If the machine is having hardware problems, the network's chances of contacting it when it's working may be very small.

Failures Involving Multiple Recipients

So far, all of the examples of failures have been for mail destined for one person. It's easy to become confused when something goes wrong with mail sent to several recipients. The returned mail might look like this:

```
Subject: Returned mail: User unknown
Status: RO


    ----- Transcript of session follows -----
While talking to ux1.cso.uiuc.edu:
>>> RCPT To:<willie_martin@ux1.cso.uiuc.edu>
<<< 550 <willie_martin@ux1.cso.uiuc.edu>... User unknown
550 willie_martin@ux1.cso.uiuc.edu... User unknown


    ----- Unsent message follows -----
Date: Thu, 7 Nov 1991 10:43:40 -0600
From: Ed Krol <krol>
To: krol@ux1.cso.uiuc.edu, willie_martin@ux1.cso.uiuc.edu
Subject: Willie do you exist?
```

Who got the mail, and who didn't? You can figure this out by looking at the "unsent message" section. The message was destined for both **krol@ux1.cso.uiuc.edu** and **willie_martin@ux1.cso.uiuc.edu**. The "Transcript of session" tells us it is complaining about **willie_martin**, and not **krol**. You can conclude that **krol** received the message safely, and that there's something wrong with

willie_ martin's address. You need only resend the message to **willie**, when you correct his address.

Last Ditch Help

By convention, every computer that exchanges mail should have a mailbox named **postmaster** defined. **postmaster** should be read by the e-mail administrator for a the host computer addressed. If you need any help with a particular machine, you can send a request to:

```
postmaster@hostname
```

Some things you might consider sending a message to **postmaster** about are:

- Help finding the e-mail address for someone you know to be using his host
- Help finding the proper gateway to use to send e-mail to strange networks
- Complaints about the actions of someone on a particular host (e.g., harassing messages)

Mail Lists and Reflectors

In an earlier section, we discussed aliases and learned how to define an alias with multiple recipients. For example, I can define a group alias for a few suspicious people:

```
alias aliens john_b@yoyodyne.com, john_w@yoyodyne.com
```

After I have created this alias, I can send a message to **aliens**, and it would be delivered both to **john_b** and **john_w**. This is a natural way to implement group discussions through electronic mail. It works fine for small groups, or for personal groups that only you use. As the group grows and other people want to use the same group definition, it turns into a maintenance nightmare. Whenever anyone is added to or deleted from the group, everyone who wants to use the alias must change the definition on his or her own mail system. "Everyone" never does, so someone gets left out on a message and there is hell to pay.

You really want a centrally maintained mailing list, so that you can make a single change that is effective for everyone. As long as you (or some other responsible person) maintains the **aliens** mailing list, everyone—senders and recipients—will be happy. This is typically implemented by a *mail reflector*. A mail reflector is a special e-mail address set up so that any message sent to it will automatically be resent to everyone on a list. For example, let's assume that we've set up a mail reflector for **aliens**, rather than a simple alias. Now I can send a message to **aliens@yoyo-dyne.com**. The mailer on **yoyodyne.com** would then take my message and resend it to **john_b** and **john_w**. It doesn't take much of a machine to act as a mail reflector, but it does take someone with system administrator privileges to set one up.* In this section, we'll tell you how to use lists that other people set up; we won't discuss how to create your own.

In the tradition of computing, we need to make things even more complex. The mail reflector we discussed above works well for a private (though large) group. What if, rather than a private list of people, it were a list available to anyone who wanted to take part in a discussion? We would like to allow anyone in the world who wants to discuss pencil collecting access to the address **pencils@ hoople.usnd.edu**, where it would be forwarded to all the other participating collectors. You would receive everyone else's messages automatically; likewise anything you send to this address would be "broadcast" to pencil lovers worldwide.

To implement such a mailing list, you would need a method for saying "Please add me to the list." Sending that message to **pencils@hoople.usnd.edu** is not a reasonable solution. It not only sends the message to the person maintaining the list, but everyone on the list as well. Doing this may work, but it is considered bad form (making you appear to be a geek among pencil collectors everywhere).

Unfortunately, the correct way to subscribe to a list depends on how the list is maintained. By convention, the Internet uses special addresses for administrative requests. Whenever you create a public mail reflector, you create a second mailbox on the same machine. This mailbox has the same name as the mailing list, with the suffix **–request** added. This special mailbox is "private"; anything it receives isn't broadcast, but instead is sent to the mailing list's maintainer. So the correct way of subscribing would be to send a message to:

```
pencils-request@hoople.usnd.edu
```

If you want to subscribe to a list on Bitnet (Internet users can take part in Bitnet discussions), you may need to deal with **listserv**. **listserv** is a software system for maintaining mailing lists (and more) without human intervention on IBM/VM machines. In this case you'd join by sending a specially formatted message to **listserv** on the computer that runs the mailing list, like **listserv@ hoople.usnd.edu**, from the account where you want to receive the mailings. The message should have the single line in it:

```
subscribe pencils your name
```

where **subscribe** is a keyword and **pencils** is the name of the group. Your name in the above example is strictly for documentation and the format doesn't really matter. Thereafter, if anyone sends messages to **pencils@hoople.usnd.edu**, you will get a copy.

Now that you can get on a list, how do you get off it, or "unsubscribe"? Mailing lists can be as annoying as any other form of junk mail. Unsubscribing is known in the

---

*One of the reasons for this is that if you create multiple mail reflectors, which have each other as members, they could send messages to each other forever.

listserv parlance as **signoff**, and is done by sending the following command to the list server:

```
signoff pencils
```

Of course, if you want to "unsubscribe" to an Internet-style mailing list, just send a message to the administrative (**list-request**) address.

If you want more information about what **listserv** can do, send the message:

```
help
```

to any list server you can find. It will reply with information about what it can do.

If you think about what happens when a mail reflector is in operation, you will realize that it isn't terribly efficient. If five people from the Yoyodyne corporation all subscribe to the **aliens** mail reflector at **hoople.usnd.edu**, five messages will be sent from **hoople.usnd.edu** to **Yoyodyne** for every original message sent to **aliens@hoople.usnd.edu**. This sends unneeded, extra traffic across the Internet. There is a way to get around this suboptimal behavior and, also, make the list a little more responsive to local personnel changes. The system administrator for **yoyodyne.com** could create a local mail reflector that only resends messages to its employees (Figure 7-1).

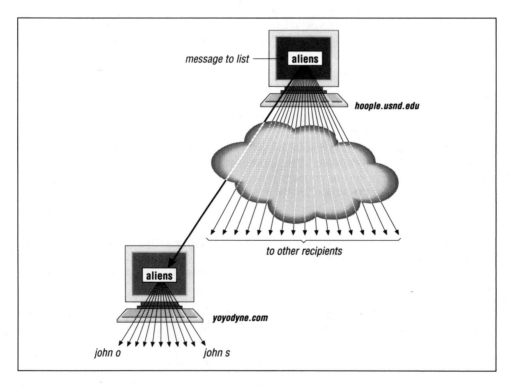

Figure 7-1: Local mail reflectors

Then he subscribes the **Yoyodyne** reflector's address to the national reflector at **hoople**. So, when a message gets sent to **aliens@hoople.usnd.edu**; one message is sent to **aliens@yoyodyne.com**; and, **yoyodyne.com** resends that message to the five subscribing employees.

A couple of final pieces of trivia about using mailing lists. First, some lists are *moderated*. Rather than automatically retransmitting all messages sent to them, a moderator screens the messages to determine whether or not they are appropriate. This is usually not a big deal, but may lead to some delays in reposting. Second, some lists do not repost mail to the submitter, so you may not get the warm fuzzy feeling from seeing your message sent back to you. If you feel you really want a copy, you can use any of the normal means to keep a copy, like ˜c or put your address in after the cc: prompt.

Finally, be careful with responding to list messages. Some messages require personal responses to the original sender; for others, it's more appropriate to send your response to the list. For example, consider a meeting announcement requesting an RSVP. Your RSVP should be sent to the person requesting the information—don't expect that everyone on the list cares that you're coming. On the other hand, replies to requests for information of general interest (e.g., "Anyone know how to make a million dollars legally?") should probably be sent to the list. Be careful about using your mailer's **reply** command. Sometimes, your reply will go to the entire list by default; other times, replies are sent to the originator by default. Exactly what happens depends on how the mail reflector was set up. A mail reflector should set the message's **From:** line to the address of the reflector, and should insert a **Reply-To:** line containing the address of the original sender. If this is done, and your mailer works correctly, the reply should go to the original sender. However, not all mail reflectors are set up correctly, and not all mailers handle **Reply-To:** lines properly. Only experience will tell you for sure. One thing about e-mail lists: you'll hear about it, via e-mail, if you do something obnoxious.

File Retrieval Using Electronic Mail

Earlier, we discussed how you can use e-mail to send a file to someone else as a substitute for FTP. The reverse is also true in some special cases: you can, on occasion, use e-mail to request and receive files from FTP archives. This requires a special kind of server. You send this server a special message, telling it which file you want it to send. Upon receiving this message, the server gets the file and sends it back to you through the mail. The reason for this service is, again, so that you can retrieve files even if the server is on another network (like Bitnet) or over a UUCP connection.

There are three ways of requesting files via electronic mail:

- Specialized "Internet-style" servers that give access to a specific set of files at one location.

- Specialized **listserv** servers that give access to a specific set of files at one location. These are functionally equivalent to the Internet-style servers, but for historical reasons, they work differently. **listserv** originated on Bitnet, where it is very widely used, since Bitnet has no equivalent to FTP.

- General FTP-mail gateways (**ftpmail**). These servers allow you to send a message describing what you want to get. The server then performs anonymous FTP for you, and mails the results back. This differs from the previous two in that **ftpmail** can get any publicly available file anywhere on the Internet.

If you have a direct connection to the Internet, you won't need to use these facilities; it's easier to use FTP directly.

Specialized Servers

The first method of retrieval is used by Internet information repositories that have to be widely accessible (most notably the NIC). To get a file from one of these Internet-style servers, send a mail message to the server in which the **Subject:** line of the mail header contains the command **send**, followed by the name of the file you want. For example:

```
% mail mail-server@pit-manager.mit.edu
Subject: send usenet/comp.mail.misc/Inter-Network_Mail_Guide
.
Cc:
```

The message's body should be "null," i.e., non-existent. This message asks the machine named **pit-manager** at MIT to send a copy of the file **usenet/comp.mail.misc/Inter-Network_Mail_Guide** back to the original sender (i.e., the **From:** line of the requesting message). If you don't have enough information, or if your request fails, a message with **help** as the subject requests information about what facilities are available through that server. One common pitfall: Filenames on Internet servers are usually case-sensitive, so be careful to use capital and lowercase letters appropriately; you must match the filename exactly.

Listserv Requests

The **listserv** commands for requesting files are similar to the commands used to do mailing list maintenance. Send your request to the name **listserv**, on the machine providing the service. The message body should have lines of the form:

```
get filename filetype
```

where **filename** and **filetype** are the two components that make up an IBM/VM filename.* For example, assume you want to get a list of files that are available about Bitnet network nodes. This list is the file *bitnode filelist*, and is available from the server **bitnic.bitnet**. To get the file, send the message:

```
get bitnode filelist
```

_____

*There is more about this in Chapter 6, *Moving Files: FTP* in the section, "Target: IBM/VM Systems."

to the address **listserv@bitnic.bitnet**. There are a couple of funny things that you'll notice the first time you try to fetch something from a **listserv** server. You will receive at least two messages back: a message acknowledging the request and telling you it will be sent, and a message that contains the requested data. The data may arrive in multiple messages because Bitnet has a limit on the size of any individual message. If the file you want is too long, it will be divided into smaller chunks. Finally, with a **listserv** request, you don't have to worry about upper and lowercase letters. **listserv** servers are not case-sensitive. All requests are converted into uppercase before being serviced.

The Ftpmail Application Gateway

You can also request a file through e-mail by using an FTP application gateway called **ftpmail**. **ftpmail** may be used to retrieve files from any **ftp** server on the Internet. Unfortunately, the command structure for **ftpmail** is different from the previous service. Requests to use the **ftpmail** service are made by sending messages to **ftpmail@decwrl.dec.com**. The subject of the message is ignored, but may be used for your reference as **ftpmail** will include your subject in return messages. For example, let's assume that you are really into juggling and want to get a copy of the Juggler's World newsletter, available in the directory */pub/juggling/jugglers-world* on the computer **piggy.cogsci.indiana.edu**. You might do the following:

```
% mail ftpmail@decwrl.dec.com
Subject: jugglers world
connect piggy.cogsci.indiana.edu    ftp from this computer
chdir pub/juggling/jugglers-world   move to target directory
get winter-91                       request the file
quit
.
Cc:
```

You can get complete information about how to use **ftpmail** by sending it a message with the single word "help" in the body, but some of the more useful commands are listed here:

connect *hostname login password*

Specifies the host to contact. Each request must have one **connect** statement in it. If you don't list a hostname with the command, **ftpmail** assumes that the file will be located on the host **gatekeeper.dec.com** (which isn't a very good assumption). Login and password are optional. If they are not given, they default to "anonymous" and your e-mail address.

binary   Specifies that the file is binary and should be encoded into ASCII before being transmitted. By default, the file is encoded with the **btoa** utility.

uuencode Specifies that binary files should be encoded with **uuencode** rather than **btoa**.

compress Specifies that binary files should be compressed with the UNIX **compress** utility.

chdir *directory*

> Changes to the specified directory when the **ftp** connection is made to the server computer.

dir *directory*

> Returns a directory listing of the specified directory. If none is specified return a listing of the current directory.

get *file* Specifies the file to be sent to you from the **ftp** server via electronic mail.

chunksize *number*

> Specifies the maximum number of characters which will be sent in any one message. If a message is larger than the specified (the default is 64000), the file is split into as many messages as required for transmission. When you receive all the pieces, you have to reassemble them in order.

quit Tells the server to terminate the request.

The **ftpmail** utility will be quite happy to mail you any file. It's up to you to tell it if it should treat it as a binary file or not. If it is binary and you don't tell it so, what you get will be useless.

## CHAPTER EIGHT

NETWORK NEWS

News Groups and News System Organization
Getting Started
Reading News
Posting Your Own Articles
Summary of Commands and Features

Let's say you have a question like: Where should I stay on my first trip to Disney World? or: Why won't my Western Digital Ethernet card work in my 286 machine with NCSA **telnet**? or: What is wrong with my laser? It won't lase.

Wouldn't it be nice to ask the world to solve your problem? Wouldn't you like to carry on a discussion about your favorite obscure hobby with obscure hobbyists worldwide? On the surface, e-mail discussion groups seem to provide all you could possibly want for worldwide discussions. As you get into it, however, you find that there is a problem with the volume of messages. There are discussions you take part in for work, and those you participate in for recreation and enjoyment. Having these messages mixed in with the messages from the big boss, which you need to react to immediately, is an information disaster waiting to happen. Network news is a way to take part in even more discussions, yet keep them organized and separate from your mail.

News has another advantage: it's ideal for browsing and doesn't require a lot of commitment. If you're marginally interested in an obscure hobby, you can "drop in" and read up on the latest discussions once a month, or once a year. You don't have to subscribe to a mailing list, and you won't receive lots of mail that's only vaguely interesting—which, at best, you'll have to delete. Of course, something about network news turns lots of these "marginal interests" into all-consuming passions. If electronic mail is the application that forces people to use the Internet the first time, net news is the application that keeps them coming back.

Network news is the Internet equivalent of a discussion group or a "bulletin board system" (BBS) like those on Compuserve or private dial-up facilities. To the user, network news organizes discussions under a set of broad headings called "news groups." A news reading program presents those discussions in an orderly way: a menu of classical music discussions, followed by a menu of pencil collecting discussions, followed by a menu of chemical engineering items, etc. Inside each news group, there are usually multiple discussions going on under specific subjects. In the classical music news group, you might see discussions of Beethoven's Ninth

Symphony, breaking in reeds for an oboe, and the children of Bach. All of these discussions will be going on simultaneously. The news reader helps you keep everything in order. It keeps track of the items you have already seen and only (by default) displays new items that have arrived since your last session. Once the news reader has shown you what articles are available for any topic, you can select and read the items that interest you. If you forget where you have seen something, you can search for an article based on its author, subject or an author-given synopsis. You can also set up your news reader to view or discard certain items automatically, based on the author's name or the article's subject.

As with most Internet applications, there are several news reading programs from which you can choose. On UNIX systems, the most common news readers are **nn** and **rn**. **rn** may be more widely used than **nn**, but I've chosen not to discuss it; it lacks a few important features, so you might find it frustrating. **rn** was written at a time when there wasn't a whole lot of news flowing around. It assumes that you want to read most items that come along in groups to which you are subscribed. Now there is so much news flowing it is easy to get inundated with stuff you don't care about. I will use **nn** to illustrate the features of the news system; it has a good set of features designed, was more to be used in a busy news environment, and is becoming very popular among UNIX users.

If you're getting started with network news, the important thing is not whether or not you use **nn**, but rather that you use a reader that supports *threads*. Threads allow you to read news items in order within a topic. (A more thorough discussion of threads will come later.) This feature is what separates the cream from the milk. **nn** is not the only reader to have this; **trn**, **tin**, and others are just as feature rich. Nowhere in the Internet are religious wars so evident as when discussing which reader is best. There tend to be a lot of similarities between different news readers, so looking at the commands and features for **nn** will give you a start on whatever full featured news reader you finally decide to use.*

News Groups and News System Organization

News groups are organized hierarchically, with the broadest grouping first in the name, followed by an arbitrary number of subgroupings. The name of each group is separated from its "parent" and its "subgroups" by a period (.), a notation you're probably familiar with by now. So:

```
rec.music.folk
```

is a **rec**reational discussion, one which most people take part in for fun, in the general category of **music**. Specifically, it's a discussion of **folk** music.

*****nn** is a very complicated program; its entry in the UNIX reference manual is over 50 pages long, significantly longer than this chapter. Therefore, we won't pretend to discuss all of **nn**'s features; we are only introducing you to the "important" ones.

Now the big question: "Just what news groups are available to me?" The answer is, of course, "It depends." It depends mostly on what computer your news reader uses for its news server. To understand this we need to look a little at how news works. Figure 8-1 shows what the news system looks like to users. You have your "news reader," which interrogates a news server to receive menus of articles, and calls for the articles themselves as required. The server collects news from a number of places: USENET, local news sources, mail reflectors, and Clarinet. It holds these articles for a certain pre-set period (controlled by the server's administrator) and eventually discards them.

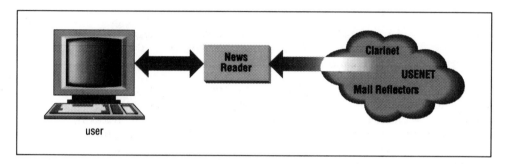

Figure 8-1: User's view of the news system

Most of the server's news groups come as part of *USENET*, a set of news groups generally considered to be of interest globally, and free. USENET is one of the most misunderstood things around. It is not a computer network. It does not require the Internet. It is not software. It is a set of voluntary rules for passing and maintaining news groups. Also, it is a set of volunteers who use and respect those rules. (If you want the whole story, get the article "What Is USENET" that's listed under News, Network in the *Resource Catalog*.) USENET is made up of seven well-managed news groups. The rules for how to use, create, and delete groups have been around since before the Internet. (Yes, USENET predates the Internet; in those days, news was passed via regular dial-up connections. In fact, there are still many sites not on the Internet that participate in USENET in this fashion.) The seven major news categories are:

comp   Computer science and related topics. This includes computer science "proper," software sources, information on hardware and software systems, and topics of general interest.

news   Groups concerned with the news network and news software. This includes the important groups *news.newusers. questions* (questions from new users) and *news.announce.newusers* (important information for new users). If you are new to USENET, you should read these for a while.

rec   Groups discussing hobbies, recreational activities, and the arts.

sci Groups discussing scientific research and applications (other than computer science). This includes news groups for many of the established scientific and engineering disciplines, including some social sciences.

soc Groups that address social issues, where "social" can mean "politically relevant" or "socializing," or anything in between.

talk The **talk** groups are a forum for debate on controversial topics. The discussions tend to be long-winded and unresolved. This is where to go if you want to argue about religion.

misc Anything that doesn't fit into the above categories, or that fits into several categories. It's worth knowing about *misc.jobs* (jobs wanted and offered) and *misc.forsale* (just what it says).

Servers can also get news groups by creating them locally. Any server administrator can create whatever groups it likes, corresponding to the interests of its users. These might include discussions of campus events, local network outages, employee announcements, etc. Although these are local groups, they can still be passed between servers that also want to carry them. Each department in a large corporation might have its own server, but they still might want to pass around the employee announcements group between themselves. They, of course, don't want it to be passed to the outside world. Local news groups are named by the local server's administrator, who must choose names that don't conflict with other news groups. Now we start getting to the confusing part. To a user, the news system looks like Figure 8-1. In actuality, it is implemented as shown in Figure 8-2.

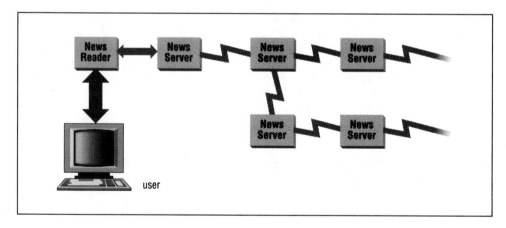

Figure 8-2: Implementation of the news system

A server's administrator makes bilateral agreements with other administrators to transfer certain news groups, usually over the Internet, between each other (known as *news feeds*). Certain servers will provide feeds for some groups, other servers for other groups. A server administrator may make any arrangements for news feeds from any servers that are necessary to provide the set of groups to be offered. Over the years, this has caused some useful local groups to be distributed almost as widely as the core USENET groups.

These are known as "Alternative News Group Hierarchies." Since they look like the USENET news groups (except that they have different names), the term USENET is frequently expanded to include these groups as well. The most common alternative news groups are:

alt Groups that discuss "alternative ways of looking at things." There are a lot of truly bizarre news groups here (including one that tracks the wanderings of an itinerant West-coast evangelist). In a few groups, the postings lack any coherence at all, and make you wonder what, er, stimulants were influencing the authors. However, there is also a lot of useful information. Some important groups (like *alt.gopher*) were created here rather than going through the bureaucracy required to create an "official" news group. (These groups sometimes migrate to official news groups as their topics gain acceptance.) On the whole, though, discussions tend to be out of the mainstream.

bionet Groups of interest to biologists.

bit The most popular Bitnet *listserv* discussion groups.

biz Discussions related to business. This news group allows postings of advertisements or other marketing materials; such activity is not allowed in other groups.

de Technical, recreational, and social discussions in German.

fj Technical, recreational, and social discussions in Japanese.

ieee Discussions related to the IEEE (Institute of Electronic and Electrical Engineers).

gnu Discussions related to the Free Software Foundation (FSF) and its "GNU" project. This includes announcements of new FSF software, new developments to old software, bug reports, and questions and discussion by users of the foundation's tools.

k12 A group dedicated to teachers and students, kindergarten through high school.

u3b Discussions related to the AT&T 3B computer series.

vmsnet Discussions of Digital Equipment's VAX/VMS operating system and Decnet.

Several of these groups are "gatewayed": in particular, the *bitnet* and *gnu* groups. This is another way of creating news groups. The output of a mail reflector or a list server can be converted into a news group. This allows people who would rather use the organizational facilities of news to take part in a mail reflector-style discussion without subscribing to the mailing list themselves. A few computers subscribe to a mailing list, reformat the mail so it's appropriate for the news system, and then distribute it to anyone who wants a news feed.

Finally, several commercial information services are distributed via network news. One example of this is *Clarinet*, which is essentially the United Press International and various syndicated columns indexed for the news system. For a server to offer this service, it must contract with Clarinet for the service; this contract places limits on where the server can distribute the group. The group is usually limited to a corporation, campus, or work group. This group is prefixed by the header *clari*.

All of these groups generate an amazing amount of network traffic; a typical server subscribes to over 1500 news groups and receives about 10 Megabytes/day.* This leads to other limitations on the news groups that are available from any particular server. A server administrator may choose not to accept a certain group because it is very active, and eats up too much disk space. This, also, limits the amount of time old news items will reside on a server. It's possible to go back and read news items you passed by earlier, provided that the server hasn't yet deleted (or *expired*) the article. The amount of time that any article remains on the system depends entirely on how long the administrator feels those items can be stored. It varies from a few days to months, and may be different for each group. This also means that if you go away on vacation, some items may come and go before you get a chance to read them. Luckily, many important work-related news groups have their conversations archived at various places. The locations of these archives are usually announced via the group.

Last, we must deal with, how can I write this delicately, censorship. Some administrators decide that some groups (especially in the *alt* category) are not for consumption by the server's clientele. So they choose not to carry them. If you are offended, you have two choices: find another server or beat up on your administrator.

These last two points are very fuzzy and lead to much animated discussion about basic freedoms. Every time some group is not offered, censorship is not the reason. A server administrator is the steward of a machine. That computer is owned by someone and it has a purpose, aside from being a news server. The administrator walks a fine line between accepting as many news groups as possible and not diverting too many machine resources to news. If you look at this logically, on most servers (other than perhaps at the Kinsey Institute) the group *sci.engr.chem* has a lot more to do with the machine's intended purpose than *alt.sex*. Hence, if disk space runs low, the group to be cut is *alt.sex*. If you use that machine as a news server, you are using someone else's property. There is no basic freedom to use other people's property. You can suggest *alt.sex* (or any other group) be carried, but not demand it.

---

*This may not sound like much, but consider that this is 10 MB being shipped to almost every server in the country daily.

Getting Started

This is probably the hardest part. The biggest problem with starting is that your client software has no idea where your interests lie. Typical network news servers offer 1500 news groups or so, and the first time you use a client, you are most likely subscribed to all of them. Most of them you will find uninteresting. The straightforward approach is to "unsubscribe" to the groups one by one. Obviously, this process is slow and boring: the client displays a page, you say unsubscribe, it says, "do you really want to," you say, "yes," repeat 1450 times. Clearly, there must be an easier way to start.

Some people never even bother to start—they just use standard UNIX commands to read news. They rely on the fact that on a computer running a news server, news items live in a directory */usr/spool/news* and just **grep** for keywords. This is OK, but from an information organization standpoint this is even worse than using an old reader like **rn**. The biggest problem with it is that it can't be guaranteed to work! If you look back to Figure 8-1, the computer having the news reader has no news files on it. Whenever you ask to read news, it asks the computer running the server for articles. So, this approach will only work if the server is running on the same system where you are trying to read news from, something which is occurring less and less these days.

Assuming you are not the type that still rolls their own cigarettes and doesn't believe in power tools, you will want to use a reader. So, let's get back to a shortcut for getting started with **nn**. We're going to discuss this shortcut even before telling you how to read news; you won't *want* to read news if you don't have some control over what you read. The shortcut is very specific to the **nn** news reader. Other news readers will have different files and utilities for handling this problem; you may have to use your ingenuity to find out what will work. This discussion may give you some insight into configuring the other news readers correctly. Whatever you do, your first step will be the same: you must tell your computer what groups you want to view.

Setting Up nn

Two files govern **nn**'s action when dealing with groups: **.nn/init** and **.newsrc**. **.nn/init** is used to set configuration variables and to tell **nn** what groups you want to read (and what groups you want to ignore). Use this file to specify which groups you never want to read. The other file, **.newsrc**, keeps track of what groups you are subscribed to and what articles in each group you have read. Use it to unsubscribe to particular groups that have not been excluded in the **init** file. Let's just start doing it step by step, explaining what is happening along the way.

1. If your home directory does not contain a subdirectory named **.nn** (you can check with a **ls –a .nn**) create one with **mkdir .nn** while you are in your home directory (you can get there with a **cd** command with no arguments).

2. Using the editor of your choice, create a file in the **.nn** directory named **init** (using the **vi** editor, give the command **vi .nn/init**). The contents of the file should look like:

```
sequence
!bionet
!gnu
(List as many groups as required)
```

The first line must be the word "sequence." Subsequent lines are the groups that you never want to subscribe to. In this case, you are excluding any groups starting with *bionet* or *gnu*. You can add any amount of detail to get the job done. For example, if you don't care about any groups about TV that might pop up, you could add lines:

```
!alt.tv
!rec.arts.tv
```

These would exclude only those portions of the *alt* and *rec* groupings. When you have listed all the groups you don't care about, exit the editor.*

3. Issue a **nn** command. When **nn** starts, immediately enter a **Q**. This quits **nn**, but not before it creates the file *.newsrc*. This file lists all the groups offered by the server you are using.

4. Edit *.newsrc*. (If you are using **vi**, use the command **vi .newsrc**, which edits the *.newsrc* file.) Your display should begin something like:

```
alt.activism:
alt.aquaria:
alt.atheism:
alt.bbs:
alt.callahans:
alt.co-ops:
alt.cobol:
alt.config:
alt.conspiracy:
alt.cosuard:
```

5. Issue a "global replace" command that turns all colons (:) into exclamation points (!). This unsubscribes you to everything by changing all colons to exclamation points. (A : after the group name flags the group as subscribed, an ! as unsubscribed.) If you're using **vi**, give a **:%s/:/!/** command.

6. Find the groups you want to participate in, either by using a search command if you know the group's name (**/***name* for **vi** users), or by scrolling through the file

---

*How do you know what groups you're not interested in? This is a chicken-and-egg problem; you don't have a news reader running, so you can use it to tell you what's available. You can make some very broad cuts on the basis of the top-level summaries we've already given, but you might want better control. One way to find out for sure is to ask your news server. Find out the name of the news server your system uses and **telnet** to its **nntp** port like: **telnet your.news.server.here nntp**. This will connect you to the server. You should then type **list news groups**, which will do just that. After you see all the groups fly by, you can exit by typing **quit**.

(use CTRL-f to move down a screen at a time in **vi**). When you find a group you want to subscribe to, change the exclamation point (!) following the name to a colon (:). By changing the ! to a :, you are flagging that group as subscribed. Repeat as necessary. For **vi** users, position the cursor over the ! and type **r:**.

7. Exit the **vi** session normally (with a **ZZ** in **vi**). This updates the actual file and terminates the **vi** editor.

You should now be subscribed to those groups whose names are followed by a colon (:) and that aren't listed in the *.nn/init* file as "don't care" groups.

These instructions are a bit more than is absolutely necessary to do a minimal job. You could easily do steps 1 and 2, cutting the number of groups to around 200; then use **nn** to unsubscribe to the rest, one at a time. Or you could do steps 3 through 7 to set up your current subscriptions correctly; in this case, you'll automatically be subscribed to any new groups that are created, and have to get rid of them by hand. Steps 1 and 2 prevent you from subscribing automatically to newly created groups in any of the categories listed in *.nn/init*. In the long run, the complete 7-step procedure does just what you want.

Reading News

Now we're through with preliminaries: selecting the news groups that you're interested in. Once you're through with this somewhat messy process, you can start the fun part: reading news and creating your own news items.

What Is a News Item?

A news item is very similar to an electronic mail message. It has the same general parts as an e-mail message: a header and a body. The body of a news item is the message's text, just as you'd expect. The header tells the news software how to spread the item throughout the Internet, and also tells you something about the item's contents. The header information is used to build an index on news servers; this index allows the clients to build menus and search for items of interest without having to pass around the complete set of articles. Thus, the header has information about the submitter, the subject, a synopsis, and some indexing keywords. The header is built when you create a new item. You needn't worry about its format, but you do need to provide the information. (The program you use to post the news will ask you for the information it needs.) You will see a header if you save an item in a file for later use, since the header is saved as well.

Each news item is considered part of a discussion *thread*. The act of creating (*posting*) a new article on a completely new topic creates a new thread. News readers who want to add their "two cents" to the discussion then make *follow-on* postings. This creates another article but tells the news software that it is part of the thread created by the original posting. This allows it to be logically tied together in the presentation.

Using a News Reader

As we said earlier, we will describe the **nn** news reader, one of the more popular news readers available for UNIX. You can expect other news readers to have features that are more or less similar; and, no matter what the commands are, the basic tasks you want to perform (select news groups and individual news items, search for different topics) will be identical. Once you understand what you should be able to do, figuring out how to make your personal news reader do it should be simple.

The **nn** news reader has two distinct phases (or modes) of operation: the *selection* phase and *reading* phase. In the selection phase, you are presented a menu of news postings in a group you subscribe to, and you select which ones you really want to read. Assume I went through the laborious news group selection process that we outlined, and ended up subscribing to the single group *rec.music.folk*. When I next give the command **nn**, I will get a menu like this:

```
% nn
News group: rec.music.folk            Articles: 6 of 6/1
a Mr. Chicago        19  World Cafe
b John Storm          8  >
c Willie Martin       4  >>
d John Bigboote      34  lyric request: HARD TIMES
e Jimmy Gretzky       ?  Jimmy Driftwood
f Jimmy Gretzky       ?  Guitar Strings
  -- 13:16 -- SELECT -- help:? -----All-----
```

The format of the listing is pretty simple. There is a title line at the top, telling you the news group that you're currently looking at. The rightmost part of the line, beginning "Articles:", tells you there are 6 articles you haven't seen in this group. The "6/1" says there are 6 total articles you haven't seen in all groups you are subscribed to; there is only 1 group with unread articles. (Of course, so far you have only subscribed to one group.) At the bottom of the screen, you see a status line. This line tells you the current time; it says that you are now in selection mode; it tells you how to get help (by typing ?); and it states that you're currently looking at the headings for all the unread articles in the news group.

The middle of the listing shows entries for the selectable articles, or news items. Each line has the following format:

```
 ID author         size  subject
```

The items in each line mean:

ID   A letter used to select (or unselect) a particular article for reading. For example, to select the sixth item on the screen, type **f**. If you change your mind, another **f** will "unselect" it. On many terminals, **nn** highlights the items which are selected by using reverse video or more intense lettering.

author   The name of the person posting the article. Most news senders will put their login name as the name in this field. Some news readers allow you to post news with a "non de plume" (e.g., Mr. Chicago above) or pseudonym. These pseudonyms are frequently used in discussions where anonymity promotes a more complete expression of opinion (like in *alt.sex*).

size   The number of lines of text in the article. Some news readers fail to provide this information when posting. This is why some of the articles have a ? in the size field.

subject   The subject of the article, as typed by the submitter. Notice that some of the article's subject entries have text, and some only have one or more > characters in that field. The lines which have textual subjects are the original postings for their thread. Lines which have a > are reactions or follow-on postings to the original. Multiple >'s flag these as follow-ons to the follow-ons. In the preceding example, item **b** is a follow-on to the original "World Cafe" posting. Item **c** is a comment on what John Storm said in item **b**.

Typing a SPACE takes you to the next step in the process. If the status line looks like this:

```
-- 09:37 -- SELECT -- help:? -----Top 6%-----
```

it is telling you that there are more articles to be scanned in "selection mode"; so far, you have only seen 6% of the selectable articles in this group. In this case, a space bar gets you the next menu (the next "page") of unread articles. If you have finished all of the selection menus, typing a SPACE displays the first article that you have selected. If you haven't selected anything, typing a SPACE will move you to the next news group that you have subscribed to. If you haven't subscribed to any more news groups, typing SPACE will exit **nn**. Of course, a **?** will get you a help menu; there are many more options.

Often, there will be more than a screen-full of news articles to scan—particularly when you've just subscribed to a new news group. To move between screens of articles, use > to move forward a page, and < to move backwards.

Now let's assume that you selected Jimmy Gretzky's second posting on Guitar Strings by typing the letter **f**. When you reached the last menu, you typed a SPACE. **nn** displays the first item you have selected, one page at a time. Here's Jimmy Gretzky's posting:

```
Jimmy Gretzky: Guitar Strings    Thu, 21 Nov 1991 16:24
I've been following this news group for a long time, to
my knowledge there's never been a discussion of guitar
strings.  I have two primary questions:
 1. What's the brand that the good people buy?
 2. How long before a gig should you change
    your strings?
Thanks for any opinions.
-- Jimmy Gretzky    "The old axe man"
-- 13:30 --rec.music.folk-- LAST --help:?--Bot--
```

Now you're in the reading mode. This means that there are a number of different options available; if you type a question mark to get help, you'll get a different list now. You can read the items you have selected by pressing the space bar until you have waded through them all. In reading mode, typing a SPACE takes you to the next page of the article you're reading, or to the next article that you have selected. If you want to move to the previous page of your current article, type BACKSPACE.

If you have selected multiple items to read, they are presented in the same order as they were displayed in the menu. This is oldest to youngest for each thread. For an original posting with follow-on's, they would be displayed in that order. If you get bored with a long item you are reading and want to skip to the next one, use the **n** command. Sometimes, after selecting a large number of articles in a thread, you may decide that the whole thread is going no where and want to skip reading the remainder of it. To do so, use the reading mode's **k** command. It skips to the next article you have selected in a different thread.

When you have finished reading all of the articles, typing SPACE will either enter selection mode for your next news group, if you have subscribed to more, or **nn** will terminate normally. (A little later we will talk about what else you may want to do.)

If you come back later and start **nn** again, you will work through a similar dialog—except that **nn** will only display news items that have arrived since your last news-reading session. This time around, you might see a subject line with both a **>** and a subject thread. These are follow-on items for a thread whose original note was not displayed because you saw it in your previous session(s).

When you're in "selection mode," you don't have to wade through the entire menu for a news group before you start to read. The commands **X** and **Z** take you to reading mode immediately and display the first article that you selected. The only difference between the commands is that **X** says you are done selecting; when you're finished reading, you will move on to the next group. **Z** returns to the selection menu for the same group after you have read the articles.

If you need to quit reading before you're finished going through all the groups, type the command **Q** in either reading mode or selection mode. This command exits **nn** normally, updating the list of news items that have been displayed. If you restart **nn** after issuing a **Q**, you will be given the option of starting at the beginning of your group list, or continuing where you left off. You do this in response to a question:

```
Enter clari.biz.market.ny (1 unread)?
```

In this example *clari.biz.market.ny* is the name of the group you were reading when you quit. Answer **y** to the question and you will be placed back in this group. Answer **n** and you start at the beginning of the groups you normally read.

Steering a News Reader

The last section took you through a typical reading session and told you some of the turns you might have taken in the process. Now that you are introduced to the news reading, let's talk about navigating. As you come back to news time and time again, your biggest problem will be the amount of information that's there for the taking. There's so much information that it's difficult to step where it is useful, without getting caught in the tar pits. How can you move back and forth to read the material that interests you, ignoring material that looks interesting but really isn't?

When you're in **nn**'s selection mode, you can:

1. Go forward and back in between groups.
2. Go forward and back within the selection menus of a group.
3. Go to reading mode.
4. Quit.

When trying to move around in **nn**, or in any news reader, it's important to think about what mode and group are you in, and where you want to go next. Groups are presented in the same order each time you enter **nn**. You will get a feel for when a group will be presented in the normal course of events. If you want to skip forward to the next group, leaving the current group untouched use **N**. If while you are skipping or after you leave a group, you decide you really ought to have read something use **P** to go back.

If you want to stay in the same group, you can page back and forth in selection menus with < and >. Once you have selected a few things, you needn't page all the way through the menu before reading. We've already mentioned the **Z** and **X** commands, which allow you to jump to reading mode directly. Use **Z** if you want to return to the same group after reading what you have already selected. **X** allows you to read, but will finish the group normally and after reading move on to the next group.

Similar options are available when you are in reading mode as well. You have the ability to move back and forth between articles you have selected with the **n** and **p** commands. You can page forward and back within an article with SPACE or BACK-SPACE. And, even if you have said you never want to return to selection mode for this group again (with an **X**), you can get back there with an equal sign (=).

All of the commands described here and more are explained more fully in a chart at the end of this chapter.

Saving News Items

After reading a news item, you will often want to store it in a file. You might want to print it, mail it to someone, or just save it for later. You can save a file while you're in reading mode by entering the **s** command, which appends the current item to the end of a file. In response to an **s**, **nn** will suggest a default filename. It picks the default filename based on the news group you are reading. It takes each sub-group as a subdirectory within the directory *News*. So if you decide to save an article while reading *rec.music.folk,* **nn** will pick the filename *News/rec/music/folk.* That is, *rec/music* is a subdirectory within *News,* and *folk* is the name of the actual file. This is a great filename for archiving because it keeps saved entries from the various news groups separate in an orderly set of files. To "accept" this filename and store the article, type RETURN. If there's already an article in *News/rec/music/folk,* **nn** adds the new article after whatever's already there; you won't lose the old article.

If you'd rather use a different name for the file, **nn** leaves the cursor positioned at the end of the filename:

```
Save on (+~|) +rec/music/folk []
```

Backspace until you erase the portion of the string you want to replace; then type the new name:

```
Save on (+~|) guitar
```

When you are satisfied with the name, hit a carriage return. In this case, the news item will be appended to the file **guitar** in the current directory.

If the file does not exist, **nn** will make sure you want to create it with the message:

```
Create "guitar" ?
```

You can respond with a **y** or **n** as appropriate. **nn** creates any directories it needs to in order create the file as requested.

Controlling What You Read

There's something you'll learn very quickly: there are very few needles in the haystack. For every news item that's truly worth reading, there are many that are a waste of time: either they're on a topic that's completely uninteresting, or an initially-intelligent discussion has degenerated into name-calling, or it's clear that the participants didn't know what they were talking about in the first place. You shouldn't be surprised, then, to learn that all news readers support some commands to limit the articles that are inflicted on you.

Subscribing and Unsubscribing

At the beginning of this chapter, we took you through a relatively laborious procedure for limiting the number of news groups that you read. We said that you "subscribed" to a limited number of groups (out of the many that are available). Just as with a magazine, you can change your subscription status at any time: you can "subscribe" to new groups, and you can "unsubscribe" to groups that you're currently receiving.

Subscribing and unsubscribing are done with the **U** command while viewing the group's selection menu. If you are subscribed to the group *alt.callahans,* issuing a **U** will unsubscribe you with the following dialog:

```
Unsubscribe to alt.callahans ?
```

If you answer **y** it will unsubscribe you.

Subscribing presents an obvious problem: if you haven't yet subscribed, how do you view the selection menu in the first place? The easiest way to do this is to start a separate **nn** session with some command line options.* You can tell **nn** to read a group even though you aren't subscribed by starting it with the command line option **–X**. Start **nn** with the command:

```
nn -X group-list
```

If you do this, you will read the groups listed in the normal fashion. For example, to subscribe to the group *alt.callahans* you would type the command:

```
nn -X alt.callahans
```

You would see the selection menu for this group's unread articles. If you then enter the **U** command, the response would be:

```
Already unsubscribed.  Resubscribe to alt.callahans ?
```

Again, answering with a **y** resubscribes you. If you list groups on the command line, **nn** only reads those groups in the session; you won't see the other groups that you've subscribed to. So you see only *alt.callahans* this time, but the next time you enter normally with **nn**, the newly subscribed group would appear in its normal place.

By the way, **–X** is useful if you want to "look in" on a group periodically, without subscribing to it. For example, you might want to read *rec.arts.poems* once a year, but you don't want to read it regularly, and you don't want it cluttering up your selection menus. Don't bother to subscribe to it; just invoke **nn –X rec.arts.poems** when the urge strikes.

Killing and Auto-selecting Items

Killing means automatically ignoring some postings within a group. You specify certain criteria. If the article meets the criteria, the news reader ignores it when building the selection menu; you will never see it. Auto-selection is the opposite of killing. You set some criteria. If the article meets the criteria, the news reader automatically "selects" the article for you when it presents the selection menu. Killing is more frequently used by far. This is because judicious use of kill criteria saves you time. There are fewer items to scan, and it takes less time to transmit menus. In this section, we will concentrate on "killing." The process for auto-selection is almost identical.

In **nn**, setting kill criteria is done in either mode. You give the news reader a word or a phrase to search for,† and tell the news reader whether you want to "kill" based on the message's contents (as given in the subject field), or the message's author.

---

*There are other ways. You can also move to unsubscribed groups using the **G** command, too. This isn't a **nn** manual, and using **G** has lot more side effects.

†In practice, this can be any string; indeed, it can be a full UNIX "regular expression." If you're not a heavy-duty UNIX user and don't want to learn about regular expressions, just search for words or phrases.

nn saves this search string in one of your startup files. In the future, whenever **nn** is creating its lists of interesting articles, it will check each article to see whether or not it matches one of the "kill" criteria. If it does, the news reader ignores the article. (Likewise, if you have specified "autoselect" criteria, **nn** automatically selects those articles for you.)

How does this work? Let's say you were reading *rec.humor* and saw this selection menu:

```
News group: rec.humor            Articles: 671 of 671/1

a willie martin      9   >>>racial
b aaly055            ?   >>>>
c Peter Johnson     39   >
d M K T             30   >>>
e M K T             13   >>>
f Earl Butz         18   >>>
...
-- 10:07 -- SELECT -- help:? -----11%-----
```

You decide you don't like racial jokes, so you want to suppress their display. Type the command **K**, which is used for *both* killing and auto-selecting. **nn** returns with:

```
AUTO (k)ill or (s)elect (CR => Kill subject 30 days) []
```

At this point, you have three choices. Type **k** to enter a slightly longer dialog about killing the topic; type **s** to enter a similar dialog about auto-selecting the topic; and type a RETURN for a "shorthand kill." The shorthand kill uses the subject of a displayed item, and remains in effect for 30 days. If you entered a carriage return, **nn** would have asked:

```
AUTO (k)ill or (s)elect (CR => Kill subject 30 days)
from article:a
```

to which you respond with an **a**, saying "don't let me see any articles with the same subject as article **a**." Now, for the next 30 days any items which are part of that thread are ignored.

In this case, you decide the default criteria are not strong enough. If someone posts a new joke with the subject "Racial Joke", you will still see it because it doesn't match your kill criterion exactly. You really want to suppress permanently any item with the word "racial" in its subject. To do this, start out with the command **K**, but don't type a RETURN; instead, enter a **k**, and the dialog continues:

```
AUTO (k)ill or (s)elect (CR => Kill subject 30 days)k
AUTO KILL on (s)ubject or (n)ame (s) s
KILL Subject: (/)racial
KILL in (g)roup 'rec.humor' or in (a)ll groups (g)g
Lifetime of entry in days (p)ermanent  (30)p
CONFIRM KILL Subject perm: racial y
```

The dialog is fairly self-explanatory, but a few points should be explained. Note that **nn** gives you the option of killing the subject either in this group only, or in all groups. Since you may want to read about racial bias on *soc.politics*, you choose to restrict the suppression to the group *rec.humor*.

The news reader also lets you set the "lifetime" of the kill: it can be permanent (i.e., forever), or for a fixed period (by default, 30 days). You may wonder why anyone would want a non-permanent kill—with racial jokes, you probably do want to banish them permanently. However, there are other reasons for "killing" articles where the same considerations don't apply. You may be generally interested in the subject, but you're not interested in the current discussion. For example, you, being quite the rocket scientist, enjoy reading *rec.models.rocketry*. An article with the subject "Designing rocket motors" appears, and you think "great". However, when you start to read the thread, you find out that it is really basic stuff and you're just not interested. You don't want to ignore articles on rocket motor design forever; you just want to wait for the current thread to die. Although it's anybody's guess how long any particular discussion will last, a 30 day kill is appropriate.

Aside from the racial example, there is another situation in which a "permanent" kill may be preferable to a temporary kill. Some groups have an internal structure. Although the group isn't divided into subgroups, the readers of the group have agreed to put certain codes into their subject lines to allow their messages to be categorized easily. For example, the *rec.arts.tv.soaps* group uses codes to indicate what soap opera is being discussed. On the selection menu, it looks like this:

```
News group: rec.arts.tv.soaps        Articles: 630 of 630/1

  a Sherri  Lewis      42   >OLTL: Blair-ramblings
  b John R. Anderson   ?    >>>>OLTL: Gabrielle's son
  c M. T. Czonka       24   >>>
  d S. A. Winslow      143  >>>DOOL: Friday 10th of January
  e Lisa J. Huff       38   AMC: Terrence Was: The Wedding
  f S. A. Winslow      18   >>>DOOL: One Stormy Night Update
  g Willie Martin      50   >GH--Faison,etc.
  h Willie Martin      126  >GH: More Ramblings
  i Liz Wolf           ?    >DOOL : please clear some things up
  j Liz Wolf           ?    >>
  k Jason Castillo     15   >>
  l Liz Wolf           ?    >OLD KL: Question

-- 13:33 -- SELECT -- help:? -----8%-----
```

In this example, if the only soap you are interested in discussing is "Days of our Lives", you could auto-kill all articles that do not contain the string "DOOL" in their subject.

If a news group has established conventions like this, someone regularly posts a key showing which flag strings to use.

Catching Up

Some time, when you are reading twenty or thirty groups regularly, you will go on vacation. You will come back to find thousands of articles in those groups waiting for you to scan. When confronted with this daunting task, you may decide that you really *do* need to read all the messages in some of those groups; but for most of them, you'd just as soon flush all of the old articles. Most news readers provide you with a facility to do this; it is generally called *catching up*. **nn** gives you this through the command line option **–a0**. To begin catching up, give the command:

```
% nn -a0
```

nn then responds:

```
Release 6.4.16,  Kim F. Storm, 1991

Catch-up on 2031 unread articles ?
(auto)matically (i)nteractive i

   y - mark all articles as read in current group
   n - do not update group
   r - read the group now
   U - unsubscribe to current group
   ? - this message
   q - quit

Update bit.listserv.cdromlan (2)? (ynrU?q) y
Update comp.dcom.lans (3)? (ynrU?q) U
Update rec.arts.disney (12)? (ynrU?q) n
Update rec.music.folk (1)? (ynrU?q) n
...
```

The first question asks whether you want to catch up automatically or interactively. An "automatic" catchup tells **nn** that you want to mark all of the unseen articles, in all groups, as "read," so you won't be bothered with them again. It doesn't do anything to change your subscription status; if you were subscribed to the group before, you're still subscribed, and you'll see any future articles that arrive. To do an automatic catchup, type **auto**.

Your other alternative is an "interactive" catchup, for which you type **i**. **nn** starts by telling you the possible responses, and then proceeds through the groups you're subscribed to, one at a time. In this case, you choose to update *bit.listserv.cdromlan* (**y**), meaning that it marks all the messages in that group as "read," but you remain subscribed to the group. You decided to "unsubscribe" to the group *comp.dcom.lans* (**U**), so you'll never see any messages from it again. You decided not to update the last two groups, meaning that you still want to read the articles that arrived during your vacation (**n**).

The next time we invoke **nn**, you won't see *comp.dcom.lans* at all; you unsubscribed to the group, so **nn** will skip it. You will see the news group *bit. listserv.cdromlan*, but only the new articles that have appeared since the "catchup."

You will also see *rec.arts.disney* and *rec.music.folk* in full, including the articles that arrived while you were away.

rot13

In an attempt to keep political pressures at bay, there is a voluntary rule that potentially offensive postings to widely read news groups should be encrypted with a code called **rot13**. The intent of **rot13** isn't to keep any information "confidential"; it is just to prevent readers from "accidentally" seeing something they would rather have avoided. If you go to the trouble of decoding the message, you deserve what you get.

You are most likely to see encrypted messages in groups like *rec.humor*. Such groups are read by a wide mixture of people, with many different tastes. In groups in the *alt* area, where some of these same topics are commonplace, it is not needed. The easily offended should not be wandering through them anyway.

A posting which is in **rot13** will usually be flagged on the selection menu line:

```
e Ed Krol          38 Joke offensive to some (rot13)
```

If you decide to live dangerously and read it, you will see a posting like this:

```
Ed Krol: Joke offensive to some ( Thu, 21 Nov 1991 16:24

Lbh qvqa'g rkcrpg or gb trg
bssrafvir va cevag, qvq lbh?
------
Ed Krol    Speaking for myself not my employer
```

Now you're curious and want to see what this is all about. To read what was written, you must decrypt it using the **D** command; this would cause the screen to be repainted with:

```
Ed Krol: Joke offensive to some ( Thu, 21 Nov 1991 16:24

You didn't expect me to get
offensive in print, did you?
------
Rq Xeby    Fcrnxvat sbe zlfrys abg zl rzcyblre
```

Notice that the entire text of the message was changed, even the signature (which was not encrypted to start with).

If you need to read some **rot13** text and you can't figure out how to make your news reader deal with it, you'll have to create your own decoding command. The code could be implemented with one of the "coding rings" found in cereal boxes. It's merely the alphabet rotated 13 letters: "a" mapped to "n", "b" to "o", "A" to "N", etc. All non-letters remain the same. (As we said, this code isn't designed to keep anything "secret"; it's just to allow readers to ignore offensive material.) In UNIX this can be translated with:

```
% tr "[a-m][n-z][A-M][N-Z]" "[n-z][a-m][N-Z][A-M]"
```

So, if you're curious, save a message and use **tr** to translate it. If you're not using UNIX, you'll have to cook up your own translation command.

Posting Your Own Articles

After reading news for a while, you might get your courage up enough to take part in a discussion. There are two basic ways of taking part: adding to an existing discussion thread or starting a new discussion.

Adding to an Existing Discussion

Let's start by adding a follow-on item to an existing discussion thread. This is a bit easier because all the work of describing the thread (i.e., building the header) is done for you. It is like replying to an electronic mail message. Remember Jimmy Gretzky's question:

```
Jimmy Gretzky: Guitar Strings     Thu, 21 Nov 1991 16:24
I've been following this news group for a long time, to
my knowledge there's never been a discussion of guitar
strings.  I have two primary questions:

1. What's the brand that the good people buy?

2. How long before a gig should you change
   your strings?

Thanks for any opinions.
--
Jimmy Gretzky   "The old axe man"
```

You, being a folk guitarist from way back, see this request for comments on guitar strings and wish to respond. So, while viewing this article, you enter a **f**, meaning "make a follow-on posting." Note that the **f** has a different meaning now that you are in reading mode. **nn** asks you:

```
Include original article? n
```

To which you responded "no," because nothing would be gained by including the questions. You then get popped into the **vi** editor* and can enter your reply by using normal editor commands. After you are done, you have something like this:

---

*If you don't like *vi*, you can give the command **setenv EDITOR emacs** (or whatever editor you like) before you start **nn** and use it instead.

```
News groups: rec.music.folk
Subject: Re: Guitar Strings
References: <1991Nov21.162445.17611@yoyodyne.com>

I've been playing acoustic guitar for a long time and
I've found one brand of strings that I think is the
best.  I use GHS Bright Bronze, which are the
mellowest-sounding I've ever found.
```

Save the file and exit your editing session normally (for **vi**, the command **ZZ** does both). At this point, **nn** will ask you what you want to do next with the line:

```
a)bort c)c e)dit h)old m)ail r)eedit s)end v)iew w)rite
Action: (post article)
```

which gives you the option of revising your posting (**e**), chickening out (**a**), or posting what you just did (with a return or an **s**). You hit a return and your posting is on the way to the world. It will take a while for it to get there, so be patient. (There are other options, obviously, but you can go pretty far without ever using them.)

Some news groups are "moderated"; that is, all items in the group are reviewed by a moderator, who relays the postings that are of genuine interest to the rest of the group. A moderated group is thus more like a magazine or journal than a free-for-all discussion. As you might expect, moderated groups have much higher "quality," albeit at the cost of spontaneity. Posting to a moderated group is no different than posting to any other group. The news servers know which groups are moderated and who moderates them; your news item will be forwarded to the appropriate moderator automatically.

Starting a New Discussion

The only difference between a follow-on posting and creating a new thread is that for a new thread, you must supply the information to fill out the header. To begin a new discussion, use the command:

```
:post
```

at any time during an **nn** session. **nn** will ask you what news group you want to post to:

```
POST to group rec.music.folk
```

In this case, you typed the name of the old folk music group, *rec.music.folk.* Notice: you don't have to be looking at the group, nor even a current subscriber to it. After you type the group's name, **nn** will ask you for the subject, keywords, and a summary of the article. These are the items which go in the header to allow searches. Finally, you need to tell the news reader how far you want your posting disseminated. This exchange looks like this:

```
Subject: Is Mike Seeger Still Touring?
Keywords: traditional
Summary: Wondering if Mike Seeger is still alive
Distribution: (default 'world')
```

The first three lines (Subject, Keywords, and Summary) are passed from news servers to the news readers; these allow other news readers to build selection menus and kill or auto-select your article. Therefore, make it good. It is all the reader has to judge whether your posting is interesting or not. (The actual text of the posting does not get sent unless someone selects an article and starts reading it.)

The distribution line gives the news system some idea about how far you would like the posting passed. You should treat this as a statement of the minimum coverage required for the article. There is no guarantee that it will not be propagated farther than you think. Once you pick a distribution that goes beyond your local server, you are depending on remote servers' configurations to be correct. This is probably too optimistic.

There is no way to find out exactly what distribution lists are available for a server. There are a set of standard distributions which are available on most servers, but they describe only wide areas. They are shown in Table 8-1.

Table 8-1: Common Distribution Keywords

Keyword	Meaning
world	Worldwide distribution (default)
att	Limited to AT&T
can	Limited to Canada
eunet	Limited to European sites
na	Limited to North America
usa	Limited to the United States
IL,NY,FL ...	Limited to the specified state

The problem comes in with smaller, local distributions whose names are made up by the local server's administrator. So only he can tell you for sure.

This is not quite as hopeless as it sounds. Most of the time, the default for the group is what you want. This is OK, even if it sounds too large. News group propagation is voluntarily arranged between sites, and most of the time a group of local interest will not be sent too far even if you specify "world" as the distribution. The person who runs a neighboring server for the Megabucks Corporation certainly doesn't want his disk filled up with discussions about the problems with dorm rooms on some remote campus. That server would be set up to ignore the group *hoople. campuslife*.

However, you should restrict distribution if you are trying to contact local people through a worldwide group. What if you wanted to find lunch hour running partners in your area? One way to approach the problem would be to assume that avid runners would read *rec.running*, and send a posting to this group. This, however, is a world wide group. If you posted a request for jogging partners to this group, you would probably get snide replies like "Sure, meet on the steps of Paddington Station at noon." Quite a jog. What you want to do is post to that group, but use a limited distribution: "campus," "local," "hoople," or whatever your local distribution identifiers are. Similarly, if you're offering an old car for sale, you might want to restrict distribution to your state (unless you're willing to deliver it): IL, NY, CA, or the proper two-letter abbreviation.

One final word of warning about the distribution. You cannot specify a distribution that does not contain your server. For example, you can't specify a distribution of "FL" while sitting on a machine in "NY." This is because news is distributed by flooding: it is "poured" into the system by your server to its neighbors, and flows outward. If you specify "FL" in a message that's distributed from "NY," about the time it gets to "NJ," machines start saying "Why did you give this to me," and throw it away.

Once the header is built, you enter the **vi** session to enter your text and proceed just like you did when writing a follow-on posting. Write your message; exit your editor; and tell **nn** whether you want to abort, send, or revise your message.

Replying Via E-mail

You sometimes want to reply to the submitter of an item privately, through electronic mail. This is useful when the comments you want to make are not of general interest, or should not be widely distributed. To make this easy, **nn** has a mail facility built into it. To invoke it, use the **r** command while reading an item. After the command, the mail interface proceeds much like a follow-on posting. For example, if you were reading the same Jimmy Gretzky item you have been reading for the last thirteen pages and typed an **r**, you would see something like this:

```
Include original article? n
```

You are then given an editing session (using **vi** or your favorite editor) with a mail header already built:

```
To: gretzky@ux.uiuc.edu
Orig-To: gretzky@ux.uiuc.edu
Subject: Guitar Strings
News groups: rec.music.folk
References: <1991Nov21.233330.1466@ux.uiuc.edu>

Are you the same Jimmy Gretzky who was in the class
of '80 at PS12 in Sheboygan?
```

Again, when you are done, exit from the editor normally. You'll return to **nn**, which will ask you:

```
a)bort e)dit h)old m)ail r)eedit s)end v)iew w)rite
Action: (send letter)
```

Of the possible responses, the most useful are to **a**bort sending the message, **s**end the message (a carriage return will do this, too), or **e**dit the message again.

Other Hints and Conventions

Here are some other gems which are known to most experienced news users:

- Read before you post. Take some time getting to know both the system and the group. If you see any postings marked **FAQ** (Frequently Asked Questions), read them. These postings may be in the group itself, or they may be in the special group *news.answers*. Your question may have already been discussed *ad nauseam*, and you will look like a novice just asking it again.

- Format your postings nicely. Use a subject which is descriptive. People will choose to read your postings based on the subject. Busy people tend to have less time to read news than they would like, so they choose items which don't appear to be a waste of time. A subject like "Question" will probably be ignored because I would have to be an expert on everything to know I could answer it. Try "Guitar String Question." Never use "gotcha" subjects (e.g., "Subject: Sex", but in the body, "Now that I have your attention, I have a question about insects"). On the other end of the posting, signatures are fine but keep them short.

- Be polite. You asked a question of the network. Someone took their time to answer, a thank-you message back is appreciated. Disagreements are fine, but attacking someone personally for their postings is not good form (although common). This is known in the trade as *flaming*.

- Post and reply appropriately. Post to the smallest distribution that will get the job done. Read the whole thread before responding. If someone asks, "What's the answer?" and someone already said "The answer is 42", you don't add anything by repeating it. Some of this will be inevitable because of the delays in news propagation, but avoid contributing to the problem intentionally. If the answer is not of general interest, reply by e-mail.

- Don't automatically include the article to which you are responding. Too many times, articles get longer and longer with each response because people include all previous discussion. The people who are reading the group chose to read your posting based on the subject. If it is a follow-on posting, they probably have read the initial postings, too (they had the same subject). Please don't make them read it again. If you want to respond point by point, edit the discussion down so only the relevant sentences are included.

- Controversy is fine, but keep it in its place. There are groups designed for pro/con discussions, and there are groups where people of a like mind meet to commiserate. Don't post anti-gun sentiments on *info.firearms*; it won't do anything but get you tons of hate e-mail. Flag opinions, which may be controversial, with IMHO (In My Humble Opinion) like "IMHO, Mossberg makes the best firearms."

- Be patient; news takes a while to be distributed. When you post something it goes into a queue on your server; it then needs to be indexed and passed on to the rest of the world. All of this is done by background tasks on the server. So your posting won't appear on your system immediately, and may take a day to get to the rest of the world. Also, don't expect responses immediately, even by e-mail. Some people feel guilty reading *rec.arts.disney* on company time. There-fore, a lot of people read recreational groups only on the weekend.

- The biggest problem with reading news is there is so much and it is all so inter-esting. It is easy to be enamored with it. Be selective about which groups you read. It could mean your job, your family, or your college career.

Summary of Commands and Features

In the following sections, we're going to summarize the **nn** commands that we have discussed. If you're not using **nn**, these lists may not be of too much value, but take heart; they do provide a "checklist" of worth-while features.

Command-line Options

In most of the previous examples, we have assumed that you invoked **nn** with no options. In reality, the general format for invoking **nn** is:

```
% nn options group-list
```

If you specify a group-list, **nn** only examines the listed groups in this session. The groups you list will only be examined if you are subscribed to them, unless you specify the **–X**. If you specify the beginning of a group in the list, all groups match-ing that beginning are examined. For example:

```
nn -X rec.arts.
```

will show you any groups beginning with *rec.arts*. If you don't specify a group list then all groups you are subscribed to are examined. Options control various aspects of the particular invocation. Some of the more useful ones are:

–a0	Used to "catch up" on all groups to which you subscribe. (Explained more fully in the "Catching Up" section of this chap-ter.)
–i	Makes searches of the **n** or **s** command case-sensitive, which means that uppercase letters and lowercase letters are considered different. Normally, case is ignored in matching.
–m	Displays all articles meeting other criteria (specified with other control-line options like a group list, **–s**, etc.) on one selection menu, rather than a menu per group. This is useful if you are searching for a particular article and don't know what group it is in. Using **–m** prevents **nn** from marking new items in this session as "seen."
–n*string*	Used to search the groups used in this invocation, and select items whose author matches the string. (Think of "n" as an abbre-viation for "name.") The string may either be a single word, like **–nkrol**, a complete name like **"ed krol"**, or a search expression like **–n/"ed.*"** to search for all authors beginning with "ed." The

search is case-insensitive, but otherwise the name has to match exactly; that is, **–n"ed krol"** won't match "Edward Krol."

–s*string*   Used to search the groups used in this invocation, and select items whose subject matches the string. The string may either be a single word like **–sgolf**, a phrase like **–s"u.s. open golf scores"**, or a search expression like **–s/"go.*"**; the latter searches for articles whose subject contains a word beginning with "go".

–x   Tells **nn** to consider all articles for display, subject to other criteria (e.g., search strings), regardless of whether you have viewed the article previously. Useful when you read an article once then want to go back and read it again. (Its use prevents **nn** from marking new items in this session as "seen".)

–X   Tells **nn** to consider groups even if you are not subscribed to them. Useful when you are looking for an article in groups to which you are not subscribed.

Here's an example. You remember having seen an interesting posting by John Wadsworth. However, you don't remember the news group it was in. But you do know it was in a news group that you regularly subscribe to. To find it, you can give the command:

```
% nn -x -n"john wadsworth"
```

We used **–x** to search all articles in all news groups that we have subscribed to, including articles we have already read. To make an even wider search that includes all articles in all groups, we could have done:

```
% nn -X -n"john wadsworth"
```

Given our example, this wider search isn't necessary; in fact, it's a waste of resources. We remember reading the article, so it must be in a news group to which we subscribe, so **–x** is appropriate.

When would you use **–X**? Let's say someone else told you about this interesting article, but she didn't remember where it appeared. In this case, **–X** is appropriate. However, you should be judicious in the use of the **–x** and **–X** options. **–x** relaxes the limits on items within groups which are searched. **–X** suppresses limits on what groups the search is conducted. If you use both parameters, the search looks at every news item on the server, and could take a long time. It would be better if you could say, "well, I'm sure that article would have appeared in one of the 'talk' groups." Then you can give the command:

```
% nn -X -x -n"john wadsworth" talk.
```

Some Selection Mode Commands

The following list shows the most important commands available to you while in selection mode. It includes all of the commands that we have covered, and a few that we haven't. There are many additional commands that we won't mention; the commands we've listed below are certainly all you need to get going, and may be all that you ever need.

lowercase letters

Used to select news items; type the ID letter that appears on the left side of the menu. If the news item is already selected, typing its ID letter will "unselect" it.

space bar

Moves to the next logical progression in the process of selecting or reading. If you're reading the selection menu, typing the space bar moves you forward to the next menu page, if one exists. If none exists, you move to the first selected item. Within a selected item, pressing the space bar moves you to the next page of that item. When there are no more pages, you go to the next item. When there are no more items, you move to the next news group. If there are no more groups, the program terminates.

<   Moves you back a page in the menu.

>   Moves you forward a page in the menu.

K   Starts the kill dialog to suppress listing of some items (see the section "Killing and Auto-Selecting Items" earlier in this chapter).

N   Moves forward to the next logical group in sequence. If items are selected they will remain selected, should you return to that group.

P   Moves backward to the previous logical group in sequence. If items are selected they will remain selected, should you return to that group.

Q   Quits the **nn** session normally. This updates the list of items shown so you won't see articles a second time.

U   Toggles subscription status of the current list. If you are currently subscribed, it will unsubscribe you. If you are currently not a subscriber, it will subscribe you.

X   Moves to reading mode if something is selected, or to the next group if not. Marks items in the menu as having been seen, so you won't see them again. After reading the articles, you won't return to the selection menu.

Z   Same as **X**, except that after reading, you **will** return to this group's selection menu.

Some Reading Mode Commands

Here are the most useful commands for reading mode. Again, we've listed all of the commands covered in the text, plus a few more; and again, there are many more commands available, but you may never need them.

space bar
> Moves down one page in the article or if on the last page of an article to the next article or menu. Note that this is different from the command used to page forward in selection mode.

backspace
> Moves up one page in the article. Note that this is different from the command used to page backward in selection mode.

=
> Switches back to selection mode for the current group from reading mode.

C
> Cancels this entry. It is a way you can retract an entry you made. People will probably see it before you retract it, so you may still catch some grief about it. This can only be used on items you have submitted.

D
> Decrypts an article posted in **rot13** to make it readable.

f
> Starts a follow-on posting to the current article (see the section, "Adding to an Existing Discussion" earlier in this chapter).

k
> Kills the remainder of the thread you currently selected. If you select an article and five follow-on articles, then decide you don't care to read them, a **k** skips those articles and any other ones in the menu for that session.

K
> Enters the kill dialog to automatically ignore or select articles (see the section "Replying via E-mail"). Remember the difference between **k** and **K**. Uppercase **K** lets you permanently kill (or auto-select) a group of articles; **k** is used to ignore follow-on articles in the current session that you don't want to bother reading.

n
> Stops reading the current article and moves to reading the next selected article.

p
> Stops reading the current article and moves to reading the previous selected article.

r
> Replies to the selected item via e-mail (see the section "Replying via E-mail" earlier in this chapter).

s
> Saves the selected item in a file (see the section "Saving News Items" earlier in the chapter).

U
> Toggles subscription status of the current list. If you are currently subscribed, it will unsubscribe you. If you are currently not a subscriber, it will subscribe you (see "Controlling What You Read" in this chapter).

Q
> Quits the **nn** session normally. This updates the list of items shown so you won't see articles a second time.

CHAPTER NINE

FINDING SOFTWARE

How Archie Works
Contacting Archie
Using Archie with Telnet
Using Archie by Electronic Mail
Archie Using a Client

Historically, one of the biggest problems on the Internet has been finding what you know exists. Anonymous FTP servers sprang up early on, giving you the ability to fetch files from repositories on the network, but the existence of those files was largely communicated by interpersonal networking. Part of the apprenticeship for a network guru was knowing enough other people and attending enough conferences to find out where things were hidden. This worked just fine while the Internet was a small network used by computer professionals. Now that the Internet is attempting to provide resources to the masses, the "good ole boys" network no longer works. Plenty of new users don't have access to an "experienced" administrator with the right contacts. And there are now so many resources online that not even the best administrator could keep track of them all. You may know that such-and-such a database or public domain program exists, but finding it is like finding the proverbial "needle in the haystack."

This sounds like a job for a computer. Enter **archie**, a system which allows searching of indexes of what files are available on public servers on the Internet. It's the place you should start if you are searching for programs, data, or text files. Currently, it indexes about 1200 servers and 2.1 million files. You ask it either to find filenames which contain a certain search string or suggest files whose description contains a certain word. It returns the actual filenames that meet the search criteria, and the name of the servers containing those files. Once you decide which of the files most likely meets your needs, you can easily move the file to your computer with anonymous FTP.

First, we'll look at how Archie works. It's so amazingly simple that it took years for someone to think of it. From there, we will move to how to use Archie. Like a lot of services on the Internet, Archie can be used in three ways. Most people use Archie through TELNET, so we will spend most of our time there. The really lucky folk have an **archie** client installed on their computer. The unlucky folk must use e-mail for their queries. After the discussion of TELNET access, we will look at these as well.

How Archie Works

If this were a murder mystery, this would be the time to unveil the killer. In the preceding chapters, I have given you all the clues necessary to build an Archie service. The answer to "whodunit?" is "some people at McGill University."

The answer to "howdunit?" is "to ask, via the network, for people who were running servers to register them." Once a month, McGill runs a program that contacts every server it knows about via **ftp** (Figure 9-1). When it contacts the server, it does a directory listing of all the files on the server, using standard **ftp** commands (**ls –lR**, to be exact). When you come along some time later and say, "find me a file which has the string 'eudora'," Archie just scans all the merged directories and sends you the filenames that match your search string, together with the server where each file is available.

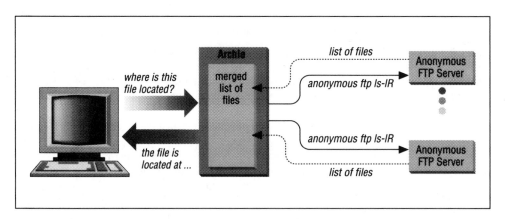

Figure 9-1: How archie works

This is the basic service that was created. It became obvious that some people chose strange, non-intuitive names for their files, like a filename of *MacPOPclient* for the Macintosh electronic mail program named Eudora. They then asked for people to send information on the major packages they provide and created a service called *whatis*. It is a set of alternative indexing keywords for files on the network. It can be used to locate software or data files even if the filename bears no resemblance to its contents. Since this service requires human intervention, it is a lot spottier, but none the less useful.

Contacting Archie

To use Archie, you must choose an Archie server. There are a number of servers, all of which are equivalent; that is, each has the same information. There aren't any "good" servers, or "special-purpose" servers. So, when you select an Archie server, your choice should be motivated by two goals: to be nice to the network, and to spread the work around.

The "nice" way to pick a server is to choose one which is close to you on the network. This is not easy to do, since you probably don't know exactly where the wires providing your Internet connection go after leaving your campus or company. The best approximation you have is to pick one that is geographically close. Using a server in Australia from the U.S. might be cool, but it is quite wasteful of slow transoceanic network links. The following table shows a list of Archie servers and suggested areas for use:

Table 9-1: Available Archie Servers

Name	Suggested Usage Area
archie.rutgers.edu	Northeastern U.S.
archie.sura.net	Southeastern U.S.
archie.unl.edu	Western U.S.
archie.ans.net	Sites connected to the ANS network*
archie.mcgill.ca	Canada
archie.au	Australia & the Pacific Basin
archie.funet.fi	Europe
archie.doc.ic.ac.uk	United Kingdom

Archie is a very popular service. It is not unusual for a server to be handling over 40 requests simultaneously. In order to protect the responsiveness of the service, some have limits on the number of concurrent requests that can be handled. If you try to use a server and hit one of these limits you will get a message:

```
Due to serious overloading on the archie server,
we have been forced to restrict the number of concurrent
interactive (telnet) sessions to 10.

Connection closed by foreign host.
```

If everyone uses the server closest to them, it naturally spreads the load around and minimizes this irritation.

---

*ANS is one of the Internet Service Providers.

Using Archie with Telnet

After you decide what server is the best one for you to use, the common way to use it is to **telnet** to that hostname. It will come back with a standard UNIX login prompt, to which you respond with the login name **archie**:

```
% telnet archie.sura.net
Trying 128.167.254.179...
Connected to nic.sura.net.
Escape character is '^]'.

SunOS UNIX (nic.sura.net)

login: archie
Last login: Mon Apr  6 12:11:44 from eeopr2.ENG.UAB.E
SunOS Release 4.1.2 (ARCHIE) #3: Sat Feb 15 15:09:08 EST 1992
            Welcome to the ARCHIE server at SURAnet

Please report any problems to archie-admin@sura.net

archie>
```

At this point, you are talking to Archie and can set parameters and make searches. You should begin by checking how string matches are done on the server you are using. This is done with the command:

```
archie> show search
# 'search' (type string) has the value 'exact'.
```

Different servers default to different types of searches. Some are case sensitive, some insensitive. Some allow full UNIX regular expression searches. The above server defaults to an "exact" match. This means you must match the filename exactly, including case. If you are browsing for software, this probably isn't what you want. If you are looking for the package Eudora, you usually want the search to match Eudora, eudora, or EUDORA.

You can change the way your search is conducted with the command:

```
archie> set search type
```

type tells the way Archie should conduct your search. It must be one of the following:

exact   The search string given must exactly match a filename.

regex   The search string is treated as a UNIX regular expression to match filenames.

sub   The search string will match a filename that contains it as a substring. The case is ignored when doing the matching. This is probably the most useful search type for general-purpose use.

subcase   The search string will match a filename which contains it as a substring. The case of the matching substrings must match as well.

In all Archie searches (even "exact" searches) there's no way to search for a file in a particular directory.* That is, if you say, "find *eudora*," Archie will find directories and files named *eudora*. There is no way you can say "find *pub/eudora*" (*eudora* in the directory *pub*). In most cases, this is reasonable: the directory structure depends entirely on the FTP server that has the file you want. If you know the directory in which a file resides, it's a good bet that you know the server, too, and don't need Archie.

When you are finished searching, you leave Archie with:

```
archie> quit
```

This terminates the TELNET session and returns you to the computer you used to contact Archie.

Searching by Filename

The most common and definitive way to look things up in Archie is to search for likely filenames. It is definitive because you know that the information you find was correct within the past thirty days. Therefore, if you find a file in the index, you will almost certainly find the same file when you go to fetch it with anonymous FTP. To begin this search, pick a minimal search string that will probably be in a filename you are looking for. Use the command:

```
archie>prog searchstring
```

to start the search. The search string is interpreted as specified by the "set search" variable.

For example, let's say someone suggested you check out the Eudora package to do electronic mail from your Apple Macintosh. You might try:

```
archie> prog eudora
# matches / % database searched:   40 / 16%
```

To show you that something is happening, the second line changes as the search progresses. It shows the number of files which contain the search string (in this case 40) and how much of the index has been searched (here 16%).

After the search is complete, the server returns a list of servers and filenames that fit the criteria. Eudora, being a very popular package, was offered by 81 servers. An abbreviated listing of this search looks like:

```
Host miki.cs.titech.ac.jp   (131.112.172.15)
Last updated 16:51  3 Mar 1992
  Location: /mac/eudora/old
    FILE  rw-rw-r--  241493  Oct 10 19:25   eudora1.2J.sit.hqx
  Location: /mac/eudora
```

---

*A newer version of Archie due out in the Fall of 1992 should make this possible.

```
        FILE  rwxrwxr-x  281139  Oct 22 02:00    eudora1.2.2.sit.hqx

    Host ee.utah.edu   (128.110.8.42)
    Last updated 02:22 17 Mar 1992
     Location: /pop3/eudora
       FILE  rw-r--r--  459636  Jan 30 00:48    eudora1.2.2.i.sit.hqx
     Location: /pop3/eudora/beta
       FILE  rw-r--r--  240607  Jan 30 00:49    eudora1.3b8.sit.hqx

    Host ix1.cc.utexas.edu   (128.83.1.21)
    Last updated 02:37 21 Mar 1992
     Location: /microlib/mac/comm
       FILE  rw-rw-r--    9660  Oct 18 12:13    eudora-12-changes.txt
       FILE  rw-rw-r--  637998  Jan 17 11:33    eudora-122-comm-1.hqx
       FILE  rw-rw-r--  535253  Oct 18 12:56    eudora-122-docs.hqx
       FILE  rw-rw-r--  555712  Oct 18 12:56    eudora-122-manual-pm.hqx
       FILE  rw-rw-r--  308680  Dec 11 09:53    eudora-122.hqx
       FILE  rw-rw-r--    5997  Feb 25 10:55    eudora-123b28-readme.txt
       FILE  rw-rw-r--  258321  Feb 25 10:54    eudora-123b28.hqx
       FILE  rw-rw-r--    4211  Feb 25 10:43    eudora-123bxx-uucp.txt
```

a file that matches the search string. The first one in the example is **miki.cs.titech.ac.jp**. Next it tells you the directory where the file resides (*/mac/eudora/old*) after the word "Location." Finally, it lists the filenames within that directory (*Eudora1.2J.sit.hqx*).

Sometimes a search will match a word in a directory path, but no filename in that directory. In this case, the location line will be the path to the directory which matched the search criterion. Instead of beginning with "FILE", the actual entries at that location will be listed:

```
    Location: /microlib/mac/comm
      DIRECTORY rwxrwxr-x    512  Jun 25  1990    eudora
```

This shows that what was found is a directory that might contain something useful. If you decide that this entry is promising, the only way you can find out what contains is to use anonymous FTP to look in the directory, with a **cd microlib/mac/comm/eudora** followed by a **dir**, to see what is actually there.

Since there are lots of anonymous FTP servers that have what you want, you now face a new problem: which one to use. This is the major problem with Archie: you get very little information to help you decide which file is best to use. Here are a couple of things to help you choose:

1. If the program is popular and runs on several kinds of computers, you have to decide which file is for each kind of computer. This is not so bad for Eudora, but when you start looking for things like *gopher* (after reading Chapter 11, *Tunneling Through the Internet: Gopher*, you'll want to) you will find the Macintosh version, a PC version, an X windows version, etc. The only help you have is to decide in Archie are the directory and filenames. There are no standards for these names, but most server administrators try to name directories in an intuitive, descriptive way. In this example, you'll find that many copies of *eudora*

reside in some sub-directory called "mac," which probably stands for Macintosh. Another clue are the filename suffixes. Certain kinds of compression and file encoding techniques are more prone to be used on certain kinds of computers. In particular, *.sit* and *.hqx* are frequently used on Macintoshes. (There is a nice table of these in Chapter 6, *Moving Files: FTP*).

2. Multiple versions of the same software may be available. With luck, a version number might be encoded in the filename, as in the following examples:

```
eudora-122.hqx
eudora-123b28.hqx
```

If some friends told you about the software, you might ask which version they are running. If you can't, you might pick the latest version possible. Again, there are no standards for how versions are encoded into the filename. You could guess that 123 is a later version than 122, and you would almost certainly be right. Sometimes, the directory name will be a clue again. At **miki.cs.titech.ac.jp** there were two directories: */mac/eudora/old* and */mac/eudora*. You might presume that the newer software is in the latter directory.

Also, remember that the term *beta* is used in software development to describe test versions. In the example, **ee.utah.edu** had two directories: */pop3/eudora* and */pop3/eudora/beta*. Unless you are adventurous, stay clear of the beta versions.

3. Pick an official looking server. (Remember the security discussion from Chapter 4, *What's Allowed on the Internet.*) Try to pick a server that is run by someone who should be in the business of delivering software, like a computer center, network provider, etc.

4. Finally, pick a server that is close. Earlier, we said that you should pick an Archie server that's relatively close to you, to minimize the total network traffic and spread the workload among the different servers. The same reasons apply here. If you look closely at the first host in the previous example (**miki.cs.titech.ac.jp**), you could figure out it is in Japan from the ending **.jp**. It would probably take longer to fetch the file from there than someplace on the same continent. Also, you might be in for a surprise: things that cross country borders sometimes get translated. You might find that *eudora*'s menu strings had been translated into Japanese!

If I were trying to decide where to pick Eudora up from the sites shown in the example, I would probably choose *eudora-123b28.hqx* from the **ix1.cc.utexas.edu** server. First, the server appears to be run by the University of Texas Computer Center, a conjecture based on the **cc** in the name. They should be distributing software. They seem organized, have a good selection including what I want (sounds just like picking a department store). I would pick that file because it is the latest version in a format I could easily deal with on a Macintosh.

Searching Using the Descriptive Index

The other type of search which can be used with Archie is a *whatis* search. It searches the so-called "software descriptions database." When administrators place files in their FTP archives, they may contribute to an index entry for the file to help people find it. The index entry creates a relationship between a filename and a set of keywords. When you do a *whatis* search, your search string is used to examine the keyword list. The search is done with the command:

```
archie> whatis searchstring
```

If the search string is contained in one of the keywords, Archie prints the name of the file and a short description. Once you have a filename that sounds appropriate, you must do a filename search to find out where it is located.

Let's say you were looking for a gene sequence map for E.Coli bacteria.* If you do a **prog coli**, Archie would return over 100 filenames. Most of the matches are obviously not what you want: the broccoli recipes, the horse colic database, etc. There are a few like *colidb* which might be good, but that's all you know. So you decide to try a *whatis* search to get more information:

```
archie> whatis coli

ECD        Escherichia coli db (M. Kroeger, Giessen)
NGDD       Normalized gene maps for E.coli, S.typh., etc.
                     (Y. Abel, Montreal)
```

The file *NGDD* looks like just what the doctor ordered. To find out where it lives you do a *prog* search, just like you did before:

```
archie> prog NGDD
# matches / % database searched:    1 /100%

Host ncbi.nlm.nih.gov   (130.14.20.1)
Last updated 02:23  4 Mar 1992
 Location: /repository
    DIRECTORY rwxrwxr-x    512  Jun 25  1990    NGDD
```

This looks even more promising now. It even comes from a reliable source, the National Institute of Health (**nih.gov**). Notice, however, that what Archie found is not a file called NGDD, but a directory by that name. So you don't quite know what you really have. You need to anonymous FTP to **ncbi.nlm.nih.gov** and go to the */repository/NGDD* (**cd repository/NGDD**) directory. Once there do a **dir** command to see what files are there.

Remember the one caveat. The "prog" index is up to date to within 30 days. The "whatis" index is not. Someone can create an entry, and sometime later delete the file. So you may occasionally find something with **whatis**, but not be able to locate it with the **prog** command.

---

*As this example shows, Archie isn't just good for looking up software; it's good for finding all kinds of resources.

Other Archie Commands

We talked about the **archie** commands which are used regularly. There are a number of other commands which can be useful on occasion. Here is a selection of the other commands you might need:

bugs   Gets you a list of the current known bugs in the Archie system.

help   Gets you a list much like this one.

list   Displays a list of anonymous FTP servers that are indexed in the Archie system.

set *variable value*   Used to set parameters used to control your Archie session. The variable name is required (there is a list of variables in the next section). The value is required only if the variable is not a Boolean (on or off) variable. For Boolean variables, **set** *variable* turns the variable on. For other variables, the value is remembered and used appropriately.

show *variable*   Displays the value of the specified variable. *Variable* is optional. If it is not specified, **archie** displays the value of all the variables. **Show**, with no variable name, is a good way to get a list of valid variable names, or to find out your server's default settings.

unset *variable*   Turns off a Boolean variable.

mail *destination*   Sends the result of the last search to an e-mail address. The *destination* is optional. If given, it is taken to be an e-mail address where the search results should be mailed. If no destination is specified, the value of the variable **mailto** is used as the destination.

servers   Gets a current list of all the known **archie** servers.

site *computer*   Lists all the files available at the anonymous FTP server named *computer*.

Archie Configuration Variables

Here is a partial list of the variables that can be manipulated with the **set**, **unset**, and **show** commands:

mailto *address*   Sets a default e-mail address; this address is used whenever the **mail** command is given without a parameter.

pager   Determines whether the output should stop whenever the screen is full. If **pager** is set, output will be held until you enter a carriage return when the screen is full. This is a Boolean variable (use **set** to turn it on, **unset** to turn it off).

maxhits *number*   Limits the amount of output to *number* entries. (*Number* must be between 1 and 100.)

sort *keyword*   Declares the order the output will be presented. For a list of what kinds of sorting are available, try **help set sort**.

search *keyword*   Sets the search type. This is explained more fully in the text.

term *type row col*   Declares that you are using a *type* terminal (e.g., **VT100**) which has *row* rows on the screen and *col* columns. The type can be any one of the typical terminal abbreviations available in UNIX. *Row* and *col* are optional. If they are omitted the standard size for the declared terminal type will be used.

Using Archie by Electronic Mail

In addition to logging into an Archie server directly, you can use Archie via electronic mail. While it's less convenient than an interactive session, there are two reasons why you might want to use mail. First, you may be forced to: your network might not allow you to contact Archie via TELNET. This would be the case, for example, if your only connections to the outside world are through UUCP or Bitnet. Many of the servers that **archie** indexes provide access through **ftpmail** (Chapter 7, *Electronic Mail*) for those networks which can't do **ftp**. Second, you may not care to wait around for Archie to do the lookup. If you hear about something great at 4:59 and have to run for the train, send an e-mail query—the answer will be there when you get to work the next morning. The same logic applies if Archie tells you that it's busy, or if it's unavailable for some reason.

Archie by mail is a subset of what is available using **telnet**. You build a message having search commands in it, and send it to:

    archie@`server`

where *server* is one of the servers mentioned earlier. Commands must begin in column one of a line. You can have as many commands as you like in a message. Any command which cannot be understood is interpreted as **help**. So if you do anything wrong, you get help whether you need it or not. Since interactive responsiveness is not an issue, the arguments all use more powerful search types like **regex**. Here are the commands that are available to you through the e-mail interface:

path *e-mail-address*   Tells **archie** to send the responses to *e-mail-address* rather than the address given in the **From:** field of the requesting message. It is useful if you are traversing e-mail gateways and not enough information is conveyed to Archie in the "From:" field for the return trip. If you send requests and never receive an answer, try specifying a very exact route back to your computer and see if it helps.

compress	Will cause the output sent to you to be compressed and uuencoded before being sent. It is suggested you use this option whenever the output you expect will exceed 45k bytes.
prog *regexp*	Looks for filenames that match the regular expression.
site *siteid*	Returns a list of all the files on the server with the specified *siteid*, which may be either a domain name or an IP address.
help	Returns a help guide for mail **archie**.
list *regexp*	Returns a list of all the servers whose names match *regexp*.
servers	Returns a list of all the known Archie servers.
whatis *keyword*	Returns a list of possible files which match the keyword argument in the **whatis** database. This can then be used in a subsequent mail message with the **prog** command to look up the location of these files.
quit	Causes processing to be terminated and any lines following this command to be ignored. This is useful if you have a signature file which may be taken as further commands.

For example, let's say you wanted to find an archive for the *sci.geo.meteorology* news group. Of course, since you are interested in meteorology in general, you might want to also go fishing and see if there are any other good meteorology files available. To do this, use your favorite mail program to construct a message like this:

```
% mail archie@archie.rutgers.edu   use any server you like
Subject:                           no subject necessary
prog meteorology
   .
```

Some time later, you would receive a message back from the server, containing the results:

```
>From archie-error@dorm.rutgers.edu Sat Apr 11 06:33:30 1992
Received: from dorm.rutgers.edu by ux1.cso.uiuc.edu with SMTP
Date: Sat, 11 Apr 92 07:32:35 EDT
Message-Id: <9204111132.AA04307@dorm.rutgers.edu>
From: archie@dorm.rutgers.edu
To: Ed Krol <krol@ux1.cso.uiuc.edu>
Subject: archie reply: prog meteorology
Status: R

Sorting by hostname
Search request for 'meteorology'

Host cnam.cnam.fr   (192.33.159.6)
Last updated 02:06  8 Apr 1992
  Location: /pub/Archives/comp.archives/auto
```

```
    DIRECTORY rwxr-xr-x  512  Feb  5 21:20   sci.geo.meteorology

  Host earth.rs.itd.umich.edu   (141.211.164.153)
  Last updated 06:48 10 Apr 1992
   Location: /mac.bin/development/libraries/MacVogl :c4/fonts
     FILE      rw------- 3034  Oct 17 06:55   meteorology

  Host pit-manager.mit.edu  (18.172.1.27)
  Last updated 06:27 26 Mar 1992
   Location: /pub/usenet
     DIRECTORY rwxrwxr-x  512  Feb 19 01:56   sci.geo.meteorology
   ...
```

Well, you found what you were looking for at **cnam.cnam.fr** in France, and at **pit-manager.mit.edu** in Massachusetts. You also seem to have come across some fonts for a Macintosh which might be useful in meteorology at the University of Michigan (**earth.rs.itd.umich.edu**). They could be worth playing around with!

Archie Using a Client

The most convenient way to do **archie prog** lookups is with the **archie** command installed on your system. If you have this command available to you, you can do searches with:

```
% archie -modifiers string
```

string is the search string, as in all the other **prog** lookups we have discussed previously. The modifiers control the type of search. Some of the modifiers available to you are:

–c   Tells **archie** to return files whose names contain the search string. Uppercase and lowercase letters must match exactly.

–e   Tells **archie** to return files whose names match the search string exactly. This is the default.

–r   Tells **archie** the search string is a UNIX regular expression.

–s   Tells **archie** to return files whose names contain the search string; and the case of the letters is ignored.

–l   Tells **archie** to reformat the output so it is suitable for input into another program.

–h*name*   Tells the **archie** client to use the specified server for the request. With many clients, you can set an environment variable to default this to what ever server you like to use. On UNIX, the variable to set is **ARCHIE_HOST**.

–m*number* Tells **archie** to return no more than *number* files. If you don't specify this parameter, Archie returns at most 95 matches.

Any given request can only include one of the **–c**, **–r**, or **–s** modifiers. If **–e** is used with any of the other search switches, an exact match is tried before doing the more time-consuming search types.

Let's see if we can find the source for the **archie** command for a UNIX workstation, just in case you might want to install it yourself:

```
% archie -s -m5 archie
Host ab20.larc.nasa.gov
 Location: /usenet/comp.sources.amiga/volume89/util
  FILE -rw-rw-r--   5015  Mar 15 1989  archie.1.Z

Host nic.funet.fi
 Location: /pub/archive/comp.sources.amiga/volume89/util
  FILE -rw-rw-r--   4991  Aug  1 1989  archie18.1.Z

Host wolfen.cc.uow.edu.au
 Location: /ab20/usenet/comp.sources.amiga/volume89/util
  FILE -rw-rw-r--   5015  Aug 16 1991  archie.1.Z
  FILE -rw-rw-r--   4979  Aug 16 1991  archie18.1.Z

Host wuarchive.wustl.edu
 Location: /usenet/comp.sources.amiga/volume89/util
  FILE -rw-rw-r--   5054  Mar 16 1989  archie.1.Z
```

When we did this search we said, "Search for filenames which contain 'archie' (**–s**), ignoring case; return the first five files you find (**–m5**)." We found five **archie** clients but they all appear to be for amiga computers. If that's what we were looking for, fine. If not, we might have to issue the search again, making **–m** bigger. I'm sure you get the idea.

One of the problems with **archie** is that the output is humanly readable, not suitable for computer processing. The **–l** modifier changes the output to give you one match per line with this format:

```
timestamp size host filename
```

This makes the output quite suitable for further filtering with some other program. For example, when we looked for a UNIX Archie earlier, we failed to find it because we restricted the search. What we decided had to be done was to expand the search and humanly peruse the output for what we wanted. Using **–l** we can unrestrict the search and let a program do the perusal for us. We do this by sending the output from **archie** into a file (*temp* in the example). Next, we use a utility like **grep** asking it to select lines which contained "unix":

```
% archie -sl archie >temp
% grep unix temp          search for "unix" in file temp
199202160011400Z    512 dorm.rutgers.edu /pub/unix/archie/
199201221103600Z    512 nic.funet.fi /pub/unix/databases/archie/
```

The first thing in each line is a timestamp which tells the time the information was gathered—it can be ignored. If you look at the first line, you can see it is a directory (because the entry ends with a slash) 512 bytes long. It resides on a host

dorm.rutgers.edu in the directory */pub/unix/archie.* We appear to have found what we needed and we only had to look at two entries rather than the 95 that **archie** returned as matches to the search. We did have to deal with a slightly less readable output format, but that was a small price to pay.

One of the other uses of this filtering is to try and find sites that are close to you. Using the same set of commands but specifying a search string of "edu" displays only the servers which are at U.S. educational institutions. For U.S. sites this is just a subset of what is available, but if you were in some other country where country codes are used pervasively, you can very effectively limit the search to your own country.

The only drawback of the **archie** command is that it can't do the other searches (**site**, **list**, **whatis**, etc.). If you want to do those, you need to use **telnet** or e-mail.

## CHAPTER TEN

FINDING SOMEONE

Why Isn't There One?
What Is There?

I t seems only natural that if the phone company can provide a "white pages" telephone directory of its customers, then the network should be able to provide one, too. Well, in fact it does. The problem is that, just like the phone company, there are multiple phone books for various parts of the Internet. It is easy to find out Willie Martin's phone number if you know he lives in Chicago. If you don't know where he lives, it is nearly impossible. The same is true of the Internet. You can probably find someone, but the more you know, the easier it will be.

In a rare attempt not to be confusing, the technical name for this service is the *white pages*, named after the phone book. On the surface, it looks like building a global white pages service should be easy; after all, we have computers. But it's not as easy as it looks. There are a couple of reasons why there is no single service for the entire Internet. First, we'll talk about this; then, we'll discuss what services are available and how to use them. More information about these white pages servers is listed in the *Resource Catalog* under "white pages."

Why Isn't There One?

A single, unified Internet user's directory doesn't exist for three reasons:

- The ease with which users change location and work habits

- Lack of standards for directories

- Worries about security and privacy

These factors delayed the creation of such a directory. Progress is being made now that some of the fundamental problems have been solved, but it is still slow. Let's examine these issues more closely.

Mobile Users

Let's consider the first point by comparing an Internet directory to the telephone directory. You want a phone. You call the company, pay them some money, give them some information, get a phone, and they put you in the directory. If you move, you cancel your service, and the company takes you out of the directory. If you stop paying your bill, the company discontinues your service and takes you out of the directory. You are forced to play the phone company's game: each time you get a new phone, you have to give them information and pay their fees. Under these circumstances, creating and maintaining a directory is easy: the phone company always has all the information it needs.

On the Internet, there is no one group to deal with, no money changes hands, and no requirement for information to be collected. If my workstation is on the network and you want to be on. I can set up an account for you in five minutes. I'll set up an account for you and, Boom! you're an Internet user with all the capabilities of the other hundreds of thousands of users. Since there is no monthly charge for the account, there is no reason to turn your account off if you stop using it. It just sits there looking like your other accounts.

This illustrates how difficult it is to keep data accurate, but it's really only the tip of the iceberg. First, almost everyone on the network has multiple accounts. Sometimes they are on co-located computers: everyone in the office has accounts on each other's workstations. Sometimes, they are widely separated: I may have an account at the San Francisco office so I can work while I am there. In either case, having an account on an Internet-connected machine makes me an Internet user. It doesn't mean I will ever use that account again. If you send an urgent e-mail message to my account at the San Francisco office, I probably won't read it until next year, when I'm there for the annual sales meeting.

In order to maintain a good directory, someone needs to maintain it; in turn, the maintainer needs the cooperation, even if it's forced, of the user. On the Internet, the first part is easy. The second is almost impossible. Many campuses and corporations maintain internal staff directories. Some of these include electronic access information and some are online. That doesn't mean the information is up-to-date. Most of the information is gathered when a person is hired and deleted when he retires or quits. Updating the information is optional and frequently not done.

Standards

One problem with computing is that if everyone does his own thing, no one else can use it easily. After some initial confusion, a standard technique for doing something emerges and is agreed to. Anyone who knows the standard can then use the service regardless of where it is located.

A long time ago (by computing standards anyway) the International Standards Organization started trying to develop a standard for directory services called *X.500*. There were some non-standard servers already, built for special groups. As the X.500 standard took longer and longer to complete, more special directory services with their own facilities got built out of need. Now X.500 is a reality, but a lot of the other services are still there working just fine. Almost every campus or corporation has its own local service. The people who use them are reluctant to change for the sake of changing. If it ain't broke, why fix it?

Security and Privacy

Remember when we discussed security and said that a common way to break into a system was to find a valid username and try common passwords? Since an e-mail address usually contains the recipient's login name, some people think making this information public is a breach of security. It makes it slightly easier for a cracker to break in. Therefore, as a matter of policy, some systems refuse to provide any information about users.

On the personal privacy side of the coin, some people believe that they should control whether or not this information is publicly accessible. In fact, some countries have very strict personal privacy laws that forbid any personal information to be released without express permission. This is not a problem for voluntary delivery systems (e.g., **whois**, which is discussed later in this chapter), where you ask to be included. But it arises with non-voluntary systems: for example, automatic inclusion in a directory. Most corporations and campuses have e-mail information gathered, but administrative procedures may not be in place to protect the users' privacy. Rather than deal with the administrative problem directly, these organizations solve it by refusing to give out any information.

What Is There?

Now let's look at what directories are available and how to use them. The facilities are not presented in any order of preference; rather, each one has its own place. You have to decide which one will most likely find the person based on what information you already know. Again remember, even the best online directory is out of date and gives only approximate information. If you really want to know for sure, personally gathered information (e.g., via a phone call, recent business card, etc.) is best.

Finding a User on a Specific System

finger is a fairly old and common UNIX facility that examines the user log in file (*/etc/passwd*) on a system. It lets you find out someone's login name (hence the e-mail address), given that you know what computer your correspondent uses and his or her personal name. In addition to giving you a valid login ID, it will tell you whether or not the user you're asking about is currently logged in to the target machine. Although this is primarily a UNIX facility, there are non-UNIX clients that allow you to make finger-style queries from other types of computers as well.

The general format of the **finger** command is:

```
% finger name@host
```

The "name" is optional and specifies the name to be searched for on the host. It returns information on all login id's that contain *name* in either the login name or username fields (usually displayed "In real life" in the output). You must give either a complete first name or a complete last name (or a complete login name); you can't give part of a name, and you have to "spell" the name correctly; you can't say "mike" if the user's real name is "Michael." If you give a login name, it has to be capitalized correctly. But if you type a "given name," **finger** ignores capitalization. (Confusing? Once you get used to it, it isn't bad.)

Host is the name of the computer where you want the inquiry to be made. Only include the **@host** if you are naming a remote host. If you are asking about someone on your local system, you can omit **@host** entirely; that is, if you don't specify a host, **finger** searches the computer on which you gave the command.

If you omit the name, **finger** lists the users who are currently logged into the *host*. (You must still include the **@** sign in the request to signify that you want the current users of a remote machine.) If you omit both the name and the host, **finger** lists everyone who is logged in to the local system.

For example, to find the e-mail address of Ed Krol you might try:

```
% finger krol@ux1.cso.uiuc.edu
[ux1.cso.uiuc.edu]

Login name: ajzxmvk          In real life: Marge Krol
Directory: /mnt/other/ajzxmvk    Shell: /bin/csh
Last login Mon Dec  3, 1990 on ttyq5 from dc-mac49
No Plan.

Login name: krol             In real life: Ed Krol
Directory: /cso/staff/krol       Shell: /bin/csh
Last login Sun Mar  8 20:01 on ttyr3 from beretta
No Plan.
```

This query found two Krols on the machine **ux1.cso.uiuc.edu**: the first is Marge Krol with the login name *ajzxmvk*; the second, Ed Krol with the login of *krol*. There is other information of interest here. If you were looking for a place to send e-mail you might glean that sending mail to **ajzxmvk@ux1.cso.uiuc.edu** is futile. The last time that login was used was in 1990. It is not a regularly used account. Ed Krol, on the other hand, has used his account last Sunday March 8 at 20:01. Using this one for e-mail probably would be successful.

On the surface, both of these logins appear to be owned by shiftless people with no plans. "No Plan" actually refers to the file *.plan*. If the files *.plan* exists in the user's home directory, **finger** displays its contents. The file *.project* is treated similarly; if it exists, its contents are displayed at the end of *finger*'s report.* Let's look at what would happen if I created those two files and did another **finger**:

---

*For this to work, the files must have world read permission and your home directory must have world read and execute permissions.

```
% finger krol@uxh.cso.uiuc.edu
[uxh.cso.uiuc.edu]

Login name: krol               In real life: Ed Krol
Office: 3337886
Directory: /cso/staff/krol       Shell: /bin/csh
On since Mar  9 19:23:37 on ttyp3 from mossberg.cso.uiu
Project: Write this damn book.
Plan:
Keep plugging away working early mornings and
weekends until it is done.
```

Notice that the contents of the *.plan* and *.project* files were displayed.

finger is often used to get a list of the people who are currently using a system. To do this, just omit the login name from your command. The following command uses **finger** to find out who's logged in to the system **uxc.cso.uiuc.edu**:

```
% finger @uxc.cso.uiuc.edu
[uxc.cso.uiuc.edu]

Login Name          Tty Idle Login       Office Phone
dxd   Deb Nongrata p0      Mar 9 19:33 1705 UCB 334-8475
opr   Operator      co 3:12 Mar 6 15:01
philh Phil Howland p2   55 Mar 9 17:52 114 DCL  245-6246
rrm   Ross Maddux  p3 5:26 Mar 9 12:15 169 DCL  245-4274
```

Notice that the output looked quite different and gave information about the current login as well as some personal information.

Finger as a General Information Server

finger's ability to dump a "plan" file provides a simple and effective way to distribute small amounts of information. It's often used for this purpose, playing a role as a very simple database server. For example, in the account for **quake@ geophys.washington.edu** someone maintains a listing of recent earthquake information in the *.plan* file. So, if you use **finger** to inquire about that login, you get something like this:

```
% finger quake@geophys.washington.edu
[geophys.washington.edu]

Login name: quake           In real life: Earthquake Info
Directory: /u0/quake         Shell: /u0/quake/run_quake
Last login Thu Mar  5 03:34 on ttyp0 from teal.csn.org
Mail last read Sun Jul 14 08:48:33 1991
Plan:
Information about Recent earthquakes are reported here
for public use.  DATE-TIME is in Universal Standard
Time which is PST + 8 hours, LAT and LON are in decimal
degrees, DEP is depth in kilometers, N-STA is number
of stations recording event, QUAL is location quality
A-good, D-poor, Z-from automatic system and may be in
error.
```

```
Recent events reported by the USGS National Earthquake
Information Center
DATE-TIME (UT) LAT   LON    DEP MAG   LOCATION AREA
92/03/04 03:49  2.6S 147.5E  33 6.5  ADMIRALTY ISLANDS
92/03/05 14:39 53.0N 159.8E  40 5.9  COAST OF KAMCHATKA
92/03/07 01:53 10.2N  84.4W  80 6.0  COSTA RICA
92/03/07 18:37  2.4S 146.7E  33 6.1  ADMIRALTY ISLANDS
92/03/08 03:43 40.2N 124.2W  10 5.2  COAST OF CALIF.
<the list continues - remainder deleted for space>
```

If you look through the *Resource Catalog*, you'll find several organizations that provide similar information through **finger**.

When Finger Fails

Finally, **finger** requires that a server be running on the target computer (on UNIX, it is named **fingerd**) to service the request. If you try to use **finger** on an uncooperative host, you will get a message:

```
% finger krol@sonne.cso.uiuc.edu
[sonne.cso.uiuc.edu]
connect: Connection refused
```

In this case there is nothing you can do. **finger** is simply unavailable on the remote computer. You might complain to the administrator—but, likely as not, the administrator has decided that running **finger** is a security risk (a point that's been hotly debated on the Net). You must try other means to find the information you require.

Whois

whois is the name of both a white pages directory and an application to access it. Whois is a directory that grew up in the Arpanet community. The directory is maintained by the DDN Network Information Center (NIC) and contains about 70,000 entries. The people listed in it are those responsible for the working of the Internet and those people doing network research. There are three ways of accessing this directory: the **whois** command, **telnet**, or e-mail.

The **whois** command is the easiest way to access the DDN's directory. In addition, since the Whois directory was one of the first white pages servers around, it became the model for other directories. These other directories can also be accessed with this same command. To use the **whois** command to look someone up, just type in the command followed by the last name of the person you are looking for:

```
% whois krol
Krol, Ed (EK10)          Krol@UXC.CSO.UIUC.EDU
   University of Illinois
   Computing and Communications Service Office
   195 DCL
   1304 West Springfield Avenue
   Urbana, IL  61801-4399
   (217) 333-7886

   Record last updated on 27-Nov-91.
```

Individual names are stored as:

```
last name, first name, titles
```

Matches always begin at the beginning of this text, so it is easiest to look up people by last name. If you are hazy about spelling you can search on a portion of the last name by ending the search string with a period. For example, the search string "*kro.*" matches all names beginning with the three characters "*kro*":

```
% whois kro.
Krokeide, Per-Arne (PK117)                              +47-2-800200
Krokoski, Chester (CK124)  OOSCT1G@GW3.ARMY.MIL         (817) 287-3270
Krol, Ed (EK10)            Krol@UXC.CSO.UIUC.EDU        (217) 333-7886
Krolikoski, Stan (SK139)   KROLIKOS@WPAFB.AF.MIL        (507) 253-7200
Kroll, Carol (CK43)        carol@CS.UTEXAS.EDU          (512) 835-6732
<only a portion of the matches>
```

If you match more than one item, **whois** gives you a shortened output format. The funny string in parentheses, like (EK10) for 'Krol, Ed', is a unique identifier known as a *handle*. If you have someone's handle, you can get his or her complete record with another **whois** command:

```
% whois \!ek10
```

Note: when you're using the UNIX C shell, you have to put a backslash (\) prior to the exclamation point to ensure the string is not processed as a history reference. You can omit the backslash if you're using some other UNIX shell (like the Korn shell), or if you're not using UNIX.

When the Arpanet was retired, the address of the NIC server was changed. Unfortunately, some old implementations still point to the old Arpanet address. If yours does, when you try to use it you will get a message:

```
% whois krol
Hi!  You have attempted to contact a whois server at
SRI-NIC.ARPA.  Your WHOIS client program is either
extremely old or your software vendor is really out
of it.  Please complain to them.  To contact the current
DDN NIC WHOIS server, it will be necessary to either:

a) Use a command-line option to tell your WHOIS client
   to connect to a different host (NIC.DDN.MIL),

b) Or, recompile WHOIS with the CORRECT name for the DDN
   NIC, NIC.DDN.MIL, in place of the ancient SRI-NIC.ARPA.

For further information about the DDN NIC, please contact
the new contractor, GSI, at 1-800-365-3642.  Thank You.
```

If this is the case, you can use **telnet** or e-mail to make your query. Or you can try to tell **whois** to go to the proper place:

```
% whois -h nic.ddn.mil name
```

Be forewarned: some **whois** clients allow this and some don't. This is really too bad because there are many whois-style services around—not just the NIC's. For a long time, **whois** was the only game in town, so many sites set up their own directory services with **whois** access. To access these special servers, issue the **whois** command with a special hostname, as in the previous example.*

You can also access the whois database at the NIC through **telnet**. Start by **telnet**-ing to the **nic.ddn.mil** address.† When you get there, you enter **whois** automatically, and can start making queries. For example:

```
% telnet nic.ddn.mil
Trying 192.112.36.5...
Connected to nic.ddn.mil.
Escape character is '^]'.

SunOS UNIX (nic.ddn.mil) (ttyrf)
* -- DDN Network Information Center  --
*
* For TAC news, type:                TACNEWS <return>
* For user and host information, type: WHOIS <return>
* For NIC information, type:          NIC <return>
*
* For user assistance call (800) 365-3642 or (800) 365-DNIC
*  or (703) 802-4535
* Please report system problems to ACTION@NIC.DDN.MIL

NIC, SunOS Release 4.1.1 (NIC) #1:
Cmdinter Ver 1.2 Wed Mar 11 15:50:15 1992 EST
@ whois
Connecting to id Database . . . . . .
Connected to id Database
NIC WHOIS Version: 2.5 Wed, 11 Mar 92 15:50:24

   Enter a handle, name, mailbox, or other field,
   optionally preceded by a keyword, like "host diis".
   Type "?" for short, 2-page details, "HELP" for full
   documentation, or hit RETURN to exit.
---> Do ^E to show search progress, ^G to abort a search<---
Whois: krol
Krol, Ed (EK10)          Krol@UXC.CSO.UIUC.EDU
   University of Illinois
   Computing and Communications Service Office
   195 DCL
   1304 West Springfield Avenue
   Urbana, IL  61801-4399
```

---

*There are lists of **whois** servers available. See the *Resource Catalog* under "white pages."

†Other **whois** servers may not allow this.

```
      (217) 333-7886

      Record last updated on 27-Nov-91.
   Whois: ^D
   @^D
   Connection closed by foreign host.
```

When you are done, you need to send two CTRL-D characters: one to end the **whois** session, and one to close the session.

As you can see, the **telnet** dialog implies that the **whois** database contains more than just people. Although it is a bit off the subject, this is worth mentioning for two reasons. First, if you make broad searches, you will probably see some odd stuff returned. Second, you may occasionally want to make some other inquiries. After the information about users, the most useful data in the **whois** database is information about network and domain ownership. Let's try to find some information about the networks at the University of Illinois. This time, let's do it by e-mail. First, construct and send a message like the following, using your favorite e-mail program:

```
% mail service@nic.ddn.mil
Subject:
whois University of Illinois
.
```

Some time later, you will get a response containing an answer to the request. Again, you can read it however you like, but it will probably look something like this:

```
% mail
"/usr/spool/mail/krol": 3 messages
>1 LISTSERV@bitnic.bitnet Fri Nov  8 16:02  128/6172 "LISTSERV FILELIST"
 2 LISTSERV@bitnic.bitnet Fri Nov  8 16:08  164/9834 "BITNODE FILELIST"
 3 service@nic.ddn.mil Thu Mar 12 03:46   36/1912 "re: whois university"
& 3
>From service@nic.ddn.mil Thu Mar 12 03:46:19 1992
Date: Thu, 12 Mar 92 04:43:46 EST
From: service@nic.ddn.mil (NIC Mail Server)
To: krol@uxh.cso.uiuc.edu
Subject: re: whois university of illinois

University of Illinois (GARCON) GARCON.CSO.UIUC.EDU       128.174.5.58
University of Illinois (UIUC)    A.CS.UIUC.EDU           128.174.252.1
University of Illinois (UIUC-UXC) UXC.CSO.UIUC.EDU        128.174.5.50
University of Illinois (NET-UIUC-CAMPUS-B) UIUC-CAMPUS-B  128.174.0.0
University of Illinois (NET-UIUC-NCSA) UIUC-NCSA             130.126.0.0
University of Illinois (NET-UIUC-NET) UIUC-NET               192.5.69.0
University of Illinois at Urbana-Champaign (UIUC-DOM)        UIUC.EDU

<output truncated for space considerations>
```

Although the example shows a query about the University of Illinois, you can certainly inquire about people in this same manner.

The USENET User List

This service is provided by MIT and contains names and e-mail addresses of USENET posters. It looks at all of the USENET news group postings that pass into MIT. This includes almost all of the normal and alternative news groups described in Chapter 8, *Network News.* When the server at MIT receives a posting, it tries to figure out the poster's name and e-mail address. If it can, it puts them in a file. Therefore, you can use this service to find the addresses of people who post to the USENET's worldwide news groups. You can search for a string which would appear in the username field of the **From:** line of a news posting. For example, if a news reader displays the poster's name as "Ed Krol," the message will probably contain a line like this inside it:

```
From: krol@ux1.cso.uiuc.edu (Ed Krol)
```

In turn, you can infer that the e-mail address **krol@ux1.cso.uiuc.edu** will probably work if you want to contact Ed Krol.

To use this service, send an e-mail message to **mail-server@pit-manager.mit.edu**. The body of the message should look like:

```
send usenet-addresses/search-string
```

Search-string is the name that you are interested in finding. The *search-string* can only be one word without spaces. Matches will not occur on a partial word. So you can't use "kro" to find "krol." For example, to look up "Ed Krol" using this technique, you could send a message like the following:

```
% mail mail-server@pit-manager.mit.edu
Subject:
send usenet-addresses/krol
.
```

Some time later, you would get a message back from the server. It will look something like this:

```
% mail
"/usr/spool/mail/krol": 2 messages 1 unread
  1 LISTSERV@bitnic.bitnet Fri Nov 8 16:02 12/617 File:LISTSERV
>N2 daemon@pit-manager.MIT.EDU Tue Mar 17 14:09 18/710 Reply from mserv
& 2
From daemon@pit-manager.MIT.EDU Tue Mar 17 14:09:00 1992
Date: Tue, 17 Mar 92 15:08:56 -0500
From: Mr Background <daemon@pit-manager.MIT.EDU>
Subject: Reply from mserv re: send usenet-addresses/krol
Reply-To: mail-server@pit-manager.mit.edu
X-Problems-To: postmaster@pit-manager.mit.edu
Precedence: bulk
To: krol@uxh.cso.uiuc.edu

krol@ux1.cso.uiuc.edu (Ed Krol) (Mar 1 92)
```

If your search request fails to locate anyone, the response will look like this:

```
From daemon@pit-manager.MIT.EDU Tue Mar 17 14:13:05 1992
Date: Tue, 17 Mar 92 15:13:00 -0500
From: Mr Background <daemon@pit-manager.MIT.EDU>
Message-Id: <9203172013.AA16508@pit-manager.MIT.EDU>
Subject: Reply from mserv re: send usenet-addresses/ekrol
Reply-To: mail-server@pit-manager.mit.edu
X-Problems-To: postmaster@pit-manager.mit.edu
Precedence: bulk
To: krol@uxh.cso.uiuc.edu
Status: RO


No matches for "ekrol".
```

Remember, this service is dependent on information in the **From:** field of news postings. Depending on how the article was posted, the name might be under the posters control. So, if Ed Krol has his news reader configured to post with an alias like "Mr. Hockey" you won't find "Ed Krol" in this directory. Of course, if you know that Ed's alias is "Hockey," you could look this up, instead.

It should go without saying that you can use any program you like to send or read the mail messages.

The Future: X.500 Directory Services

None of the services we have mentioned so far "scale well." That is, **whois**-style directories work just fine for 70,000 entries, but would fail horribly if asked to list millions of users. As is often the case, the Internet is the victim of its own success; when **whois** was planned, no one thought that the database would ever have 70,000 entries, to say nothing of the millions of Internet users who aren't listed.

At the beginning of this chapter, we mentioned the X.500 directory service, adopted by the Organization for International Standardization (OSI). Unlike **whois**, X.500 does scale well. Unfortunately, although it solves this problem, the standard offering is very cumbersome to use directly. Therefore, it will probably never see widespread use by the general population. To deal with these problems, NYSERnet and PSI developed a "friendlier" interface, called **fred**. **fred** makes X.500 usage a bit more intuitive and obvious. You do need to know something about the philosophy of X.500 to use **fred**. So, first we will sketch out what X.500 is like; then we will talk in detail about using **fred** in the PSI X.500 pilot project.

Native X.500

Let's go back to our first analogy: the phone company. If you were looking up Willie Martin in Chicago, you could start at one end of the shelf and look at each phone book sequentially, but it would take all day. Instead, you could find the U.S. section, within that find the Illinois section, then find the Chicago directory and finally look up Willie. This is know as a tree structure. Figure 10-1 shows how to model a collection of phone books as a "tree."

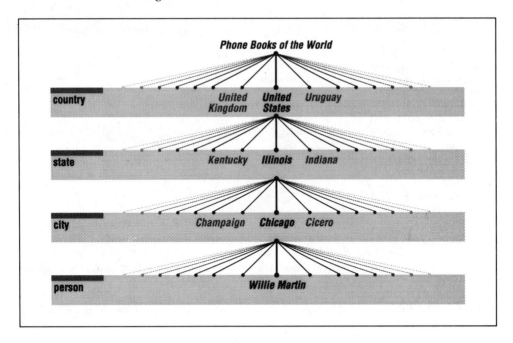

Figure 10-1: Phone book structure

If you want to find a person, you start at the top and pick the most likely path. When you finally get to a node at the bottom which has directory information, you can look up Willie. The path from the top of the tree to the bottom should identify a particular Willie:

```
World,US,IL,Chicago,Willie Martin
```

This points to your Willie, not the one in Grovers Mills.

X.500 views "the white pages problem" as a library of telephone books. Each participating group has responsibility for its own directory, just like Illinois Bell is responsible for the Chicago phone book. Figure 10-2 shows the tree structure for the X.500 directory service. The structure is very similar to our "phone book" model, though the labels for each level are different. The levels shown are fairly static. At the organization level, each organization has responsibility for its own lower structure. This is analogous to the set of phone books for Illinois. Any changes to the books, or to their structure, are made by Illinois Bell. Any changes in an organization get made by the organization's administration.

Therefore, with the X.500 service, once you know the right organization you can probably find the name you want without trouble. If you like, you can poke around and find out about the organization's internal structure, but you don't need to. Limiting your search to the organization will suffice for doing queries.

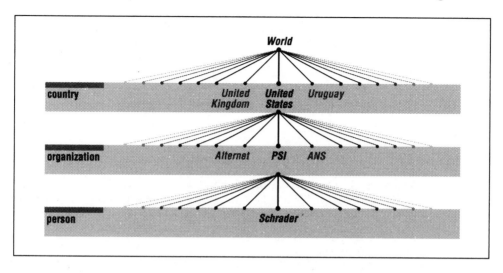

Figure 10-2: X.500 tree structure

How does this work? If I were searching for my buddy Bill Schrader, who works for Performance Systems International, I would type something like:

```
c=US@o=PerformanceSystemsInternational@cn=Schrader
```

As you can see, direct X.500 has a fairly complex syntax. You might not have considered **whois** terribly "friendly," but X.500 is worse! (To be fair, X.500 was designed to be used by computers, rather than people. And, as we know, computers aren't terribly bothered by complexity.)

Fred Via Telnet

fred provides an intuitive way to do simple lookups with X.500. In its easiest form, you can just type in the name of someone you want to look up. However, to make the search efficient, **fred** makes some assumptions about where to look—otherwise, it would have to work through the entire X.500 database, which is a little like looking through all the phone books in the world. **fred** searches for names within a particular *area*. By default, its area is the organization that is running **fred**. This is probably not what you want, so you need to go through a two-step process:

1. Find a likely organization to look in.

2. Look up the person within that organization.

How does this work in practice? **telnet** servers for **fred** are available at either of the two following machines:

```
wp.psi.com
wp2.psi.com
```

When you **telnet** to one of these machines, log in with the name **fred**. No password is required. It looks like this:

```
% telnet wp.psi.com
Trying 192.33.4.21...
Connected to wp1.psi.net.
Escape character is '^]'.

SunOS UNIX (wp1.psi.net)

login: fred
Last login: Thu Mar 19 15:54:25 from 149.23.1.2
SunOS 4.0.3c (WP_PSI_BOOTBOX) : Tue Dec 17 12:20:46 EST 1991

Welcome to the PSI White Pages Pilot Project

Try   "help" for a list of commands
      "whois" for information on how to find people
      "manual" for detailed documentation
      "report" to send a report to the white pages manager

To find out about participating organizations, try
     "whois -org *"

   accessing service, please wait...

fred>
```

Once you gave the login name "fred," you were logged in without a password, and the **fred** software was available to you.

Let's say you want to look up your old friend Bill Schrader again. You remember he changed jobs, and now works for the firm "Performance something or other." How do you find him? First you need to find the organization's exact name. Let's look at all the organizations that start with the letter "p". This can be done with the command:

```
fred> whois p* organization -org *
```

This command says: "find all the entries starting with "p" (**p***) of type *organization*." In doing the search, the system will consider any organization on record (**–org ***). Note the use of the * as a wildcard to match any string of zero or more characters. The results of this search would be:

```
3 matches found.
1. Performance Systems International    +1-703-620-6651
2. Portland State University           +1 503-725-3000
3. Princeton University                +1 609-258-3000
```

Number one looks like a good candidate for Bill's employer. Let's display it to be sure:

```
fred> whois "performance systems international" -org *
Performance Systems International (1)
1-703-620-6651 (Corporate Offices)
     aka: PSI

PSI Inc.
  Reston International Center
  11800 Sunrise Valley Drive
  Suite 1100
  Reston, VA 22091
  US

Telephone: 1-703-620-6651 (Corporate Offices)

          +1 800-836-0400 (Operations)
          +1 800-82PSI82 (Sales)
          +1 518-283-8860 (Troy Office)
          +1 408-562-6222 (Santa Clara Office)
FAX:      +1 703-620-4586

value-added provider of networking services

Locality:   Troy, New York
            Santa Clara, California
            Reston, Virginia

Name:     Performance Systems International, US (1)
Modified: Mon Sep 23 15:00:31 1991
     by: Manager, Performance Systems International,
         US (4)

<some of the entry deleted for space considerations>
```

Note the line "aka: PSI." This tells you that you can save typing by using the three letter abbreviation instead of the full name.

Finally, let's try to look up Bill:

```
fred> whois schrader -org psi
```

In this example, you specified that the search should be limited to Performance Systems International (**-org psi**). Here is the successful result:

```
Trying @c=US@o=Performance Systems International ...
William Schrader (8)                    wls@psi.com

President

Chief Executive Officer
PSI Inc.
  Reston International Center
  11800 Sunrise Valley Drive
```

```
     Suite 1100
     Reston, VA 22091
     USA

   Telephone: +1 703-620-6651 x310
   FAX:       +1 703-620-4586

   Locality:   Reston, Virginia

   Picture:    (No display process defined)

   Name:     William Schrader, Reston,
               Administration,
               Performance Systems International,
               US (8)
   Modified: Thu Feb  7 07:49:48 1991
         by: Manager, Performance Systems International,
               US (4)
   fred> quit
```

Since you found what you were after and were finished using **fred**, the last line of the above example was the command **quit**. This ends the **fred** session and logs you out, returning you to the system you started from.

We just demonstrated the obvious way of performing a lookup. However, it is a bit roundabout. You could actually have made the lookup with one command. If you specify more than one organization, **fred** will ask you which ones you really want to use. So, you could have given a command like this:

```
   fred> whois schrader -org p*
```

This command tells **fred**: "Look up 'schrader' in every organization that begins with a "p." It then displays the organizations that meet the criteria and asks you if they should be searched:

```
   try c=US@o=Performance Systems International [y/n] ? y
   William Schrader (2)                           wls@psi.com

   President

   <all the same stuff from before deleted>

   Modified: Thu Feb  7 07:49:48 1991
         by: Manager, Performance Systems International,
               US (3)

   try c=US@o=Portland State University [y/n] ? n
   try c=US@o=Princeton University [y/n] ? n
```

One interesting feature of the **fred** system is that it can match names phonetically. This can only be used when the search string contains no wildcards (i.e., *****). Normally this feature is "off," but you can turn it on with the command:

```
fred> set soundex on
soundex     = on                              use soundex for matching
```

So, if you don't know how to spell a name but can make a good guess, you can still look someone up. Let's look up Bill again, but using an even more compact syntax with "sounds like" matching turned on:

```
fred> whois schraeder, psi
William Schrader (2)                          wls@psi.com
        aka: William L. Schrader
<again the same old stuff>
```

Notice that the name was spelled incorrectly, but almost right, and the match succeeded.

Wildcards are a bit different in **fred** than you would likely assume. They are not UNIX "regular expressions," or even the customary "shell wildcards." There is a single wildcard character, *, which matches zero or more characters. It can only be used at the beginning or the end of a search string. Therefore, the following strings both could match "Schrader":

```
*rader
schr*
```

Finally, remember that this is part of an X.500 pilot project. Some sites participate in the project, but their X.500 servers may not be running all the time or be stable. Since **fred** may need to contact the X.500 servers at various organizations, you might get a message like:

```
fred> whois braun -org merit
Trying @c=US@o=Merit Computer Network ...
*** Service error : Unavailable ***
```

This means that the server that's responsible for the organization "merit" was unavailable; you had better try other means to find your name. (If merit's server is only temporarily out of commission, you might try the same query a few hours later.)

Fred Via E-mail

In a pinch, you can access **fred** via e-mail. To do so, send mail to **whitepages@wp.psi.com**; the message's subject line should be your request:

```
% mail whitepages@wp.psi.com
Subject: whois schrader, psi
.
Cc:
Null message body; hope that's ok
```

Sometime later, you will receive a response through the mail. Of course, this is not quite as convenient as interactive access, but it can be used from computers that can't access the Internet interactively (e.g., Bitnet computers).

Fred as an Application

fred is actually a network application, just like TELNET, FTP, etc. As such, it can be run on any computer on the Internet and can reach out across the network to query other X.500 servers. In reality, there aren't many computers running **fred** that aren't already part of the X.500 project. The reason for this is that the service is not yet static enough to interest a lot of people—it is just too new.

If you do find yourself on a computer that has *fred* installed, the usage will be the same with one slight exception: the default area for the search will be different. It will probably be an organization defined by whoever installed the software.

Knowbot Information Service

The Knowbot Information Service (KIS) is an experimental white pages meta-server. That is, it does not itself hold any white pages data. It knows about other servers, and allows you to query them all through one set of commands. You say "find krol" and it contacts **whois** servers, X.500 servers, **finger** servers, and so on. You don't have to think about what tool to use; Knowbot does that for you.

On the surface, this sounds so nice that you're probably wondering why I bothered talking about the other servers. For two reasons: First, Knowbots are actually an area of research that far exceeds just white pages services. (It is talked about more generally in Chapter 14, *Other Applications*). KIS is one of the first Knowbot applications. Since the area is so new, any part of it may change or become unavailable for a time. I didn't want you to be caught high and dry should this occur.

The second is that the Knowbots "ease of use" philosophy currently is somewhat constrained by practicality. KIS could easily be made to access every host on the Internet when looking for a person, The search would take days. Therefore, it can use these services, but only if they are targeted at certain subsets. It can use **finger**, but only if you tell it what host to inquire on. It can use X.500, but only if you tell it an organization. In short, you have to know enough about these services to use them through KIS, but why bother? It is far easier to inquire with **finger** directly than to access KIS and have it do it for you.

Nevertheless, Knowbots is useful because it knows how to access some unusual directories. One service it can access is the MCImail directory, which contains information about users of MCI mailboxes. The other unusual directory it knows about is the RIPE directory. RIPE is a society to promote IP networking in Europe. The directory contains the names and addresses of IP networking people in Europe. Let's see how it works.

KIS can be used with **telnet**. You **telnet** to port 185 of either of these addresses:

```
nri.reston.va.us
sol.bucknell.edu
```

On UNIX, this would usually be done with the command:

```
% telnet sol.bucknell.edu 185
```

The easiest way to use it is to type the name you want to find at the prompt. For example, let's look up "krol" again, but using KIS:

```
% telnet sol.bucknell.edu 185
Trying 134.82.1.8...
Connected to sol.cs.bucknell.edu.
Escape character is '^]'.
Knowbot Information Service (V1.0). Copyright CNRI 1990. All Rights Reserved.
Try ? or man for help.
> krol
Name:         Ed Krol
Organization: University of Illinois
Address:      Computing and Communications Service Office,
              195 DCL, 1304 West Springfield Avenue
City:         Urbana
State:        IL
Country:      US
Zip:          61801-4399
Phone:        (217) 333-7886
E-Mail:       Krol@UXC.CSO.UIUC.EDU
Source:       whois@nic.ddn.mil
Ident:        EK10
Last Updated: 27-Nov-91.
> quit
```

Notice that the *Source* field of this entry shows that the data came from the **whois** database at **nic.ddn.mil**. However, the output format is very different from a **whois** command. KIS takes your Knowbot requests and reformats them to make queries of the actual servers. It then takes their output and formats it uniformly. This again makes it nice for you since the data is always presented in a standard manner.

You can make as many requests as you like in this fashion. When you are done you can exit by issuing the **quit** command.

If your request was not serviced at the NIC, the Knowbot would have gone ahead and tried a number of other places. Unless you tell it otherwise, it will try, by default, the following directories:

1. DDN NIC whois
2. MCImail
3. RIPE

CHAPTER ELEVEN

TUNNELING THROUGH THE INTERNET: GOPHER

The Internet Gopher
Finding Internet Resources
Gopher Development

In the past few chapters, we talked about tools that allow you to do particular tasks: find people, software, or data. The next three chapters introduce you to some tools on the horizon that can do a lot more. They try to be "friendly" and help you to search a variety of online resources. To understand what each of these tools does, think of your local public library. It's convenient, and has a fairly good collection on its shelves. It also belongs (most likely) to a system of cooperating libraries. The library in the next town belongs to the same system and has a lot of the same material as yours. But it also has some different materials. If your library doesn't have something, the neighboring library will honor your library privileges. You don't even need to visit the other library in person. You talk to your local librarian, arrange an inter-library loan, and the materials you need are shipped from the next town to you.

This chapter discusses **gopher**, a lookup tool that lets you prowl through the Internet by selecting resources from menus. If you want to use one of the resources that Gopher presents, it helps you access it. This is like helping you browse the remote library's card catalog and automatically sending the material you want. It doesn't really matter where the library is located, as long as it is part of the Gopher system.

In the next chapter, we'll look at Wide Area Information Servers (*WAIS*). This service helps you search indexed material. You can search for particular words or phrases; it gives you a list of online files that contain those words. WAIS is like walking into a library with a quote ("these are the times that try men's souls"), and having the library automatically check out everything that contains it.

In Chapter 13, *Hypertext Spanning the Internet: WWW*, we'll discuss the newest arrival from the Internet's toolshop: the World-Wide Web. On the surface, the Web looks like a variation on Gopher: it's another menu-based service that helps you access different resources. However, the Web is based on a much more flexible "hypertext" model that allows cross-references, or links, between related resources. And, unlike the Gopher, the Web is a "read/write" resource (at least potentially). It really offers a different paradigm for working: if you have a Web server and a hypertext editor, it will support all kinds of collaboration and joint authorship. Admittedly, Web servers and hypertext editors are scarce; but the potential here makes the World-Wide Web one of the most interesting new tools on the Internet.

The Internet Gopher

Gopher, or more accurately, "the Internet Gopher," allows you to browse for resources using menus. When you find something you like, you can read or access it through the Gopher without having to worry about domain names, IP addresses, changing programs, etc. For example, if you want to access the online library catalog at the University of California, rather than looking up the address and **telnet**ting to it, you find an entry in a menu and select it. The Gopher then "goes fer" it.

The big advantage of Gopher isn't so much that you don't have to look up the address or name of the resources, or that you don't have to use several commands to get what you want. The real cleverness is that it lets you browse through the Internet's resources, regardless of their type, like you might browse through your local library with books, filmstrips, and phonograph records on the same subject grouped together. Let's say you're interested in information about the American West: history, climatological data, minerology, and so on. You can use Gopher to wander around the Internet, looking for data. By looking through a menu of "online catalogs" or "libraries," (the exact menu item will vary, depending on your server), you see that the University of California is available, and you know that its collection of Western Americana is very strong; so you access the catalog and try to look up any books that are relevant. (You may even be able to use Gopher to arrange inter-library loans if the library permits it through their online catalog.) A search of FTP archives finds you some data about the relationship between drought cycles and snow pack, which is interesting; looking further, you could probably find some meteorological statistics from the time of the Gold Rush.* Yes, you still need to know what you're looking for, and a little bit about where the resource might be located; but Gopher makes the search less painful.

To think about how to use Gopher, it's best to return to our well-worn library image. Think of the pre-Gopher Internet as a set of public libraries without card catalogs and librarians. To find something, you have to wander aimlessly until you stumble on something interesting. This kind of library isn't very useful, unless you already know in great detail what you want to find, and where you're likely to find it. A Gopher server is like hiring a librarian, who creates a card catalog subject index. You can find something by thumbing through the subject list, then showing

---

*I don't know if such a database exists—but you could certainly use Gopher to check. A little experience will teach you a lot more than this book.

the card to the librarian and asking "Could you help me get this, please?" If you don't find it in one library, you can electronically walk to the next and check there.

Unfortunately, Gopher services did not hire highly trained librarians. There's no standard subject list, like the Library of Congress Subject Headings, used on Gophers to organize things. The people who maintain each server took their best shot at organizing the world, or at least their piece of it. It's the same state we would be in if one library had things filed under a subject called "Folklore, American" and another had the same works under "Funny Old Stories." Each server is a bit different—you have to approach each one with an open mind.

Gopher does not allow you to access anything that couldn't be made available by other means. There are no specially formatted "Gopher resources" out there for you to access, in the sense that there are FTP archives or white pages directories.* But, once you find something you want to "check out", Gopher will also help you with that. Gopher knows which application (**telnet**, **ftp**, white pages, etc.) to use to get a particular thing you are interested in and does it for you. Each type of resource is handled a bit differently. However, they are all handled in an intuitive manner consistent with the feel of the Gopher client you are using.

If you've followed the discussion so far, you should realize that it doesn't really matter what Gopher server you contact first. Your home server only determines the first menu you see. The other menus all come from whichever server is appropriate at that point. Each server, like every library, has a unique collection which it can provide.† Popular files, like collections of frequently asked questions, may be in several places. Obscure collections of data might only have a single server. If you don't find what you want at your initial library, you can search elsewhere. When you find what you like, get it by inter-library loan. With libraries this can take a while; with Gopher, getting material from somewhere else is instantaneous.

Finally, the system is smart enough to enforce licensing restrictions. Some software or resources (e.g., online newspapers) may only be licensed for use within a particular city or campus. You may access a remote Gopher server, but it may prevent you from accessing a particular resource because you are not local. This is annoying, but license enforcement is a major stumbling block to delivery of online information. Gopher seems to have taken a step in the right direction.

Gopher is a lot harder to talk about than to use. So, if you are mildly confused, just press on. Find a **gopher** client and play with it! The information is there for the taking. It's there to be used. No one is watching you and laughing at your mistakes. So make some!

---

*Some files might only be available through Gopher, but that is strictly a security issue. If you access those files through Gopher, they come to you via **ftp**.

†In reality, the collection might be housed elsewhere, but you don't care—it will be fetched automatically should you request it.

Where the Gopher Was Born

The name "Gopher" is an interesting pun. It started out as a distributed campus information service at the University of Minnesota, home of the "Golden Gophers." Since its primary function is to "go fer" things, the name **gopher** was coined.

The service was designed so that each piece of a bureaucracy could have control over its own server and data. That is, the school administration could have a computer in the administration building which could deliver information on administrivia. The athletic department could have a sports schedule server in its offices. Each academic department could provide a server with a class schedule; and so on. There could be as many servers as there were groups who wanted to provide them.

Gopher's developers then created a special application that could guide students to the information with no training. To do this, they organized the system by topic so that it looks like one large database, rather than hundreds of smaller databases. It can access files in FTP archives, phone numbers from white pages servers, library catalogs and other databases with special-purpose (TELNET-based) servers, whatever. Only the Gopher knows where the data really is, how to access it, and that there are multiple servers providing it.

It didn't take much effort to see that if this could work for a bunch of servers in various departments, it could work for servers all over the world. All it took was the Internet to connect them all together. In the space of about 18 months, the Gopher system has gone from one site to over 100 sites.

Finding a Gopher Client

To access the Gopher system, you need a **gopher** client program. The special client software must be installed on a computer which is on the Internet. There are free **gopher** clients for just about any computer you might have: UNIX, Macintosh, IBM/PC, X Windows, VAX/VMS, VM/CMS, and probably more by now.

Each client has the "look and feel" of the system it runs on. If you are an IBM/PC user, the PC version will work just like other PC applications. The Macintosh version will look like a hypercard stack with buttons to push. The X-windows version also has a "point-and-click" interface. The source for this software is **boombox.micro.umn.edu**, in the directory *pub/gopher.* You can get what you need from there via anonymous FTP. If you'd rather, you could use **archie** to find other sources for the client software.

Whichever client you decide to install, it will be pre-configured with the Internet address of some home server. Since all servers are public, it doesn't really matter where it points initially. You can start the client, get a menu, and use **gopher**.

When you have some experience, you can decide which Gopher server you want to be your home and change the configuration accordingly.*

As in the other chapters, to illustrate **gopher** I had to pick a client. I chose to use the UNIX non-graphical version (sometimes called the *curses* version because it uses UNIX's standard terminal interface package curses). I chose this version for two reasons. First, all it requires is a terminal emulator. You don't need a mouse or a super graphics monitor. Second, when you're starting off with **gopher**, you're more likely to access the client on a "public" client computer somewhere, rather than setting up a new client on your own system. If you use **telnet** (or a dial-up modem) to access a Gopher server on a remote system, you're most likely to see the UNIX curses client.

There are two "public" **gopher** clients I know about. These are **consultant.micro.umn.edu** and **gopher.uiuc.edu**. You can try **gopher** out on either of these before you go through the trouble of installing a client. Just **telnet** to them and use the login name "gopher". If you do try this, you will find that the interface you will be using will be the curses **gopher**, which is used in this chapter.

Almost anything that you can do on one **gopher** client you can do on another. It may be a bit easier if you have a mouse, but it works just fine without one. Ultimately, the choice of a client isn't important; find one that suits your taste.

How Gopher Works

When you first start up a **gopher** client, it contacts its home server and asks for its main menu. The server sends the menu, and the client displays it for you. When you select one of the items on the menu, your client asks the server for more information about the item. The server tells your client what kind of thing your selection represents (e.g., a text file, a directory, a host, a white pages server, etc.), the IP address of a server for that item, a port number to use, and a directory path to a file. The IP address could be the server itself, if that's where the resource resides; it could just as easily be another server somewhere else. It doesn't matter; the client does the same thing wherever it is. Your client then saves its current position (in case you want to return), takes this new information and contacts the new server. The process repeats as before.

Eventually, you will choose a resource rather than a menu. Your **gopher** client will choose an appropriate utility for dealing with the resource you select, whatever it is. If it is a file, the client **ftp**s it for you. If the resource is a "login" resource (i.e., a system you can log in to), it creates a TELNET session. If it's a collection indexed by Archie or WAIS, Gopher uses Archie or WAIS to find out what's relevant. The **gopher** client you are using allows you to speak to it in a screen oriented, menu-driven fashion. It takes what you say and turns them into real commands for the appropriate application. So, if you are in Gopher, you will never have to type an **ftp get** command.

---

*How you change the configuration varies from client to client. Check the documentation that comes with the client you have installed.

Finding Internet Resources

Getting started is easy. To start a **gopher** client on UNIX, give the command:

```
% gopher
```

Whatever server you use, your first menu will look something like:

```
            Internet Gopher Information Client v0.8


                         Root Directory

     --> 1.  Welcome to the U of Illinois Gopher.
         2.  CCSO Documentation/
         3.  Computer Reference Manuals/
         4.  Frequently Asked Questions/
         5.  GUIDE to U of Illinois/
         6.  Libraries/
         7.  National Weather Service/
         8.  Other Gopher and Information Servers/
         9.  Peruse FTP Sites/
         10. Phone Books/


     Press ? for Help, q to Quit, u to go up        Page: 1/1
```

If your initial client resides at the University of Minnesota, you may find items in the menu about Minnesota campus events. If you use University of Illinois, you will find items of interest to their students. In addition to these "local interest" categories, though, you will always find a few topics of general interest (for example, items 6, online library catalogs; 7, current weather and forecasts; and 9, software and data sources), and a way to reach other servers (item 8). You're also likely to find some introductory information (item 1). Usually it will be pretty obvious what an item is from the menu entry. If it isn't, try accessing it and see if it's interesting.

gopher keeps track of two types of entities: directories and resources. These things are flagged on the menus. This client uses a slash at the end of a line to denote a directory.* A directory is really equivalent to another menu. That is, if you select a directory and access it, you'll see another menu—this time, one that's more specific to your topic. (Selecting item 8 will give you a menu of other Gopher servers.)

With this Gopher implementation, you move between menu items by typing the line number you want, or by using your terminal's arrow keys to move up and down the screen. (On a version with a graphical interface, you'd point at the item you want and click a mouse button, or something along those lines.) As you move around the menu, the arrow on the left will show you which item is selected. If you are interested in "Frequently Asked Questions," you would move the cursor (i.e.,

---

*Fancier clients (like Macintosh or X clients) will most likely use an icon or something pictorial to denote a directory.

the arrow) to number 4.* Notice that the line has a slash (/) on the end of it, meaning that it's a directory; expect another menu when you access it. When you want to access this directory or any other type of resource you have selected, type a carriage return. In this case, your screen will change to:

```
             Internet Gopher Information Client v0.8

                    Frequently Asked Questions

     --> 1.   About Frequently Asked Questions.
         2.   New Users/
         3.   AIX and IBM RS6000/
         4.   Binaries Sent via News or E-mail.
         5.   Bulletin Board Systems.
         6.   C Language/
         7.   Consumer Information/
         8.   Credit/
         9.   E-mail Questions/
         10.  Experienced Internet User Questions.
         11.  FAQs from Finland/
         12.  File Compression Questions/
         13.  GNU EMACS/
         14.  Glossary of Networking Terms.
         15.  Home Owner/
         16.  How to find sources.
         17.  Internet Naming Conventions/
         18.  LISP/


     Press ? for Help, q to Quit, u to go up        Page: 1/2
```

You can do several other things while sitting on a menu. Sometimes menus won't fit onto a single screen. The "Page" item in the lower right-hand corner shows you how much more material there is, and where you are. (This example happens to be page 1 of 2.) To move between pages, press the < key to move backward and > to move forward. If you find yourself somewhere you didn't want to be, or if you decide that you're done with a topic, you can move "up" to where you came from by pressing the **u** key. If you did this now, you would move back up to the main menu. When you are done with **gopher**, press the **q** (quit) key to exit.

Looking at Text Files

The first menu we looked at only showed us directories. But this second menu (Frequently Asked Questions) has some entries that end in periods rather than slashes. These are text files. To read a text file, just "access" it just like you did a directory: make the arrow point to it and press your RETURN key. For example, let's say you want to peek at the "Glossary of Networking Terms." Type **14**, which is the number

---

* "Frequently Asked Questions" (or FAQs) are, in net-speak, lists of common questions organized by topic. There are thousands of such lists scattered in various archives; many are "published" periodically through the USENET News. These lists exist so that users can solve the most common problems themselves, rather than asking an expert (who probably answers the same question 100 times a day).

prefixing the line. When the **gopher** client detects a numeric key, it changes the bottom line from "Press ? for Help . . . " to:

```
Move To Line: 14
```

It stays in this mode until a RETURN is typed. The carriage return moves the selection arrow to line 14 and returns the bottom line to its standard format. Entering one more carriage return "accesses" the document; you'll see something like this on your screen:

```
Network Working Group                    O. Jacobsen
Request for Comments: 1208                 D. Lynch
                        Interop, Inc.
                        March 1991


           A Glossary of Networking Terms

Status of this Memo

    This RFC is a glossary adapted from "The INTEROP
    Pocket Glossary of Networking Terms" distributed
    at Interop '90.  This memo provides information
    for the Internet community.  It does not specify
    an Internet standard.  Distribution of this memo
    is unlimited.

Introduction
--More--(1%)[Press space to continue, 'q' to quit.]
```

The UNIX **gopher** client honors the PAGER environment variable. This is the UNIX facility to determine how a program should act when it displays text that's longer than your screen. If you have this variable set, **gopher** will use the pager you have specified (e.g., **more** or **pg**). For example, to use the utility **more** as your pager, give the following command before starting **gopher**:

```
% setenv PAGER more
```

If PAGER isn't set, this **gopher** client uses the internal pager seen here; typing a SPACE advances you to the next screen of text. Clients that are more window-oriented use a scrollbar to page back and forth.

When you get to the end of the article (by pressing the space bar) or quit (by pressing **q**), **gopher** asks what you want to do next:

```
Press <RETURN> to continue, <m> to mail, <s> to save: []
```

Type a carriage return if you want to return to the menu from which you selected this item. If you want a copy of the document you are looking at, you can get one either by e-mail or as a file. You can e-mail a copy of the file to yourself (or anyone else) by pressing **m**. You'll see a prompt like this:

```
Mail document to: []
```

Then type your e-mail address,

```
Mail document to:krol@ux1.cso.uiuc.edu
```

followed by a RETURN. Eventually, you'll receive the document as an e-mail message to you; you can read it and save it with your favorite e-mail program, just like any other message.

Alternately, you can save a copy of the item in your file space on the computer running the **gopher** client. This might not be of much use if you are using a "public" client, since you won't have any file space on the client's computer.* If you ran the client on some computer that allows you to create files, you can wander the world collecting souvenirs as you go. When you get home, you can admire your collection. To save a file, press **s**. **gopher** will ask:

```
Enter save filename: []
```

Type the filename you want for the saved article. **gopher** saves the article in the "current directory" that was in effect when the **gopher** client started. You may use any legal filename; the name may contain directory components (for example, *rfc/1208*). If you use a pathname like this, the directories must already exist.† It doesn't matter what Gopher server you happen to be using or where the data resides: **gopher** knows how to move the file to the computer that's running your client.

In the next few sections, we'll visit a few other menus. These should give you a feeling for how to navigate through Gopher, and what kinds of information you're likely to find.

White Pages Servers

In Chapter 10, *Finding Someone*, we discussed "white pages" services, which are essentially electronic phone books. However, we omitted one important class of service, commonly called "CSO name servers."‡ Normally, you need a special client program to use these name servers. The software for this client is, for the most part, only available at the sites that use this directory service, so it's not widely available. However, Gopher knows how to perform CSO name server lookups; so, once you're comfortable with Gopher, you can access another fifty or so online directories to search for people.

---

*In this case, you would be limited to using e-mail to get copies of resources you find.

†Many **gopher** implementations don't know how to create directories as required.

‡They are so named because they were developed from the CSnet name server code at the Computing Services Office of the University of Illinois, Urbana.

Item 10 on our main menu was labeled "Phone Books." If you select this item, you will see the following selection menu (or something like it):

```
              Internet Gopher Information Client v0.8

                    Phone Books

  --> 1.  U of Illinois at Urbana-Champaign <CSO>
      2.  Australian Defense Force Academy, New South Wales <CSO>
      3.  Brown University <CSO>
      4.  Eastern Illinois University <CSO>
      5.  Massachusetts Institute of Technology <CSO>
      6.  Northwestern University <CSO>
      7.  Notre Dame University <CSO>
      8.  Princeton University <CSO>
      9.  Roskilde Universitetscenter <CSO>
      ...
```

The **<CSO>** suffix at the end of each line tells you that these all represent CSO-style white-pages servers. The entries are mostly large universities, where CSO servers are most popular. If you access one of these items, just like you accessed the file we used in the previous example, you can look things up in the selected directory.

For example, let's say that you accessed the server for the University of Illinois by entering a carriage return. Now you get a new menu for entering search criteria:

```
              Internet Gopher Information Client v0.8

                U of Illinois at Urbana-Champaign

      1. Name    :
      2. Phone   :
      3. E-Mail  :
      4. Address :

     Press 1-4 to change a field, Return to accept fields and continue
```

Type the number for the information you want to enter: that is, if you know the person's name, type **1**; if you know the person's phone number, type **2**; and so on. The cursor will move to the corresponding portion of the screen. Type the words you want to search for.

CSO's search rules make sense, but they're a little different from what you might be used to. Each word in the name is taken as an item, with wildcard characters allowed.* The words in the search string must all be found in the target for the target to match. Substrings don't automatically match. If you met Ed Krol over a beer, and tried to look up "Ed Krol" when you got thirsty, you would likely be drinking alone. "Ed" would not match "Edward" or "Edwin", and his first name is not "Ed."

---

*For review: * matches any sequence of characters. [*list*] matches any single character between the brackets (e.g., [abc] matches a, b, or c.). CSO name servers do not honor UNIX regular expressions or the ? wildcard character.

Therefore, it is usually safer to search for wildcarded first names like "Ed*." Order and case are not important. That is:

    1. Name   : **Ed* Krol**

would match "Edward M Krol", because both "Ed" followed by any characters and "Krol" were in that name. Similarly,

    1. Name   : **Krol Ed***

would also work. Notice also, that you needn't match every word in an entry, like the middle initial "M." After entering either of these strings, type a carriage return to "enter" the item. Another carriage return begins the search, which would return:

```
    --------------------------------------------------------
         alias: e-krol
          name: krol edward m
        e-mail: krol@ux1.cso.uiuc.edu
         phone: (217) 333-7886
       address: 1121 dcl, MC 256
             : 1304 w springfield : urbana, il 61801
    department: computing and communications services office
         title: asst director

Press <RETURN> to continue, <m> to mail, <s> to save:
```

As with the text file that we retrieved earlier, you can either continue (i.e., look up another address), save this output in a file, or mail it to yourself.

One quirk of CSO-style servers is that they only index entries based on some fields in an item. You might have inferred, incorrectly, that you could find the person whose address is "1121 DCL" by filling in line 4 and doing the search. You can't, because there is no index for the data based on the address. Your search must be based on the person's name, phone number, or e-mail address. You can use any fields, however, to further constrain a search. For example, let's say you got a note from your secretary saying "L Ward at 244-0681 called." You don't recognize the name; after playing telephone tag for a while, you decide to try e-mail. So you do a lookup on "L* Ward":

    1. Name   : **L* Ward**

The result is:

```
query name=L* Ward

Too many entries to print.
```

The search was too broad and the server is refusing to print all the matching entries (you are usually limited to about 20). You can further constrain the search by adding the telephone number:

```
                Internet Gopher Information Client v0.8



                 U of Illinois at Urbana-Champaign

      1. Name    : L* ward
      2. Phone   : 244-0681
      3. E-Mail  :
      4. Address :



         Press 1-4 to change a field, Return to accept fields and continue
```

Now you'll be rewarded with a single matching entry:

```
      ---------------------------------------------------------
             alias: l-ward1
              name: ward lynn e halpern
            e-mail: ux1.cso.uiuc.edu
             phone: (217) 244-0681
           address: 1541 dcl, MC 256
                  : 1304 w springfield
                  : urbana, il 61801
        department: computing services office
             title: res programmer
             hours: 7:30am - 6pm"ish" (Mon-Fri)

      Press <RETURN> to continue, <m> to mail, <s> to save:
```

Moving to Other Servers

By poking around with **gopher** on your home server, you might find 80% of everything you ever wanted to find. Now you need to find the other 20%. You can do this by poking around on other servers. **gopher**'s main menu will usually have an entry that looks something like:

```
   --> 8.  Other Gopher and Information Servers/
```

The wording may change from server to server. Sometimes it may be one level down in menus, underneath "Other Services" or something like that. It may be hidden, but it's always there.

Moving from one server to another isn't different from any other search: you look through menus and pick a resource. So after picking the "Other Gophers" entry, you may have to go through a few screens to find one you want. Some servers break them up alphabetically, according to the server's name:

```
1.  Gopher Servers (A-G)/
2.  Gopher Servers (G-T)/
3.  Gopher Servers (U-Z)/
```

Some break them up by geographical area, usually continent. Move around until you find an entry you want to try:

```
--> 1.  CICNET gopher server (under construction)/
    2.  CONCERT Network -- Research Triangle Park, NC, USA/
    3.  Cornell Information Technologies Gopher (experimental)/
    4.  Cornell Law School (experimental)/ ...
```

Notice that other servers are flagged as directories: their menu entries end in a slash. If you think about it, this makes sense—if you access any of these servers, you get a menu of services. It's not important that the services are provided by another server.

From the list above, you might be able to gather that some servers are general, like the one we have been using. Some, like the server at the Cornell Law School (number 4), have a particular focus. On a "focused" server, you might not find any of the specific items we've seen so far, like the glossary of network terms, or a general directory of white pages services. But you will always find a way to move to other Gophers. If your interests lie in the area of one of these special servers, you might consider making it your home base; the Cornell Law School server would be an obvious choice if you're specifically interested in legal questions. It can place much of the information you need for day-to-day existence at your fingertips—and someone else maintains it for you!

Index Searches

If you poke around in Gopher long enough, you might find some "questionable" items, like #3 below:

```
Internet Gopher Information Client v0.8

            Drosophila

    1.  About Drosophila Gopher.
    2.  Drosophila Archive/
--> 3.  Drosophila Stocks (genotype,breakpt,...) <?>
```

What does this mean? Gopher isn't sure what this item is?

Not at all. The symbol **<?>** refers to a type of entry that we haven't seen yet. These are *indexed directory* resources. In a normal Gopher directory (/), you select the directory and see a menu of everything in it. Index resources work similarly, except that the menu only shows a subset of the directory's contents. The subset that you see is based on a keyword search. For example, assume that you're a biologist and need to find a strain of Drosophila that has purple eyes. After finding the

"Drosophila" menu, you select resource #3: "Drosophila Stocks"; you'll see this display at the bottom of the screen:

```
Index word(s) to search for: []
```

Gopher leaves the cursor at the end of the query line; now you can type keywords:

```
Index word(s) to search for: purple
```

When you type RETURN, **gopher** searches the index and builds a "custom" directory menu that only contains items matching your search criterion. In this case, then, you'll see a new menu that only contains items that match the keyword "purple":

```
             Internet Gopher Information Client v0.8

         Drosophila Stocks (genotype,breakpt,...): purple

    --> 1.  Genotype: D. mauritiana  pr-3.
        2.  Genotype: D. simulans  pur osp-3.
        3.  Genotype: D. simulans  pur e.
```

This menu isn't any different from the other menus. You're looking at a collection of files (the entries end in periods). Therefore, selecting item 1 just displays the file:

```
>>>
Genotype: D. mauritiana  pr-3
Comments: Coyne stocks, 1990; purple eye
Stock #:  2520  Stock Center: Bloomington

Press <RETURN> to continue, <m> to mail, <s> to save: []
```

(If you're a biologist, you presumably know how to use this information!)

Indexed searches are a great feature, but there are some tricks. The Gopher interface is very general and, as with anything very general, there are several causes for confusion. First, you have no idea what kind of computer or software is really doing the search. Gopher can do searches through Archie servers, WAIS servers, and others. Each of these servers has its own search rules, and interprets keywords differently. Some, like Archie, will only let you search for a single word. Some servers accept strings of keywords, but the meanings of these keywords may change as you move from index to index. For example, consider the string:

```
bush and quayle
```

Does this mean that for the search to match, the item must contain the words "bush", "and", and "quayle"? Or is the "and" a directive telling the server to find entires that contain the word "bush" and the word "quayle"? You don't know, and can't tell beforehand.

Another problem is that Gopher tends to reduce the search capabilities of different servers to the intersection of their features. You get to use the features they all have in common, not the best of any one. For example, you can access WAIS servers through Gopher. WAIS searches are extremely powerful, much more sophisticated than anything you've seen so far. (You should be drooling by now!) However, if you use a WAIS server through Gopher, much of its power is lost because you can't use all its facilities with Gopher's simple line-oriented keyword interface.

You may also find that the resources which are most useful to index also tend to have licensing restrictions. Most of the time, you're allowed to search the database, but you're not allowed to see the information that you find. For example, the University of Minnesota's Gopher server has the UPI press feed (the same thing as the Clarinet news group) as an indexed resource. You can access it:

```
Internet Gopher Information Client v0.8

                    UPI News

        1.  About UPI News.
   --> 2.  Search Today's News <?>
        3.  Search entire news archive <?>
        4.  Search last month's news archive <?>
        5.  Search this month's news archive <?>
        6.  Stories/
```

And search it for "clinton":

```
Index word(s) to search for: clinton
```

It gives you a menu of articles that match the search key:

```
Internet Gopher Information Client v0.8

            Search Today's News: clinton

   --> 1.  Today/biz/Israeli report: Pan Am security was lax before bombing.
        2.  Today/feature/PEROT CAN CASH IN BY IGNORING ISSUES.
        3.  Today/news/What Newspapers Are Saying.
        4.  ..news/Israeli report: Pan Am security was lax before bombing.
        5.  Today/news/UPI NEWS AT A GLANCE.
        6.  Today/news/Voters still unhappy with their choices.
        7.  ..news/Florida Perot supporters say they've got enough signatures.
        8.  ..Bush, Clinton get big wins but Perot could be a factor in th.
        9.  Today/news/Clinton takes campaign to Congress.
```

But, when you try to read an article, you get:

```
We cannot off campus allow connections to this server.
Sorry

Bummer.....

Press <RETURN> to continue, <m> to mail, <s> to save: []
```

This is because the license that allows the University of Minnesota to have the UPI news feed online forbids them from distributing it off campus. The Gopher knows where you are coming from, and enforces this restriction.

These problems are a minor price to pay for this facility. (Keep in mind that the alternative to licensing restrictions is not unlimited access to data; in reality, the alternative would be no data at all.)

With a little experience, you will hardly notice the differences in how searches work. Here are a couple of hints to help you through:

- Gopher searches are always case-insensitive; uppercase and lowercase letters are considered the "same."

- When you approach a new index, keep the search simple. If you want articles containing "bush" and "quayle," just look for "quayle." He is likely to appear in fewer articles, hence the resulting menu will be shorter. If your search is too broad, no harm done, the menu will just be longer.

- If you use a particular resource regularly, take 15 minutes to experiment. Find an article and read it. Jot down a few terms from the article. Try a few searches with multiple keywords, including some with "and", "or," and "not" in between them. See what happens; are words like "and" considered part of the search string, or are they keywords? Remember that the rules change from resource to resource; that is, two different resources that you access from the same Gopher server may behave differently.

- If you move from Gopher server to Gopher server, the way a search is conducted for a similarly named resource may vary. If you always use a resource from the same Gopher server, the search semantics will remain the same.

- There is no obvious way to cancel a search once you have started. If you react instinctively with a CTRL-C, you will cancel the **gopher** client. The best you can do is let it complete and give you some bizarre collection of menu items.

FTP Through Gopher

Now that you know about Gopher and indexes, you can use Gopher as an alternative interface for FTP. Gopher's FTP features currently allow you to move files from anonymous FTP servers to the computer running your **gopher** client. (I'd say "your own computer" but at first, it's more likely that you'll be using a "public-access" **gopher** client on some other system. This is one of the motivations for running the client on your computer or workstation—you can move files to it.)

If you look back to Gopher's menu, you'll see an item labeled "Peruse FTP Sites." On our **gopher**, it's item 9. The name may change from client to client, but you should be able to recognize which item we mean. Once you've selected this item, you'll see one of two types of menus; which menu you'll see depends on how your Gopher server works with FTP sites. Some servers use FTP directly, in which case you'll see an alphabetic list of sites, annotated with their holdings:

```
          Internet Gopher Information Client v0.8


                    Peruse FTP Sites


     --> 1.  About Peruse FTP Sites.
         2.  About Anonymous FTP.
```

```
   3.   a FTP sites/          sites starting with "a"
   4.   b FTP sites/          sites starting with "b"
   5.   c FTP sites/          sites starting with "c"
   ...
```

If you see a menu like this, you'll have to search through a series of menus to find the server and file you want. In this case, let's say that you're looking for information about the effect of snow pack on drought, and that you vaguely remember that the files you want are on a server whose name starts with "c." So you select the menu for the "c" servers:

```
          Internet Gopher Information Client v0.8

                     c FTP sites

      1.   c.scs.uiuc.edu 128.174.90.3      adventure, dungeon, world,/
      2.   cadillac.siemens.com 129.73.2.39      unknown/
      3.   caf.mit.edu 18.62.0.232      giraphe3/
      4.   calpe.psc.edu 128.182.62.148   GPLOT, GTEX/
      5.   calvin.nmsu.edu 128.123.35.150   unknown/
      6.   casbah.acns.nwu.edu 129.105.113.52    unknown/
      7.   casper.na.cs.yale.edu 128.36.12.1      multigrid repository/
  --> 8.   ..Drought info for/
      9.   cayuga.cs.rochester.edu 192.5.53.209    JOVE, NL-KR mail list/
     10.   cc.curtin.edu.au 134.7.70.1      internet access sw, chemical/
      ...
```

You're lucky: **gopher** has suppressed the hostname because it's too long, but the annotation shows that item 8 is a likely source. It doesn't matter that the name is truncated; internally **gopher** knows how to access the source. So select item 8, and type a RETURN:

```
          Internet Gopher Information Client v0.8

          caticsuf.cati.csufresno.edu 129.8.100.15
                  Weather/Drought info for

      1.   bin/
      2.   dev/
      3.   etc/
  --> 4.   pub/
      5.   usr/
```

Now you have contacted an FTP server that might contain the data you want (its name is **caticsuf.cati.csufresno.edu**). You need to find out more precisely what information it has that's useful. To search through this server's files, you (again) use a series of **gopher** menus—not FTP-style **ls** or **dir** commands. The first thing to look for is a *README* file, if it exists. Unfortunately, it doesn't. So, knowing a little about FTP, you guess that the *pub* directory (item 4) is a good place to start. When you select item 4, you see lots of subdirectories, including these:

```
    4.  beer/
--> 5.  drought/
    6.  ethics/
```

The *drought* entry looks appropriate, so you select it. You get another directory; this time, you find an entry on *snowpack*, which is just what you're looking for. If you select that item, Gopher will display it on the screen and ask whether or not you want to save it or mail it elsewhere. What's interesting about this process is that the machine you're receiving the file from doesn't belong to the Gopher system at all; it's just an anonymous FTP server somewhere.

Of course, the process we just described really isn't all that convenient. Gopher makes the search a little more convenient, but you still have to know (or at least, have an idea) which server has the data you want. That's where the other kind of FTP menu comes in. Some Gopher servers use **archie** to look up FTP resources. This builds an indexed resource, accessible by menu, of the entire world's supply of anonymous FTP servers! If the Gopher server you are using is using one of these, you will see a menu like this:

```
            FTP Sites

--> 1.  Read Me First.
    2.  Exact Word FTP Search <?>
    3.  Partial Word FTP Search <?>
    4.  University of Minnesota - Gopher, POPMail/
    ...
```

We're no longer looking at "raw" directories, as in the previous example; we're looking at indexed directories, accessed via Archie. That is, rather than traversing a series of menus to find a server, you can use a Gopher-style "indexed directory" search to find the file you want. You're actually using Archie—but, as you'd expect, Gopher hides the details of Archie from you.

Notice that you can perform two kinds of searches, corresponding to two of Archie's search types: you can perform exact string matches (#2) or Archie substring searches (#3). If we pick #3, Gopher responds:

```
Index word(s) to search for: []
```

To which we respond:

```
Index word(s) to search for:snowpack
```

After the search is completed, we get a menu:

```
Internet Gopher Information Client v0.8

    Partial Word FTP Search: snowpack
```

```
--> 1.  caticsuf.cati.csufresno.edu:/pub/drought/snowpack  General Info.
    2.  caticsuf.cati.csufresno.edu:/pub/drought/snowpack.
```

This menu shows us two items, both of which match the search criterion we specified. If we select #2 we get the same item we found previously:

```
                    DEPARTMENT OF WATER RESOURCES
                    Hydrology and Flood Operations

                      WATER SUPPLY CONDITIONS
                        as of March 15, 1991

   Precipitation,  Northern Sierra 8-station index:
       Mar 1 - Mar 15:  12.1" (est.)
       March average:    7.0"
       Pct of Mar avg:  172%
 ...
```

Don't be surprised if you see both interfaces: an Archie-like indexed directory, plus an alphabetical list of FTP servers. Archie's resource list is probably more reliable, but both are useful in their own way. The indexed list is obviously appropriate if you're looking for information about a particular topic, and don't know where to find it. The alphabetical list may be easier if you already know where the data is (you don't have to try constructing an appropriate search), or if you've heard that the FTP server at **hoople.usnd.edu** has some great stuff, and you'd like to check it out.

Gopher works just fine for text (ASCII) files, but binary files are more troublesome. To handle a binary file appropriately, **gopher** must be able to guess the file's type, based on extensions to the name (e.g., *.tar.Z*, *.hqx*, etc.). If it finds one, **gopher** flags it for you with the **<BIN>** suffix. There is a lot of development in this area; the way **gopher** handles these files may vary from client to client. For example, the Macintosh client may work perfectly with binary files, and unpack them if they end with the extension *.hqx*. The UNIX version may transfer the files in binary but leave them intact. The X version may throw up its hands and say "I'm sorry; no can do binary." All of this may change in the future (hopefully for the better), so just try it, and see what happens.

Even if your **gopher** client refuses to handle binary files (or if it tries, but does something unreasonable), it still isn't useless. The equal sign (=) command shows, technically, what **gopher** is doing. If you are positioned on a resource like #2 and press the = key, you'll see something like this:

```
Name=snowpack
Type=0
Port=7997
Path=caticsuf.cati.csufresno.edu@/pub/drought/snowpack
Host=gopher.uiuc.edu

Press <RETURN> to continue, <m> to mail, <s> to save: []
```

The important thing here is "Path." It tells you exactly where the resource is located. Even if **gopher** can't transfer the file for you, you still know that the hostname is

caticsuf.cati.csufresno.edu. You can use anonymous FTP to access this host, and then **cd** to *pub/drought*. You can then do whatever is necessary with *snowpack* using normal FTP commands to get it to your home system. There you could do whatever decoding is necessary to make the file usable.

Using Telnet Through Gopher

Finally, at least for now, Gopher can connect you to resources using **telnet** as an interface. You do this in the same fashion as every other resource: find an interesting resource by walking through the menus, and then "select" it. For example, while browsing through a menu under the title "Libraries", you notice the resource below:

```
--> 23. University of California MELVYL <TEL>
```

This is an online, TELNET-style interface to the University of California's card catalog. The marker **<TEL>** at the end of the entry tells you that this is a "telnet" resource. When you select this kind of resource, **gopher** gives you a warning and help screen:*

```
         Warning!!!!!, you are about to leave the Internet
          Gopher program and connect to another host.
      If you get stuck press the control key and the ] key,
                  and then type quit

              Now connecting to melvyl.ucop.edu

                  Press return to connect:
```

Gopher gives you this warning because it loses control of your session once **telnet** starts; it regains control when **telnet** finishes. If you get hung up somewhere in TELNET, you're on your own. Control right bracket is the common way to get to **telnet**'s command mode.†

Depending on the resource, the warning screen may have some hints about how to use it. For example:

```
    Use login "Guest"
```

or:

```
    When you get connected do a "DIAL VTAM"
```

In other cases, you are on your own. You may need to contact the site to arrange an account. Just because you are getting there through **gopher** doesn't mean you bypass security.

---

*This facility is very different in the Macintosh Hypercard Gopher.

†If you are using **telnet** to get to **gopher** in the first place, remember the cautions about escape characters when running multiple TELNET sessions! Also, note that public Gopher servers usually won't allow you to access a TELNET resource. To get to TELNET resources, you need your own client.

Now that you have read the warnings, if you enter another carriage return you get connected to the selected resource:

```
Trying 31.1.0.1...
Connected to melvyl.ucop.edu.
Escape character is '^]'.

DLA LINE 145 (TELNET) 06:56:54 05/06/92    (MELVYL.UCOP.EDU)

Please Enter Your Terminal Type Code or Type ? for a List of Codes.

TERMINAL?
```

When you are done and log out, you will return to **gopher** and to the menu where you selected the resource.

Gopher Development

Since the Gopher service is still under development, the features that are available are changing—hopefully for the better. Client programs for other types of computers are being developed by volunteers. Also, as they are developed some may have different features. Some clients may omit certain features; other clients may have strange implementations of some features. So be forewarned; if you expect some surprises, you'll be able to deal with them without too much trouble.

One useful feature that might not be in all clients is a "bookmark." If you played with **gopher** a bit, you have probably noticed that the menu structure can be inconvenient. From any given menu, you can only go up and down in the menu "tree." If you have gone though ten menus to get to where you are, and you suddenly decide to look somewhere else, you can only go up and up and up and up . . . . Once you have gone up enough, you can move to a new menu and start going down. For example, recall the "non-Archie" FTP example. To find the *snowpack* data file, you started with a menu of all FTP servers whose names begin with "c"; you moved to a menu for the site you wanted; you moved to the *pub* directory; and after moving through a few other menus, you finally arrived at *snowpack*. What if you found *snowpack* and discovered that it wasn't what you wanted? You only had two options: quit or retrace your steps.

A bookmark allows you to remember where you have been. If this client had a bookmark facility, you could have placed one at the "FTP servers" menu. **gopher** would then remember this position. When you were done, rather than retracing your steps, you would tell **gopher**, "go to that bookmark", and you would be there immediately. Bookmarks are usually available only on "point-and-click" style **gopher** clients, like the Macintosh, X, PC/DOS, etc.

We also mentioned that you may find features with "strange" implementations. The Macintosh Hypercard client provides a good example of this. It cannot start a TELNET session for you. However, it does show TELNET resources, and allow you to select them. When you select a TELNET resource, the **gopher** client creates a TELNET configuration file. You must leave **gopher** and open the configuration file, which then starts the **telnet** program and connects you to the appropriate server. This must be done "outside" of the **gopher** client. It helps you along, but doesn't quite do everything as an integrated package.

Aside from the uneven development of what is there now, people are considering the future of Gopher. There are already audio resources available though Gopher: resources that when you select them, your computer plays or speaks them instead of displaying them on the terminal. I didn't talk about them because they don't work well over long distance networks. They will improve. Also on the horizon are images, resources that you select to see a picture. Some Gopher servers and clients may start supplying images by the end of 1992.

A Last Word

I hope I've given you some idea of what's available through Gopher—that is, almost everything. One thing that I can't give you is a better sense of how Gopher is organized: for example, where to look if you're an archaeologist, or a financial analyst, or a software developer, or a Dante scholar. Gopher may help to guide you to the resources, but you still have to know your resources fairly well. In a traditional library, there's no substitute for browsing through the stacks and seeing what looks interesting. The same is true for Gopher: there's no substitute for exploring. Not only will you become familiar with the various commands, you'll also find out where the "good stuff" is. And you'll probably find some useful services that you didn't know existed.

## CHAPTER TWELVE

SEARCHING INDEXED DATABASES: WAIS

How WAIS Works
Getting Access
Adding Sources

WAIS (pronounced "wayz") is another of the Internet's new services. It's great for searching through indexed material and finding articles based on what they contain. That is: WAIS lets you search through Internet archives looking for articles containing groups of words.

WAIS is really a tool for working with collections of data, or databases. To many people, databases connote a file full of numbers—or, once you've seen a little of what WAIS can do, a set of articles about some topic. That's too narrow a view. WAIS can deal with much more; the format of the information presented doesn't matter much. It doesn't really look at the data in the process of a search, it looks at an index. If you or someone else took the trouble to build an index, WAIS can select information and present it to you regardless of its format. It's most common to see indexes for various kinds of text (articles and so on); but you can build an index for anything. For example, someone could build an index from the descriptions of great works of art; the data tied to the index could be the works of art themselves, stored in some standard graphical format (e.g., GIF). You could then search for "gothic," and up would pop Grant Wood's painting "American Gothic." There are many such indexes built from data that is available elsewhere, (such as **whois** and **archie** indexes). Some of them are good and some are not, but you can search them and frequently come up with what you want.

I confess that I dislike the "official" terminology used to discuss WAIS. The database language is overly abstract, and prevents you from seeing what WAIS can do. I like to think of WAIS databases as private libraries devoted to a particular topic: for example, a library of architectural building standards and codes. Since I find this an easier way to view things, that's how we'll talk about them for the rest of the chapter.

Like Gopher, WAIS allows you to find and access resources on the network without regard for where they really reside. In Gopher, you find resources by looking through a sequence of menus until you find something appropriate. WAIS does the same thing, but it does the searching for you. You tell it what you want; it tries to find the material you need. A **wais** command is essentially: "find me items about this in that library." WAIS then looks at all the documents in the library (or libraries) you gave it, and tells you which documents are most likely to contain what you want. If you like, WAIS then displays the documents for you.

There are more than 250 free WAIS libraries on the network now. Since they are maintained by volunteer effort and donated computer time, coverage tends to be spotty. For topics where there are a lot of willing volunteers, coverage is good: as you'd expect, there are many libraries for computer science, networking, and molecular biology. Some literature libraries exist, such as Project Gutenberg's collection and various religious texts. Coverage in the social sciences is pretty thin at this time; however, libraries are always being added. There is a way to ask: "Is there a library for this topic?" So, you can easily check whether or not WAIS has any resources that are relevant to you.

Some commercial information products, like the Dow Jones Information Service, provide their product through a WAIS interface. You have to pay a fee to use services like this. Once you've arranged for payment, these services are no different from the free network WAIS services.

We'll introduce you to WAIS by discussing how it works. There are some good and bad points about how WAIS does its job. It takes a little practice to get WAIS to do what you want; you have to ask it the right questions. It's a bit easier to understand how to construct these questions if you know what WAIS does with them. Once that is behind us, we can do some searches. Finally, you can use WAIS to build and search arbitrary private libraries; we'll touch on that briefly.

How WAIS Works

WAIS is a distributed text searching system. It is based on a standard (named Z39.50*) that describes a way for one computer to ask another to do searches for it. WAIS is one of the first systems based upon this draft standard. At this point, it's also the most common.

To make a document available through a WAIS server, someone must create an index for that server to use in the search. For textual information, every word in the document is usually indexed. When you request a search from a **wais** client, it contacts the servers that handle the libraries you suggested. It asks each server, in turn, to search its index for a set of words. The server then sends you a list of documents that may be appropriate, and a "score" telling how appropriate it thinks each one is. The scores are normalized, so that the document that best matches your search

---

*Z39.50 is a draft ANSI standard for requesting bibliographic information. It has been under development for a long time within the library and computing communities.

criterion is given a score of 1000; others get proportionally less. So, if you say, "Find me documents that contain 'bush' and 'quayle,'" WAIS looks in the index and counts how many times each document contains the word "bush," the word "and," and the word "quayle." The sum of these counts, weighted slightly by what the word is, is converted to a score for a document. After all the libraries are searched, WAIS gives you the titles of the documents that received the highest scores. There's a limit to the number of documents it reports—usually, between 15 and 50, depending on which client you use. You then can pick which documents to view, and WAIS will display them for you.

You should see a problem already. How many times can you conceive of selecting a document because it contained the word "and"? You might have thought that "and" meant the logical *and* operation in WAIS. In fact, there are no special words in WAIS; every word counts some amount in the ranking. A document that contains 1000 matches for "and," but no matches for "bush" or "quayle" might just have the best score; or, more likely, a score high enough to place it in the top 10. Remember that WAIS is a pretty new facility, and all the kinks haven't been worked out. As the software matures, some of these problems will be resolved.

A second problem that may not be as obvious is that WAIS lacks "contextual sensitivity." You could ask WAIS to find articles containing the words "problem children," but it would also be just as happy with an item containing the sentence, "The children had a problem, they'd lost their lunch money." You can't tell WAIS that the words must occur in a certain order, and you can't provide any information about the context in which they occur.

Finally, once a search has taken you astray, you can't tell WAIS to exclude any "wrong turns" or portions of a source. That is, you can't give a command like, "find articles with the words 'problem children,' but throw out articles that contain references to lunch." There is also no way to ask, "What's been added to this source since last year?" This makes it hard to do searches repeatedly in a changing source. If your source were papers from a journal, there is no way to say, "Look for the articles which were published since the last time I checked."

So much for the bad aspects. Even with these flaws, you'll find that WAIS is one of the most useful lookup tools on the Internet. And it's possible that future versions of WAIS will solve these problems. WAIS has one really unique feature going for it: *relevance feedback*. Some clients allow you to find articles that are similar to the articles you've already found. Let's say your search for "problem children" turned up an article titled "Educational Problems In Gifted Children," in addition to the spurious "lunch money" article. "Education Problems . . ." happens to be exactly what you're looking for. Relevance feedback allows you to take some text from that article and have WAIS extract good words from it to use in future searches. These searches can be done either within the same source or in a different source.

Getting Access

Accessing WAIS is a lot like accessing Gopher. In order to use it, you need to have a computer running a **wais** client program. You can install the client program on your own workstation, or you can access a computer that already has the client installed and run it there. Again, as with Gopher, there are **wais** clients for most standard operating systems and computers: Macintosh, DOS, X Windows, NeXt, UNIX, and so on. In all the other sections of the book, I have always said, "I'll illustrate with the UNIX version so nothing special is required to run it." Well, I could do that with WAIS, too. There is a UNIX character-oriented interface called **swais**. To use this system, **telnet** to either **quake.think.com** or **nnsc.nsf.net**, and login as **wais**:

```
% telnet quake.think.com
Trying 192.31.181.1...
Connected to quake.think.com.
Escape character is '^]'.

SunOS UNIX (quake)

login: wais
Welcome to swais.
Please type user identifier (i.e user@host):
krol@ux1.cso.uiuc.edu
TERM = (unknown) vt100
Starting swais (this may take a little while)...
```

If you want to glance at the instructions, you can get help with a **?**. Use a **q** to exit. However, I would not wish this interface on anyone. The program tends to die on you, it uses the ancient UNIX **ex** editor to display articles, you can't save questions or documents, and relevance feedback is missing.

All of the functionality of a public SWAIS server can be also accessed through Gopher servers.* Most Gopher servers have a line something like this on the main menu:

```
9.   Other Gopher and Information Servers/
```

If you access that line, the next menu will have an entry:

```
6.   WAIS Based Information/
```

This item allows you to do WAIS searches of all of the free sources, but through the Gopher index interface. The only thing you can't do with this facility is search multiple sources at one time.

You might want to use one of these public servers the first time to try things out. If you decide you want to use it regularly, get yourself a better client (like Gopher, **wais** clients are getting better all the time). They are all available for free from

---

*You can also access WAIS through the World-Wide Web, which we'll discuss in the next chapter.

various places. You can use **archie** to find them. Many are available via anonymous FTP, from the machine **think.com**. Look in the directory *wais*.*

Since I didn't want to use the character-oriented version, **swais**, I had to pick one. I chose the X version (**xwais**) this time. It has all the features you'll want, and it is reasonably similar to the other window-based versions. As with the other software we've discussed in this book, the choice of a **wais** client is primarily a matter of taste.

Formulating a WAIS Search

Now that we're through the preliminaries, let's get started. In order to get properly started, though, you need to make a leap of faith and forget how you would normally deal with computer databases. When many users try WAIS for the first time, they ask the question "What libraries of documents are out there, anyway?" This is the wrong approach. People are used to relying on the computer for some tasks and their brain for the others. The brain is usually responsible for scanning lists to look for interesting items. In order to use WAIS most effectively, you must trust WAIS and let it do the scanning for you.

When you start the **wais** client for X, **xwais**, the first thing you'll see is the "main window," which appears in Figure 12-1. **wais** clients maintain two libraries: a library of questions and a library of sources.† This window shows both. The "Questions" section at the top contains identifiers for queries you may want to make again. If you want to see what is new in a particular field every month, all you need to do is re-execute the search in its original form, or modify it and issue it again. Here we see one saved question, named *child-sources*.

The "Sources" section, just below the questions section, is for source library maintenance. It shows a scrolling list of libraries that your client knows how to locate and search.

The "Questions" and "Sources" sections each have three buttons to select from:

New   Creates a new question or source window.

Open   Displays an existing question or source that you have previously selected. To select a source or a question, "click" on it with the mouse then "click" the **Open** button. This button is used to change and re-execute a question, or to change source entries.

Delete   Deletes an existing question or source that you have previously selected.

---

*Much of the development work for WAIS is done at Thinking Machines. Their massively parallel processors make very good WAIS servers.

†These libraries are stored in directories named *wais-questions* and *wais-sources* in the home directory for the account you use to run the client.

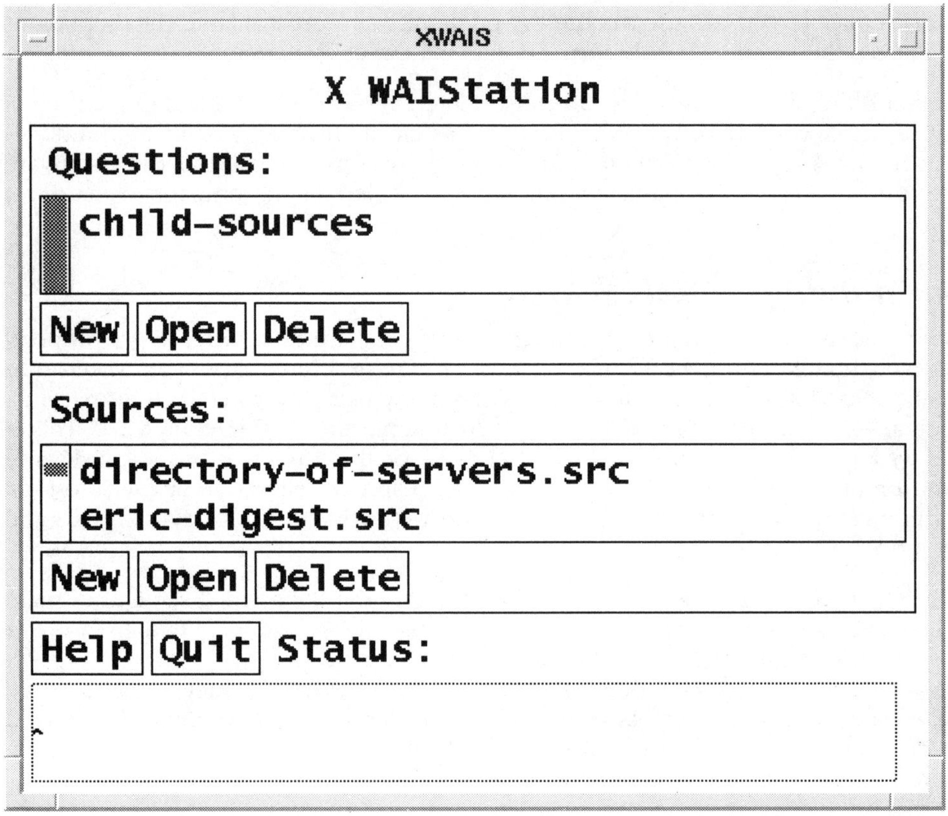

```
┌──────────────────────────────────────────────────────┐
│ ─         ▓▓▓▓▓▓▓▓▓▓     XWAIS     ▓▓▓▓▓▓▓▓     ◄  ▢  │
│ ┌────────────────────────────────────────────────────┐ │
│ │                X WAIStation                        │ │
│ │ ┌────────────────────────────────────────────────┐ │ │
│ │ │ Questions:                                     │ │ │
│ │ │ ┌────────────────────────────────────────────┐ │ │ │
│ │ │ │█ child-sources                             │ │ │ │
│ │ │ │█                                           │ │ │ │
│ │ │ └────────────────────────────────────────────┘ │ │ │
│ │ │ ┌────┐┌────┐┌──────┐                           │ │ │
│ │ │ │New ││Open││Delete│                           │ │ │
│ │ │ └────┘└────┘└──────┘                           │ │ │
│ │ └────────────────────────────────────────────────┘ │ │
│ │ ┌────────────────────────────────────────────────┐ │ │
│ │ │ Sources:                                       │ │ │
│ │ │ ┌────────────────────────────────────────────┐ │ │ │
│ │ │ │▪ directory-of-servers.src                  │ │ │ │
│ │ │ │  eric-digest.src                           │ │ │ │
│ │ │ └────────────────────────────────────────────┘ │ │ │
│ │ │ ┌────┐┌────┐┌──────┐                           │ │ │
│ │ │ │New ││Open││Delete│                           │ │ │
│ │ │ └────┘└────┘└──────┘                           │ │ │
│ │ └────────────────────────────────────────────────┘ │ │
│ │ ┌────┐┌────┐                                       │ │
│ │ │Help││Quit│ Status:                               │ │
│ │ └────┘└────┘                                       │ │
│ │ ┌────────────────────────────────────────────────┐ │ │
│ │ │^                                               │ │ │
│ │ └────────────────────────────────────────────────┘ │ │
│ └────────────────────────────────────────────────────┘ │
└──────────────────────────────────────────────────────┘
```

Figure 12-1: Main window

At the bottom of the window there are two buttons. **Help** gets you help if you click on it. **Quit** terminates **xwais** when you are done.

There is a list of public WAIS libraries in existence, but that list is also a WAIS library itself. So, if you know about the one library, the *directory-of-servers*, you've got it all. But instead of reading the list of libraries yourself, you should start your search by asking WAIS: "What library do I look in for 'gifted children'?" To start the process, click the **New** question button. This displays another window, with a template for asking a question.

So, now it's time to compose a question. Before starting, I'll give you a clue. "Gifted children" is much too narrow a term; if you look for libraries that are appropriate for "gifted children," you're not likely to find any. This makes sense, if you think about traditional (books and paper) libraries: there are probably very few libraries in the country with "gifted children" in their name (if any). If you had an index of important special collections, you'd probably find a few that contained the words "gifted children," but (again) not too many. If you restricted your search to these libraries, you'd miss many libraries with excellent social science collections, some of which may be more useful than the special-purpose libraries. WAIS is no different. The right way to find an appropriate library is to use really broad terms. Think about what kind of people would worry about gifted children. You might think of social workers, educators, parents, etc. Since adding more terms to a search in WAIS makes it easier to match, try to search the *directory-of-servers* with your relevant terms:

```
social work
education
parenting
```

Type your keywords into the "Tell me about:" window, as shown in Figure 12-2.

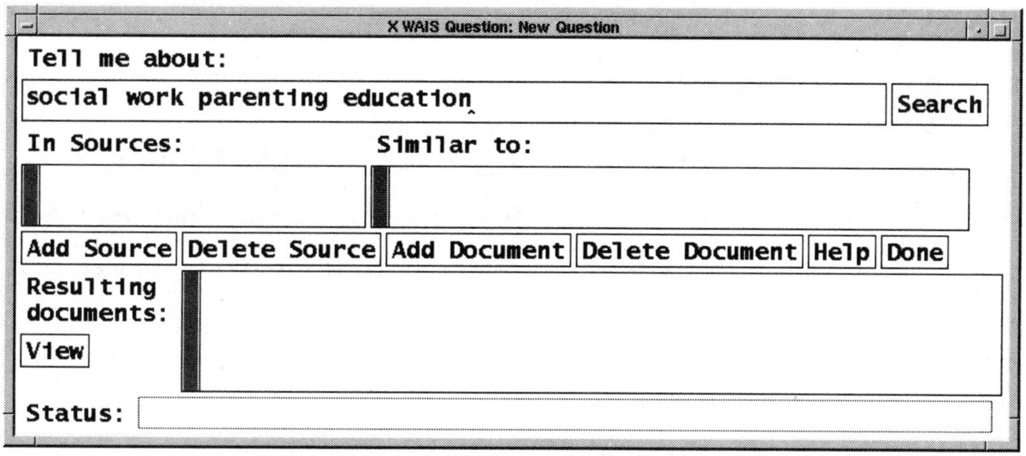

Figure 12-2: Directory-of-servers query

After you've filled in the relevant terms, click on the **Add Source** button. This creates a "pull-down" menu of all the libraries listed in your clients library of sources, shown in Figure 12-3.

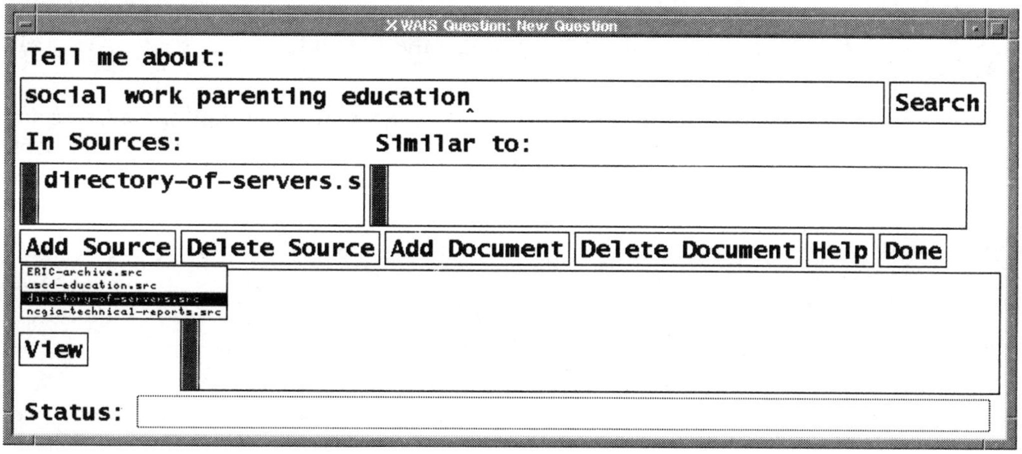

Figure 12-3: Selecting a source

Move the arrow to the *directory-of-servers*, which will appear in reverse video, and let the button go; the *directory-of-servers* will appear in the "In Sources:" box. Now you're ready to run your query. So, with bated breath, push the **Search** button.

If you did things correctly, WAIS will fill in the "Resulting documents:" section of the window. This is shown in Figure 12-4.

```
┌─────────────────────── X WAIS Question: New Question ──────────────────────┐
│                                                                            │
│  Tell me about:                                                            │
│  ┌──────────────────────────────────────────────────────┐ ┌─────────┐     │
│  │ social work parenting education                      │ │ Search  │     │
│  └──────────────────────────────────────────────────────┘ └─────────┘     │
│  In Sources:              Similar to:                                      │
│  ┌─────────────────────┐  ┌────────────────────────────────────────────┐  │
│  │ directory-of-servers.s│ │                                            │  │
│  └─────────────────────┘  └────────────────────────────────────────────┘  │
│  ┌──────────┬─────────────┬──────────────┬─────────────────┬────┬─────┐   │
│  │Add Source│Delete Source│ Add Document │ Delete Document │Help│Done │   │
│  └──────────┴─────────────┴──────────────┴─────────────────┴────┴─────┘   │
│  Resulting    1000    986 ascd-education.src    /proj/wais/wais-sources    │
│  documents:    625    518 ncgia-technical-reports.src   /proj/wais/wai    │
│  ┌────┐        375   1020 ERIC-archive.src    /proj/wais/wais-sources/     │
│  │View│        375   1 2K eric-digest.src    /proj/wais/wais-sources/      │
│  └────┘                                                                    │
│  Status: ┌────────────────────────────────────────────────────────────┐   │
│          └────────────────────────────────────────────────────────────┘   │
└────────────────────────────────────────────────────────────────────────────┘
```

Figure 12-4: Results of directory search

Look at the first result:

```
1000  986 ascd-education.src /proj/wais/wais-sources
```

The 1000 is its score; this score indicates that it fit your search criteria better than any other source, not that it was a "perfect match"—but you're more likely to find interesting articles here than anywhere else. The size is listed next: 986 characters.* The name of the index, "ascd-education.src," sounds promising. When you make your next search, looking for actual articles (rather than promising libraries), you'll select "ascd-education.src" in the "Add Source" menu, and add it to your search list, "In Sources." At the end of the line, you see the filename of this source. You can ignore this for now.

If you scrolled down the list of prospective sources, you would find their scores fall off significantly after the top four. So, you decide to draw the pass-fail line there, and use the top four for the real search:

```
ascd-education.src
ncgia-technical-reports.src
ERIC-archives.src
eric-digest.src
```

---

*This is the size of the item you found. In this case it is the size of the server descriptor. The 986 characters has nothing to do with the size or completeness of the ascd-education library itself.

Now that you've successfully searched for something, it's really tempting to click the **Done** button and get rid of the search window. Don't be so hasty. You'll need this information again in a bit. The *directory-of-servers* is like the Yellow Pages telephone directory. It tells you what telephone numbers to call for different services, but it doesn't call them for you. The *directory-of-servers* likewise tells you where to look to find what you want. You'll need to take the sources you just found, and use them in the next search. Leave the window on the screen and you won't have to write those four libraries on a piece of paper to use them.

It's time to think about what we just accomplished. There are a couple of obvious questions which WAIS users ask at this point. First: "How do the *directory-of-servers*, the library of sources, and the 'In Sources:' area of a question relate?" To make sense of this, you need to keep in mind what you know and what your client knows. In the beginning, you know what you want to ask but don't know where to tell your client to look. Your client knows how to look in all the servers listed in its library of sources, but you have to tell it which ones. The *directory-of-servers* solves this quandary by suggesting where you should send your client looking. Once you've found out which libraries are useful, you can fill in the "In Sources" part of a question and send WAIS off. On occasion, you may find that a search through the *directory-of-servers* suggests libraries that your client doesn't know about. Perhaps they are new and your client's source library doesn't have its entry yet (remember, your client can only search libraries found in its Sources library). For now, let's assume that any source suggested to you by *directory-of-servers* is in your client's library of sources.

The other second question is simply "Why did we bother?" Why didn't we just tell WAIS to "look everywhere"? There are several reasons. First, selecting sources is one way of choosing where your interests lie. If you ask WAIS to look up items about "cars," you could get articles on toys, automobiles, and Computer Aided Registration Systems (CARS). Selecting some suitable libraries, like "automobile-repair-records," focuses your search.* Wading through hundreds of articles to decide which are relevant is a waste of your time—that's what WAIS is supposed to do. Second, searching everywhere could take a long time. You don't go to the library and start at one end of the shelves looking at every title to find something of interest. You know automobile repair starts at 629.28, so you find that section, and browse only that section.

Now that we've got these questions out of the way, let's get back to behavior problems: how do we compose an appropriate question? The real search is similar to the directory search with which we started. Go to the main menu and click the **New** button in the question area. Now you have a new question menu; fill in some relevant keywords:

```
behavior problems in gifted children
```

---

*I used this for illustration; I don't think this library exists—yet.

Then you fill in the sources section. That is, you fill in the "phone numbers" you found above from the "yellow pages." You do this as before, with the pull down menu under "Add Source", but you need to do it four times, once for each source. Now you are ready. You click the **Search** button and off you go. In a bit, the results return as shown in Figure 12-5.

```
┌──────────────────────────────────────────────────────────────────────┐
│  ─                    X WAIS Question: New Question          │ ▼ │ □ │
├──────────────────────────────────────────────────────────────────────┤
│  Tell me about:                                                        │
│  ┌──────────────────────────────────────────────────┐  ┌────────┐     │
│  │ behavior problems in gifted children_            │  │ Search │     │
│  └──────────────────────────────────────────────────┘  └────────┘     │
│  In Sources:              Similar to:                                  │
│  ┌───────────────────────┐ ┌──────────────────────────────────────┐   │
│  │█ ERIC-archive.src     │ │█                                     │   │
│  │  ascd-education.src   │ │                                      │   │
│  └───────────────────────┘ └──────────────────────────────────────┘   │
│  ┌──────────┬─────────────┬──────────────┬───────────────┬────┬─────┐ │
│  │Add Source│Delete Source│Add Document  │Delete Document│Help│Done │ │
│  └──────────┴─────────────┴──────────────┴───────────────┴────┴─────┘ │
│  Resulting     █ 1000 10.0K ed265936.edo   /var/spool/ftp/pub/databases/│
│  documents:      1000  8.6K Children's Peer Relationships.              │
│  ┌────┐          1000 63.2K 90-9.txt   /home/ncgia/ul/ftp/pub/tech-repor │
│  │View│           958 148.5K 89-1.body.txt   /home/ncgia/ul/ftp/pub/tecl │
│  └────┘                                                                 │
│  Status: ┌──────────────────────────────────────────────────────────┐ │
│          └──────────────────────────────────────────────────────────┘ │
└──────────────────────────────────────────────────────────────────────┘
```

Figure 12-5: Behavior problems result

Now that's what you wanted: a set of articles which sound interesting. (If you want to see more of the titles, you could expand the window horizontally.) The item's size field tells you the size (in bytes) of what will be fetched. If you click on "Children's Peer Relationships" and push **View**, WAIS will fetch the article (8.6K characters worth) for you and display it in another window. This is shown in Figure 12-6.

```
┌──────────────────────────────────────────────────────────────────────┐
│  ─                1000 8.6K Children's Peer Relationships.   │ ▲ │ □ │
├──────────────────────────────────────────────────────────────────────┤
│  ┌──────────────────────────────────────────────────────────────────┐ │
│  │█ Children's Peer Relationships.                                  │ │
│  │  Author(s): Burton, Christine B.                                 │ │
│  │  Publication Year: 86                                            │ │
│  │                                                                  │ │
│  │  Children's friendships have inevitable ups and downs. Yet the f │ │
│  │ of satisfaction and security that most children derive from inte │ │
│  │ with peers outweigh periodic problems. For a number of children, │ │
│  │ peer relations are persistently problematic. Some children are a │ │
│  │ rejected by peers. Others are simply ignored, or neglected. It e │ │
│  │ that some popular children have many friends but nevertheless fe │ │
│  │ and unhappy.                                                     │ │
│  │                                                                  │ │
│  └──────────────────────────────────────────────────────────────────┘ │
│  ┌───────────┬─────────┬──────────────┬────┐                          │
│  │Add Section│Find Key │Save To File  │Done│                          │
│  └───────────┴─────────┴──────────────┴────┘                          │
└──────────────────────────────────────────────────────────────────────┘
```

Figure 12-6: Article you retrieved

This menu lets you do four things, in addition to reading the article:

Add Section   Adds a previously selected section of the article to the relevance feedback section of the question window. (This is the **Similar to:** field, shown in Figure 12-5.)

Find Key   Skips forward in the text to the next word in the document that was part of the search and highlights it.

Save to File   Saves the article in a file on the computer running the client. The client will ask you for a filename. WAIS then stores it by that name in a directory, *wais-documents*, under your home directory.

Done   Gets rid of the article and the window.

Finally, with your problem solved you can push the **Done** button on the question window. WAIS will ask you if you want to save the question. If you do, you need to provide a filename. After saving a question, it will appear in your "question library." Next time you want to ask the same question just select it and "click" **Open**.

Refining a Search

Relevance feedback lets you use the results of a search to further refine the search. You do this by selecting items, either in whole or in part, that you have already found and moving them to the **Similar to:** area of the question window. If you want to use the whole article, you select the article on the question screen and click **Add Document**. The result of this action is shown in Figure 12-7.

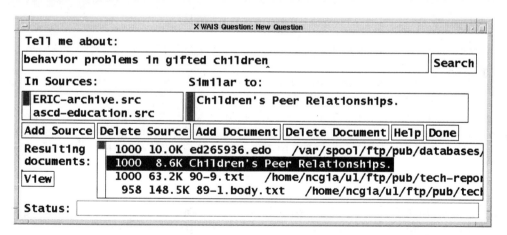

Figure 12-7: Feedback search setup

In this example, you selected "Children's Peer Relationships" as the most appropriate article to use.

To use a portion of an article as feedback, you must be viewing the document. Select the text you want with the mouse arrow: pressing the button at the beginning of the text to be used, moving the arrow to the end of the passage and letting the button up. This highlights the text. Then click **Add Section** in the view window. When you move back to the question window, the feedback section would refer to the selected portions of the document. You can select multiple pieces of the same article, or of different articles, in the same manner. When you are done selecting, click **Search** to try the search again, but with the added selection criteria.

NOTE

Relevance feedback is the section of clients undergoing the most development. If a client is going to die on you, this is where it will happen. If your client runs into trouble, check whether a newer one is available.

When Searches Don't Go as Planned

Sometimes your searches won't retrieve what you want; you may get articles that are unrelated, or you might find nothing at all. There are two possible problems: you either used inappropriate keywords or incorrect sources. That's one reason why most WAIS clients let you save your questions. Some questions are hard to construct. Once you have one that works, you may not want to let it go. Even if you don't want to ask the same question next time, you may find it easier to modify an old search than to start from scratch. It is not unusual to do a search many times, modifying it slightly each time until you get what you want.

Of course, saving your searches doesn't solve the problem at hand: searches that aren't effective in the first place. The only real solution is to keep trying until you find something that works. However, we can give you some hints about how to proceed:

- If the search results are reasonable, but not what you really want, refine the search, either by adding keywords yourself or using relevance feedback.

- View an article even if it is not what you really want. It may give you some ideas about terms that are appropriate to the field you are searching. You won't find many matches for "God" in the Koran, but if you try "Allah" you will. WAIS does not automatically try synonyms. This technique might also turn up some variant spellings ("behavior" vs. "behaviour") or relevant synonyms (like "Llah").

- If WAIS doesn't find anything, and if you're confident of the sources, try a simple search first, for which you're sure there will be some articles. Look at the results; this may give you some clues about the best words to search for.

- If you keep getting irrelevant articles, try to limit the number of sources you use. Sometimes sources will be highly rated, but provide irrelevant articles. Unfortunately, WAIS doesn't tell you which source a particular document came from. You might be able to guess by looking at the article's filename, to see if it correlates to a source's name, or the source's filename. Don't count on being able to do this. If you need to, you can delete a source and try the search again. If it's better, leave it out. If it's worse, put it back and delete another.

Adding Sources

When we composed the question about "behavior problems in gifted children," we first looked up some interesting source libraries in the "directory-of-servers." We then used the "Add Source" menu to add these to the source list for our "real" question. Now it's time to ask: how does a source get onto the "Add Source" menu?

In our example, we assumed that the **wais** client already knows about all the sources—at least, all that were interesting to you. This is normally a good assumption. However, you'll occasionally find sources that your **wais** client doesn't already know about. These sources may show up in the *directory-of-servers*, and therefore may appear in searches through the directory, but you won't find them on the "Add Source" menu. (It's also possible to discover sources that aren't even listed in the *directory-of-servers*; we'll describe that situation later.) Remember that the *directory-of-servers* is like the phone book's Yellow Pages; likewise, the "Add Source" menu is like a set of "speed dial" buttons. If you look up your favorite pizzeria in the Yellow Pages, you'll find it listed there; but you could just press the speed dial button on your phone (you probably programmed it last year). However, if you want to try a new pizzeria, you'll have to look it up in the yellow pages *and* program it into your phone.

To see why this analogy is relevant, think about what the *directory-of-servers* is. It's just another library (or database). The actual information isn't on your client—it's on some server in some remote part of the world (probably Cambridge, where Thinking Machines is located). You can make WAIS searches on that server, and dig up any information that it knows about. And, from time to time (fairly often, in fact) people create new WAIS libraries, tell the folks at Thinking Machines who maintain the *directory-of-servers*, and these new sources appear in there. Your client doesn't know anything about these new sources, any more than your phone automatically knows about every number in the Yellow Pages. How could it? You find a new library in the library of servers, and you'd like to use it; but your local client doesn't even know the name of the system on which to find it. This information is available, but it's all in Cambridge.* How do you tell your **wais** client about the new library?

This is called "saving," or "adding," a source. It's really quite easy. Most **wais** clients let you copy a source entry directly. Let's say your question to the *directory-of-servers* about "social work" accidentally turned up a strange source called *beer.src*, with a fairly low score. This probably isn't relevant, but you think it's interesting; it might contain recipes for home-brew, or something else you'd like. You ignored it when you were looking up articles about "behavior problems in gifted

---

*It's actually a credit to WAIS that this is so confusing. If we had to think in detail about what information was where, and who knew what, everything would be clear. After all, if someone told you "There's a great new FTP archive about gerontology," you'd know that you don't have enough information to use the archive; you'd immediately ask "where?" But WAIS really gives you the illusion that all the data is available locally. You still have to ask "where" (or get WAIS to ask "where") but it almost seems like you shouldn't have to.

children," but now you want to see if you can find a new recipe for lager. So you pop up a new question window, and start searching the "Add Source" menu. Surprise! *beer.src* doesn't show up. With our X client, all you have to do is go back to the menu where you searched the *directory-of-servers* for relevant libraries—i.e., the question in which you discovered this new library. Click on *beer.src*, and then "view" the library. You'll see a new window with a description of the library. This window will have a button labeled **Save**. If you click that button, your client will save the source automatically. You don't need to type anything.

Now you can go back to your new question. This time, when you search through the "Add Source" menu, you'll see *.beer.src*. Your client now "knows about" it; you've added it to the "speed dialing" library. Add it to your search list, just like any other source.

New Sources That Aren't in the Directory-of-Servers

Most of the time, you'll discover new sources through the *directory-of-servers*." However, on occasion you'll find one through other means. You might be prowling through a news group, and see a message like this:

```
I just created a new and most wonderful source:

(:source
      :version  3
      :ip-name "nic.sura.net"
      :tcp-port 210
      :database-name "/export/software/nic/wais/databases/ERIC-archive"
      :cost 0.00
      :cost-unit :free
      :maintainer "info@sura.net"
      :description "ERIC (Educational Resources Information Center) Digests

Information provided by EDUCOM

ERIC Digests are:

- short reports (1,000 - 1,500 words) on one or two pages, on topics
  of prime current interest in education.
- targeted specifically for teachers and administrators, and other
  practitioners, but generally useful to the broad educational community.
- designed to provide an overview of information on a given topic,
  plus references to items providing more detailed information.
- produced by the 16 subject-specialized ERIC Clearinghouses, and reviewed
  by experts and content specialists in the field.
- funded by the Office of Educational Research and Improvement (OERI),
  of the U.S. Department of Education (ED).

Created with WAIS Release 8 b4 on Apr 10 13:02:45 1992 by lidl@nic.sura.net
")
```

Most of this message (everything following the first line) is a standard WAIS descriptor for the source. To tell your client about this source, go to the "sources" section of the main menu. Click the **New** button. After you push that button, **xwais** will put up a blank template for you to fill in the information necessary to add a source.* If you were to fill in the template given for the "ERIC-archive" source shown in the previous example, it would look like Figure 12-8. Retyping the source by hand may be painful, but if you're using a window system, you should have a copy/paste mechanism to move large chunks of text automatically.

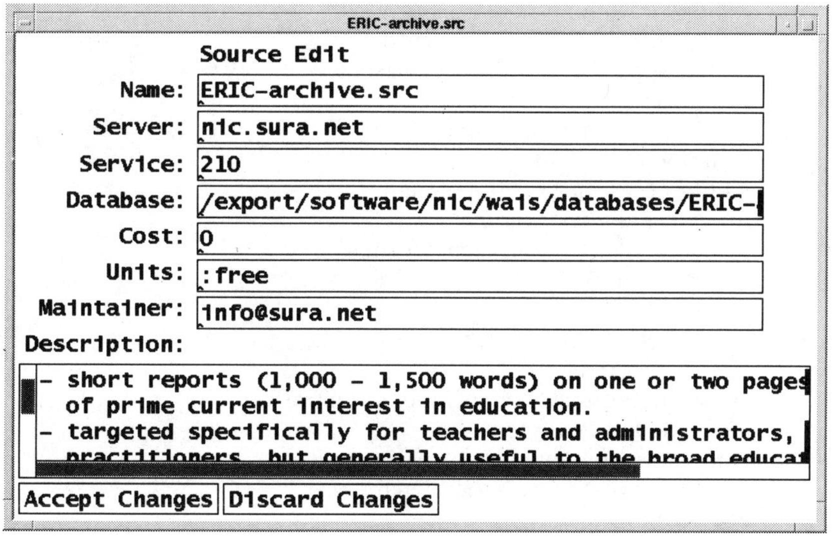

Figure 12-8: Source maintenance window

When you are done adding or changing an entry for a source, you can either save your changes, or throw them away by using the **Accept Changes** or **Discard Changes** button, at the bottom of the window.

Building Your Own Sources

Frequently, the same software servers that provide **wais** clients also provide programs and documentation that allow you to create your own sources and offer your own servers. One of these, **waisindex**, takes a set of files and builds an index from them. It knows about various forms of data: normal text, various text formatters (e.g., LaTeX), mail folder format, etc. These formats are shown in Table 12-1, waisindex Input Formats.

---

*Before copying the source descriptor by hand, though, it might save you some work to search the *directory-of-servers* to see whether or not it's been added "officially" to the list. Anyone who creates a new library is supposed to tell Thinking Machines. This doesn't always happen, but it's worth checking.

Table 12-1: Waisindex Input Formats

Name	Description
text	Simple text files
bibtex	BibTeX / LaTeX format
bio	Biology abstract format
cmapp	CM applications from Hypercard
dash	Entries separated by a row of dashes
dvi	dvi format
emacsinfo	GNU documentation system
first_line	First line of file is headline
gif	gif files, only indexes the filename
irg	Internet *Resource Catalog*
mail_digest	Standard internet mail digest format
mail_or_rmail	mail or rmail or both
medline	medline format
mh_bboard	MH bulletin board format
netnews	Net news format
nhyp	Hyper text format, Polytechnic of Central London
one_line	Each line is a document
para	Paragraphs separated by blank lines
pict	pict files, only indexes the filename
ps	Postscript format
refer	refer format
rn	Net news saved by the rn news reader
server	Server structures for the directory-of-servers
tiff	tiff files, only indexes the filename
ftp	tiff files, only indexes the filename

So if you want to build a WAIS index for the e-mail you receive, you can. It's really beyond the scope of this book to tell you how to do this. Many people find that once they learn WAIS, it is a valuable tool for searching many other things. If you'd like to experiment, look for **waisindex** via **archie**. It is also part of the distribution package for UNIX WAIS servers available by anonymous FTP to **think.com** in the directory *wais*.

CHAPTER THIRTEEN

HYPERTEXT SPANNING THE INTERNET: WWW

Getting Started
The Web and Gopher
Using WAIS Resources
Other Internet Resources
Navigating the Web
Where the Web Is Going

The World-Wide Web, or WWW, is the newest information service to arrive on the Internet. The Web is based on a technology called *hypertext*. Most of the development has taken place at CERN, the European Particle Physics Laboratory; but it would be a mistake to see the Web as a tool designed by and for physicists. While physicists may have paid for its initial development, it's one of the most flexible tools—probably the most flexible tool—for prowling around the Internet. Like Gopher and WAIS, the Web is very much under development, perhaps even more so. So don't be surprised if it doesn't occasionally work the way you'd like. It's certainly worth playing with.

To try the Web, **telnet** to **info.cern.ch**. This will automatically drop you into a public-access client program (or *browser*, to use the Web's terminology).* This is a "line-oriented" browser that will work with a traditional terminal. Several other browsers are available; if you decide to install your own (and that's highly recommended if you want to use the Web frequently), you can choose between the line-oriented browser, several browsers for the X Window System (the one called "Viola" or "ViolaWWW" is probably the most feature-rich), the NeXT UNIX workstations, the Macintosh, and PCs.†

---

*More precisely, a *browser* is any program for reading hypertext. Web clients are basically hypertext readers, so they're called browsers.

†One good software source is the anonymous FTP site **info.cern.ch**. Look in the directory *pub/WWW/bin*; you'll see directories for several different machines. In any of these directories, the file *www* is the line-oriented browser. *viola* and *erwise* are X-based browsers.

227

What Is Hypertext?

Hypertext is a method of presenting information where selected words in the text can be "expanded" at any time to provide other information about the word. That is, these words are *links* to other documents which may be text, files, pictures, anything. For the sake of illustration, let's assume that your library had a hypertext card catalog. If you pulled up the card for a particular book it might look like:

```
TITLE:    The river and the prairie : a history
          of the Quad-Cities, 1812-1960
AUTHOR:   Roba, William Henry.
PUBL.:    (Davenport, Iowa) : Hesperian Press,
DATE:     1986

SUBJECT:  Quad Cities (Iowa-Ill.)--History.
          Davenport (Iowa)--History.

FORMAT:   157 p. : ill., map ; 24 cm.
CONTENTS: Includes bibliographical references and notes.
```

If the italicized words were links, you could expand the author's name and get a biographical sketch. If you expanded "prairie," you might end up in a hypertext Oxford English Dictionary and see:

```
prairie ('pre&schwa.rI). Also 8, 9 parara, pararie, praira, 9 praire,
prairia.  a A tract of level or undulating grass-land, without trees,
and usually of great extent; applied chiefly to the grassy plains of
North America; a savannah, a steppe.
```

Since this is another hypertext document, there are links in it as well. You could plunge deeper by expanding "savannah," ending up in a hypertext encyclopedia positioned at a whole article on savannahs. You can repeat the process as long as you like, getting deeper and deeper into a topic.

Hypertext is a fairly new concept. There isn't a lot of true hypertext available on the Internet, yet. The big problem is a scarcity of tools to build the linked structure. Most of the hypertext documents available now were painstakingly built by hand. Hypertext editors are just being written: one is currently available for NeXT workstations, and the Viola package for X windows will get one soon. So, as time goes on you will begin to see more and more about hypertext.

In this chapter, we'll focus on the line-oriented browser—but you should be aware that the others are available. The others are prettier and fancier, and certainly worth using if you can; but the line-oriented browser is very usable.

Getting Started

What is WWW about? It's an attempt to organize all the information on the Internet, plus whatever local information you want, as a set of hypertext documents. You traverse the network by moving from one document to another via "links." For example, using the line-mode browser at CERN, you might see something like this:

```
CERN is the European Particle Physics Laboratory in Geneva, Switzerland.
Select by number information here, or elsewhere.

Help[1]                   About this program

World-Wide Web[2]         About the W3 global information initiative.

CERN information[3]       Information from and about this site

Particle Physics[4]       Other HEP sites with information servers

Other Subjects[5]         Catalogue of all online information by subject. Also:
                          by server type[6] .

1-7, Up, Quit, or Help:
```

This is CERN's current "home page." Your home page is the hypertext document you see when you first enter the Web. The bracketed numbers are links. To follow any link, just type the number, followed by a RETURN. On a graphic browser, the links would "highlight" words; to follow a link, just click on the word. For example, to see what other subjects are available, type **5** RETURN. Here's what you get:

```
                  INDEXES OF ACADEMIC INFORMATION

Information categorised by subject. See also by organization[1] ,
protocol[2] , and commercial[3] online data. Mail us if you know of online
information not in these lists....

Aeronautics              Mailing list archive index[4] .

Astronomy                A sample collection of astronomical images[5] , (Also
                         available in GIF[6] format);  Not yet browsable
                         directly using W3.

Bio Sciences             See separate list[7] .
 ...
```

Have you guessed? Typing **4** would get you to resources about Aeronautics. The Web is about the simplest of any Internet tool to use. For comparison, Figures 13-1 and 13-2 show the same two screens from the Viola browser.

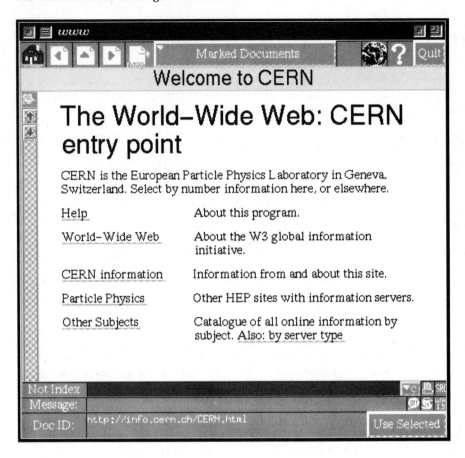

Figure 13-1: CERN home page, using Viola

After clicking on the phrase "other subjects," you'll see the same "Academic Information" menu.

By the way, this "index of academic information" is, in itself, a great service. It's a very useful way to see what kinds of resources are available at a glance.

Any of these hypertext pages can be changed, hopefully for the better, at any time. It's important to realize that the home page, the index of academic information, and everything else that's available is not "built-in" to your browser. They are just hypertext documents that can be modified at will. Some screens aren't even documents in the traditional sense (i.e., files that exist on some system's disk); they are generated "on the fly" by gateways between the Web and other services. Therefore, don't be surprised if you see text that doesn't match our sample screens. The Web is constantly changing; that's part of its beauty.

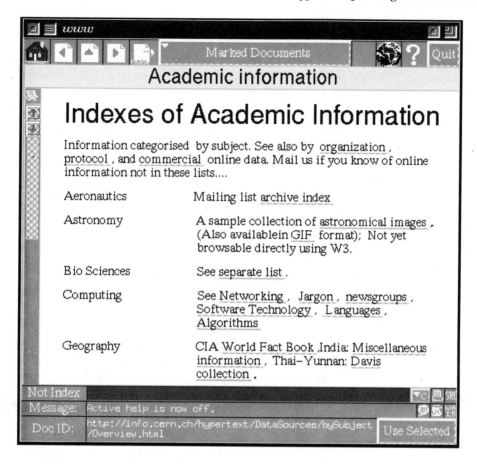

Figure 13-2: Academic information, using Viola

The Web and Gopher

You may be asking what's so great about this. After all, what we've done so far isn't all that different from what you can do with Gopher. The Web appears to have a subject-oriented flavor, which is an advantage, but at first glance, it doesn't seem fundamentally different.

That's really not true, though. While there are a lot of similarities, the Web and Gopher differ in several ways. First, the Web is based on hypertext documents, and is structured by links between pages of hypertext. There are no rules about which documents can point where—a link can point to anything that the creator finds interesting. So a text about chemistry might point to a periodic table entry for Lithium, which might in turn point to some other articles discussing the properties of Lithium, which might point to an FTP server containing spectral data for various Lithium compounds. A link can even point to a relevant sentence in the middle of an article; following the link will point you to the relevant point in the article.

The Gopher just isn't as flexible. Its presentation is based on individual resources and servers. When you're looking at an FTP resource, this may not make much of a difference; in either case, you'll see a list of files. But the Gopher doesn't know anything about what's inside of files; it doesn't have any concept of a "link" between something interesting on one server, and something related somewhere else.

Second, the Web does a much better job of providing a uniform interface to different kinds of services. Providing a uniform interface is also one of the Gopher's goals; but the hypertext model allows the Web to go much further. What does this mean in practice? For one thing, there are really only two Web commands: follow a link (which we've already demonstrated) and perform a search (which we'll discuss momentarily). No matter what kind of resource you're using, these two commands are all you need. With Gopher, the interface tends to change, according to the resource you're using.

Simple as the Web is, it's still flexible. For example, the Web allows you to read USENET news. If you read any news, you've probably noticed that each posting contains references to other messages. A client restructures news postings as hypertext, turning these cross-references into links: so you can easily move between original postings, follow-ups, and cross-references, just by selecting links. The Gopher doesn't have any way of organizing news articles; they're just "there."

Finally, the Web eliminates the barrier between your data and "public data." If you set up a WWW server and an appropriate hypertext editor, you can integrate your own personal notes into the Web. (Your notes, of course, remain private; but they can have links to public documents.) Ten years ago, a few dozen boxes full of index cards was *de rigeur* for anyone writing a dissertation or an academic book. With the Web, a few hypertext documents make that all obsolete. Rather than copying a quote and sticking it into an index box, you can just create a link from a "notes file" to the document you're quoting. Using WWW for your own editing is beyond the bounds of this book, but it's an important topic, and something that should become easier in the future. (Today, browsers are pretty much read-only tools; in the future, though, browsers and editors will be integrated.)

At this point, the World-Wide Web really hasn't been exploited fully, making it seem more like Gopher than it really is. The Web, being a hypertext system, requires hypertext documents, and there aren't a whole lot of them out there. You can look at a lot of "normal" resources (FTP archives, WAIS libraries, and so on), some of which have been massaged into Hypertext by a clever server; but you won't find a lot of "true hypertext" (meaning material that was written and intended as hypertext). Hypertext is used primarily as a way of organizing resources that already exist—there aren't that many true "hypertext resources."

To get a feel for what the hypertext world looks like, spend some time reading the WWW documentation. That's probably the easiest and most accessible source of true hypertext.* I highly recommend this exercise, even if you don't care about the documentation itself; it's a good way to see what's possible.

Using WAIS Resources

Many of the resources available through the World-Wide Web are WAIS resources. We've already seen what WAIS is, so perhaps the best approach would be to search for something concrete. Imagine that you're an economist and need some accurate data about France. There are several places to look. But, while scanning the index of academic information, your eye falls on the CIA World Fact Book:

```
Geography                  CIA  World Fact Book[14], India: Miscellaneous
                           information[15] , Thai-Yunnan:  Davis collection[16],
```

It certainly looks like you might find something useful there! So, after selecting item 14, you see the factbook's "cover page":

```
                           CIA

Connection Machine WAIS server.  Operated between 9AM and
9PM East coast time.  The 1990 World Factbook by the CIA which
contains a
good description of every country.  The entry for WORLD is also
particularly good.

Descriptions of 249 nations, dependent areas, and other entities with
information on population, economic condition, imports/exports, conflicts
and wars, and politics.  Produced annually by the
CIA.  Search 'World Factbook' for table of contents.

FIND <keywords>, 1, Back, Quit, or Help:
```

To search a database (in this case, a WAIS database), just type **find** followed by the keywords you want to search for.† You can use **f** as an abbreviation for **find**; you can even omit the command entirely, if your keywords don't overlap with any commands.

Here's the frustrating part. We type **find france**, and get a list of 40 documents: various obscure French territories, former colonies, countries with territorial disputes involving France, and so on. There are so many listings that WAIS hits its built-in limit (40 items) without finding what you want. Obviously, this is a WAIS problem, rather than a limitation of the Web. It's hard to construct an appropriately narrow question. Relevance feedback would really help here, but it's not yet possible to use that feature within the Web.‡

---

*Some other "true" hypertexts are available, but they are largely in specialized areas, like physics.

†On an X-based browser, you would see a keyword entry box at the bottom of the screen; on the NeXT, a WAIS search is represented by a pop-up menu.

‡But it is possible to create a link to "the result of a WAIS search": whenever you open the link, WWW performs the search, and shows you the documents that match. This feature is similar, though not quite identical, to the ability to save a WAIS query.

So we really need a better question. **find france economy** doesn't really help—virtually every article in the database will have something about the economy. An inspired guess: how many articles would refer both to France and to Paris? Let's see:

```
FIND <keywords>, 1-40, Back, <RETURN> for more, Quit, or Help: find france paris
                                                    france paris (in CIA)

                         FRANCE PARIS

Index CIA contains the following 40 items relevant to 'france paris'.

France  Geography Total area: 547,030 km2; land area: 545,630 km2; includes
                      Corsica[1]
                      Score: 1000, lines: 415

France  Geography Total area: 547,030 km2; land area: 545,630 km2; includes
                      Corsica[2]
                      Score: 1000, lines: 415


French Guiana (overseas department of France)[3]
                      Score: 1000, lines: 299


   ...
```

By constructing a somewhat contrived question, we've managed to get the article we wanted—the factbook's main entry about France—at the top of the list. Let's see what we've managed to dig up:

```
FIND <keywords>, 1-40, Back, Up, <RETURN> for more, or Help: 1
                                                        Document

0000073CIA
920120
CIA World Factbook 1991
France

Geography
Total area: 547,030 km2; land area: 545,630 km2; includes Corsica
and the rest of metropolitan France, but excludes the overseas
administrative divisions

Comparative area: slightly more than twice the size of Colorado

Land boundaries: 2,892.4 km total; Andorra 60 km, Belgium 620 km,
Germany 451 km, Italy 488 km, Luxembourg 73 km, Monaco 4.4 km,
Spain 623 km, Switzerland 573 km

Coastline: 3,427 km (includes Corsica, 644 km)
   ...
```

If you read through enough of this, you'll eventually find statistics about the French economy. You'll also find estimates of the number of Communists around, the size of the armed forces, and other statistics of understandable interest to the CIA.

I intentionally picked a slightly difficult problem so you could see how WAIS searches are refined. Ironically, looking for a "first world" country with a long history is likely to be more difficult than looking for an obscure third-world country: searches for obscure entities are, by nature, more tightly focused. Experience will help you with the inspired guesses; further development will improve the quality of the servers and clients.

Despite these kinds of problems, the World-Wide Web and WAIS really are a natural pair. With some improvements to the browsers (for example, incorporating relevance feedback) and perhaps some improvement to WAIS, WWW could easily become the ideal WAIS client.

The WAIS Directory of Servers

It's possible to search the WAIS directory of servers directly. You can either look up WAIS servers explicitly (there's an item for WAIS servers on many "home pages") or you can look for any WAIS resource. Once you've found a WAIS resource, you'll see (on its cover page) a link to the directory of servers. If you select this link, you'll see a description of the directory of servers; you can then search the servers for whatever topic interests you. In the example below, we search for WAIS libraries relevant to classical literature:

```
FIND <keywords>, 1, Back, Quit, or Help: find classical literature

              CLASSICAL LITERATURE

Index directory of servers contains the following 9 items relevant to
'classical literature'.

indian-classical-music.src[1]
                Score: 1000, lines:  30
bryn-mawr-clasical-review.src[2]
                Score:  400, lines: 107
bionic-algorithms.src[3]
                Score:  333, lines:  18
  ...
```

We're interested in looking up articles about Plato, so the Bryn Mawr Classical Review looks like what we want. Selecting item 2 gets us to strange nowhere-land:

```
FIND <keywords>, 1-9, Back, Up, <RETURN> for more, or Help: 2
The index cover page has been retrieved. Please see the index itself[1]
[End]
```

This is an intermediate step that will soon be eliminated. Logically, it's the same as copying a list of interesting WAIS libraries into your next WAIS query. For the time being, just select 1; this gets you to the review's cover page:

```
                     BMCR

The _Bryn Mawr Classical Review_ is a review journal of books in Greek and
Latin classics.
```

```
    In its new format the BMCR will distribute reviews as they become
    available:  that is, as soon as they have been submitted and gone through
    the minimal editorial massaging (inserting missing commas, removing
    libelous assertions) that we do.
    FIND <keywords>, 1, Back, Up, <RETURN> for more, Quit, or Help:
```

Now you can type **find plato**, and get a list of relevant articles. We're back in familiar territory.

Don't hesitate to use the directory of servers if the Web drops you into some strange place that you weren't expecting.

Other Internet Resources

At this point, we've really covered all you need to know: how to select a resource, and how to search an index. You can do anything—you can access virtually any resource on the Internet—with these two commands. (The same "find" command is used to search any kind of index, not just WAIS indexes). However, it still helps to know a little bit about what you're accessing. In the next few sections, we'll look briefly at how to work with specific kinds of resources using the World-Wide Web.

FTP Resources

As you'd expect, the World-Wide Web's interface to FTP resources is fairly simple. An FTP server is represented as a series of menus; each item in the menu is a link to either a directory or a file. When you select a directory, you see another menu. When you select a file, the browser displays the file's contents. For example, let's say you find your way to "Project Gutenberg"; it's on the "Academic Information" menu that CERN offers. After selecting Project Gutenberg, you'll see a menu like this:

```
                          FTP Directory of
     //mrcnext.cso.uiuc.edu/gutenberg                          /GUTENBERG

     Parent Directory[1]          LIST.COM[2]     ETEXT92[3]    etext92[4]
     AAINDEX.NEW[5]   etext91[6]  NEW.GUT[7]      freenet[8]    incoming[9]
     usonly[10]       articles[11]

          [End]
     1-11, Back, Up, Quit, or Help:
```

Selecting *etext92* lists the books that were published in 1992:

```
     FTP Directory of //mrcnext.cso.uiuc.edu/gutenberg/etext92
                      /GUTENBERG/ETEXT92

     Parent Directory[1]          t[2]            AAINDEX.NEW[3]  LIST.COM[4]
     aesopa10.txt[5] aesopa10.zip[6]  census00.txt[7] crowd10.txt[8]  crowd10.zip[9]
     duglas10.txt[10]             duglas10.zip[11]                opion10.txt[12]
```

```
opion10.zip[13] plrabn10.txt[14]              plrabn10.zip[15]
...
[End]
1-40, Back, Up, Quit, or Help: 1-40, Back, Up, Quit, or Help:
```

A rather messy directory listing! By selecting *aesopa10.txt*, you'll see Project Gutenberg's transcription of Aesop's Fables. You have to page through several screens of propaganda and legal notices (an artefact of the Gutenberg project, not the Web) before you get anything interesting. But with enough patience, you'll find it:*

```
The Cock and the Pearl

A cock was once strutting up and down the farmyard among the
hens when suddenly he espied something shining amid the straw.
...
```

The Web can also search for FTP resources via Archie. An Archie search is similar to a WAIS search—in fact, an Archie search *is* a WAIS search. The Archie database is converted regularly into a WAIS library, which you can search using the **find** command. The best way to get to an Archie server is to find the menu item that says "Catalogue of online information . . . by server type."

Beware: there's a catch. On an FTP server, most (if not all) files are compressed in one way or another: they're binary files. The Web doesn't, at this point, try to be "smart" and uncompress the files for you. So if you read the file, you'll dump a lot of garbage to your screen, possibly resetting it in some strange way. It's better to use the > command, which we'll discuss below, to save the file.

Telnet Resources

The Web also includes links to TELNET resources. These are handled pretty much in the same way as with Gopher: your browser will start a TELNET session, and you'll temporarily "drop out" from the browser while you work with the TELNET server.

For security reasons, you're not allowed to access TELNET resources from a public browser (like the one at **info.cern.ch**). If you try, you'll see a polite message like this:

```
Sorry, but the service you have selected is one
which you have to log in to.  If you were running WWW
on your own computer, you would be automatically connected.
For security reasons, this is not allowed when
you log in to this information service remotely.

You can manually connect to this service using telnet
to host tycho.usno.navy.mil, username ads.
```

Get your own browser and try again.

---

*A "search" capability will be added to Web browsers in the very near future.

USENET News

As we've said, you can use the Web to read USENET news. A client converts each posting into a hypertext, which allows you to move easily from posting to reply. It's easy to follow a "thread," and then wander back to the original message—in fact, easier than it is with most news readers.

You've already seen how to select items from hypertext menus, so we won't bother to review that. Reading news isn't different from anything else. It is worth mentioning some of the things you can't do, though. Web browsers are not full-fledged news readers. They don't keep track of which news postings you've seen or haven't seen, and they don't let you reply to news postings or create new postings. There's no reason why they can't and, in the future, they probably will. All that's needed is someone to write appropriate browser software.

White Pages

The Web also includes a number of "white pages" resources. By convention, hypertext articles prepared for the Web have the author's initials in the bottom left corner. These initials are a link to information about the author; just select this link, and you'll see the author's full name, phone number, and so on.

You can also access online telephone directories. To search these, you type **find** followed by the person's name. Notice that there's no apparent distinction between a white pages search and a WAIS search, or any other search operation: to the user, they're the same. A "yellow pages" is available, in addition to the "white pages": it is based on function and title rather than name.

Most home pages have a link to one (or more) telephone directories. Of course, the directories that are provided have a lot to do with the server you use; if you use the CERN server, you'll currently find a lot of information about physicists. More general services, like **whois**, aren't yet available, though I'd expect to see them in the not-too-distant future.

Navigating the Web

With the ASCII browser, you'll see a line like this at the bottom of every page of hypertext:

```
1-7, Back, Up, <RETURN> for more, Quit, or Help:
```

These lines summarize some of the commands that are available for moving from one document to another. They're the most useful. Most simply, typing a number selects a document; **Back** returns you to the previous document; **Up** moves to the previous page of the current document; **RETURN** takes you to the next page of the current document; **Quit** exits the Web; and **Help** shows you a help screen.

However, these simple commands aren't really enough; if you reach a dead-end, you may not want to type **back** 30 times before returning to some recognizable point. Therefore, there are number of navigational short-cuts:

Home   Moves you to the "home page," which is the page you saw upon entering the Web. If you use an "off the shelf" browser, it will probably be the introductory page from CERN.

Recall   The **recall** command is the equivalent of the **gopher** bookmark. It lets you return to any of the documents you have already visited. This is a much more convenient way of navigating than simply crawling back and forth. By itself, **recall** lists the documents you have already visited, together with a number:

```
Back, Up, Quit, or Help: recall

Documents you have visited:-

R  1)   in Welcome to CERN
R  2)   in User Guide for the WWW Line Mode Browser
R  3)   Commands -- /LineMode
R  4)   in Welcome to CERN
R  5)   in Academic information
R  6)   in Commercial data available through WWW-WAIS
R  7)   abstracts index
R  8)   in batch (in abstracts)
R  9)   Document
```

To return to any of these documents, give the command **recall**, followed by the document's number. In this example, **recall 7** will take you back to the "abstracts index." To save typing, you can abbreviate the command to **R 7**.

Next   Goes to the "next" article in a list of articles. Or, more precisely, follow the "next" link. Let's say that I'm looking at a hypertext article about shale. I see something interesting, so I follow some link to another article—say, the 7th. The **next** command takes me to the "next" link from my previous article (in this case, the 8th link from the original article about shale). This command comes in handy if you want to read the responses to a news posting message in order.

Previous   Goes to the "previous" article in a list of articles; similar to **next**.

Top   Moves to the beginning (first screenful) of the current document.

Bottom   Moves to the end (last screenful) of the current document.

               There's more to life than moving around; you may want to print a document, or save your own copy of it. So there are a few more commands:

Print   Prints the current document. (Your administrator may need to fiddle with things to make it work properly.) This command is only meaningful if you're running your own browser. Obviously, if you're using a public browser, like the one at CERN, printing a document somewhere in Switzerland isn't going to help much.

> *filename*   Saves the current document in the local file *filename*. Only available on UNIX systems. Again, it's only meaningful if you're running your own browser.

>> *filename*   Appends the current document to the local file *filename*. Only available on UNIX systems.

| *unix-command*

"Pipes" the document into the given UNIX command. For example, you might pipe a large document (like the cross-reference index to the CIA world fact-book) into a UNIX **grep** command to eliminate the entries you don't care about. Only available on UNIX systems.

Commands like **next**, **up**, and so on can be abbreviated; you only need to type enough letters to distinguish the commands from others. In most cases, the first letter is sufficient.

Creating Your Own Home Page

The home page provided by CERN is a good entry point into the Web; it points you to a lot of resources fairly quickly. However, there are lots of reasons to want your own home page. You may be a doctor with absolutely no interest in physics; you may therefore want a home page that takes you directly to subject headings for biology, medicine, and related topics. Or you may notice that you head straight for the "academic information" menu whenever you enter the Web. Why not make that your home page, instead of the default?

You can use any page of hypertext that's accessible to the Web as your home page. Let's say that you want to use the "academic information" menu for your home page. How do you do that? All you need to do is tell your browser where to find the home page. On UNIX systems, set the environment variable WWW_HOME to the file's "document address." A file address is an awkward mouthful, but it's not too terribly hard to work with. To find the address for "academic information," just start your browser;* work your way to the "Index of Academic Information"; and give the **help** command. You'll see something like this:

```
1-40, Back, <RETURN> for more, Quit, or Help: help

WWW LineMode Browser version 1.2a:     COMMANDS AVAILABLE

You are reading
  "Academic information"
```

---

*If you're just installing a browser and don't have any home page, you may get an error message. In this case, just **telnet** to **info.cern.ch** and use the public browser.

```
whose address is
   http://info.cern.ch/hypertext/DataSources/bySubject/Overview.html
...
```

The big long thing is the document address. So, to set your home page, give the command:

```
% setenv WWW_HOME \
http://info.cern.ch/hypertext/DataSources/bySubject/Overview.html
```

The next time you start your browser, your first page of hypertext will be the "Index of Academic Information."

By the way, here's one other good use for document addresses. If you want to tell your friends about an interesting server or service that you've just discovered, just send them the address of a reasonable home page through e-mail.

Where the Web Is Going

We'll close our discussion of the Web by talking a bit about where it is going. We'll discuss a few desirable (but still unimplemented) features, and a few features that exist already, but are still under-used.

Other Kinds of Documents

The current browsers focus mostly on textual documents. However, this isn't inherently a limitation: it's just that textual documents are easiest to deal with. Browsers and servers are being developed that can deal with other kinds of files: for example, postscript files, video, sound, word processor output, etc. In the future, you may be able to say, "When I select a postscript file, send it to the printer automatically; when I select digitized sound, decode it and send it to my stereo" and so on. The trick is figuring out what kind of data any file represents and then handling that data reasonably.

Making Your Own Links

If I'm reading an interesting article about shale, and it calls to mind something I read elsewhere, can I put in a link from the "shale" article to that other article? Or can I create a link from this document to some comments of my own? This would be an obvious help in organizing research. Unfortunately, you can't; at least, not yet. To put a link into a document, you need write access. So, while you can annotate any documents you own, you can't make annotations on documents that are already "out there." Private links are a desirable feature, so they may be implemented later.

Collaborating with Others

Potentially, the Web can become a way to structure your workplace. If you have a server and a hypertext editor, you can use the Web to write proposals, status reports, and so on; your colleagues can use the Web to insert their own comments or questions; and so on. It can be used for collaborative authorship: several people can jointly write a paper or presentation.

Hypertext Editors

At this time, hypertext editors, which are needed to take full advantage of the Web, are scarce. The WWW browser for the NeXT workstation incorporates a hypertext editor; the Viola browser will eventually add a hypertext editor. For the moment, if you don't have a NeXT, you're out of luck. If you poke around in the online help long enough, you'll find a description of HTML, the markup language. If you're really bold, you can create hypertext "by hand." But that's beyond the scope of this book. We expect that use of the Web will really explode once hypertext editors are available. For the moment, though, it's hobbled by the lack of editors.

In the future (i.e., after "simple" hypertext editors are available), special-purpose editors designed for collaborative work may be developed. This is clearly an exciting research topic; although there are some ideas, no one yet knows exactly what such an editor would be like.

How Can I help?

Obviously, software developers (particularly in the area of hypertext editors) are still needed. But there are many more mundane needs. Creating texts (even "plain" texts) and making them available via FTP servers is a help in its own right. People are also needed to maintain information in a particular subject area. The online documentation for the Web contains information about what kinds of help are needed, and who to contact.

In short, the Web is much more than a lookup service. It's really a way to structure information. It's one of the newest and most exciting developments on the Net. Check it out.

CHAPTER FOURTEEN

OTHER APPLICATIONS

The R Commands
X Windows
Disk and File Sharing
Time Services
Fax Over the Internet
Diversions
Robotic Librarians

We have covered all of the standard, system independent, and useful software that an average Internet user needs to make the network useful. There are many other Internet facilities that don't fit these categories. Some of them are useful, but system-specific (e.g., can only be used between UNIX systems). Some are useful to system administrators and software developers, but not to a "general purpose" user. And some are just plain useless. Notwithstanding these problems, no book on the Internet could be complete without introducing a few such applications.

This chapter is a brief introduction to the clutter of "miscellaneous" applications that you'll find. The facilities discussed are treated unevenly. Some facilities are really useful to normal network users, and are discussed in detail. Some of the other facilities may be useful, but require a third-order guru with "root" or "system" privileges to implement. In these cases, I've only given a brief, conceptual explanation—enough so that you'll know what exists, and what to ask for.

The R Commands

The "R" commands are a time-honored part of the BSD (Berkeley) UNIX system. These commands are networking versions of other standard commands. Most of them are based on common UNIX commands, like **cp**, which copies files. The command **rcp** is just the obvious network-based extension of **cp**: whereas **cp** copies files within one computer's filesystem, **rcp** copies files from one system to another via the network—similar to **ftp**. Likewise, the **rlogin** command is a network-based version of **login**—which makes it similar to **telnet**.

You're probably asking the obvious questions. Why would you ever need these UNIX-specific commands? What's wrong with **ftp** and **telnet**? Strictly speaking, you don't need the **R** commands; you can get by with the "standard" Internet utilities just fine. However, the **R** comands are more convenient if they are available. They have a simple command-line interface, and if set up appropriately, they eliminate the need to log in to the remote system. As we talked about in Chapter 4, *What's Allowed on the Internet*, this feature can also be a big security risk.

Because of their origins in BSD UNIX, the **R** commands aren't available on every system. You can only assume that they'll work if *both* computers (the local system and the remote system) are running some variant of BSD UNIX. The **R** commands are included with most (but not all) networking packages for System V UNIX. They are also included with some (but not most) networking packages for non-UNIX systems. As you might expect, details of the commands (and, in some cases, which commands are implemented) vary from one version to another.

Security and Validation

All of the **R** comands involve multiple computer systems: the system on which it is issued (the local system), and one or more remote systems, accessed through the network. I mentioned above that they can be a security problem because they can "short circuit" the normal login procedure. Security on the local system isn't a problem; if you're giving commands at all, you must have logged in first. The local system knows who you are, and what you're allowed to do. The security problem is on the remote system, which isn't normally in the habit of giving people access without prior screening. Security on the remote system is governed by two files, */etc/hosts.equiv* and *.rhosts*.

There may be one */etc/hosts.equiv* file for any computer. Keeping this file up-to-date is the system administrator's job. If your local computer's name is listed in the *hosts.equiv* file on some remote computer, then anyone on your local system can execute **R** commands on the remote system without having to give a password, provided that he has an account with a matching login name on the remote system. You'll be put into the remote system's account with the matching name. You'll be able to access any file that you could access when you're logged in directly. More colloquially, we say that the computers are "equivalent."

If this sounds confusing, an example will clarify things. **system1.usnd.edu** is a computer with two accounts, Ren and Stimpy. Another computer, **system2.usnd.edu** has two accounts with the same names. Its */etc/hosts.equiv* file contains the line:

```
system1.usnd.edu
```

In this case, Ren on **system1.usnd.edu** could use **R** commands to execute commands under the Ren account of **system2.usnd.edu** without having to give a password. The same is true for Stimpy: when he's logged into **system1**, he can use the Stimpy account on **system2** without providing a password.

However, the reverse isn't true. **System1** doesn't have a *hosts.equiv* file, so neither Ren nor Stimpy can execute **R** commands on **system1** from **system2**. These facilities need not be symmetrical—and, in practice, they rarely are. Note, too, that I haven't said that Ren and Stimpy can't use the **R** commands. I've only said that they won't have password-free access. If an **R** command doesn't give you password-free access, it will ask for the password when it is necessary.*

The file *.rhosts* offers similar functionality, but is maintained by any user for his or her own account. It allows the owner of an account to grant access to any other user without requiring a password. The account names no longer have to match. Let's say the owner of the account Ren created a file *.rhosts* in his home directory on **system1.usnd.edu**. This file contains the following line:

```
system2.usnd.edu Stimpy
```

With this line, Stimpy on **system2.usnd.edu** can access Ren's account on **system1** without a password. You may have as many entries in your *.rhosts* file as you like, one per line.

As we've said, this is a security hole. If someone breaches security on one computer, he can also bypass security and gain access to another computer as well. For this reason, */etc/hosts.equiv* is rarely used. *.rhosts* files are used regularly, but caution should be maintained. You should regularly examine your *.rhosts* file to make sure you want to continue granting access to the accounts listed. Also, be aware that anyone who breaks into your account can modify your *.rhosts* file to guarantee continued access to any accounts he has stolen.

Finally, you should be aware that some system administrators forbid users from creating *.rhosts* files, and may have "search and destroy" programs to delete them. I won't debate the wisdom of this policy. But I will suggest that, if such a policy is in effect, you obey it.

Remote Login

The **R** equivalent to the **telnet** command equivalent is called **rlogin**. Like **telnet**, it lets you start a terminal (login) session on a remote computer. The most common form of the command is simply:

```
% rlogin hostname
```

The **hostname** is the name of the computer you wish to contact—for example, **system2.usnd.edu**.† If you have password-free access, the next thing you'll see is a

---

*Unfortunately, because **rcp** doesn't know how to ask for a password, you can only use it when the remote system is configured to allow you password-free access.

†If the remote computer is in the same "domain" as yours—i.e., if everything after the "local" name matches—you should be able to abbreviate the full name to something like **system1** or **system2**.

prompt from the remote system, after it executes the user defined auto-log in procedures defined in the files *.cshrc* and *.login*. Here, Ren on **system1** logs onto **system2**:

```
system1% rlogin system2.usnd.edu
system2% whoami
Ren
```

You've bypassed the "login" step entirely. The **whoami** command tells you your login name (Ren), which should normally be the same login name that you had on **system1**. It's instructive to compare this to **telnet**: after the command **telnet system2.usnd.edu**, you'd still have to give a login name and a password. With **rlogin**, you don't have to worry about that: you're ready to start typing commands immediately.

What if you don't meet the criteria for password-free access? In this case, you'll see a "password" prompt:

```
system1% rlogin system2
Password:                               type the password here
Last login: Thu Jun  4 03:32:30 from MacEd
system2%
```

Notice: this time I didn't specify **usnd.edu** because it was the same on the local and remote systems.

If you want, you can log into a different account on the remote system. If Ren wanted to log into Stimpy's account, he would add the account name after the system name, using the **–l** option:

```
% rlogin system2 -l Stimpy
```

Again, whether or not **rlogin** will ask for a password depends on the *.rhosts* file in Stimpy's home directory on **system2**. If it had an entry like this:

```
system1.usnd.edu Ren
```

system2 would grant access to Stimpy's account without a password.

When you are done, you log out in the normal manner. After you log out, you return to the system where you issued the **rlogin** command.

One advantage of **rlogin** over **telnet** is that it automatically forwards your terminal environment to the remote computer. So, if you have an odd terminal like a Whizbang 23 with 132 columns and 60 rows and you've told the local system about it, when you **rlogin** to a remote system, the remote system will automatically know about your terminal.*

---

*Not quite true. The remote system will know what your terminal *is*—but it may not know how to handle it. An appropriate terminal description must exist on the remote system. It doesn't do the remote computer any good to know that you're sitting in front of a Whizbang 23 if it doesn't know what that terminal's properties are. Most UNIX systems come with a broad database of terminal descriptions, though, so you should be in good shape most of the time. The way UNIX terminal descriptions work is *way* beyond the bounds of this book; if you're curious, see the Nutshell handbook *Termcap and Terminfo*.

Escape Sequences

When we were discussing TELNET, we told you how to "escape" and return to **tel-net**'s command mode. This would let you run commands on your local system without terminating your session on the remote system. **rlogin** has the same kind of feature: you can temporarily suspend a session or terminate it abruptly by using a "tilde escape" sequence (a beast we met in the chapter on electronic mail). These are command sequences beginning with the character tilde (~), often pronounced "squiggle."

The tilde escape sequences are:

~CTRL-z   Suspend the remote login session. You'll instantly return to your local system. However, the remote session isn't terminated; you can return to the remote system by typing **fg**.*

~.   Abort the remote login session. This is similar to a **logout**, except more brutal. If possible, use the regular **logout** command; only use ~. if you're stuck.

The tilde must be the first character on the line—otherwise, **rlogin** will think you're typing normal text. If it doesn't hurt what you are doing, it's a good idea to type a RETURN before issuing one of these commands.

One warning: if you're new at this, it's easy to get excited and create a dozen or so **rlogin** sessions to the same host. You start one; suspend it; forget it's there; start another one; and so on. While this isn't particularly harmful, it's not good style. If you don't think about what you're doing, it's also easy to **rlogin** to some system; **rlogin** back to the first system; then **rlogin** to the second again; *ad infinitum*. This is also a bad practice, and wastes network resources, too: every character you type has to go back and forth between the two systems like a ping-pong ball. If you find yourself doing this often, you need to learn about **~CTRL-Z**.

Moving Files

As I said earlier, you can move files between systems using the **rcp** command. Access to remote filesystems is governed by the *.rhost* and */etc/host.equiv* files, just as with **rlogin**. The syntax of the **rcp** command is:

```
% rcp source-file destination-file
```

Source-file describes the file to be moved; *destination-file* tells **rcp** where to put the new copy. Both arguments have two kinds of information: the name of a file (or a

---

*Two notes. First: This requires a feature known as "job control," which isn't supported on many System V UNIX implementations. Second: by **CTRL-Z** we mean "the suspend character," which is almost always set to **CTRL-Z**. However, it can be set to other values—so beware.

directory) and the name of a computer. This requires a new syntax, in which the file specification has two distinct parts:

```
hostname:filename
```

If you just give a *filename*, **rcp** will assume that you mean a file on your local system. Neither the *source* nor the *destination* need be local—often, they're not. You can copy a file from your local system to a remote system, or from a remote system to a local system, or from one remote system to another remote system.

This can most easily be understood through a couple of examples. All of the following commands were issued from Ren's account on **system1.usnd.edu.**:

```
% rcp program  system2:program              #1
% rcp system2:thesis/data  data.old         #2
% rcp system2:data  ux1.cso.uiuc.edu:data.old #3
```

Example #1 copies the file *program* to a file with the same name on **system2**. The file is put in Ren's home directory. (This is the equivalent of an **ftp put** command.) Because you didn't specify the whole domain name for **system2**, it is assumed to be in the same domain as **system1**—i.e., the full name of the remote system is **system2.usnd.edu**.

Example #2 copies the file named *data* in the *thesis* directory on **system2** to the file *data.old* on **system1** in Ren's directory. In this case, the file is moving from the remote system to a local system.

Finally, in #3 you copy a file named *data* on **system2** to the file *data.old* on the computer **ux1.cso.uiuc.edu**. The copy does not need to involve files on the system issuing the commands.

When you use **rcp**, you can copy any files that you have "read" access on the remote system. This is determined by the account you're using on the remote system—which is the account of the same name on your local computer.* So, in example #2, **system2** must allow Ren to read the file *thesis/data*; otherwise, the **rcp** command will fail.

This limitation (to a single remote account) sounds like a real pain. In real life, it's not as bad as it sounds—that's all you can do on the local computer, anyway. If the file permissions are set up carefully (which may require some cooperation from several different system administrators), you should be able to access what you need. It's obviously helpful to have the same login name on every system you use. It's also a good idea to have groups structured reasonably.† For example, if Ren and

---

*Similar, though somewhat more complicated rules, determine whether or not you're allowed to copy the file to the destination. In any case, though, there's nothing especially "network-ish" to this. If the destination computer would allow you to copy the file with **cp**, you should be able to copy it with **rcp**.

†UNIX has three sets of file permissions. One set determines what the owner of the file can do to it (read, write, or execute it). Another set determines what the public can do to it (world permission). Finally, there's something known as "group permission." The idea is that if you are part of a project team, you might give all members of the team access to a file, but not the general public.

Stimpy tend to work on the same files, they should be put into the same group; that will make it easier for them to move files back and forth. (If you don't understand UNIX groups, look at any book on System Administration. The Nutshell Handbook, *Essential System Administration*, is a good choice.)

So far, we've only shown **rcp** with "relative" pathnames which (implicitly) start at your home directory on the remote machine. There's no reason you can't use an "absolute" pathname, as in the following command:

```
system1% rcp prog system2:/staff/Stimpy/prog
```

This command will work correctly if you're allowed to write the file *prog* in the directory */staff/Stimpy*.

The most interesting feature of **rcp** is its ability to copy a directory, including all the files contained in it. You do this by adding the **–r** switch to the command. In the following example, you can see that there is a directory on **system1** named *resources* containing quite a number of files:

```
% ls resources                              check files locally
README          foo.ms          prompt          text
data            geography.us    split.output
data.add        macros          splitter
% rcp -r resources system2:book/resources   copy the directory
% rlogin system2                            login to system2
Last login: Tue Jun  9 05:35:15 from uxh

% ls book/resources                         Yes! there they are
README          foo.ms          prompt          text
data            geography.us    split.output
data.add        macros          splitter
```

This directory is copied to **system2** with the single **rcp** command. If there are any subdirectories within *resources*, they'll be copied, too.

Distributing Files

Copying files from here to there is nice as far as it goes, but there are times when it would be nice if it were more automated. A common problem that falls into this category is maintaining a set of files on various computers. This problem doesn't ring a bell for you, huh? Well, consider Archie again. How do all the Archie servers in the world get copies of all the information they provide? They could all go out and gather it themselves, but that would be wasteful of the Archie servers, the FTP servers, and the network. It would be better for one server to gather the information and give the necessary files to all the other servers periodically.* So, once a week you need to pass five or six files to ten or twelve computers. It sounds like a boring

---

*This is not how the Archie system really works. It certainly could. I am only using it as an example to illustrate the problem.

job, doesn't it? The sort of thing you're likely to forget if you're the slightest bit busy? That's why **rdist** was created.*

rdist is a sophisticated (and complicated) program. If the *.rhosts* file on each computer is set up correctly, **rdist** allows you to move groups of files to any number of computers on the network. The movement is controlled by a command file. From the command file, you can direct it to rename files as they are moved, conditionally move files based on modification dates, and notify people of the updating. I'm not going to show you how to use **rdist** in all its glory. Most people will never need it. I'm only going to give a quick and fairly simple example that should be sufficient for most problems you will ever face. If you need more, check the **rdist** documentation.

For an **rdist** example, let's think about designing a simple "Archie." Let's assume that data is gathered in two files, *archie.dat* and *whatis.dat*, on the computer **archie.mcgill.ca**. Once a week, you need to give these files to the secondary systems **archie.unl.edu** and **archie.sura.net**. Implementing this with **rdist** is very simple:

- First, you need to make sure the *.rhosts* files on the destination computers allow the access. So use **telnet** or **rlogin** to access these hosts, and make sure that they're set up correctly.

- You need to create an **rdist** control file, which we'll call *moveit*. The control file basically tells you what files you want to distribute, and where you want to distribute them. Here's the listing; everything after a pound sign (#) is a comment:

```
(whatis.dat archie.dat) ->              # files to move
        (archie.unl.edu archie.sura.net) # destination hosts
        notify archiemgr;               # send email to archiemgr
```

Notice the "notify" statement. It directs **rdist** to send a message to the account "archiemgr" whenever **rdist** updates the files. Since there is no hostname appended to the login name, **rdist** sends the message to "archiemgr" on each of the computers it touches.

- Now that you've set up the control file, you just need to give the **rdist** command whenever you want to transfer the files:

```
% rdist -f moveit
updating host archie.unl.edu
updating: whatis.dat
updating: archie.dat
notify @archie.unl.edu ( archiemgr )
updating host archie.sura.net
updating: whatis.dat
updating: archie.dat
notify @archie.sura.net ( archiemgr )
```

---

*By the way, **rdist** is one of the few **R** commands that doesn't have a "non-network" analogy. There's no such thing as *dist*—it really isn't needed.

- In real life, typing **rdist** every week is almost as bad a burden as distributing the files by hand. So you'd probably run **rdist** through the UNIX **cron** facility. It allows you to schedule a program to run at a given time or regular intervals (like every Sunday at 3 A.M.). We won't discuss **cron** here—it has nothing to do with networking. See the documentation, or any book on system administration, for more information.

X *Windows*

The X Window System is not a network application in itself. It is a special way of delivering network applications. It is an industry-standard way of displaying graphical information and reading information from graphics and keyboard devices.

To understand what the X Window System does, you need to understand the problem it solves. One long standing problem with computer graphics is that every graphic display is different. To drive a Tektronix graphics terminal, for example, you need completely different commands than to drive a Hewlett-Packard display. A third graphics display would be different again.* So, if you bought some fancy program to display car crash simulations, you might have to buy a special graphics display to run it; this would probably be a different display from the one you used to do stress analysis; and so on. Each program might only know about a few of the many output devices available.

MIT did some thinking about this problem and suggested the following approach. What if:

- we designed, not as hardware but as a set of software facilities, a mythical graphics device with all the bells and whistles you might want.

- programs wrote software to drive this mythical device, not particular hardware.

- software was written for each workstation to translate mythical terminal commands into actual commands to drive their particular display.

Then, any software that could drive the mythical terminal could be used on any computer that simulated the mythical terminal. The mythical terminal was dubbed an X-terminal.

It turns out that describing, programming, and setting up a computer for the X windows environment, as the system is called, is not easy. But, lucky for you, using it is a snap. Each application you use under X has the same look, feel, and features. So once you learn the X Window System, you can easily figure out how to use any application that runs under it. You have a standard set of buttons and menus available to you, regardless of what you are doing.

---

*The same actually is true of normal terminals, like a VT100. However, normal terminals are "more or less" the same; they differ mostly in their advanced features. Certainly all character-based terminals take the same approach: you send them characters, they display them on the screen. With graphics terminals, there's really no common ground. Each manufacturer's terminal is completely different from everyone else's. As a result, software to support all the different types would be unmaintainable.

To use X, you need a suitable display, mouse, and software for your workstation. All the necessary pieces are available to make most any computer work in the X environment. As I said before, you may need some help getting all set up to use X,* but once you start you should feel comfortable pretty quickly. Most of the time, you would use the same commands you always did, except that some of them are preceded with an "x," like **xgopher** or **xwais**.

If the X applications are running directly on the computer driving your X-display then things work just fine. If, however, you are using the applications on a remote system through TELNET you may run into some difficulty. The X application needs to know the IP address and some other information about the display you want it to use. With UNIX, this is normally conveyed to the application through the environment variable DISPLAY, which is set by the X system software on your home system when you begin your X session. The problem is that some TELNETs don't pass this variable to the remote system when you log in there.† All you need to do to get around this problem is to set the variable appropriately on the computer running the application.

For example, assume you normally use **ux1.cso.uiuc.edu** for all your computing with X. You decide to try **xwais**, but find it doesn't have the client installed. So you **telnet** to **wais.uiuc.edu**. When you fire up **xwais**, you get the message:

```
Error: Can't Open Display
```

To solve this problem, you only need to set your DISPLAY variable. The problem is: what to set it to? The easy way to find out is to print it on your original system before you do the **telnet**:

```
% printenv DISPLAY
ibmxtrm1.cso.uiuc.edu:0.0
% telnet wais.uiuc.edu
```

Once TELNET has established a connection and you've logged in to the remote system, you need to give another **setenv** command to set DISPLAY properly. Just set it to the same value you got above:

```
% setenv DISPLAY ibmxtrm1.cso.uiuc.edu:0.0
```

Disk and File Sharing

Up to this point we have always talked about copying a file from a remote system in order to use it—or putting that file back onto the remote system to make it available to someone else. But it's possible to do better. The next logical step would be to use the file where it is. That is, why can't you just use the network to make a disk somewhere on the network appear to be part of your computer's hardware? Then

---

*O'Reilly publishes the definitive set of X manuals, should you really get into it.

†Since TELNET predates the X system, the ability to do this was added as a standardized extension. Not all vendors have embraced this standard.

you could access it just like any other disk, without having to know special commands. You might not even know, or care, where the file was physically located. If it's on your local system, that's fine; if not, it still "looks like" it's on the local system.

As you might expect, there are a few ways of doing this. Just like e-mail, there are two basic approaches: those that grew up in the Internet community, and those that grew up in the LAN/microcomputer community. The basic functionality of these approaches is identical. Depending on what type of computer you're using, your computer sees a disk file structure like */remote/*... (UNIX), a D: disk (DOS), or an icon (Macintosh) for another disk. The differences lie in the software required.

The Internet approach is the network filesystem, *NFS*. It was championed by Sun Microsystems and is a UNIX-oriented approach. If you're using a UNIX workstation, you probably have the necessary software already. For most other systems, NFS implementations are available for an extra cost. It requires careful cooperation between the managers of all the systems sharing disks. As a result, NFS can be hard to set up when the systems can't be tailored easily to fit the NFS environment. The biggest advantage of NFS is that it was based on the Internet protocols from the beginning. As a result, you can use it to access disks anywhere that the Internet reaches (provided, of course, that the necessary arrangements have been made in advance). The drawback is that performance could be very slow: it's limited by the rate at which you can move data across the Net.*

Approaches that have grown out of the LAN/microcomputer community are based on so-called "LAN Operating Systems" like Novell Netware or Microsoft LAN-manager. These products were designed for file sharing within a local area network. The competitive pressures of the marketplace made the manufacturers design for access speed. The speed issue forced them to use proprietary network protocols optimized for a particular hardware and software platform. They were not designed for generality: they were stripped bare to work fast. Since LAN operating systems were designed for the small business market, they did not consider UNIX worthy of support. And they didn't use the Internet's TCP/IP protocols, so they were inherently limited to a local network.

Over time, these two camps have grown together. Some third-party vendors now provide NFS support for non-UNIX computers, and gateways to support NFS in other environments, like Appletalk. Coming from the other direction, many LAN operating system suppliers now allow their products to use TCP/IP, hence the Internet, as a transport medium. Some have also begun to offer NFS support.

In either case, it is nice to know these facilities exist as a tool to solve certain problems. However, before you can use any of these facilities, some system administrator will have to make the necessary arrangements. So, if you think you need these

---

*A newer alternative to NFS—namely the "Andrew Filesystem," also called AFS and sometimes called DFS—will solve some of these problems. AFS has been in use in some research environments for a while, but solid commercial products are just coming to market.

facilities, give your local administrator a call. It is beyond the scope of this book to tell you which approach is best and how to install it.

Time Services

Computers have had built-in clocks since the early days of computing. They were used for a variety of reasons, but mainly to help figure out what happened when something went wrong: did event A happen before event B, or after it? What if you start two jobs: one to create a file and one to use it, in that order. The second job fails because the file was not found. To see what happened, you check the log to see whether the second job ran faster than the first, and tried to use the file before it was created.

Before networking, time synchronization didn't matter much. Whenever you needed to compare two times, the times that you were comparing were all taken from the same clock. It didn't really matter if that clock was inaccurate; it would still tell you that event A took place before event B. With the advent of network, the same problems existed, but you started to compare events that happened on different computers. Each computer's clock was set by a half-asleep myopic operator, who typed in the time from the wall clock when the system booted. Needless to say, there was a lot of error entering this data. So, the times on various computers never really were the same. Did event A really occur before B? You never really knew, particularly if the times were close.

In order to get around this problem, a program called **timed** was developed for UNIX. **timed** just runs in the background and watches clocks. It contacts other **timed** programs running on other computers on the same local network, and compares their clocks. Each computer adjusts its clock slowly until the whole network reaches some average network time. From then on, **timed** continues monitoring to make sure the clocks stay synchronized, making slight modifications if needed.

This was good as far as it went. The next problem was: how do you synchronize clocks on computers that are widely separated? How do you keep a computer in California synchronized with a computer in Massachusetts? This problem is much harder: you have to account for the time the synchronizing messages take to reach their destination, including (if you really need accuracy) the time it takes for an electrical signal to travel down a wire at the speed of light. To handle this case, a more advanced service was developed: the network time protocol, or NTP. NTP uses time servers at various points on the Internet. These time servers listen to time synchronization broadcasts from the U.S. Naval Observatory, and make them available to computers that need them.* This is a really hard problem, considering that the network distributing the information has variable delays. So a lot of fancy computations are done to derive some statistically reasonable time to the requesting computer.

---

*You can set your personal clock to this time source, too. See Standards—Automated Data Server of the U.S. Naval Observatory in the *Resource Catalog*.

These are really neat things, but in reality, using them may be beyond your control. In order to set up either **timed** or NTP, you need to be a system administrator. For NTP, you also need to find a willing time server. (It's possible to buy the necessary hardware and software to become your own time server, but this costs tens of thousands of dollars.) However, if you're likely to need such services, you should know that they exist.

Fax Over the Internet

These days everyone seems to have access to a FAX machine. To use one, you need a communications medium. Since the Internet is a communications medium, you would assume the technologies should merge: it should be easy to send FAX transmissions over the Internet. Well, the technologies are indeed merging, but certainly not as smoothly nor as quickly as you would anticipate. The reason for this is, I think, primarily a "not invented here" phenomenon. The people who developed FAX are making money hand over fist because it works fine over phone lines. They aren't primarily computer networking people, and they're perfectly happy sending FAX transmissions over the phone. On the other hand, computer people have viewed FAX as a lesser service because the documents are not machine readable, merely machine transferable and displayable. That is, you can't fax a document to a computer and then edit it with a text editor. What's there is not text, but a picture of the page. It's only us guys who might find the facility useful who are tugging at the coat tails of the manufacturers saying, "pardon me, but can you make FAX work over the Internet?"

As I said, the technologies have merged to a limited extent. You can take a file (either a text file, or a file in any number of standard display formats) and send it via a modem to a FAX machine. Likewise, you can receive a FAX and have it placed in a file, where you can examine it with a display program. All the software you need is available commercially. If you poke around, you should be able to find the necessary software on the Net for free. (Try **transit.ai.mit.edu** in *pub/systems/fax-3.2.1.tar.Z.*)

The ability to send FAXes over the Internet means that you can transfer the "fax" file by whatever means to another system across the Internet and then view or re-fax it via a local phone call, thus saving long distance charges. A working group of the IETF, the technical advisory body for the Internet, is studying the problem and intends to define a standard for Internet FAX transmission. Unless you send lots of FAXes, you can probably wait for this to be completed. The trouble you would have to go to make this work now probably isn't worth the effort. Well, libraries send lots of FAXes. Many journals are transferred from library to library via FAXes.* To save on long distance charges, the Big 10 Universities decided it was worth it and funded Ohio State University to build network FAX machines for each of their libraries. This system is being deployed. It may lead to more faxing over the Internet in the future, but it isn't yet clear where this service is headed.

---

*Libraries that do this have made special arrangements with the publishers for paying copyright fees.

Diversions

Many ways to waste time, both yours and the network's, are available on the Internet. Some people read recreational news groups. Others talk to other people or play games. There is fairly wide disagreement by system administrators about the validity of these uses. For this reason, I don't want to encourage you. But if I didn't tell you about them, you'd find out they exist on your own.

Conversations with Others

Several facilities allow you to "connect" to someone at some other Internet site and type messages back and forth. These facilities are generically called **talk** (for two-way conversations) or **chat** (for group discussions). Of course, communications are what you make of them. **talk**s and **chat**s can be business oriented, helping you win the Nobel prize. Or someone may be giving you grief because your team lost the big playoff game. They can be used either way, so it is hard to condemn or restrict their use.

Talking

The UNIX **talk** program is probably the most common application used for direct communication with others. To use **talk**, two people must agree to communicate with each other. The process starts when one person calls the other, using **talk** to set up the communications link. Let's say that Stimpy on **cat.nick.org** wants to talk to Ren on **chihuahua.edu**. He starts by issuing the command:

```
% talk Ren@chihuahua.edu
```

If Ren is logged in, a message like this will appear on his screen:

```
Message from Talk_Daemon@chihuahua.edu at 13:15 ...
talk: connection requested by Stimpy@cat.nick.org.
talk: respond with:  talk Stimpy@cat.nick.org
```

Just in case Ren doesn't notice, the terminal's "bell" will beep a few times. If Ren wants to talk back, he must issue the command **talk Stimpy@cat.nick.org**. When he does this, a connection is made and the screen clears. The screen is then divided vertically into two halves. Anything Stimpy types to Ren is displayed on the top half of his screen, and the bottom half of Ren's screen, and vice versa. In this example, Stimpy's screen would look like this:

```
[Connection established]
Joy, Joy, Joy




------------------------------------------------------------
What is it, man!
```

Stimpy typed everything that appears above the line; Ren's replies appear below the line. It's a little hard to describe how this works, but you'll get use to it fairly quickly once you try.

talk displays everything you type one key at a time, as you type it in. You can't edit something before you send it off, as you can with mail. **talk** doesn't even wait until you finish typing the line. So if you are a bad typist, the other person can see how slow you type, and every mistake you backspace over. This can be dangerous. Ill-advised comments still appear for an instant, even though they are erased. So, if you type "get off my case" while you're talking to the big boss, you're in trouble. Even if you change your mind and backspace over it, you've already dug your grave. It was displayed long enough for her to read it.

talk pages (the message and the bell) can be irritating: for example, you may not want one appearing suddenly on your screen when you're proofreading the final copy of a report. This is easily prevented. The command:

```
% mesg n
```

disables incoming **talk** conversations; you can still call other people, and they can connect to a call you make. The only thing that is affected is your ability to receive **talk** messages initiated by someone else. This remains in effect until you logoff or give the command:

```
% mesg y
```

If you are not participating, the requesting person will get the message:

```
[Your party is refusing messages]
```

Some programs, like text formatters, may put your session into **mesg n** mode for you. They do this so their output won't be messed up by random **talk** messages. When they finish, they return you to the state you were in before you invoked them.

There is no way for a caller to know if your refusal is temporary or permanent. If you try to contact someone and see that he's refusing messages, you can only try again later, send electronic mail, or make a phone call.

NOTE

Some **talk** programs are incompatible. If you have trouble communicating with someone using **talk**, you might try looking for another version called **ntalk**. The problem is that older versions tend to send characters out in a manner that is specific to a particular vendors hardware.

Chat

chats are generalizations of **talk** where multiple people converse at once. You can think of this as an electronic cocktail party without drinks. Groups gather to **chat** about various subjects. You can feel free to wander from group to group and take part as you like. Sometimes you might feel the need for a private conversation with someone in the discussion—i.e., drop out of the "chat" and revert temporarily to a two-person "talk." All this is possible within the framework of **chat** facilities.

Some **chat** facilities are quite open, allowing discussions about any topic (or no topic) at all. Most Freenets include **chat** facilities where users gather to discuss the local weather and whether the Peoria Rivermen will win their big game. Other topics (whatever is on anyone's mind) might be discussed in separate groups at the same time. At the other extreme, some **chat** facilities are "directed": they're restricted to a particular topic. One such facility is the discussion group in the SpaceMet resource, where people can gather to talk about space exploration. They are not so much restricted by "law" as they are by audience. If you go to SpaceMet to try and talk hockey, you will feel as lonely as a social scientist at a computer science faculty cocktail party.

One of the most popular general **chat** facilities is the Internet Relay Chat or *IRC*. It consists of a number of channels; each channel has a particular topic. A person can be talking and listening on multiple channels at once, either to the whole channel or to a single person. Here is a small piece of the "Sherwood" channel (I have no idea why it is called that), just so you can see what it looks like:

```
*** krol!krol@ux1.cso.uiuc.edu has joined channel #Sherwood
*** Topic: Welcome to the mystical forest of Sherwood!
*** = #sherwood : krol Lucky @dicky Sunshine
<Lucky!frittes@ux3.hoople.usnd.edu/#sherwood> I am dusting the keyboard..yeah,
<dicky!tannenbaum@lab.gov/#sherwood> hello krol
<Lucky!frittes@ux3.hoople.usnd.edu/#sherwood> Hi krol
<Lucky!frittes@ux3.hoople.usnd.edu/#sherwood> *sigh*
>#Sherwood> hi all - just seeing whats happening in sherwood
*** APerson!daemon@general.MiamiOfIndiana.edu has joined channel #sherwood
<APerson!daemon@general.MiamiOfIndiana.edu/#sherwood> I know, 10 minutes to
+my final final.
<Lucky!frittes@ux3.hoople.usnd.edu/#sherwood> what school. pm?
<APerson!daemon@general.MiamiOfIndiana.edu/#sherwood> William and Mary.
<Lucky!frittes@ux3.hoople.usnd.edu/#sherwood> oh.
<Lucky!frittes@ux3.hoople.usnd.edu/#sherwood> Good luck, what's it in?
<Sunshine!KAM@student.WatsamattaU.edu/#sherwood> pretty school
```

The top three lines are headers sent to me when I joined the group. I was announced to everyone on it, given the topic, and told who else was there (all in nicknames). After that come a stream of messages in the order they are received. Messages from each group I have joined are interspersed, so the screen can get rather confusing. To help me sort it out, each message has the channel named, (e.g., #sherwood). That's about all there is to say. There used to be public IRC computers you could **telnet** to, but most of these have been removed from service. You'll have to find your own client program. If you think this is for you, look for a program called **irc** on a computer you can use, or look at the news group *alt.irc* to see how to become active. Sources for client software and the locations of **chat** servers are regularly posted to this group.

There are no standards for how **chat**s should work, so everyone is different. Fortunately, the software is pretty user-friendly, and online help is usually available. So, if you are interested, feel free to try one out.

Multi-person Games

Computer games have been around for a long time. However, the past few years have spawned a number of person-to-person games played via the computer. These range from traditional games, like Chess and Go,* to real-time simulation games, to multi-user dungeon (MUD) games. The traditional games are not really a problem on the network, since they consume few resources. The others, however, have the ability to consume both computers and networks.

In real-time simulation games, each player is the commander of something (like the starship Enterprise or an F16 fighter). The players all take part in a simulated battle, complete with cockpit displays and visual effects. These games were really designed to be played over LANs because of their high-speed communication requirements. They require more speed than most inter-campus Internet connections provide. As a result, if you play these games over the Internet, two things will happen:

- You will get other network users (and maybe some administrators) mad at you, because you're dragging the network's performance down.
- You will lose. You are at a competitive disadvantage, because the speed with which you can react to threats is limited by your link to the Internet's speed.

Multi-user dungeons are less hoggish, but still considered a waste. In these games, patterned after Dungeons and Dragons, you meet other dungeon explorers and wander through a simulated dungeon. While wandering, you might meet other groups, monsters to fight, and treasures to find. As you do these things, you gain experience and get more powerful.

Again, play if you must, but be discreet and considerate. There is no inalienable right to play games on the Internet.

Robotic Librarians

We've talked about Knowbots in Chapter 10, *Finding Someone*, as a white pages server. This is only a minor use of the Knowbot concept. The model for Knowbots is a reference librarian. You don't go into a library and ask, "I need to know this. Could you look it up in that book?" If you knew where to look it up, you could do it yourself. (Beside, this is what WAIS does.) You ask only, "I need to know this." The reference librarian is trained to know how to find it. Robotify this model and you have a Knowbot.

Knowbots are generally thought of as software worms that crawl from source to source looking for answers to your question. As a Knowbot looks, it may discover more sources. If it does, it checks the new sources, too. When it has exhausted all sources, it comes crawling home with whatever it found.

---

*Check out Recreation—Games in the *Resource Catalog.*

Clearly, this is a very futuristic view of the information retrieval problem. It is probably an idea whose time has not quite come. There are pilot projects and research in the area, but the fields of networking, computing, and information science are not quite ready to support them. Perhaps they will by the fourth edition of this book.

CHAPTER FIFTEEN

DEALING WITH PROBLEMS

The Ground Rules
Gather Baseline Information
The Battleplan
Talking to Operations Personnel
Dealing with Coaxial Ethernets
Token Ring Notes

The network is not infallible. You will eventually walk up to your workstation and type:

```
% telnet ux1.cso.uiuc.edu
Trying 128.174.5.59...
```

You wait and wait until finally after a few minutes it prints:

```
telnet: Unable to connect to remote host: Connection timed out
```

Now what?

You don't have to be an ace network technician to deal with this situation, but you do need some guidance about managing in the face of adversity. First, we'll talk about what usually breaks, then what you need to know to attack a problem. After that, I'll give you a reasonable approach to deal with common network problems. It's not an exhaustive guide. I could easily construct scenarios that would lead you astray with this approach, but they would not be common in real life. Finally, I'll give you some hints about how to deal with some common LANs.

If you are easily offended, you may be upset by some of the suggestions in this chapter. Don't be. When the pressure is on, people lose common sense. If you read this chapter when there is nothing wrong (and you should) you might think "I'm not stupid. Of course I'd check the power cord." I don't think you are dumb. When you are in the swamp up over your knees, it's very easy to forget the most common-sense trouble spots.*

The Ground Rules

When you're thinking about what's wrong with the network, there are two rules to keep in mind:

1. The cheaper the component, the more likely it will fail and the less likely it will be noticed by someone who is able to fix it.

2. You need to know what's right before you can figure out what's wrong.

What do these rules mean? The Internet is frequently described as an amorphous cloud, as in Figure 15-1.

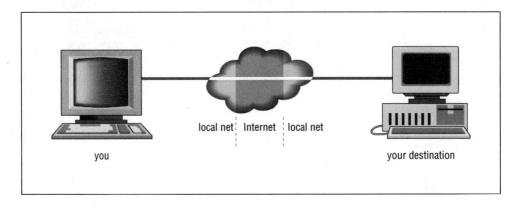

Figure 15-1: The Internet cloud

Think about this cloud in the context of rule #1. As you move away from your workstation, you know less and less about what happens to your packets; you enter the cloud. As you get closer to the cloud, components get more expensive. Inside the cloud are a bunch of expensive computers and telephone lines. If one of them fails a lot of people could be affected: a campus or even an entire country could be disconnected. So the cloud is monitored continuously and built as redundantly as possible. If something goes wrong, technicians notice and take corrective action immediately.

On the other extreme, you are probably sitting at a $5000 workstation talking to a network over a $150 Ethernet interface connected to a $5 piece of cable running across the floor. If something happens to these, no one except you will notice.

---

*You might also be offended if you're an experienced administrator; a lot of the solutions here are, admittedly, simplistic. Remember that this chapter isn't for you; you'll get to do your job if the techniques in here don't work. If I can cut down your work load significantly, I feel I've succeeded.

In between, an area of reduced visibility, there will be a campus or corporate network connecting you to the Internet cloud. It is medium-priced, fairly well protected, and frequently monitored during business hours.

Most unexpected network outages occur fairly close to the ends: either around your computer or the one you are trying to reach. It may be in your computer or between your computer and the wall, but the closer you get to the cloud, the less likely the problem is to occur. This doesn't mean that problems are "always your fault." There is a destination computer sitting just as far from the cloud as you are, but somewhere else in the world. The problem is just as likely on the other end. And, on rare occasions, there are problems in the "cloud" itself. But that should be your last assumption, not your first.

When something goes wrong, your major goal is not fixing the problem. If you can, great, but more often than not, the problem will be something you can't control. Although you are close to the point of failure, much of the time fixing it will be beyond your means. This isn't necessarily because you're not a skilled technician; it's a function of failure probabilities, how things are built, and who has spare parts. Even if the problem occurs in your building, it could be in a locked network closet. This is where the cloud starts: wherever the network gets beyond your control. Your goal is finding out when you can expect it to be fixed. Do you sit in your office at midnight banging on the return key, or do you go home and watch David Letterman? If it's 10 P.M. and you deduce that the problem's a bad cable, you can go home; the guy who has the key to the supply cabinet won't be back until morning. If you learn that you're accessing a service that's temporarily off-line until 11 P.M., you might stick around and play some network Go.

Even if you can't fix the problem, you can help by narrowing down the area to be searched by others. When a technician is handed a stack of trouble tickets with equal priorities, it's natural to work on the most specific problem first. What would you do if someone handed you some assignments, and one said "It don't work," while the other said "Bad Ethernet cable—needs new one"? You could go to the second and fix the problem in five minutes, making someone happy. The other might be just as easy, or it might take hours—you don't know. If you attack them in the opposite order, both users could be unhappy for a long time. The problem gets even worse if there are multiple technicians responsible for different pieces of your connection (e.g., one does PC Ethernet cards, another does cables)—you have to call the right one. The moral is simple: even if you can't fix the problem, the more you know, the better the service you'll get.

Now we start getting into rule #2. You need to learn a little about your network and your network neighbors while the network is running correctly. When things go wrong, a few simple tests will show you what's changed. You don't need anything special for these tests. You already have the tools you need: a **telnet** program and your eyes.

Gather Baseline Information

To do any reasonable amount of network troubleshooting, you need to push the cloud back a bit. You need some information on your local connection to the network, and the router that connects you to the rest of the Internet. If you push back the cloud, every network in the world looks something like Figure 15-2.

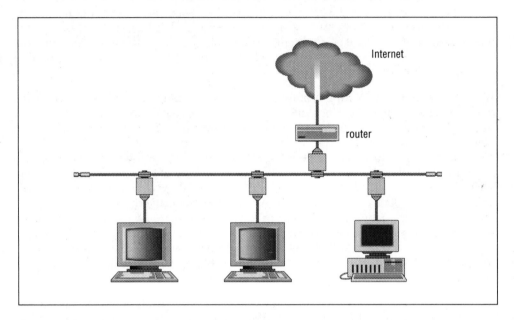

Figure 15-2: Network schematic

The technology may change from place to place. The wiring might be thin coax Ethernet, phone wire Ethernet, token ring, or something else. In any case, a wire connects your computer to something else. You need to find out a little about the "something elses": who is responsible for them, and how fast those responsible respond. So right now, go shopping for the following items:

1. The IP address of your computer and another computer on the same LAN. (There may not be any others.)

2. The IP address of the router closest to your computer that is responsible for connecting you to something larger (the router in Figure 15-2).

3. A list of who to call, by hour of day and day of the week, when something goes wrong with your LAN (item 1) and item 2 (your closest gateway). These aren't necessarily the same person.

4. The state of the status lights on any networking equipment you have access to.

These points are just guidelines. What is appropriate varies from connection to connection. For small sites or dial-up users, there may not be any other IP addresses, and there might not be anyone local to call: just you and your service provider. For really large sites, the network infrastructure may be complicated, but so is the support structure. The heartening thing is that the more complex your network is, the more local help you are likely to find. In a really large network, "who to call" is probably a single phone number, answered 24 hours per day, seven days a week. In almost every case, the information required is quite manageable, but you need to modify the shopping list based on how your connection is made.

Don't underestimate the importance of items 1 and 2: the numeric Internet address of your system, a neighbor's, and the closest router. Elsewhere, we've always used computer names to contact things, rather than IP addresses. Troubleshooting is the exception to this rule. In order to use a name to make contact, your computer may automatically seek out a Domain Name Server to convert the name to an address. This requires a healthy network. If your net is in sad shape it won't be able to do this; the tests you run using a name will be meaningless. An IP address is immediately usable, so it eliminates one source of error.

The Battleplan

Let's get back to the task at hand. You walked into your office to work on the big project at 10 P.M. and you can't connect to the "Federal Information Exchange." Your first question should be "do I have time to fiddle with the problem?" If the project is really important, you might not want to waste an hour worrying about a network problem. It might be better to try using your buddy's computer in the next office (he's not using it—he has a life). If his connection works, then you can get your work done. You also have a clue to the problem: something's wrong with your computer or its connection to the network.

Well, your buddy's office is locked and you have to get the report out tomorrow. So let's look at the problem. Throughout this discussion, we need to assume that your connection has been working and just quit. It's beyond the scope of this book to tell you how to configure your system for the first time. Your service provider or corporate/campus network group should help you with this.

Know Hours of Operation

The computers that provide network resources range from personal computers to gigantic mainframes. Most of these, along with the network control computers, require some kind of periodic maintenance. Most sites schedule maintenance during odd hours, like 2 A.M. Saturday morning, when the network load is usually light. However, scheduled "down time" varies from resource to resource. If you use a resource regularly, you should try to find out what its hours are supposed to be. You may save yourself a midnight attempt to access a resource that isn't available, anyway. Also, remember the Internet is worldwide. Friday during business hours in the United States is 2 A.M. Saturday morning in Japan.

If you are trying sources randomly, you don't have this luxury. If these attempts are in the middle of the night, however, you run a greater risk of finding a computer out of service. The computer may be down for scheduled maintenance, or it may have crashed, and no one is around to bring it back up. Remember, many resources are volunteer efforts. If the last volunteer locks up the office and goes home at five, it could be the next morning before someone can restart a crashed application.

Read the Error Message

When some people get an error message, they become so flustered that they only see:

```
ERROR - glitzfrick framus gobbledegook
```

Relax, read the error closely, and write it down. You need to write it down so if you have to report it to someone you have the exact text of the message. Nothing is more frustrating, for the network technician and the network victim, than a message like "It said 'error something something something'." Before you start calling out the troups, you might be able to fix your own problem. Even if you don't understand the whole message, you should be able to pick out a couple of words to help you along. Several words and phrases crop up regularly: "unknown," "unreachable," "refused," "not responding," and "timed out." Let's try and deal with each of these, mapping them into some telephone call scenarios.

unknown   You called directory assistance and asked for Willie Martin's phone number. The operator responded "I'm sorry; there is no listing for Willie Martin." This problem usually shows up when your computer tries to convert a name into an IP address. You told the computer to call **ux1.cso.uiuc.edu**. It tried to find the address, but was told that the computer didn't exist. Either you misspecified the name (e.g., spelled it wrong) or the computer couldn't convert it. This might be because your computer doesn't use the Domain Name System, but rather the old system in which all names are looked up in a file (under UNIX, */etc/hosts*).* There could also be a problem with the Domain Name System. This is almost certainly something you can't handle; get on the phone. In a pinch, if someone can tell you the IP address you need, you could use it and bypass this problem.

unreachable   You dialed the number and get the message "I'm sorry; the number you have reached is out of service." This is a real network problem. A portion of the network is down. The network is telling you, "I know where you want to go, but you can't get there from here." If this happens, there is nothing you can do: call for help.

refused   You tried to make a person-to-person call, got to the correct number, but the person you want is not there. The computer at the far end needs to accept connections for a particular service (e.g., TELNET). Your computer successfully contacted the destination

---

*UNIX systems will probably have an */etc/hosts*, with one or two entries in it, even if they are using the Domain Name System. So, if you find */etc/hosts* but there are only two entries, don't conclude that you're not using DNS. You're almost certainly wrong. For that matter, even if you find a huge host table, you still can't conclude that you're not using DNS—that table might be left over from the "olden days."

computer and asked to make the connection to a service, but the destination said "no." There are several possible reasons for this. The computer may be running, but not available for user access. This is frequently the case during maintenance periods or while doing filesystem dumps. It's also possible that the service has been cancelled: i.e., the system's manager has decided not to provide it. For example, you might hear that a great game is available if you **telnet** to **game.edu** at port 5000. When you try this, you get a "connection refused" message. This probably means that the computer's owner decided not to allow game playing anymore.

timed out This may mean that you called and no one answered, or that you were put on hold indefinitely. When TCP, through whichever application you are using, sends messages to a remote computer it expects responses in a reasonable length of time. This is usually a few minutes. If it doesn't get one, it gives up and sends you this message. It usually means that the destination computer or a piece of the network is dead. This can happen in the middle of some ongoing conversation. Try again in about ten minutes. This is long enough for most things to recover from a crash automatically, if they are going to. If it still doesn't work, investigate further. (You would get this message if the network cable suddenly fell off your computer.)

not responding This is very similar to a "timed out," but the conversation is happening with UDP rather than TCP. (Different applications use different protocols. From your point of view, it shouldn't matter.) It does mean that packets were sent to the remote site and nothing came back. As with the "timed out" message, try again in about ten minutes. If it still doesn't work, investigate further. (Again, you'd get this message if the network cable suddenly fell off your computer.)

Did You Change Anything?

If you've ever used a computer, or helped others use computers, the following dialog should come as no surprise:

> "It stopped working."
> "Did you change anything?"
> "No, it was working yesterday and then it just stopped."
> "You're sure?"
> "Well, I did change the screen color in my configuration file,
>   but that wouldn't affect it."

If it worked yesterday and doesn't work today, something has changed. It may be your computer, it may be the network, it may be the destination. Changes you've made are the easiest to undo, but the hardest to acknowledge as a problem. People change things on their computers because they're trying to accomplish something. If

I tell you that your changes caused some problem, you'll probably think that I'm trying to impede progress. But in many cases, your recent changes probably *did* cause the problem. If you have changed anything, a file or some hardware thingy, and your network connection hasn't worked right since, don't consider it unrelated even if the relationship appears remote. Before looking anywhere else, try to undo the change. You only have to go back to your old version of *config.sys* (or whatever the file might be). You did copy *config.sys* to *config.bak* before you made the changes, didn't you?

A good rule of thumb is to assume that the problem is at your end of the connection before you suspect problems at the other end. Make sure your end is working correctly before looking elsewhere. "Why?" you ask. "Didn't you say that the problem is equally likely to be at the far end?" Yes, that's true. But think about this: the far end is as likely to be in Japan as in Chicago, and almost certainly isn't close to you. Before making a long distance phone call to Japan, make sure that the problem's not on your end.

Try a Different Destination

Since you didn't change anything, you need to find out what has changed. First, try accessing a different destination. You don't even have to leave your seat. Look in the *Resource Catalog* and pick any destination that allows TELNET access; then **telnet** to it. If you get through, the problem is probably at the first destination you tried to reach. A successful **telnet** to any remote destination tells you that your system is working, and the network as a whole is working. If you are desperate to use that resource, you can call them up and ask them what the story is. Or you could just call it a night. In any case, your network connection is working just fine. Once the "remote end" gets its act together, you should be able to reach it.

Just to be comprehensive, I'll repeat a tip I gave earlier. If you get the message with a phrase like "host unknown" in it, your computer is having trouble looking up the Internet address of the remote system you want. Make sure you spelled the name correctly. Then see if you can find the (numeric) Internet address of the remote system. Using the numeric address should solve your problem.

Try Your Neighbor's System

Since you are still reading, I assume that didn't fix it. Earlier, I suggested that you go to your buddy's office, and try again. If you can get to whatever resource you want, you know two things:

- You can work until the office's owner shows up in the morning.

- The problem is most likely with your workstation—it certainly isn't with the resource you want to access, or the network.

If you can't reach the resource you want, your local network or (in rare circumstances) the Internet itself is in trouble. Eventually, you'll need to call someone and ask for help. But there are still a few things to check.

Try to Reach a Local System

On the shopping list, we told you to get the IP address of another computer on the same local network. Here's where you use that information. Try to **telnet** to that machine. You should see its login prompt:

```
% telnet 192.33.44.56
Trying 192.33.44.56
Connected to 192.33.44.56
Escape character is '^]'.

login:
```

If you get this far, you've proven that your system is probably working. If you can reach local systems but not remote systems, the problem is most likely somewhere on your local net—very likely a router, or some other piece of hardware that connects your network to the rest of the Internet. If you know a lot about how your local net is structured, you can make lots of experiments and maybe even pinpoint the trouble spot. However, that's not really your job. It's time to start making phone calls.

Look Around Your Office

Now, assume that the finger of Murphy's law is pointing directly at you—or your computer. It's time to start looking around your office. In World War II, the problem was gremlins. They caused bombs not to explode, engines to stop, etc., all for unknown causes. For the network, the problem is usually people: janitors, office-mates, you. It's amazing how many network problems are caused by damage to that $5 piece of wire between your computer and the wall. Janitors knock it out with a broom, or you roll over it a hundred times with a chair wheel and cut it. If you find something obviously wrong (for example, thick Ethernet transceiver cables* on the back of a computer have this tendency to fall off), fix it (or get someone to fix it).

CAUTION

If you are on a coaxial cable Ethernet (a round cable running to your computer, not a flat one) don't do anything until you read the section on dealing with Ethernets later in this chapter.

If you have access to any networking equipment, look at it. Do the lights look normal? Are they on at all? If none of the lights are on, check the power to the unit. If they are on, but abnormal, there is probably nothing you can do except note the colors of the lights and call someone for help.

There is one situation where you might be able to help yourself out. Are you on a *10baseT* Ethernet† or a token ring LAN? These are probably the most common types

---

*A 15 pin connector explained more fully later in "Dealing With Coaxial Ethernets"

†This is an Ethernet that uses normal telephone wiring and modular phone jacks, like the ones your home telephone uses to plug into the wall. They are also referred to as Ethernet on *UTP*, unshielded twisted pair.

of local area networks in the Internet these days, so the odds are pretty good that you fit into this category. For both kinds of network, each computer plugs into a separate port (plug) in a box called a "multiport repeater" (if you're on an Ethernet) or "media access unit" (MAU, for a token ring). Each port usually has a status light next to a plug. Locate the plug next to your computer's connection.* Is the light next to the cable from your computer red or off, and are the lights next to the other cables green? If so, try moving your plug to a vacant port. Did the new port's light turn green when you plugged your cable in, or did it remain red or dark? If it is now green, leave it there and try your computer again. You may have been plugged into a bad port and have bypassed the problem. If the new light turns red or remains unlit, it means that there is something wrong with the wire to your computer, or the interface card in it. Unless there is something obviously wrong, like a loose cable, it's hopeless to proceed without some other test equipment. (If you are on a token ring LAN, there is a section on token ring hints later in the chapter.)

Check Your Local Connection

If you can't get through to any remote destination, but you can connect to computers in your local "group," the problem is somewhere between your computer and the router that connects your group of computers to the Internet. "Group" is a pretty fuzzy term. You may be in a group by yourself, particularly if you connect using a dial-up, SLIP, or PPP connection. Your "group" may be a large number of computers sharing a local network and connected to an on-site router; at the extreme, your "group" may be a whole campus or corporate network.

Now, you have to figure out whether the problem is within your area (your LAN or computer), or somewhere further away and out of your control. In this case, what you should do depends on how you're connected to the Net. Dial-up connections, in which you get network services by logging in to some "directly connected" computer over a modem, are significantly different from "direct connections." With SLIP or PPP you have the worst of both worlds: you have to use the dial-up debugging techniques until the connection gets made and then deal with problems as if you had a dedicated connection. This is because these protocols set up temporary IP protocol connections between your computer and the service providers, just like if you had a dedicated connection.

Dial-up Connections

Once again, by "dial-up connections" we mean that you dial into some other computer over a phone line; log into it as a regular user; and use that computer's network services. What happens if you can't log into the remote computer? The problem is clearly not with the Internet, since you haven't gotten anywhere close to it.

---

*If you can't find your computer's connection, call it a day (or a night). Wiring closets are often messy places. If the cables aren't clearly labelled, or if there isn't an up-to-date map telling you what each cable is, don't touch anything. I'm also assuming that you properly have access to the network equipment. In many cases it's locked away to prevent random people (i.e., you) from moving wires. If you do take it upon yourself to move some wires, be sure to tell the person responsible for the network what you did, so he can get the port fixed and update any documentation necessary.

Again, most problems fall into a few common categories. Although the symptoms and remedies listed below aren't exhaustive, they should take care of most situations:

Phone Doesn't Dial

There is a problem in either your terminal emulator software, or between your computer and the modem. Your terminal emulator and modem are speaking different speeds or using different data formats. Check that out. It could also be that the location of the modem is not what your software thinks it is. (PCs have two communications ports, called COM1 and COM2; you have to pick the one your modem is plugged into. A similar thing happens on Macintoshes with the "phone" or "printer" plug. For that matter, most UNIX systems have two or more terminal connectors on the back.) Other possibilities are that your telephone line is dead, or the phone cable isn't plugged into the modem or the wall, or the modem isn't plugged into the computer. Even if you *know* that everything is wired correctly, checking never hurts. Also: find the phone jack where your modem plugs into the wall. Try plugging a regular telephone into the jack. Do you get a dial tone? If not, call the your phone company.

Ring, No Answer

Check the number you dialed. Was it correct? If you dialed correctly and the remote system doesn't answer, the remote system may be down, or its modem may be bad. Check the published hours of operation to make sure it should be up. If it should be working, try the same phone number a few times. Better yet, if you have any alternate numbers, try them. If you have two phones available, try dialing the number with the phone not connected to the modem. While it is ringing, dial with your modem phone and see if it gets through. (Sometimes if there are multiple phone lines through one number, one bad line will always answer the call. If you keep it busy with some other phone, your modem call might get to a good one.) Even if you get through eventually, call your service provider and report the problem so it can be fixed.

Answers, Then Nothing

Here's one common scenario: the modem dialed correctly, the remote system answered, the modems whistled a few tones at each other, and you got the message "Connected" (or its equivalent) on your screen. Then nothing happened; everything went dead. This usually points to a problem with your service provider's gear. Either the provider's modem is bad, or the port on the computer it is connected to is bad. Either way, the only thing you can do is call in and report it. You might try again a few times. If you have an alternate number, try it. Getting a different modem to answer might bypass the problem.

There's one other possibility. There are certainly modems that "don't like to talk to each other," particularly if they're made by different manufacturers. However, we're assuming that you're trouble-shooting a connection that has worked for you in the past. Unless you've just bought a new modem, incompatible modems probably aren't the problem.

LAN, PPP, or SLIP Connections

If you're directly on some kind of local network, or if you connect to a service provider using PPP or SLIP, your situation is somewhat different. Try and **telnet** to the closest router that services you. You should know this address—it was on the shopping list at the beginning of the chapter! If the router responds at all, then your computer and connection are OK. The problem is in the "cloud"; it must be solved by whoever worries about the router and the network that it's connected to. This could be your service provider, the networking staff for your campus or corporation, or (if you have a large in-building network) someone in your department.

Note that we said, "If the router responds at all." You might see a login prompt, or just the message "connection refused." Both of these are equally good responses. You don't know how to log in to the router, or the router may not be interested in letting anyone log in—who cares? To get either of these messages, you had to traverse your local network connection and get to something bigger. It isn't your problem. Call the appropriate person and report it.

Some Consolation

It may sound like there's not much you can do. In some senses, that's true. Think of your washer, dryer, or VCR. If they break, you can make sure all the plugs and hoses are tight, or maybe pull out a jammed cassette. There are a few things you can fix. But, much of the time, there is nothing you can do but call up the lonesome Maytag repairman and talk about the problem knowledgeably. As we said earlier, even if you can't solve the problem yourself, the more information you can gather, the better service you'll get.

Talking to Operations Personnel

Whenever pilots talk on the radio to air traffic controllers, they are taught that every message should say:

- Who you are
- Where you are
- What you want to do

These same guidelines apply to calling network operators. First, they need to know who you are—otherwise, they can't ask you for more information, or tell you that they've solved the problem. "Where you are" (the name of your computer and possibly its IP address) and "what you want to do" (the name of the remote computer and the service you want to get) allow operators to figure out the path your communications should take. This is the essential data necessary to diagnose and solve a problem. However, it is the minimum required. In addition, keep in mind why you've called the network operators. If you've followed our short procedure above, remember what you've done, why you did it, and what the results were. Why are you convinced that the problem isn't on your desktop? The answer to this question contains very important clues about the nature of the problem.

The operator you call should be the one operating the network closest to you. Your local network operators are the only ones who monitor connections to your campus or building. It isn't like calling up the President of GM to get some action on your car. In the network world, a national operator only knows about his network's connection to regional networks. Once he or she determines that the NSFnet, or NREN, or whatever isn't at fault, he will call the regional network responsible for your connection. In turn, the regional network will call your campus or corporate networking center. Very likely, they will then call you. Save yourself some time: start at the bottom.

Dealing with Coaxial Ethernets

Traditional coaxial cable Ethernets are special because, in many cases, fiddling with the wiring can break the network for other working computers. An Ethernet that uses coaxial cable has two parts: the *bus* and a number of *taps* (shown in Figure 15-3). The bus is the cable which snakes from computer to computer. There are two kinds of cable: "thick" and "thin." In thick Ethernets, the cable is about 3/8 inch in diameter, and yellow or orange with black marks every two meters. Thin Ethernets usually use grey, white, or black cable 1/5 inch in diameter. Each end of the bus must have a special "cap" called a *terminator*. Between the two terminators may be a number of taps. A tap is where one computer connects to the network. For thick Ethernets a tap is built in the *transceiver*, a little box a bit bigger than a pack of cigarettes hanging off the cable. This box allows your computer to connect to the Ethernet. A *transceiver* or *AUI* cable runs between it and your computer. For thin Ethernets, a tap looks like a "T" made of metal tubing, shown in Figure 15-4. It's usually located on the back of your computer. In this case, there is still a transceiver but it is built into your computer.

If your computer only has a transceiver cable port, it might have an external transceiver next to the cable, just like a thick Ethernet would have.

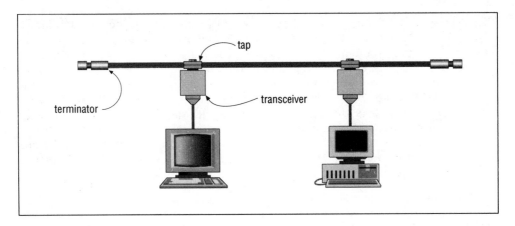

Figure 15-3: Typical thin Ethernet

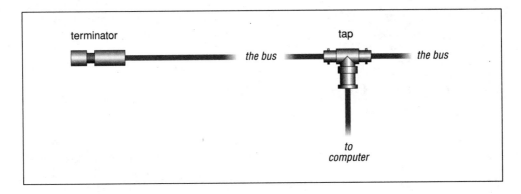

Figure 15-4: Thin Ethernet--tap and terminator

Why do you care so much about the parts of an Ethernet? Whatever you do, the bus must always remain "electrically intact." This means that there must be an unbroken connection from one end (one terminator) to the other. If the bus is broken for any reason, it stops working for *everyone* connected to it.* So, by improperly disconnecting the Ethernet cable in your office, you can easily make enemies out of friends. Two rules for dealing with Ethernets will get you through most situations:

---

*You might think that the network would still work, although in pieces: two computers should still be able to communicate if they're both on the same side of the break. Sorry. Life isn't so simple.

1. You can do anything to the connection from your Ethernet tap to your computer without affecting other people.

2. If you need to break the bus for repairs, warn others and make it quick.

Rule #1 is pretty straightforward. If you need to disconnect your computer from the network, leave the "T" in the cable, and disconnect the vertical part of the "T" from the computer (shown as "to computer" in Figure 15-4). On thick Ethernets, leave the tap and transceiver in the cable, but disconnect the transceiver cable.

The second rule is a bit harder. You must recognize that there are times when it's necessary to do things to the bus. If it's damaged or cut and everyone is down, it is not an issue. It's down and you're doing everyone a service by fixing it. If it's working for everyone but you, you have a problem. This is quite common if a thick Ethernet transceiver dies. Fixing your connection could take everyone off the air. In this case you have two choices: do it when they're not around or do it so fast they hardly notice.

Since most protocols, like TCP, are designed to deal with communication glitches of short duration, you can break an Ethernet for ten seconds or so without permanently impacting peoples work. Whatever they're doing will stop momentarily, but that's it. If you break their connection for too long, first they will notice the lack of response, then later (usually over a minute) TCP will "time out."

NOTE

Whether or not you should touch the cable at all depends on your environment. On some networks, the policy might be "no one but a cable technician or network administrator touches the wiring." Abide by your local rules.

Token Ring Notes

If you are on a token ring net, here are a few pointers. First: some MAUs don't have status lights. On these, you have no help figuring out if your port is bad or not. If you're desperate, you might just try plugging your computer into a vacant port.

Second: If you move the plug on a MAU, you may need to reboot your computer before you try again. (On some systems, you may only need to restart the Internet software.) The software has to perform a special "ring insertion" to become active on the network. A ring insertion only happens once, when the software first starts running. Your system won't automatically notice that it's back on the network, and try to insert itself again. So if you change the cabling, you need to force a ring insertion before you can be active on the network. This may be possible within your TCP/IP software package. If you can't figure out how to do it gracefully, a reboot always works.

In any case, try and leave the network in the same configuration that you found it in (with perhaps some bad cables replaced and now in working order).

THE WHOLE
INTERNET

CATALOG

RESOURCES ON THE INTERNET

Stalking the Wild Resource
How We Did It
Using the Catalog

Up to this point, I've spent a lot of time telling you "how to" on the Internet. Now it's time to give you some "to what" advice. Remember, there is no official list of Internet resources. Anyone who has an Internet connection can decide to provide some service and put it on-line without telling anyone. So the trick is: how do you find out what's available? First, we'll discuss how to use the tools we've covered to find resources. Next, we'll talk about how we built the resource catalog. Then we'll introduce the format and use of the catalog (in the Sears catalog, this section would be called "how to order"). Finally, you can start shopping in the catalog itself.

Stalking the Wild Resource

In the chapter on Gopher and WAIS, I drew some analogies between the Internet and a library without a card catalog. It's time to start thinking about that again. You may be without an official card catalog, but you are not without tools. The major tools at your disposal are your friends, network news and mailing lists, and the Archie, Gopher, WAIS, and World-Wide Web services. Let's look at how each of these may be used to find the resource of your dreams.

Friends

Your friends are your friends because you have interests in common with them. In addition to your regular friends, through e-mail you will make a set of network friends. These friends may be looking for the same things you are; or even if their interests differ, they may be aware of resources that you want. In the real world, a friend who knows you are into female mystery writers might tell you "Sara Paretzky has a new book out": he knows you are interested, and will appreciate the tip. In the network world, a friend who knows you are interested in agriculture resources might send you a message saying "Have you seen 'Not Just Cows', the Internet ag resources guide?" He, being a pencil collector, would love to hear from you if you found a complete pencil pricing database. Life on the network is not all that different from "real life."

Network News and Mailing Lists

Network news and mailing lists are resources themselves. Newsgroups are shown in the catalog by topic. Lists of mailing lists are compiled and are listed under Network Information. These resources are also gateways to other resources. If you are interested in pencil collecting and follow the rec.pencil-collecting group (or a mailing list—same facilities but different technology) for a while, one of three things will happen. First, someone might post a news item announcing a great find, like "Pencil Collecting Database Found." Second, these great finds will probably be collected into a group of frequently asked questions (FAQ). FAQs are posted to the newsgroup or news.answers periodically (usually monthly).* By reading the FAQs you can instantly be brought up to date on whatever the newsgroup is discussing.

If you don't find what you want in a FAQ, you can "go fishing" for an answer. Write a posting to the pencil-collecting newsgroup (or mailing list) asking "Does anyone have a database of current pencil prices?" It is easy to cast out and see what you can catch.

Archie

Archie (discussed in Chapter 9) is primarily a service to locate files by name. It makes a slight attempt to allow searches by topic, but this facility is limited and dated. However, in reality Archie is more general-purpose than this description implies. People who maintain anonymous FTP servers try to name things logically. Frequently, they use the structure of a filesystem to help organize: related files are stored in the same directory, which will probably have a useful name. In these cases Archie doesn't tell you exactly what you want to know, but gives you an idea where you might look. For example, to locate pencil collecting information you might try the following command:

```
% archie -s pencil

Host blandsworth.usnd.edu
    Location: /pub
        DIRECTORY drwxr-xr-x   512  May 17 05:19  pencils
```

You didn't search for a particular topic, you searched for a file starting with "pencil." What Archie found was not a file, but a directory named */pub/pencils*, on the computer **blandsworth.usnd.edu**.

At this point you don't know if there is anything useful to you on that computer or not. But—let's face it—how many people would create a directory named *pencils* for numerical analysis software? Not many. There's a good chance that this directory will contain something to do with pencils—maybe not exactly what you're looking for, but probably something interesting. All you need to do is **ftp** to **blandsworth.usnd.edu**, login as "anonymous", **cd pub/pencils**, and do a **dir**. Poke around a bit. It may contain good stuff or it may not. It is a reasonable place to start.

---

*FAQs have been archived, so they are available when you want them via **ftp**. See News, Network-USENET Periodic Posting Archives in the catalog for their location.

Gopher

Gopher (in Chapter 11) can be used to access other resource finders like Archie and WAIS. It can also be used by itself; Gopher menus are themselves pointers to resources. When looking for resources with Gopher, two general areas are of interest: the list of other Gophers available, and the list of information services provided by that particular Gopher.

There are getting to be more and more specialized Gopher servers around. Someone sees the power Gopher could bring to a community, so he or she builds a Gopher server tailored to that community. The person responsible for the server is on the lookout for more information sources in the area of interest. If you can find a Gopher server that has a collection you like, you can stay up to date by dropping into that server every now and then. To find a server that appears to have similar leanings to your own, just start from any server; find the list of "other Gopher servers"; and page through it. There are lots of them but, if you are lucky and patient, you might find the University of Minnesota Pencil Collection Gopher. Well, that might be pushing it a bit, but there are already specialized Gopher servers for soil science, history of science and law. Pencil collecting can't be far behind.

If you can't find a specialized server to your liking, try dropping into one of the better general purpose servers, like the CONCERT Gopher server. It seems to specialize in having menu items for as many services as it can find. Remember that if you find an interesting resource through a Gopher server, you can either continue to use that resource through Gopher, or you can ask Gopher how to access the resource directly.* If Gopher accesses the resource through TELNET, you can just start **telnet** manually and skip the Gopher menus.

WAIS

The directory of servers makes it easy to find any WAIS service (Chapter 12). Some of the servers are actually indexes into other services. For example, the whole of the Archie database or the archives of many newsgroups can be searched through WAIS. This allows you to use the extended search capabilities of WAIS to look for things you might want.

The World-Wide Web

The World-Wide Web (Chapter 13) is also a great way to hunt for useful resources. Not only does it have resources of its own, but it allows you to use all the other search services. There are several subject-oriented menus, like the "Index of Academic Information"; these are maintained by volunteers, and are improving with time.

---

*If you're using the ASCII ("curses") **gopher** client, use the = command.

How We Did It

How did we create our resource catalog? We did all of the above.

1. We listened to newsgroups and mailing lists looking for interesting announcements.

2. We used what we learned to find other lists and used their information.

3. We looked for sparse areas in the catalog and used Archie to perform subject searches (e.g., **archie -s music**). With that information, we then looked at the anonymous FTP servers to see if there was anything interesting in them.

4. We looked at every Gopher server available at the time and tried to list any unique services we found.

5. We included a summary of the most useful WAIS services from the directory of servers.

What Is a Resource?

What we included as a resource varies from subject to subject. There are subjects, like the Internet itself and computer science, where thousands of important files are scattered throughout the Internet, almost randomly. We chose not to include such resources; anyone can find these with Gopher or WAIS. There are other groups for which the sole motivation to be on the Internet might be to access one particular file; we tried to include these. In general, we included the most unique and interesting things we could find. Within each subject, resources were "graded on the curve." There was no absolute measure for what's "interesting."

We biased our choices in favor of resources that anyone could use, or that could be used on the spur of the moment from the network. A prime example of this would be computational resources. We didn't list the NSF supercomputer centers, even though they were one of the prime reasons why the network became ubiquitous. Anyone who wants to do heavy-duty research computing can request time on a supercomputer, but they are not for everyone to use. If you are a valid user, the center will supply you with lots of documentation about how to use it. You can't just decide "I think I'll play on a Cray today."

On the other hand, there are a few sites which offer free UNIX computing. That is, anyone can **telnet** to them and run limited programs. With the emphasis on "anyone," we included such resources.

Finally, we tried to be "broad" rather than deep. In one respect, this book is an argument about why you should use the Internet. And the simplest argument for using the Net are that there are loads of resources interesting to all sorts of people, not just "geeks with pocket protectors." To prove this, we've tried to hit as many different and diverse topics as possible. If we've succeeded, even Internet veterans should be surprised at what we've found.

Accuracy and Permissions

We verified that every listed resource was working and available at some time during the year or so when we were gathering information. That doesn't mean that these resources are still available, or that the usage information is still the same. There were times when the access information changed in the two weeks between the time we discovered the resource and the time we actually tried it. If we could figure out how to use a resource we included it; if not, we chucked it.

For this reason, we included references to other resource directories and guides. They have the advantage of being online, hence easily updatable. This doesn't mean they are actually updated frequently. There's really no way to tell whether any online database is more or less up-to-date than this catalog. Online indices are usually maintained by volunteer effort; you never know how much effort the volunteer has to expend.

Remember: a resource that is publicly accessible isn't necessarily a public resource. This caused me a bit of trouble. If I stumbled upon a good resource, how could I decide if it was intended to be public? The rule of thumb I used was that a public resource had to fall into one of these categories:

- Commonly known within the community (e.g., frequently mentioned and discussed in newsgroups).

- Listed in other resource guides or catalogs.

- Easily found with public index utilities (e.g., Gopher, WAIS)

I ran across a few resources that didn't fall into these categories, were subject to restrictions, or seemed "dangerous" to the offerer. In these cases, I asked the owner if he or she would like to see the resource listed. Usually the answer was "yes." If the answer was no, the resources are still available on the Internet. But you aren't hearing about them from me.

Using the Catalog

I tried to group the resources into the areas where they belonged, but then what do I know? In some cases, there are related but slightly differing subjects. One is frequently for the "lay user", like "Health." Here you find ways to get information about general good health and nutrition. There's another category called "Medicine," which has more academic information. Under this category, you might find information about the Food and Drug Administration, new and ongoing medical research, and similar material. Certainly not what you need to plan a nutritious lunch. Similarly, there are separate categories for "Aeronautics" (academic) and "Aviation" (material for airplane pilots). So, if you find the dry and boring material on some topic, but not the fun stuff, you are probably looking in the "academic" category. Try a more common word or phrase.

If you already know the name of some resource and would like to see if it's listed, you might start at the index. All the entries in the resource guide are listed there. So if you have a resource that you like and want to see where I put it, work backwards.

Topics Covered

Here's a summary of the topics that are covered in the resource catalog.

Table 1: Internet Topic Areas

Aeronautics and Astronautics	Library and Information Science
Agriculture	Literature
Anthropology	Mathematics
Astronomy	Medicine
Aviation	Molecular Biology
Biology	Music
Chemistry	Network Information
Computer Science	Network Organizations
Computing	Network Services
Cooking	News, Network
Education	Nutrition
Electrical Engineering	Oceanography
Engineering	Pets
Environment	Physics
Forestry	Political Activism
Freenet	Popular Culture
Gardening and Horticulture	Recreation, Games
Genealogy	Recreation, Sports
Geography	Reference Books
Geology and Geophysics	Religion
Government, U.S.	Resource Directories
Health	Science Fiction and Fantasy Literature
History	Science
Hobbies and Crafts	Society and Culture
Humanities	Standards
Internet	Travel
Journalism	Weather, Meteorology, and Climatology
Law	White Pages
Libraries	Zymurgy

By the way, we've included a handy "quick reference bookmark" in the back of the book. We hope to save you from leafing back and forth between the catalog and the chapters, looking up syntax of the commands you need to use.

AERONAUTICS & ASTRONAUTICS

News Groups:
sci.[space, astro, aeronautics]

NASA News

A short listing of current happenings at NASA. If you're interested in the space program, this is a great way to stay up-to-date. On a typical day, you'd find out about expected launches, or (perhaps) progress in a Space Shuttle mission.

Access via: *finger nasanews@space.mit.edu*

NASA Spacelink

Entries about the history, current state, and future of NASA and space flight, provided by the NASA Marshall Space Flight Center. Also, some classroom materials and information on space technology transfer. This is a particularly valuable resource for educators.

Access via: *telnet spacelink.msfc.nasa.gov*; login *newuser*; password *newuser*

Information: Phone: (205) 544-6531

Shuttle and Satellite Images

The following FTP sites make available photographs and other images taken from the Space Shuttle, Magellan and Viking missions, and other good stuff. The data formats vary; check any README files, or other descriptive files, that are available.

Access via: *ftp sseop.jsc.nasa.gov*; login *anonymous*
Note: Space shuttle images.

ftp ames.arc.nasa.gov; login *anonymous*;
cd pub/GIF
Note: Images, news from lots of missions. Also look in *pub/SPACE/GIF and pub/space/CDROM*.

telnet sanddunes.scd.ucar.edu
Note: E-mail *kelley@sanddunes.scd.ucar.edu* for login, password, and manual.

ftp pioneer.unm.edu; login *anonymous*; cd *pub/info*

Note: Absolutely necessary to look at *beginner-info* to get started.

ftp iris1.ucis.dal.ca; login *anonymous*; cd *pub/GIF*
Note: Similar to data at *ames.arc.nasa.gov*; restrict use to 5-8 P.M. Atlantic time.

Space FAQ's

Have you ever thought about becoming an astronaut? Here's where to find out what's required. Fifteen lists of "Frequently Asked Questions" are available. The lists are on topics ranging from "Astronomical Mnemonics" to "Orbital and Planetary Launch Services"—including "How to become an Astronaut." Other files include a report on tidal bulges, information on interpreting satellite weather photos, and databases on constellations and nearby stars. The *README* file describes what's in the individual files.

Access via: *ftp ames.arc.nasa.gov*; login *anonymous*; cd *pub/SPACE/FAQ*

SpaceMet

A bulletin board system for exchanging information about space exploration from the view of science educators. Has information on past, current, and future NASA plans. Also contains information on curriculum planning. There is a section on events and meetings, but it is pretty local to the Northeastern U.S.

Access via:
telnet spacemet.phast.umass.edu

Concert gopher/Internet Information Servers/General Information Servers

*A*GRICULTURE

News Groups: *misc.rural*

Advanced Technology Information Network

Any farmer knows that farming isn't a "mom and pop" business any more; it's high-tech, and it's important to keep up with the latest developments. This resource, and the others in this group, will help you to stay up-to-date. A fairly complete agricultural information service offers market, news, events, weather, job listing, and safety information. Offered by the California Agricultural Technology Institute, so there is a "west coast" bias to the information. Also contains information on trade, exports, and biotechnology.

Access via: *telnet caticsuf.csufresno.edu*; login *super*

AGRICOLA

Agricola contains citations to agricultural literature in the National Agricultural Library and other institutions. It also includes references on nutrition, agricultural economics and parasitology. The last five years worth of data are kept online. Available only to patrons who may use the Iowa State Library.

Access via: *telnet isn.iastate.edu*; to dial respond *scholar*; enter terminal type; to command respond *scholar*; database *agri* Note: Logging off is a bit of a pain—know how to disconnect before you start.

Automated Trade Library Service

Up-to-date information on agricultural exporting. Part of Advanced Technology Information Network.

See: Agriculture - Advanced Technology Information Network

Commodity Market Reports

Commodity reports compiled by the U.S. Department of Agriculture Market News Service. Twelve hundred reports covering the U.S., updated daily.

Access via:
WAIS *agricultural-market-news.src*

Information:
E-mail: *wais@oes.orst.edu*

MAPP

The national cooperative extension family database. Contains research briefs, bibliographies, census data, reference materials, and program ideas for Extension professionals and family educators.

See: Agriculture - PEN Pages

Not Just Cows

A guide to resources on the Internet and Bitnet in agriculture and related subjects. Compiled by Wilfred (Bill) Drew.

Access via: *ftp ftp.sura.net*; login *anonymous*; cd *pub/nic*; get *agricultural.list*

ftp hydra.uwo.ca; login *anonymous*; cd *libsoft*; get *agriculture_internet_guide.txt*

ftp ftp.unt.edu; login *anonymous*; get *agriculture-internet.txt*

Information:
E-mail: *drewwe@snymorva.bitnet*

PEN Pages

A complete information server concerning all aspects of rural life. Sections on commodity prices, family farm life, seniors on the farm, news, and nutrition. Also, provides various announcements by the USDA including its CITExtension newsletter. Service provided by the Pennsylvania State University, so some information may be specific to that region.

Access via: *telnet psupen.psu.edu*
Note: Use your two letter state abbreviation as your login name.

Trees

See: Forestry - Trees

U.S.D.A. Research Results

Summaries of recent research results from the USDA's agricultural and economic research services. Updated at least bimonthly.

Access via: WAIS *usda-rrdb.src*

Information:
E-mail: *wais@esusda.gov*

ANTHROPOLOGY

Aboriginal Studies

A collection of records from the Aboriginal Studies Electronic Data Archive at the Australian Institute of Aboriginal Studies and the Australian National University.

Access via:
WAIS *ANU-aboriginal-studies.src*

Excerpt from **Pen Pages**, *7/14/92:*

ADAPTING HOMES FOR ELDERLY

Since most information about a person's surroundings comes through eyesight, reduced vision problems related to aging are often compounded by the interior design of a home. The yellowing of the eye's lens produces less contrast between objects and makes it harder to see colors in the blue-violet range. Using warm colors in the red and yellow range are more comfortable for elderly persons. The use of contrasting colors helps to make distinctions and judgements easier for elderly persons. For example, the use of contrasting colors can separate the floor from the baseboard. Also, using floor coverings that are different in color and texture could help an elderly person identify danger areas such as stairways.

Source: Sarah Drummond, Assistant Extension Specialist, Oklahoma
----
Editor: J. Van Horn, Ph.D., CFLE, Professor, Rural Sociology Dept. of Ag. Economics and Rural Sociology, Penn State May 1992
PENpages Number: 085072114

Keywords: AGRICULTURAL-EC-RUR-SOC, ELDERLY, HOME, HOUSING, MAPP, NEWS, SAFETY, VANHORN-JAMES

Thai Yunnan Project

Annotated bibliography and research notes collection of the Thai-Yunnan Project, Dept. of Anthropology, Australian National University, GPO Box 4, Canberra ACT 2601. Lots of data on ethnic groups of southeast Asia, including languages, religions, customs, etc.

Access via: WAIS *ANU-Thai-Yunnan.src*

Information: Phone: +61 6 249-9262; E-mail *gew400@coombs.anu.edu.au*

ASTRONOMY

News Groups: *sci.[astro, astro.fits, astro.hubble]*

Astronomical Databases

This FTP site includes several databases of astronomical objects, including the Yale Bright Star catalog, the Saguaro Astronomy Club databases, and an asteroid database. Some IBM PC software for using these databases is also available.

Access via: *ftp mandarin.mit.edu*; login *anonymous*; cd astro

ftp pomona.claremont.edu; login *anonymous*; cd yale_bsc

Lunar and Planetary Institute Information

Information about NASA's Lunar and Planetary Institute and its services. It includes a bibliographic database, and allows access to an electronic journal, "The Lunar & Planetary Information Bulletin." There is also a service called IRPS, which is the "Image Retrieval and Processing System." It is possible to order and (with the appropriate software) display digital images of the planets. Primarily of use to researchers in lunar or planetary studies.

Access via: *telnet lpi.jsc.nasa.gov*; login *lpi*

Concert gopher/Internet Information Servers/General Information Servers

NASA/IPAC Extragalactic Database

The NED database contains information about over 200,000 astronomical objects. Also, abstracts and bibliographies of astro-nomical publications.

Access via: *telnet denver.ipac.caltech.edu*; login *ned*

Concert gopher/Internet Information Servers/General Information Servers

National Space Science Data Center

The interface to many NASA data catalogs and centers. This system allows you to connect to facilities like Astronomical Data center, access the CANOPUS newsletter, and get data from and about various satellite sensors.

Access via: *telnet nssdca.gsfc.nasa.gov*; login *nodis*

Southwest Research Data Display and Analysis System

Provides access to data returned by the Dynamics Explorer satellites. Raw datasets are available; in addition, there are interactive tools for displaying the data under the X window system. The data are of particular interest to physicists interested in magentic phenomena.

Access via: *telnet espsun.space.swri.edu 10000*

Space Telescope Science Institute

Information about the Hubble Space Telescope and the Space Telescope Science Institute. Includes instrument reports, ample data, grant information, FAQ lists, long and short range plans, software, etc.

Access via: *ftp stsci.edu*; login *anonymous*

AVIATION

News Group: *rec.aviation*

Aeronautics Archives

A group of aviation archives. Among other things, these archives include *rec.aviation* postings, aircraft specifications, FAR's, and reviews of flight simulation software.

Access via: *ftp rascal.ics.utexas.edu; login anonymous; cd misc/av*

WAIS *aeronautics.src*

DUAT

Pilot flight services via the Internet. It provides pilots with weather briefings and flight planning services. You must be a pilot (or a student pilot) to use this resource.

Access via: *telnet duat.contel.com*
Note: For certificated pilots only.

telnet duats.contel.com
Note: For student pilots.

BIOLOGY

Biotechnology Information

A set of services in the area of biotechnology. Of particular note is the electronic publication of Biotech Briefs. This is a twice-monthly publication of reviews of trade, professional and popular literature concerning biotechnology (e.g., DNA fingerprinting).

See: Agriculture - Advanced Technology Information Network

Drosophila Stocks

A list of sources for Drosophila (fruit flies, to the uninitiated) with various traits. The sources are indexed by trait.

Access via: *IUBio Biology Archives Gopher/Drosophila*

Pictures

A set of "fun" pictures of various animals and plants. All these files are in a standard graphics format (gif).

Access via: *IUBio Biology Archives Gopher/Images*

TAXACOM FTP Server

An information service for systematic biology. Data includes back issues of the journal Flora Online, Beanbag, a newsletter for legume researchers, Taxonomic standards, and many other resources for taxonomists. The *README.TAX* file serves as a table of contents.

Access via: *ftp huh.harvard.edu; login anonymous; cd pub*

News Group: *sci.bio.technology*

CHEMISTRY

News Groups: *sci.[chem, engr.chem]*

CompoundKB Database

See: Molecular Biology - CompoundKB Database

EC Enzyme Database

See: Molecular Biology - EC Enzyme Database

Periodic Table of Elements

What else can you say?

Access via: *University of Minnesota Gopher/Libraries/Reference Works*

Molecular Graphics Software

Contains various pieces of the *raster3D* application for molecular graphics, including several previewers.

Access via: *ftp stanzi.bchem.washington.edu; login anonymous; cd pub*

COMPUTER SCIENCE

News Groups: *comp.[ai, arch, cog-eng, compilers, compression, databases, dcom, editors, graphics, human-factors, lang, lsi, multimedia, music, parallel, programming, protocols, realtime, research, robotics, security, simulation, specification, terminals, theory, windows]*

Communications of the ACM

An experimental server offering the *Communications of the ACM*, from April 1989 to April 1992. It is unclear whether this will be offered in the future.

Access via: WAIS *cacm.src*

Computer Science Archive Sites

This is a list of 70 sites that provide collections of computer science technical reports through anonymous FTP. This list is regularly posted to the news group *comp.doc.techreports*.

Access via:
WAIS *monashuni-techreports.src*

Computer Science Paper Bibliography

The file is a list of journal articles from many computer journals. You can either get the entire list via FTP, or use WAIS to search for interesting articles.

Access via: *ftp cayuga.cs.rochester.edu; login anonymous; cd pub; get papers.lst*
WAIS *monashuni-papers.src*

Computer Science Tech Reports

A collection of technical reports, abstracts, and papers in Computer Science.

Access via:
WAIS *Comp-Sci-Tech-Reports.src*

Information:
E-mail: *farrell@coral.cs.jcu.edu.au*

INRIA Bibliography

The library catalog of the French *Institut National de la Recherche en Informatique et en Automatique* (INRIA). The institute's mission is to provide for the management and knowledge transfer of scientific and technological information. The database, which is updated nightly, contains 6000 research reports, 4300 Ph.D. theses, 2500 conference proceedings, 280 periodical subscriptions, and 300 videos. Keywords and catalog entries are in French.

Access via: WAIS *bibs-zenon-inria-fr.src*

Information:
E-mail: *doc@sophia.inria.fr*

Neural Networking Collection

A collection of literature, bibliographies, and indexes for the study of neural networks.

Access via: *ftp archive.cis.ohio-state.edu; login anonymous; cd pub/neuroprose*
WAIS *neuroprose.src*

Repository of Machine Learning Databases and Domain Theories

The repository contains documented datasets and domain theories to evaluate machine learning algorithms in various areas. Some of the areas available are materials science, games, medicine, mechanical analysis, pattern recognition, and economics.

Access via: *ftp ics.uci.edu; login anonymous; cd pub/machine-learning-databases*

Information:

E-mail: *ml-repository@ics.uci.edu*

SGML

Information about SMGL (Standard Generalized Markup Language). SGML is a standard that provides a uniform way of formatting textual documents, so that they can be read by different document processing tools.

Access via: WAIS *SGML.src*

SIGHyper

Documents produced by the SGML Users' Group's (SGML-UG) Special Interest Group on Hypertext and Multimedia (SIGhyper).

Access via: WAIS *SIGHyper.src*

COMPUTING

News Groups: *comp.sys.[3b1, acorn, alliant, amiga.*, apollo, apple2, atari.*, att, cbm, cdc, concurrent, dec, encore, handhelds, hp48, hp, ibm.pc.*, ibm.ps2.*, intel, isis, laptops, m6809, m68k, m88k, mac.*, mentor, mips, misc, ncr, next.*, northstar, novell, nsc.32k, palmtops, pen, prime, proteon, pyramid, ridge, sequent, sgi, sun.*, super, tahoe, tandy, ti, transputer, unisys, xerox, zenith]*

ASCII Table

The title sums it up!

Access via: *University of Manitoba Gopher/Computer Bits 'n Bites/Misc/ASCII Table*

Applications Navigator

An "extended archie" for Connection Machine massively parallel applications. Authors of software submit descriptions of software they are willing to share to this server. Others can use the WAIS server to search these descriptions for relevant software. The author, status, and restrictions are stated along with descriptions of what the application does. The database contains many different kinds of applications, ranging from fluid flow simulations to "artificial life" codes.

Access via:
WAIS *Applications-Navigator.src*

CERT Security Advisories

Security has become a really hot topic in the last five years. Whether you're trying to protect your system from bright high school "crackers" or professional spies, it's certainly something you should keep informed about. CERT, the Computer Emergency Response Team, is a national focal point for security-related problems. When the CERT finds a security related problem, it issues warnings to various mail lists. This is an indexed archive of those warnings. All system administrators should be aware of this archive!

Access via: WAIS *cert-advisories.src*

To receive advisories as they are issued, send e-mail to *cert@cert.sei.cmu.edu.*

CERT

CERT, the Computer Emergency Response Team, is a federally funded group charged with dealing with computer and network security problems. Their server has papers about security concerns, tools to evaluate security, and an archive of alerts about current break-in attempts.

Access via: *ftp cert.sei.cmu.edu; cd pub*

Excerpt from **Computer Ethics Archive**, *7/1/85:*

Computer Crime and Unlawful
Computer Access

According to Section 21-3755 of
the Kansas Criminal Code, which
went into effect July 1, 1985,
computer crime is:

(a) Willfully and without authorization gaining or attempting to gain access to and damaging, modifying, altering, destroying, copying, disclosing, or
taking possession of a computer,
computer system, computer network, or any other property;

(b) using a computer, computer
system, computer network, or any
other property for the purpose
of devising or executing a
scheme or artifice with the intent to defraud or for the purpose of obtaining money, property, services, or any other thing
of value by means of false or
fraudulent pretense or representation; or

(c) willfully exceeding the
limits of authorization and
damaging, modifying, altering,
destroying, copying, disclosing,
or taking possession of a computer, computer system, computer
network, or any other property.

Compression and Archival Software Summary

A table listing available software, by type of computer, to do and undo archiving and compression. For example: if you use an IBM PC running MS/DOS, and you want to read a UNIX compressed file, what software do you need? Where would you get the software? The more you use the Internet, the more this table will help you.

Access via: *ftp ux1.cso.uiuc.edu;* login *anonymous; cd doc/pcnet; get compression*

Computer Ethics

Contains the computing ethics policies of over thirty universities. It also includes a bibliography, the Bitnet abuse policy, and relevant laws covering computer crime from Canada and several states in the U.S.

Access via: *ftp ariel.unm.edu;* login *anonymous; cd ethics*

Free Software Foundation

The Free Software Foundation (FSF) is an organization devoted to the creation and dissemination of software that is free from licensing fees or restrictions. Software is distributed under the terms of the "General Public License," which also provides a good summary of the Foundation's goals and principles. The FSF has developed the GNU Emacs editor, in addition to replacements for many UNIX utilities and many other tools. A complete UNIX-like operating system (HURD) is in the works. FSF software is available from many places; the archive listed below is probably the most complete and up-to-date. In addition to the software itself, a number of position papers for the FSF are available.

Access via: *ftp prep.ai.mit.edu;* login *anonymous; cd pub/gnu*
Note: The file *COPYING* contains the general public license.

Information:
E-mail: *gnu@prep.ai.mit.edu*

HP Calculator BBS

A bulletin board system by HP to support their calculator customers. Programs, hints, and question/answer facilities are available.

Access via: *telnet hpcvbbs.cv.hp.com;* login *new*

Information System for Advanced Academic Computing

An information service for IBM customers to promote the use of their high-end computers in research and education.

Access via:
telnet isaac.engr.washington.edu
Note: Must apply for an account; can take a few weeks.

Information:
E-mail: *isaac@isaac.engr.washington.edu*

League for Programming Freedom

The League for Programming Freedom is an organization that opposes software patents and interface copyrights. They maintain an archive of position papers and legal information about important test cases.

Access via: *ftp prep.ai.mit.edu*; login *anonymous*; *cd pub/lpf*

Information:
E-mail: *league@prep.ai.mit.edu*

NeXT.FAQ

A set of frequently asked questions about NeXt computers, dealing with hardware, software, specialized jargon, and configurations.

Access via: WAIS *NeXT.FAQ.src*

Information:
E-mail: *akers@next2.oit.unc.edu*

O'Reilly and Associates, Inc.

 Source code for examples in the X series and Nutshell handbooks; archives of the Davenport group (online publishing); online catalog for all ORA books.

Access via: *ftp ftp.ora.com*; login *anonymous*; *cd pub* Note: For online examples.
telnet gopher.ora.com; login *gopher*;
Note: For online catalog.

Information:
E-mail: *bookquestions@ora.com*

PC Magazine

Electronic versions of the PC Magazine published by Ziff Davis.

Access via: *ftp wuarchive.wustl.edu*; login *anonymous*; *cd mirrors/msdos/pcmag*
Note: This is just one of many places this is available. Find others with *archie pcmag*.

Public UNIX Access

A few sites on the Internet are "freeish" public UNIX servers. The number of concurrent users is limited. On some servers, priority is given to "patrons" who make donations to keep the service alive.

Access via: *telnet nyx.cs.du.edu*; login *new*

telnet hermes.merit.edu; host *um-m-net*; then *g*; login *newuser*

San Diego Super Computer Documentation

Primarily designed as a service to their own users; a lot of the information is not relevant to the average person. However, it is a free place to look at Cray documentation. If you want to find out what it's like to use a supercomputer, you can look here.

Access via: WAIS *San_Diego_Super_-Computer_Center_Docs.src*

Supernet

A bulletin board system for people doing supercomputing. General areas of postings include a research register, job bank, supercomputing journal review, and software.

Access via: *telnet supernet.ans.net*; login *supernet*

Concert gopher/Internet Information Servers/General Information Servers

The Jargon File

This is a computing jargon dictionary. It was the basis for the book "The New Hacker's Dictionary."

Access via: WAIS *jargon.src*

Excerpt from **The Jargon File**, *8/19/92:*

```
blow out: vi. Of software, to
fail spectacularly; almost as
serious as {crash and burn}.
See {blow past}, {blow up}.
```

UNIX Manual

The standard UNIX reference manual, but available as a WAIS service. If you hate using **apropos** or **man -k** to find relevant man pages, and if you can't stand permuted indices, here's your chance to use something better. The manual currently appears to be for SunOS 4.1.

Access via: WAIS *unix-manual.src*

UNIX Booklist

A compilation of UNIX and C book titles, along with pertinent information for locating them (including ISBN, publisher, and ordering information where available). Also includes short reviews and summaries of book contents. Maintained by Mitch Wright in his spare time. He encourages contributions and corrections.

Access via: ftp *ftp.rahul.net*; login *anonymous; cd pub/mitch/YABL; get yabl.Z*

Information:
E-mail: *mitch@yahoo.cirrus.com*

UNIX Reference Card

A good source of basic UNIX commands.

Access via: ftp *ucselx.sdsu.edu*; login *anonymous; cd pub/doc/general*

UUNET FTP archives

One of the largest archives of free source code and USENET news available. The file *ls-lR.Z* is a compressed master list of everything that's vailable. You can also search the UUNET archives using WAIS; see the next item.

Access via: ftp *ftp.uu.net*; login *anonymous*

WAIS Software Search Sources

The three WAIS sources given here fairly well cover how to use WAIS to search for files. **uunet.uu.net** is a server which contains a good set of up-to-date software, primarily for the convenience of their clients. Archie is, of course the WAIS-indexed version of Archie's anonymous FTP index. Finally, *wuarchive.src* contains the contents of the software archive maintained by Washington University. Between these three sources, you can find almost any generally available software.

Access via: WAIS *uunet.src*
WAIS *archie-orst.src*
WAIS *wuarchive.src*

COOKING

News Group: *rec.food.cooking*

Home brewing

See: Zymurgy

Info and Softserver

A general information server at the University of Stuttgart. Has a collection of recipes and a cookbook online. Instructions are presented in German. Recipes are in both German and English.

Access via: telnet *rusmv1.rus.uni-stuttgart.de*; login *infoserv; cd cookbook*

LOUBIA BIL LUZ—Algerian green
beans with almonds. This is a
variation on an Algerian recipe
from Rose Dosti's Middle Eastern
Cooking. Since when is North
Africa in the Middle East? You
may well ask.

Serves 4
1 lb fresh green beans (500 g)
4 cups water (1 liter), salted
3 Tbsp peanut oil (50 ml)
1 clove garlic mashed
1/2 tsp ground cumin (2.5 ml)
1/4 tsp paprika (1 ml)
1/4 tsp ground cloves (1 ml)
1 Tbsp slivered almonds (15 g)

Clean and trim green beans. Simmer in lightly salted water until just tender, about 30-45
minutes. Drain and put in serving dish. Put remaining ingredients (except almonds) in a
saucepan over medium heat and
cook for two minutes, stirring
constantly. Add the almonds and
stir briefly to coat. Pour the
oil mixture over the green beans
and toss gently until beans are
thoroughly coated. Serve warm.

Canned green beans are not an
acceptable substitute in this
recipe. Powdered garlic is probably OK.

Difficulty: easy.
Time: 10 minutes preparation, 50
minutes cooking.
Precision: approximate measurement OK.

Author: Karen Kolling, DEC Systems Research
Center, Palo Alto, California, USA
kolling@src.DEC.COM decwrl!decsrc!kolling

Recipe Archives

These are mostly recipes which have passed
through *rec.food.cooking* over the past
years. You might also look for the file
beyond.ps.Z, a cookbook in compressed
postscript (must be printed on a postscript
printer), on *mthvax.cs.miami.edu*.

Access via: *ftp gatekeeper.dec.com;* login
anonymous; cd pub/recipes
Note: Organized by title.

ftp mthvax.cs.mimai.edu; login *anonymous;
cd recipes*
Note: Organized by main ingredient.

WAIS *usenet-cookbook.src*
Note: Searchable through WAIS.

Recipes

A set of recipes searchable by keyword and
contents.

Access via: WAIS *recipes.src*

EDUCATION

News Groups: *k12.ed.[art, business,
comp.literacy, health-pe, life-skills, math,
music, science, soc-studies, special, tag,
tech] and k12.lang.[art, deutsch-eng, esp-
eng, francais, russian]*

ERIC Digests Archive

Short reports of 1500 words or less, of interest to teachers, administrators, and others in
the field of education. The reports are typically overviews of information on a given

topic. Reports were produced by the ERIC Clearinghouses, funded by the U.S. Department of Education.

Access via: WAIS *ERIC-archive.src*
WAIS *eric-digest.src*

Educational Leadership

An experimental server of the ASCD publication *Educational Leadership.* Contains copyrighted articles from the last two years.

Access via: WAIS *ascd-education.src*

Information:
E-mail: *bhughes@pc.maricopa.edu*

Federal Information Exchange

An information liaison between various government agencies and the higher education community. Provides timely information on Federal education and research programs, scholarships and fellowships, surplus equipment, funding opportunities, and general information.

Access via: *telnet fedix.fie.com*; login *fedix*

International Centre for Distance Learning

This database concentrates on "distance learning": correspondence courses, courses offered via television or audio tape, and other forms of "remote education." The database includes descriptions of "distance-learning" programs, and secondary literature about distance learning. The courses cover all academic disciplines (humanities, arts, sciences, engineering, agriculture, medicine, social sciences), all educational levels (from primary to post-graduate) and are taken from all parts of

the world. From looking at this list, it's immediately obvious that "distance learning" is particularly important in the Third World.

Access via: *telnet sun.nsf.ac.uk*; login *janet*; Hostname: *uk.ac.open.acs.vax*; username *icdl*
Note: Free access ends September 1, 1992; registration and fee will be required.

Information:
E-mail: *n.ismail@vax.acs.open.ac.uk* (comments on database)

E-mail: *l.r.a.melton@vax.acs.open.ac.uk* (enquiries)
Phone: +44 908 653537

Kidsnet

This is the indexed archive of the Kidsnet mailing list. Kidsnet is a list to foster international networking for children and educators. To join send a message to *kidsnet-request@vms.cis.pitt.edu.*

Access via: WAIS *kidsnet.src*

Minority Online Information Service

Information about Black and Hispanic colleges and universities. Includes information on faculty, academic programs, degrees granted, and specialties. Part of the Federal Information Exchange.

Access via: *telnet fedix.fie.com*; login *molis*

National Education Bulletin Board System

A semi-closed system for NESP educators to discuss topics of interest to them. There is a public guest account, but it only provides limited access. Anyone in the NESP can request an account.

Access via: *telnet nebbs.nersc.gov*; login *guest*

Excerpt from **Kidsnet***, 7/28/92:*

```
Notes in a bottle.  Hello! You
have just uncorked a bottle you
saw floating in the Sea of FrEd-
Mail. And in this bottle are our
notes!  Please, write to us! We
want to hear from you! We want
to know how far this bottle
traveled and who you are!

We aren't shipwrecked or any-
thing. Just a little bored.

We are students at Morrill
Middle School in San Jose, Cali-
fornia.  Each one of us has an
electronic mail account at the
port of CHALK on the Sea of
FrEdMail. To write to Chip
Brown, for example, from FrEd-
Mail, toss your bottle in this
direction:  CBROWN@CHALK.
```

Software and Aids for Teaching of Mathematics

A collection of software to aid in the teaching of mathematics at the college and university levels. Also includes newsletters, reprints, and other material of interest in the area. Most of the software is for IBM PC compatibles. Other computers may be supported in the future.

Access via: *ftp wuarchive.wustl.edu;* login *anonymous; cd etc/math*

Information:
E-mail: *husch@wuarchive.wustl.edu*

SpaceMet

See: Aeronautics and Astronautics-SpaceMet

ELECTRICAL ENGINEERING

Electromagnetics Resources

A server with papers, conference information, and mailing lists organized around the study of electromagnetics.

Access via: *ftp ftp.eng.auburn.edu;* login *anonymous; cd pub/electromagnetics*

ENGINEERING

News Groups: *sci.[engr, engr.chem, engr.biomed]*

CERCNET

A gathering place for people interested in concurrent engineering. Under the auspices of the Concurrent Engineering Research Center, funded by DARPA. It has bulletin boards, conference and training schedules, and a job registry.

Access via: *telnet babcock.cerc.wvu.wvnet.edu;* login *cercnet*

Information:
E-mail: *jrs@cerc.wvu.wvnet.edu*
Phone: (304) 293-7226

ENVIRONMENT

News Groups: *sci.environment*

Biosphere Newsletter

Issues of the Biosphere newsletter online, plus the "Earth Day, 1991" bibliography.

Access via: *ftp mthvax.cs.miami.edu;* login *anonymous; cd pub/biosph*

Carbon Dioxide Information Analysis Center

CDIAC is part of Oak Ridge National Laboratory. It provides information to researchers, policymakers and educators about atmospheric changes and climate change (in particular, "global warming"). Contains both data and scientific papers in this area. In addition to information about carbon dioxide levels, there is also information about CFCs (chlorinated fluorocarbons) and other gasses. Sponsored by the U.S. Department of Energy.

Access via: *ftp cdiac.esd.ornl.gov*; login *anonymous; cd pub*

Environmental Protection Agency Library

A catalog to the holdings of the EPA's national library. The database has "subsections" for material on hazardous waste, lake management and protection, and chemical agents. The library includes EPA reports and many other kinds of documents. Includes abstracts.

Access via: *telnet epaibm.rtpnc.epa.gov*; select "public"

ERIN

Newsletters in postscript format from the Environmental Resources Information Network, an Australian remote sensing and environmental monitoring group.

Access via: *ftp huh.harvard.edu*; login *anonymous; cd pub*

Pesticides

An agricultural extension bulletin written by Sue Snider and Mark Graustein. This bulletin explains what a pesticide is, the laws which regulate pesticides, and their uses, benefits and detriments.

Access via: *University of Delaware Gopher/Agricultural Extension Information: AGinfo/Extension Bulletins*

Excerpt from **Pesticides (Univ. Delaware Agricultural Ext)**, *7/16/92:*

Although consumers may feel helpless in controlling pesticide residues on foods, there are some things you can do to reduce the amount you potentially could consume.

1) Wash all produce thoroughly. Either wash under running water or in water. Lift the food out of the water rather than allowing the water to drain through the produce since this will allow substances to resettle on the food. Also, wash in several changes of water.

Although some individuals have suggested washing produce in soap, no government agency (FDA, EPA, or USDA) recommends using soap on any food product. Because of the porous nature of food and the many cracks and crevices that may be present, soap residues may be difficult to remove. The safety of soap residues on food has not been determined.

2) Peel or remove the outer leaves of produce. This can also reduce the residue levels.

3) Eat a variety of foods. If only a few foods are consumed, there is a greater chance that you will be exposed to only a few pesticides and possibly in larger quantities than if you eat a variety of foods.

4) If you have a home garden, read and follow the directions for each pesticide. Not only is the amount to apply and the time period before harvesting important, but the pesticide should be used only on the fruit or vegetable listed on the label.

South Florida Environmental Reader

An archive of back issues of the South Florida Environmental reader. The reader is now distributed in electronic form only.

Access via: *ftp mthvax.cs.miami.edu;* login *anonymous; cd EnvironmentalReader*

Send message to *listserv@ucf1vm.bitnet;* body of message should contain *SUB SFER-L first-name last-name*

United Nations Rio Summit Agenda

The agenda of the United Nations Conference on Environment and Development (known as Agenda 21) held in the summer of 1992.

Access via: WAIS *unced-agenda.src*

Water Quality Education Materials

A set of educational materials on U.S. water quality assessment, maintenance and improvement, provided by the Cooperative Extension System.

Access via: WAIS *water-quality.src*

FORESTRY

Social Sciences in Forestry

An annotated bibliography of the Forestry Library at the University of Minnesota, College of Natural Resources. The bibliography covers many areas of forestry, including the history, legislation, taxation, social and communal forestry, and agroforestry.

Access via: *University of Minnesota, College of Natural Resources Gopher/Social Sciences in Forestry*

Trees

Various kinds of information about trees including care and maintenance, planting, selection, and signs and symptoms of tree problems, thanks to the University of Delaware Agricultural Extension Service.

Access via: *University of Delaware Gopher/Agricultural Extension Information: AGinfo/Brochures and Other Publications*

FREENETS

Freenets are grassroots efforts to provide networking services to an urban community, with access either at public libraries or by dialing in. It's also possible to access Freenets through the Internet. Freenets are usually organized around a model town that you "walk" through. You can stop at the "courthouse and government center" and discuss local issues with the mayor. Or you could stop by the "medical arts building" and discuss health issues with a health professional. Aside from discussions, there are usually bulletin boards, electronic mail, and other information services. There are some real hidden gem resources on some freenets. These are indexed separately. Anyone can use a freenet as a guest, but guest privileges are limited; for example, you can't use e-mail and a few other things. The software they use is menu-driven and designed for ease of use. So give them a try. If you think you'd like to organize a freenet for your town, contact Dr. T. M. Grundner at *aa001@cleveland.freenet.edu.*

Cleveland Free-Net

The original freenet and still the hub of freenet development.

Access via: *telnet freenet-in-a.cwru.edu*

telnet freenet-in-b.cwru.edu

telnet freenet-in-c.cwru.edu

Heartland Freenet

A freenet centered in Peoria, Illinois. Has typical freenet things, plus information about recreation and jobs in the State of Illinois.

Access via: *telnet heartland.bradley.edu*; login *bbguest*

Lorain County Freenet

A freenet centered in Elyria, Ohio.

Access via: *telnet freenet.lorain.oberlin.edu*; login *guest*

Tri-State Online

A freenet centered around the Cincinnati, Ohio area.

Access via: *telnet 129.137.100.1*; login *visitor*

Youngstown Freenet

A freenet centered in Youngstown, Ohio.

Access via: *telnet yfn.ysu.edu*; login *visitor*

GARDENING & HORTICULTURE

The Gardener's Assistant

A shareware program for the personal computer that assists one in planning and planting a garden. You feed it a bunch of information, and it tells you what type of plants to grow, when to plant, and how to care for it. Registration information is available.

Access via: *ftp wuarchive.wustl.edu*; login *anonymous*; *cd mirrors/msdos/database*

Horticultural Engineering Newsletter

Issues of the publication are available. Contains information on greenhouses, seeds, and other technical information about horticulture techniques.

See: Agriculture - PEN Pages (Under the Rutgers University section)

GENEALOGY

Genealogical Information

Genealogical information of all types can be found here. Genealogy database programs, lists of various genealogical societies, magazines and newsletters are included along with cemetery information. There is also information on the National Genealogical Society and a list of tips for beginners.

Access via: *ftp hallc1.cebaf.gov*; login *anonymous*; *cd genealogy*
Note: All files which are not programs have a *.zip* extension.

GEOGRAPHY

CIA World Map

The CIA map database comes in two flavors. The complete database is large (roughly 10 Megabytes), and is broken into five pieces for convenience. A smaller version, which only draws map outlines (coastlines, islands, lakes, and political boundaries in the Americas), is also available. Both versions include a map drawing program.

Access via: *ftp hanauma.stanford.edu*; login *anonymous*; *cd pub/World_Map*; start with *get README*
Note: Some lists say that this site will be discontinued soon, but the data will be moved elsewhere.

Geographic Server

An interface to data supplied by the U.S. Geodetic Survey and the U.S. Postal Service. You make requests which look like the city line of addresses (e.g., Casslake, MN). It returns latitude, longitude, population, zipcode, elevation, etc. Output is designed to be used with a client, but it is usable by inspection.

Access via: *telnet martini.eecs.umich.edu* port *3000*

GEOLOGY & GEOPHYSICS

News Groups: *sci.geo.geology*

Computer Oriented Geological Society (COGS)

The archives of the Computer Oriented Geological Society's bulletin board service. It contains lots of interesting material, including application forms for membership in the society. One file that's particularly worth having is *internet.resources.earth.sci*. This is a detailed list of many resources available, including many data archives, digitized maps, bibliographies and online publications. There's also a lot of software available, for disciplines like Geophysics, Geochemistry, Hydrology, Mineralogy, Mining, oil exploration, etc. There are also a number of Landsat images available.

Access via: *ftp csn.org*; login *anonymous*; cd *COGS*

Information:
E-mail: *cogs@flint.mines.colorado.edu*
Phone: (303) 751-8553

Earthquake Information

Information about recent earthquakes. Location, magnitude, and accuracy are given for each event.

Access via:
finger quake@geophys.washington.edu

USGS Geological Fault Maps

A digital database of geological faults, covering the United States. Includes software to draw maps from the faults. The raw data isn't in any standard format (it appears to be latitude/longitude pairs), so you'll need the mapping software. The directory *pub/summary* at this site contains another interesting database: records of California earthquakes.

Access via: *ftp alum.wr.usgs.gov*; login *anonymous*; cd *pub/maps*

USGS Weekly Seismicity Reports

Weekly reports of seismic activity (earthquakes, volcanos, etc.) and maps for Northern California, the U.S., and the World.

Access via: *Northwestern University, Department of Geological Sciences Gopher/USGS Weekly Seismicity Reports* Note: The *weekmap.dos* file is in ASCII format.

GOVERNMENT, U.S.

FDA Electronic Bulletin Board

A bulletin board containing information on FDA (Food and Drug Administration) actions, congressional testimony, news releases, consumer information, AIDS, and veterinary medicine. For example, you can use this database to find out what drugs have been approved recently.

Access via: *telnet fdabbs.fda.gov*; login *bbs*

Index to U.S. Government Programs

An index of government program abstracts.

Access via: WAIS *US-Gov-Programs.src*

NIH Guide to Grants and Programs 1991

Old and incomplete, but perhaps useful online version of the National Institutes of Health Guide to Grants and Programs for most of 1991. The guide contains the text of notices, announcements and RFAs of interest to biomedical researchers.

Access via: WAIS *NIH-Guide.src*

NSF Awards

This is a subset of the STIS service. It consists of the abstracts of the awards made by NSF since 1990.

Access via: WAIS *nsf-awards.src*

NSF Publications

Publications of the National Science Foundation. They can be searched. However, if you are interested in a particular award and know its number, you can shorten the search by using the number as a search key: just omit spaces and punctuation. For example, use nsf9110 for NSF 91-10. This is also a subset of the STIS service.

Access via: WAIS *nsf-pubs.src*

National Archives

The National Archive's Center for Electronic Records provides a historical repository for significant electronic records collected by the Federal government. Although the records are not available through the Internet, inquiries can be made through the noted e-mail address. A writeup of the services provided is available.

Access via: *ftp ra.msstate.edu*; login *anonymous; cd docs/databases; get national.archives.*

Information:
E-mail: *tif@nihcu.bitnet* Phone: (202) 501-5579

Science and Technology Information Service

STIS provides information about programs sponsored by the National Science Foundation. The NSF Bulletin, Guide to Programs, program announcements, press releases, and a listing of awards are available.

Access via: *telnet stis.nsf.gov*; login *public NSF Gopher*

Social Security Administration

Lots of documents about social security, as you'd expect. You'll find listings of social security publications, speeches and testimony by members of the social security commission, press releases, etc. However, the archive certainly isn't limited to social security information; there are a lot of other government documents, along with random collections of information, like an archive of news postings on carpal tunnel syndrome.

Access via: *ftp soaf1.ssa.gov; login anonymous; cd pub*

State Department Travel Advisories

The periodic advisories from the U.S. State Department warn about areas in which foreign travel is dangerous. If you like to travel to out-of-the-way places, this resource is invaluable!

Access via: *University of Minnesota Gopher/Libraries/Reference Works*

Zipcode Guide 1991

A list of postal zipcodes for the U.S. from 1991. The format is:

00401:Pleasantville, NY
00501:Holtsville, NY

Access via: *ftp oes.orst.edu; login anonymous; cd pub/almanac/misc; get zipcode.txt.Z*
Note: UNIX compressed format.

WAIS *zipcodes.src*

HEALTH

News Groups: *sci.[med.aids, med.physics, med], k12.ed.health-pe*

AIDS Information Resource

See: Society and Culture - Queer Resources Directory

AIDS Treatment News

An online newsletter on the treatment of AIDS.

Access via: *Louisiana Tech University Gopher/Electronic Media Sources/ISSN Serials*

Carpal Tunnel Syndrome

See: Government

Conversational Hypertext

A "natural language information system." I don't know if this is more interesting as an example of a hypertext application, or as source of information. At any rate, information on AIDS and Epilepsy is currently available, along with the Canadian Department of Communications.

Access via: *telnet debra.doc.ca; login chat*

Great Beginnings

A newsletter on the care and feeding of infants and young toddlers. It includes information about parental expectations, typical behavior, home-made toys, language games, and so on.

Access via: *University of Delaware Gopher/Agricultural Extension Information: AGinfo/Newsletters/Great Beginnings*

Handicap News BBS Archive

A collection of information and sources for and about the disabled. The archive includes legal and medical data, in addition to information about social services.

Access via: *ftp handicap.shel.isc-br.com; login anonymous*
Note: Start with README to find your way around.

Excerpt from **Great Beginnings**, *7/20/92:*

```
HOMEMADE TOYS THAT TEACH:
EGG CARTON FUN

Why?
This toy can help toddlers learn
about shapes and colors, and
teach them to understand simi-
larities and differences.

Materials
Cardboard egg carton (don't use
styrofoam; children can easily
break off and swallow pieces)
Poster paint or crayons Magazine
pictures

Making the Toy
Color the inside cups of an egg
carton different colors with
crayon or with watercolor
paints. Use bright colors — red,
blue, green, yellow. Cut circles
out of cardboard small enough to
fit into the cups. Color the
circles with colors that match
the painted cups.

Playing
Place the circles on the table
or floor. Ask your toddler to
put the circles in the cup of
the same color: the red circle
in the red cup, the blue circle
in the blue cup, and so on.
```

National Family Database (MAPP)

MAPP contains research briefs, bibliographies, census data, reference materials, program ideas, etc., on topics related to families. The material is oriented towards cooperative extension professionals and family educators. There's also information here about senior citizens, youth development (the latter provided by 4-H).

See: Agriculture - PEN Pages

HISTORY

News Groups: *soc.history*

Historical Documents

Many historical documents and speeches, including the Declaration of Independence, Bill of Rights, Surrender Documents, "I have a dream . . . ," The Gettysburg Address, and others are available from many Internet servers. They are part of project Gutenberg, and also available on many Freenets in the "Freedom Shrine."

Access via: *University of Minnesota Gopher/Libraries/Electronic Books/By Title/Historical Documents*

Mississippi State History Archives

This is an FTP site that contains many resources related to the study of history. It includes the National Council of History's Education newsletter (in the directory *newsletters*, files beginning with *NCHE*), materials on the Vietnam War, various bibliographies, and other material. Aside from the material on Vietnam and the NCHE newsletter, there doesn't appear to be any particular theme to what's available: there's material on medieval studies, French socialism, Andrew Jackson, the American Indian movement, and other topics scattered around. If you're a historian, it's worth 10 minutes of your time to see what's available here.

Access via: *ftp ra.msstate.edu*; login *anonymous; cd docs/history*

HOBBIES & CRAFTS

News Groups: *alt.[aquaria, magic, sewing], rec.[antiques, aquaria, collecting, crafts.brewing, crafts.misc, crafts.textiles, folk-dancing, gambling, gardens, guns, juggling, models.railroad, models.rc, models.rockets, photo, radio.amateur.misc, radio.amateur.packet, radio.amateur.policy, radio.cb, railroad, roller-coaster, woodworking]*

```
>> call kc1nb
Call-Sign: KC1NB
Class: ADVANCED
Real Name: MICHAEL K LOUKIDES
Birthday: SEP 18, 1955
Mailing Address: 229 BRANFORD RD
310, NORTH BRANFORD, CT 06471
Station Address: SAME AS MAILING
ADDRESS
Valid From: JAN 3, 1989
To: JAN 3, 1999
Records Last Processed: JAN 3,
1989
```

Ham Radio Callbook

The national ham (amateur) radio call sign index. You can look up hams by callsign, name, or area.

Access via: *telnet callsign.cs.buffalo.edu* port *2000*

Hockey Cards Mailing List Archive

A mailing list dedicated to hockey card collectors. People to trade with and checklists are available. Subscribe with *hockeyrequest@yahoo.cirrus.com.*

Access via: *ftp ftp.rahul.net;* login *anonymous; cd pub/mitch/hockey;* start with *get README*

Information:
E-mail: *mitch@cirrus.com*

Juggling FTP Archives

A set of resources for the juggling enthusiast. Has such resources as Jugglers World Newsletter, lists of vendors, festivals, clubs. Also, some information on the International Jugglers Association.

Access via: *ftp piggy.cogsci.indiana.edu;* login *anonymous; cd pub/juggling*

Information:
E-mail: *terry@piggy.cogsci.indiana.edu*

HUMANITIES

American Philosophical Association Bulletin Board

News of the American Philosophical Association, information about conferences, information about other philosophical societies, a "white-pages" service, bibliographies, discussion groups, and news. There's a listing of grants, fellowships, and academic positions. Note that the log-on message states that the service will be changing significantly (and improving) shortly.

Access via: *telnet atl.calstate.edu;* login *apa*

Information:
E-mail: *traiger@oxy.edu*

ANU SocSci Netlore

A collection (600Kb) of documents, notes, hints and net-lore dealing with the information resources, e-mail and networking procedures of significance to academic researchers in the fields of the Social Sciences, the Arts and the Humanities.

Access via: WAIS *ANU-SocSci-Netlore.src*

Information: Phone: +61 6 249-4600
E-mail: *wais@coombs.anu.edu.au*

Humanist

Contains Volumes 2 through 5 of the Humanist discussion list of interest to humanities scholars especially those interested in computer applications in the humanities.

Access via: WAIS *humanist.src*

Research and Education Applications of Computing in Humanities Newsletter

Various issues of the newsletter are available.

Access via: *ftp ra.msstate.edu;* login *anonymous; cd docs/history/newsletters* Note: Various files beginning with *REACH.* *

INTERNET

See: Network - various headings

JOURNALISM

Journalism Periodicals Index

Over 10,000 citations from the Index to Journalism Periodicals by the Graduate School of Journalism at the University of Western Ontario. This may become a fee based service in the future. To start try searching for "helpinfo." To receive further information, or to request a subscription, contact:

Heather York-Marshall
Co-ordinator, Resource Centre
The Graduate School of Journalism
Middlesex College
The University of Western Ontario
London, Ontario, Canada N6A 5B7
Phone: (519) 661-3383 ext. 6661

Access via:
WAIS *journalism.periodicals.src*

Wall Street Journal Sample

A few months of old Wall Street Journals online as an experiment to see how one might use an online newspaper completely indexed. This is not particularly of any use as news, but it is a reasonably good source to hone your WAIS searching skills.

Access via:
WAIS *wall-street-journal-sample.src*

LAW

News Group: *misc.legal*

Columbia Index to Hispanic Legislation

Data provided by the Library of Congress to Columbia Law School concerning hispanic oriented legislation.

Access via:
WAIS *columbia-spanish-law-catalog.src*

Information:
E-mail: *willem@lawmail.law.columbia.edu*

Columbia Law Library Catalog

A subset of 175,000 records from Columbia law school's online card catalog. The data from a standard LC formatted USMARC cataloging tapeset.

Access via:
WAIS *columbia-law-library-catalog.src*

Information:
E-mail: *willem@lawmail.law.columbia.edu*

Cornell Law Gopher

A specialized gopher server devoted to law. It includes an index of legal academia, an archive of the "law-lib" mailing list, the "teknoids" mailing list (which has lots of articles about computer applications used in law), and other services of interest.

Access via: *Cornell Law School Gopher*

Corporation for Research and Educational Networking (CREN)

CREN is the corporation that runs BITNET. It has asked its attorneys to research their liability in using the network to access foreign countries. These files are specific to BITNET, but are probably applicable to the Internet as well.

Access via: *mail listserv@bitnic.bitnet;
body of message should contain 3 lines:get legal commerce; get legal gtda; get legal counsel*

Hong Kong Laws

An archive provided by "The Alliance of Hong Kong Chinese in the United States," including the Basic Law of Hong Kong. There are several files, including the Hong Kong Bill of Rights. This resource also contains articles on human rights issues in Mainland China, and software for displaying articles written in Chinese.

Access via: *ftp ahkcus.org*; login *anonymous*; *cd hongkong/political*

Law Employers

A service under construction which lists major legal employers in U.S. and U.S. firms overseas. As time goes on, the descriptions will be refined.

Access via: WAIS *law-employers.src*

Information:
E-mail: *willem@lawmail.law.columbia.edu*

Project Hermes

A posting of recent U.S. Supreme Court decisions. The Supreme Court decided to promote timely distribution of its decisions by allowing selected computer services to access these decisions online at the Supreme court and download them. Project Hermes is one such service.

See: Freenet - Cleveland Freenet
Note: Part of the "Courthouse".

Access via: WAIS *supreme-court.src*

Sydney University Law School FTP Archive

Contains an interesting collection of various U.S. laws. The laws are both state and federal. Organized both by state and topic.

Access via: *ftp sulaw.law.su.oz.au*; login *anonymous*; *cd pub/law*
Note: README file claims all files are compressed even though their name does not flag them as such.

U.S. Judges Clerkship Requirements

There is an entry for each federal and upper level state court. It describes the requirements to apply for clerkship in each of the courts as of January 15, 1992.

Access via: WAIS *us-judges.src*

Information:
E-mail: *willem@lawmail.law.columbia.edu*

Washington and Lee Law Library

A mixed collection of legal data. Text of some laws can be found, along with some information on conferences and meetings.

Access via: *telnet liberty.uc.wlu.edu*; login *lawlib*

ftp liberty.uc.wlu.edu; login *anonymous*; *cd pub/lawlib*

LIBRARIES

News Groups: *soc.libraries.talk*

So many library catalogs are available through the Internet that we won't list them all; you can find them conveniently through Gopher, or through the "St. George" listings discussed below. We will list a few catalogs that are of special interest. It's worth making a few comments on what you're likely to find:

- Most libraries are adding all new books to their online catalogs, but only gradually entering their old books (if at all). Therefore, some library's catalog may tell you they don't have a copy of *Gulliver's Travels*. Don't believe it; this only means that they haven't bought a copy recently. Likewise, rare books, special collections, and other "interesting" material may not be represented online.

- Traditional card catalogs usually have fairly good descriptions of the books. Online catalogs are, for the most part, much more skimpy. This isn't a great step forward, but there's not much you can do about it. Many libraries no longer maintain their traditional catalogs.

- The plus side is that many library catalogs aren't just catalogs: they provide other important resources, like bibliographies, subject indices, abstracts, and online periodicals. Some even provide dictionaries and encyclopedias. There may be a great deal of information at your disposal.

CARL (Colorado Association of Research Libraries)

The CARL catalog provides much more than a simple library catalog: it's what a library catalog *could be*. CARL offers much more than a catalog of virtually every academic library in Colorado. It also offers a wide assortment of online text, indices of model school programs, online book reviews, facts about the metropolitan Denver area, and a database on environmental education. We could have cross-references to CARL from almost every section of this catalog. It's worth spending a few minutes browsing, just to see what you'll find—even if you don't live in Colorado.

Access via: *telnet pac.carl.org*

Internet Accessible Library Catalogs and Databases

Several hundred online library catalogs are available through the Internet. Art St. George and Ron Larsen's guide to library catalogs and databases is probably the most complete and up-to-date guide to these libraries.

Access via: Send message to *listserv@umnvma.bitnet*; body of message should contain *get library package*

WAIS *online-libraries-st-george.src*

ftp ariel.unm.edu; cd library; get internet.library

Library Catalogs Accessible Through telnet

If you don't want to look through the massive St. George listing, Gopher offers a good shortcut.

Access via: *University of Minnesota Gopher/Libraries/Library Catalogs Via Telnet*

Library of Congress Records

The catalog and records of the Library of Congress.

Access via: *telnet dra.com*
Note: Must use VT100 emulation.

University of Minnesota Gopher/Libraries/Library of Congress Records

Reader's Guide to Periodical Literature

Yes, that old workhorse, the *Reader's Guide to Periodical Literature*, is available on the Internet. In case you've forgotten, it's a topic-oriented index to virtually all general-interest magazines published in the U.S.: *Time*, *Popular Mechanics*, etc. You can search it electronically, by author, title, subject, keyword, and so on.

Access via: *telnet lib.uwstout.edu*

RLIN (Research Libraries Information Network)

One of the largest online "catalogs of catalogs," encompassing most major research libraries in the United States. It's also interesting because it contains many special resources, including an index of architectural periodicals; a database of research in progress; and (eventually) the "Medieval and Early Modern Data Bank."

Access via: *telnet rlg.stanford.edu*; must register first; fee charged.

Information:
E-mail: *bl.ric@rlg.stanford.edu* Phone: 800 537-RLIN

UNT's Accessing On-Line Bibliographic Databases

A list of online bibliographic databases (library catalogs online). Several files of note:

libraries.txt	ASCII version
libraries.ps	Postscript version
libraries.wp5	WordPerfect 5.1 source (transfer in binary mode)
libraries.con	WordPerfect 5.1 concordance file (binary mode)
libraries.adr	Numeric IP addresses of Internet libraries
libraries.contacts	Contacts for some of the Internet libraries

Access via: *ftp ftp.unt.edu*; login *anonymous*; *cd library*

Information:
E-mail: *billy@unt.edu*

LIBRARY & INFORMATION SCIENCE

ANU Pacific Manuscripts Microfilm Catalog

Complete annotated catalogue of the microfilms collection of the Pacific Manuscripts Bureau (PAMBU), Research School of Pacific Studies, Australian National University, GPO Box 4, Canberra ACT 2601.

Access via:
WAIS *ANU-Pacific-Manuscripts.src*

Information: Phone: +61 6 249-2521
E-mail: *pambu@coombs.anu.edu.au*

Current Cites

A monthly publication of the University of California, Berkeley, Library. It contains selected articles on electronic information technology.

Access via: WAIS *current.cites.src*

Information:
E-mail: *rtennant@library.berkeley.edu*

Directory of Electronic Journals and Newsletters

Information about existing electronic journals and also tips for starting and running new ones.

Access via: Send mail to *list-serv@acadvm1.uottawa.ca* with the commands *GET EJOURNL1 DIRECTRY* and *GET EJOURNL2 DIRECTRY* in the message body.

ISSN's for Electronic Serials

A listing of ISSN numbers and titles of available electronic serials, including *Public-Access Computer Systems Review* and *ALCTS Network News*. Many of the serials themselves are directly available.

Access via: *Louisiana Tech University Gopher/Electronic Media Sources/ISSN Serials*

Libraries and Information Resources Networks: a Bibliography

Access via: *ftp csuvax1.csu.murdoch.edu.au*; login *anonymous*; *cd pub/library*; *get stanton.bib*

MC(2)—Meckler's Electronic Publishing Service

A project to make Meckler publishing and some of its journals available online. The MeckJournal is available online, plus catalogs and ordering information.

Access via: *telnet nisc.jvnc.net*; login *nicol*; select *MC2* with arrow keys

ftp ftp.jvnc.net; login *anonymous*; *cd meckler*

Newbooks

Bibliographic information reported to the Cataloging in Publication program. It is provided as is, without warranty.

Excerpt from **Meckler's Electronic Publishing Service**, *7/15/92:*

An electronic publishing division has been established and through Meckler's link with Princeton University's JvNCNet it offers a service called MC(2). Currently featured on the MC(2) electronic system is the complete catalog of Meckler Information Technology Publishing, full conference programs for four technology conferences (Virtual Reality, HD WORLD, Electronic Networking and Publishing '92, and Computers in Libraries Canada), as well as five-year indexes to two of its monthly publications.

The editors of MeckJournal are announcing a Call for Contributions to a special issue entitled, "Real-World and Utopian Models of Electronic Publishing in the Library and Research Community." Contributions can range from sketches, reflections, and projections, to fully developed and workable schemes for commercial and non- commercial network-based publishing. Among topics for consideration are:

1. the development of the Electronic Book industry; 2. copyright protection and payment modes (e.g., licensing agreements); 3. document delivery (e.g., bitmapped vs. digitized text); 4. the future of traditional publishing and publishers; 5. library management of electronic documents; 6. electronic publishing in 2002; 7. the changing texture of education, research, and academic life; 8. the role of print in the future of publishing; 9. WAIS, Z39.50, and hardware/software publishing formats; and 10. libraries and academic research departments as publishers.

Access via: *Washington & Lee University Gopher/other useful things/Newbooks (CIP data)*

PACS-L Listserv Archives

An indexed version of the archives of this popular mailing list concerning libraries and library automation. To subscribe to the list, send a message to *listserv@uhupvm1.bitnet* with the text "SUBSCRIBE PACS-L *yourname.*"

Access via: WAIS *bit.listserv.pacs-l.src*

LITERATURE

News Groups: *rec.arts.books*

Athene Magazine

Athene and InterText, electronic magazines dedicated to short fiction, are archived here.

Access via: *ftp quartz.rutgers.edu;* login *anonymous; cd pub/journals*

Bryn Mawr Classical Review

Mostly a review journal of Greek and Latin classics, this database also includes public interest articles on the classics.

Access via:
WAIS *bryn-mawr-classical-review.src*

Information:
E-mail: *bcmr@brynmawr.edu*

Classical Chinese Literature

A library of Chinese classics, as posted on the Chinese Poem Exchange Network. Includes texts ranging from the ancient Chinese philosopers to the present. It appears to be organized by dynasty. The poems are in Chinese; software for displaying the texts is also available at this site.

Access via: *ftp ahkcus.org;* login *anonymous; cd gb/poem*

Dante Project

Contains reviews of Dante's Divine Comedy by various historical authors. A useful service for Dante scholars, but the user interface is very confusing.

Access via: *telnet library.dartmouth.edu*; type *connect dante*

Poetry

A collection of poems by Emily Bronte, Burns, Byron, T.S. Eliot, Frost, Yeats, and others. The WAIS index *poetry.src*, which is a different resource, provides the poems of Shakespeare, Yeats, Elizabeth Sawyer, and others.

Access via: *U.C. Berkeley Open Computing Facility Gopher/OCF On-Line Library/Poetry*

WAIS *poetry.src*

Project Gutenberg

Project Gutenberg is an ambitious non-profit and volunteer effort to get as much literature as possible into machine readable form. The following are some of the texts available:

> Shakespeare, complete works
> Alice in Wonderland
> Through the Looking Glass
> The Hunting of the Snark
> The CIA World Factbook
> Moby Dick
> Peter Pan
> The Book of Mormon
> The Federalist Papers
> The Song of Hiawatha
> Paradise Lost
> Aesop's Fables
> Roget's Thesaurus
> Frederick Douglass
> O Pioneers!

Manuscripts are in text only, with no special formatting. Filenames vary from server to server, but usually will have a mnemonic name followed by a version number (e.g. *alice28.txt*). The higher the version number, the more verification of the electronic text has been done. Since the text takes up a lot of disk space, some servers don't store the entire archive, and some compress the texts.

Newsletters of the society, an index and a README file are available on the *mrcnext.cso.uiuc.edu* source.

Access via: *ftp mrcnext.cso.uiuc.edu*; login *anonymous; cd etext*

ftp quake.think.com; login *anonymous; cd pub/etext*

*University of Minnesota
Gopher/Libraries/Electronic Books
WAIS proj-gutenberg.src*

Information:
E-mail: *hart@vmd.cso.uiuc.edu*

MATHEMATICS

News Groups: *sci.[math, math.num-analysis, math.stat, math.symbolic, math.research], k12.ed.math*

Centre International de Rencontres Mathematiques Bibliography

The bibliography of the CIRM in Marseille. Index words are in French.

Access via: WAIS *bib-cirm.src*

Information:
E-mail: *rolland@cirm.univ-mrs.fr*

e-MATH

e-MATH is an Internet node that provides mathematicians with an expanding list of services that can be accessed electronically. e-MATH is intended as an electronic clearing house for timely professional and research information in the mathematical sciences. Some of the current services are the AMS (American Mathematical Society) membership database, employment opportunities, publication ordering, author lists, meeting notices, and a directory of journals and newsletters.

Access via: *telnet e-math.ams.com*; login *e-math*; password *e-math*
Concert gopher/Internet Information Servers/General Information Servers

Information:
E-mail: *support@e-math.ams.com*

Software and Aids for Teaching of Mathematics

See: Education - Software and Aids for Teaching of Mathematics

MEDICINE

Alcoholism Research Data Base

A database of articles and other information related to alcoholism and other forms of substance abuse.

Access via: *telnet lib.dartmouth.edu*; select file *cork*

Family Medicine Discussion Archives

The archived mailings from the FAM-MED listserv. These are discussions about uses of computers and networking to help in the teaching and practice of family medicine. It includes lists of bulletin board services related to medicine.

Access via: *ftp spinner.gac.edu*; login *anonymous*; cd *pub/fam-med*; get *000read-me-fam-med.txt*

Food and Drug Administration

See: Government - The FDA Electronic Bulletin Board

MEDLINE

The MEDLINE database contains article citations and abstracts, indexed from over 4000 journals in medicine and related health sciences. Several university libraries provide access to MEDLINE; however, access is normally limited to students, faculty, and staff. We've listed several libraries that provide MEDLINE. If you don't have ties to one of these institutions, check with your own library.

Access via: *telnet melvyl.ucop.edu*
Note: University of California

telnet lib.dartmouth.edu
Note: Dartmouth

telnet library.umdnj.edu; login *LIBRARY*
Note: University of Medicine and Dentistry of New Jersey

telnet utmem1.utmem.edu login *HARVEY*
Note: University of Tennessee, Memphis

National Library of Medicine Educational Technology Network

Many forums and discussion groups on medical technology and medical education. There are specific discussion groups on radiology, computer-assisted instruction, nursing, hardware and software.

Access via: *telnet etnet.nlm.nih.gov;* login *etnet*

Online Mendelian Inheritance in Man

Catalogs autosomal dominant, autosomal recessive, and X linked Phenotypes. Much of the data is copyrighted by Johns Hopkins, but non-commercial scientific use is allowed with attribution. Before other than casual use of the database, you should look at the full licensing notice in the *directory-of-servers.src* for this database.

Access via: WAIS *online-mendelian-inheritance-in-man.src*

MOLECULAR BIOLOGY

Arabidopsis Research Workers List

A "white pages" listing of research workers involved with Arabidopsis.

Access via: WAIS *bionic-arabidopsis.src*

Bionic Algorithms

Database of literature references to molecular biological algorithms courtesy of EMBNET.

Access via: WAIS *bionic-algorithms.src*

Bionic Directory of Servers

A directory of WAIS servers targeted at molecular biology servers.

Access via:
WAIS *bionic-directory-of-servers.src*

Bionic Sequence Analysis Bibliography

An EMBNET index to sequence analysis literature.

Access via:
WAIS *bionic-sequence-bibliography.src*

Biosci Mailing List Archives

The contents of the BIOSCI mailing lists and news groups since 1989.

Access via: WAIS *biosci.src*

Bioscience Documents

A collection of documents collected from the BioSci network.

Access via: WAIS *bionic-biosci-docs.src*

CompoundKB Database

Peter Karps database of 981 metabolic intermediate compounds.

Access via: WAIS *biology-compounds.src*

EC Enzyme Database

This database contains the EC enzyme database of Amos Bairoch release 6.00

Access via: WAIS *EC-enzyme.src*

EMBNET Database

The EMBNET database for molecular biologists working with artificial intelligence originally maintained by Larry Hunter.

Access via: WAIS *bionic-ai-researchers.src*

Enzyme Class Index

An index of enzyme classes to be used with the EMBNET Enzyme Database.

Access via: WAIS *bionic-enzclass.src*

Enzyme Database

The enzyme database constructed by Amos Bairoch. This is also part of EMBNET.

Access via: WAIS *bionic-enzyme.src*

GenBank (Bacterial Division)

The Bacterial Division of Genbank (release 64). Done as an experiment to see if WAIS is useful in the Genbank environment.

Access via: WAIS *Molecular-biology.src*

GenBank

Genbank contains all published nucleic acid sequences. Searches may be based on accession number, description, locus name, keywords, source, organism, author, and title of journal article.

Access via: *IUBiology Gopher/Genbank Sequences*

Molecular Biology FTP and Server List

A list of molecular biology FTP sites, their IP numbers, and what information can be found. Databases and both small and large FTP sites are included.

Access via: *ftp ucselx.sdsu.edu*; login *anonymous*; cd */pub/doc/netinfo/molecular-biology.resources*

Molecular Biology Journal Contents

EMBNET index of literature references, taken from tables of contents of molecular biology journals.

Access via:
WAIS *bionic-journal-contents.src*

Molecular Biology Journal References

References to such journals as NAR, EMBO, and CABIOS updated weekly, Mondays 3 A.M. to 6 A.M. PST (unavailable during this period).

Access via:
WAIS *biology-journal-contents.src*

Information:
E-mail: *biosci@genbank.bio.net*

Molecular Biology List of Databases

Pointers to databases for molecular biologists.

Access via:
WAIS *bionic-databases-limb.src*

PROSITE

PROSITE is a collection of protein patterns, sites and sequences. It comes from the printed dissertation by Amos Bairoch, PROSITE: a dictionary of sites and patterns in proteins in Nucleic Acids Res. 19:2241-2245 (1991). It contains 530 entries that describe 605 different patterns. A more detailed description of contents, copyrights, and hints for use are contained in the description in directory of servers for *prosite.src* and the PROSITE documentation within the database found with the search words: PROSITE documentation help.

Access via: WAIS *prosite.src*

REBASE Restriction Enzyme Database

Version 9110 of this database by Richard Roberts. Keywords are strings of amino acids like CCCGGG. To specify restrictions sites, use the up-arrow key to signify the site.

Access via: WAIS *rebase-enzyme.src*

MUSIC

News Groups: *alt.[emusic, exotic-music], k12.ed.music, rec.music.[afro-latin, beatles, bluenote, cd, christian, classical, compose, country.western, dementia, dylan, early, folk, funky, gaffa, gdead, indian.classical, indian.misc, industrial, info, makers, marketplace, misc, newage, reviews, synth, video]*

Acoustic Guitar Digest

An electronic magazine for the acoustic guitar enthusiast.

Access via: *ftp casbah.acns.nwu.edu; login anonymous; cd /pub/acoustic-guitar*

Guitar Chords and Tablature

Guitar tablature and chords for songs of many popular artists from current to old, electric to acoustic. Entries are submitted by the people on the net who have worked out the tab or chords. Submissions copied from books are not allowed. Organized by artist/group.

Access via: *ftp ftp.nevada.edu; login anonymous; cd pub/guitar*

Indian Classical Music

A database of Indian CDs. Coverage is best for Hindustani music, but it also includes some Karnatic CDs. Try searching for Shankar to get a flavor for what is there.

Access via:
WAIS *indian-classical-music.src*

MIDI Information

Archives of technical documents and discussions about MIDI (Musical Instrument Digital Interface). MIDI is a common interface for computer-assisted music.

Access via: WAIS *midi.src*

University of Wisconsin-Parkside Music Archive

A general source for many types of music information, both recorded and home-made. Items include information on building classical CD collections, lyrics, guitar chords, and pictures of artists.

Access via: *ftp ftp.uwp.edu; login anonymous; cd pub/music*

NETWORK INFORMATION

AARnet Resource Guide

Information compiled about computing, networking, and libraries in Australia.

Access via:
WAIS *aarnet-resource-guide.src*

Com-priv Mailing List Archive

An indexed archive of the discussions related to commercialization and privatization of the Internet from the com-priv mailing list.

Access via: WAIS *com-priv.src*

Information:
E-mail: *archivist@archive.orst.edu*

Computer Ethics

Although primarily oriented towards computer centers, this source does have some information relevant to users of campus and national networks.

See: Computing - Computer Ethics

Domain Names and Organizations

This allows you to ask questions like "what organization uses the *domain uiuc.edu*?" Or "what is the domain name for the University of Illinois at Urbana-Champaign?"

Access via:
WAIS *domain-organizations.src*

Fidonet Node List

This is, essentially, a list of Fidonet addresses. Given the name of a person or organization on Fidonet, you can look up the relevant Fidonet node name; then convert the node name into an Internet address, as described in Chapter 7, *Electronic Mail*. This list is only for personal use, and may not be redistri-

buted. Commercial use of the nodelist is prohibited. Other use without express written consent is not allowed. For other use, please contact Fido Software, Box 77731, San Francisco, CA 94107 U.S.A.

Access via: WAIS *fidonet-nodelist.src*

Information:
E-mail: *David.Dodell@f15.n114.z1.fidonet.org*

IETF Documents

The IETF is the voluntary engineering group for the Internet. It produces various working group and planning reports. This service contains the text of those reports.

Access via: WAIS *internet-documents.src*
WAIS *ietf-docs.src*
WAIS *netinfo.src*
WAIS *netinfo-docs.src*

IETF Drafts

Whereas IETF Documents contains the official documents that have been received by the group, this contains the documents under construction. This is where you look if you want to find out where the Internet is heading.

Access via: WAIS *internet-drafts.src*
WAIS *ietf-drafts.src*

Internet Mail Guide

A detailed description of how to address electronic mail so that it will get from any network to any other network. This list includes lots of very small networks, special interest networks, and corporate networks, in addition to the "well known" networks like MCI, CompuServe, etc. Updated monthly. For experimental software (written in *perl*) to query this list, send mail to John J. Chew at *poslfit@utcs.utoronto.ca*.

Access via: *ftp ftp.msstate.edu; login anonymous; cd /pub/docs; get internetwork-mail-guide* *ftp ariel.unm.edu; login anonymous; cd library; get network.guide*

List of Bitnet and EARN Sites

A list of all the nodes on Bitnet and its European counterpart, EARN.

Access via: WAIS *bitearn.nodes.src*

Matrix News

Matrix News is a newsletter of the Matrix Information and Directory Services, Inc. The topics concern current and future network applications. Articles are copyrighted, but may be used freely with attribution. They may not be sold. Complete use of information can be found by searching for copyright.

Access via: WAIS *matrix_news.src*

Information:
E-mail: *mids@tic.com*

Network Information Center Online Aid System

NICOLAS is an online facility to help with network problems. This service is only for the use of NASA employees, researchers, and contractors. Its most interesting facility is in the E-mail section, called the Address Matrix. It lets you specify a source and destination network and tells you how to format the e-mail address.

Access via: telnet *dftnic.gsfc.nasa.gov*; login *dftnic*

NorthWestNet User Services Internet Resource Guide

Is a book much like this one, which contains information on network use and resources available. Files are in postscript and some are compressed.

Access via: *ftp ftphost.nwnet.net; login anonymous; cd nic/nwnet/user-guide; get README.nusirg*
Note: README file contains information on the other files available.

RFC (Request for Comments)

RFCs are the documents that define the Internet. They talk about how it works, how to use it, and where it is going. Most RFCs are fairly technical. There are over 1200 RFCs. An index is in file *rfc-index.txt*. Some RFCs are distributed in text, and some in postscript. The text documents have names of the form *rfcnnnn.txt*. Postscript RFCs are in files named *rfcnnnn.ps*. In either case, *nnnn* is the number of the RFC you want. Many computers only archive partial sets. The sources listed here are "official" servers with complete sets. For more information on fetching RFCs, send an e-mail message like:

> mail *rfc-info@isi.edu*
> Subject: *getting rfcs*
> help: *ways_to_get_rfcs*

Access via: *ftp nic.ddn.mil*; login *anonymous; cd rfc*

ftp.nisc.sri.com; login *anonymous; cd rfc*

ftp nis.nsf.net; login *anonymous*; password *guest; cd rfc*
Note: This is a VM/CMS server - filenames are different.

ftp nisc.jvnc.net; login *anonymous ; cd rfc*

ftp wuarchive.wustl.edu; login *anonymous; cd doc/rfc*
Note: Files are compressed with *.Z* endings.

ftp src.doc.ic.ac.uk; login *anonymous; cd rfc*
Note: Files are compressed with *.Z* endings.

ftp nisc.sri.com; login *anonymous; cd rfc*

ftp nnsc.nsf.net; login *anonymous; cd rfc*

E-mail: *mail-server@nisc.sri.com*
Note: The message body should contain *send rfcnnnn.txt*.

WAIS *internet-rfcs.src*

WAIS *rfc-index.src*
Note: This is just a search aid to the index of RFC's.

Zen and the Art of the Internet

This is the well-received booklet by Brendan Kehoe about using the Internet. It is a good introduction to the topic, told in a readable fashion.

Access via: WAIS *zen-internet.src*

ftp ftp.cs.widener.edu; login *anonymous*; *cd pub/zen*
Note: Available in various formats.

NETWORK ORGANIZATIONS

Internet Society

The Internet Society is an international professional organization established to encourage the evolution, standardization and dissemination of techniques and technologies which allow diverse information systems to communicate. The Society publishes newsletters, organizes conferences, and manages e-mail distribution lists to educate a worldwide community about the global network of networks known as the Internet which links more than four million users and one million computers. The Society sponsors the Internet Architecture Board and its Internet Engineering and Research Task Forces, and maintains liaison with other international organizations and standards bodies as part of its effort to assist in the evolution and growth of the critically important infrastructure represented by the Internet.

Information:

E-mail: *isoc@nri.reston.va.us*
Phone: (703) 620-8990

NETWORK SERVICES

News Groups: news.[announce.important, announce.newusers, newusers.questions, answers, groups, future, lists, software.readers, sysadmin, misc]

Campus Wide Information Systems Listserv Archive

An indexed archive of the Campus Wide Information Systems listserv. A good place to look for discussions of information delivery software, like Gopher, WAIS, and WWW.

Access via: WAIS *bit.listserv.cwis-l.src*

List of Lists, News Groups, and Electronic Serials

A compilation of lists of lists of news and mailing lists, both on Bitnet and the Internet. There is a lot of overlap among the sources, so if you search you will likely find something multiple times. Most valuable as a "master list" of all known electronic mail discussion groups.

Access via: WAIS *lists.src*

Prototype WAIS Ftp Server

Sort of "archie meets ftp," with a WAIS interface. Here is the description from directory of servers:

This server searches README files throughout the entire FTP directory tree. When an interesting file is found, it should be used as a relevance feedback document. When the search is re-done, the user will get a listing of the FTP directory in which the README file resides. The user can then retrieve files from that directory. Text files are returned as type TEXT, all other files are returned as type FTP.

Access via: WAIS *quake.think.com-ftp.src*

NEWS, NETWORK

News Groups: *news.answers, news.newusers.questions*

News Posting Service via E-mail

These servers allow you to post to USENET news groups even if you aren't part of the USENET system. Remember to include your e-mail address in your posting so you can get replies. Use dashes in the groupname rather than periods: for example, *rec-music-folk* rather than *rec.music.folk.*

Access via:

mail groupname@cs.utexas.edu
mail groupname@pws.bull.com

Excerpt from **USENET Software: History and Sources**, *7/22/92:*

```
The current release of B News is
2.11, patchlevel 19.  Article
format is specified in RFC 1036
(see below).  B News has been
declared "dead" by a number of
people, and is unlikely to be
upgraded further; most new sites
are using C News (see next para-
graph).
```

USENET Software: History and Sources

A frequently updated list and comparison of news reading software. A good place to start if you are unhappy with the news reader you are currently using, and want to see what alternatives are available.

Access via: *ftp pit-manager.mit.edu;* login *anonymous; cd pub/usenet/news.answers/usenet-software; get part1*

USENET Frequently Asked Questions

Reading any relevant FAQ lists before posting a question to USENET or a mailing list is highly recommended! The only problem is: where do you find the relevant list? This WAIS library is a convenient way to search through most lists. Contains the FAQ postings from USENET news groups. Search for "faqlist" to get a list of what is available. Search for FAQ's of a particular news group by deleting the periods in a news groups name (e.g., use "scispace" to search for the group *sci.space*).

Access via: WAIS *usenet-FAQ.src*

Information:
E-mail: *rhys@cs.oz.au*

USENET Periodic Posting Archives

A repository of the periodic informational postings of the news groups. There is a directory corresponding to each news group name. The directory contains a file with the same name as the subject line of the posting.

Access via: *ftp pit-manager.mit.edu; cd pub/usenet*
WAIS *jik-usenet.src*

What is USENET?

A long explanation trying to explain what the USENET news system is, how it is managed, and how it got to be the way it is.

Access via: *ftp pit-manager;* login *anonymous; cd pub/usenet/news.announce.newusers; get What_is_USENET?*

NUTRITION

News Groups: *rec.food.[cooking, receipes, drink, veg]*

Cholesterol

An explanation of what cholesterol is, where it comes from, and how it affects the body.

Access via: *University of Delaware Gopher/Agricultural Extension Information/Extension Bulletins/Cholesterol*

International Food and Nutrition Database

IFAN is a collection of contributed articles and other publications concerning food and nutrition. Some of the interesting contents are the last few issues of *The Nutrition Letter*, and some papers on special nutritional requirements of HIV infected individuals.

See: Agriculture - PEN Pages

OCEANOGRAPHY

Bedford Institute of Oceanography

Existing for the purpose of exchanging scientific data and programs with other marine scientists, the Habitat Ecology Division of the Bedford Institute of Oceanography developed the BSIM simulation package, and has files of the Uniforum Atlantic minutes. This server also has information on fishery science.

Access via: *ftp biome.bio.dfo.ca; login anonymous; cd pub*

Oceanic

The Ocean Information Center Bulletin Board provided by the University of Delaware. Has very technical and organizational material about various oceanographic experiments, field trials, and meetings.

Access via: *telnet delocn.udel.edu; login info*

Concert gopher/Internet Information Services/General Information Servers

PETS

News Groups: *rec.[pets.birds, pets.cats, pets.dogs, pets.herp, pets]*

The FDA Electronic Bulletin Board

This more general bulletin board contains information on veterinary drug usage.

See: Government, U.S.—The FDA Electronic Bulletin Board

PHYSICS

News Groups: *sci.[physics,space]*

HEPnet Through World-Wide Web

Physics resources are a bit hard to come by, on the Internet: physicists have their own network, called HEPnet, which uses a different set of protocols. However, the World-Wide Web provides access to many resources through a gateway—which you'd expect, since it was spawned at CERN, the European high energy physics laboratory. WWW currently provides access to information from CERN, DESY (a German physics lab), NIKHEF (Dutch physics center), SLAC (Stanford Linear Accelerator) and Fermilab.

Access via: *www*
Note: A good home page is *http://info.cern.ch./hypertext/DataSources/bySubject/Physics/HEP.html.*

Non-linear Dynamics Archive

Contains pre-prints of papers, abstracts, software, and other material related to non-linear dynamics. Apparently organized according to the institution that the software or paper came from, so you'll need to look at the *README* file to figure out what's available.

Access via: *ftp lyapunov.ucsd.edu: login anonymous; cd pub*

Information:
E-mail: *mbk@inls1.ucsd.edu (Matt Kennel)*

POLITICAL ACTIVISM

News Groups: *alt.activism, misc.activism.progressive*

Addresses, Phone and Fax Numbers (U.S. Gov't, etc.)

Addresses of Senate members, telephone and FAX numbers for the House of Representatives, and FAX numbers for various communications companies.

Access via: *ftp wuarchive.wustl.edu; login anonymous; cd doc/policy/academic/civics*

ftp pit-manager.mit.edu; login anonymous; cd pub/activism/congress

Congressional Contact Information

Contains the names, addresses and phone numbers of members of Congress. It can be searched by name, city, state, or postal code.

Access via: WAIS *congress.src*

Environmental Activism Server

What's your favorite cause? This server carries information on all sorts of causes, ranging from "Agran for President '92," to "Earth First!" to the invasion of Iraq, to U.S.—Japan trade. It also includes lists of government telephone numbers, to articles and judicial decisions on the environmental movement.

Access via: *pencil.cs.missouri.edu; login anonymous; cd pub/map*

Excerpt from **U.S. Government Addresses, Faxes and Phone Numbers**, *7/24/92:*

```
House of Representatives faxes and phones:
All numbers are in Washington, DC area code 202
```

NAME	STATE	FAX	PHONE
Young, Don	AK		225-5765
Bevill, Tom	AL	225-0842	225-4876
Browder, Glen	AL		225-3261
Callahan, Sonny	AL		225-4931
Dickinson, William L.	AL		225-2901
Erdreich, Ben	AL		225-4921
Flippo, Ronnie G.	AL	225-4392	225-4801
Harris, Claude	AL	225-0175	225-2665
Alexander, Bill	AR	225-6182	225-4076
Anthony, Beryl, Jr.	AR		225-3772
Hammerschmidt, John P.	AR	225-7492	225-4301
Robinson, Tommy F.	AR		225-2506
Kolbe, Jim	AZ		225-2542
Kyl, Jon	AZ		225-3361
Rhodes, John J.	AZ		225-2635
Stump, Bob	AZ	225-6328	225-4576
Udall, Morris K.	AZ		225-4065

Right to Keep and Bear Arms

An index to files related to the "right to keep and bear arms."

Access via: WAIS *rkba.src*

ftp pit-manager.edu; login anonymous; cd pub/rkba

POPULAR CULTURE

News Groups: *alt.fan.*, alt.tv.*, rec.arts.*, rec.music.**

Monty Python

A large collection of Monty Python sketches.

Access via: *U.C. Berkeley Open Computing Facility/OCF On-Line Library/Python*

SOUND, News, and Arts Newspaper

A newspaper/magazine published electronically and in print from Omaha, Nebraska. The table of contents of a recent issue includes such titles as "Censorship in the NEA" and "Give us a taste of Beer, Chrome, and Elections."

Access via: *University of Nebraska, Omaha Gopher/Sound, News and Arts Newspaper*

The Simpsons Archive

Everything you wanted to know about the Simpsons. Play dates, credits, bibliographies, episode summaries, etc.

Access via: *ftp ftp.cs.widener.edu; login anonymous; cd pub/simpsons*

WAIS simpsons.src

Unplastic News

An electronic magazine containing random quotes, criticism, songs, short stories, or whatever happens to be submitted. Unplastic

News exists to provide entertainment and to facilitate communication.

Access via: *ftp ftp.eff.org*; login *anonymous*; *cd pub/journals/Unplastic_News*

RECREATION, GAMES

News Groups: *rec.games.[backgammon, board, board.ce, bridge, chess, corewar, cyber, design, empire, frp, go, hack, misc, moria, mud, mud.lp, netrek, pbm, pinball, programmer, rogue, trivia, vectrex, video, video.arcade]*

Internet Chess Servers

A server that allows you to meet and play chess with other people. If you prefer, you can just "watch." Players may register with the server, allowing them to save games and participate in a rating system. However, you don't need to register to play.

Access via: *telnet eve.assumption.edu* port *5000*

Information:
E-mail: *shaheen@eve.assumption.edu* (for registration)

Internet Go Server

A computer that allows you to meet other people and play "go" with them. Watching and kibitzing on other games is allowed. Anonymous access is not allowed, but you can create a free login name the first time you access the server.

Access via: *telnet lacerta.unm.edu* port *6969*
Note: Use your name for login.

Simulated Conversations

The Conversational Hypertext server offers some simulated conversations, some of which are similar in flavor to fantasy games. They are a *big* improvment over the time-honored (but rather worn) psychoanalysis simulations.

Access via: *telnet debra.doc.ca*; login *chat*

RECREATION, SPORTS

News Groups: *rec.[climbing, hunting, juggling, kites, motorcycles.dirt, motorcycles.racing, running, scuba, skate, skiing, skydiving, windsurfing] and others in rec.sport.* *

Aikido Dojo List

A list of known Aikido dojos by continent. Affiliation is flagged in the list as well.

Access via: *ftp iuvax.cs.indiana.edu*; login *anonymous*; *cd pub/aikido*
Note: Various files in this directory.

Biking Information (Canada)

Lots of good stuff for bicyclists. There's a program for computing a bicycle's power output (and other software), several pictures (in GIF format), some articles collected from *rec.bicycling*, and some materials on bicycling to Nova Scotia.

Access via: *ftp biome.bio.dfo.ca*; login *anonymous*; *cd pub/biking*

Biking Information (Norway)

A program called Bike Manager, instructions for making your own brake booster, and the "Great Trail of Strength Report" for 1991 can be found here.

Access via: *ftp ugle.unit.no*; login *anonymous*; *cd /local/biking*

Scuba Diving Information

Lots of information about scuba diving, including reviews of different places to go, condition reports, news about equipment. A lot of the stuff has been collected from *rec.scuba*, but there's other material available, too. Anyone want to go to Vanuatu?

Access via: *ftp ames.arc.nasa.gov*; login *anonymous*; *cd pub/SCUBA*

Information:
E-mail: *yee@ames.arc.nasa.gov*

Ski Conditions

See: Weather - Weather Underground

Skiing FAQ

A list of frequently asked questions about skiing, as well as ski information for Utah, Idaho, and Wyoming. The Utah information is the most complete.

Access via: *ftp ski.utah.edu*; login *anonymous*; *cd skiing*

Windsurfing

You want to windsurf in Corpus Christi, TX, or down the Columbia River Gorge? How about information on windsurfing shops and launch sites in the San Francisco Bay area? This, along with phone numbers for various wind reporting stations, windsurfing bitmaps, and hot topics of discussion are located here.

Access via: *ftp bears.ece.ucsb.edu*; login *anonymous*; *cd pub/windsurf*

REFERENCE BOOKS

CIA World Factbook

The CIA maintains a dossier on every country in the world. This is the 1990 version of that dossier, describing 249 nations. Each entry contains information about population, economic condition, trade, conflicts and politics. There's lots of stuff you won't find here—like the number of nuclear warheads aimed at the Pentagon. But you will find lots of basic information about almost any country you can think of.

Access via: WAIS *world-factbook.src*

Concise Oxford Dictionary, 8th edition

The concise Oxford English Dictionary is available to be searched. You specify words and it returns the entries.

Access via: *telnet info.rutgers.edu*; select *library* then *reference*

Oxford Dictionary of Familiar Quotations

A search interface to the book. You can give words to search for, and it returns referenced quotes containing those words.

Access via: *telnet info.rutgers.edu*; select *library* then *reference*

Excerpt from **Oxford English Dictionary**, *7/17/92:*

```
Menu> dictionary
Word (? for help): hacker

Concise Oxford Dictionary, 8th Ed., Copy-
right 1991 Oxford Univ. Press

/hacker/ <<"h&k@(r)>> n.
1. a person or thing that hacks
or cuts roughly.
2. [Computing][colloq.] a person
who uses computers for a hobby,
esp. to gain unauthorized access
to data{new from OED 2/e Apr89}.
```

Oxford Thesaurus

The thesaurus is available to be searched. You specify words and it returns alternates.

Access via: *telnet info.rutgers.edu*; select *library* then *reference*

Roget's Thesaurus

One of the Project Gutenberg texts. Available either as a file or as a searchable text through WAIS or Gopher.

Access via: WAIS *roget-thesaurus.src*

See: Literature - Project Gutenberg

RELIGION

News Groups: *soc.religion.[christian, eastern, islam]*

ANU Asian Religions Bibliography

A collection (450Kb) of bibliographic references to selected (mainly Buddhist) Asian religions. From documents deposited with the Coombspapers Social Sciences Research Data Bank, Research Schools of Social Sciences and Pacific Studies, Australian National University, GPO Box 4, Canberra ACT 2601.

Access via:
WAIS *ANU-Asian-Religions.src*

Information: Phone: +61 6 249-4600
E-mail: *wais@coombs.anu.edu.au*

King James Bible

A complete King James Bible, with cross reference and lexicon.

Access via: *ftp wuarchive.wustl.edu*; login *anonymous*; *cd pub/bible*
Note: Start with *README.Z file*.

WAIS *bible.src*
Note: Available 9 A.M. - 9 P.M. EST.

Koran

M. H. Shakir's translation of the Holy Qur'an published by Tahrike Tarsile Aur'an, Inc., New York. It was scanned from the text and may not be free of scanning errors. There is a file containing each chapter, and a README file to help.

Access via: *ftp quake.think.com*; login *anonymous*; *cd pub/etext/koran*

WAIS *Quran.src*

Religious Studies Publication Journal—CONTENTS

This journal is designed to facilitate the dissemination of Religious Studies publications and resource information.

Access via: *Louisiana Tech University Gopher/Electronic Media Sources/ISSN Serials*

The Book of Mormon

See: Literature - Project Gutenberg

Access via: WAIS *Book_of_Mormon.src*

Torah

The Torah, Prophets, and Writings from the Tanach in Hebrew can be found along with a Hebrew quiz, and a Biblical Hebrew Language tutorial. The README file contains a description of the other files.

Access via: *ftp nic.funet.fi*; login *anonymous*; *cd pub/doc/bible/hebrew*

RESOURCE DIRECTORIES

Archie File Index

The data available through the SURAnet Archie server is available through WAIS. The format of an entry is:

host: directory/ . . . /filename size timestamp

Access via: WAIS *archie-orst.edu.src*

Information:
E-mail: *archivist@archive.orst.edu*

Directory of WAIS Servers

This is a list of all known servers for the WAIS system in offered as a WAIS database. (Explained more fully in the text.)

Access via:
WAIS *au-directory-of-servers.src*
WAIS *directory-of-servers.src*

HYTELNET

HYTELNET is a menu-driven version of **telnet**. It offers much of the functionality of Gopher's **telnet** interface. This is an index of all the servers it knows about. You can use it to find library catalogs, bulletin boards, campus information servers and other telnet sites.

Access via: WAIS *hytelnet.src*

Inet Services

A voluntarily compiled list of Internet services, commonly referred to as the "Yanoff list." It gives a short description of each service and access.

Access via: *ftp csd4.csd.uwm.edu;* login *anonymous; cd pub; get inet.services.txt*

Information:
E-mail: *yanoff@csd4.csd.uwm.edu*

Internet Information Search

Many of the standard help texts and guides like the *Hitchhikers Guide to the Internet, Zen and the Art of the Internet, Netiquette,* and others are indexed and contained here.

Access via: WAIS *internet_info.src*

Listserv Groups

A directory of the listservs, or discussion groups, available on BITNET. It includes the name of the listserv and address, the listserv contact person, and a short, topical description of each list. Instructions on signing on and off some of the lists are included.

Access via: *ftp lilac.berkeley.edu;* login *anonymous; cd netinfo*

NNSC Internet Resource Guide

The NSF Network Service Center asks people offering a service on the Internet to submit a description of the service. These are collected in this database.

Access via:
WAIS *internet-resource-guide.src*
UC Berkeley Open Computing Facility Gopher/OCF Help System/The Outside World

NorthWestNet User Services Internet Resources Guide

See: Network, Information

Not Just Cows

See: Agriculture - Not Just Cows

Online Resources Mailing List

The indexed archives of the Online mailing list. It is a place where people announce and report on various commercial and pay-for-use services available on the Internet. To join the mailing list, send a request to *online-request@uunet.ca*.

Access via: WAIS *online@uunet.ca.src*

SCIENCE FICTION & FANTASY LITERATURE

DargonZine

DargonZine is an electronic, fantasy fiction anthology magazine. The archive contains the magazine, subscription information and a very good description of DargonZine.

Access via: *ftp ftp.eff.org*; login *anonymous*; *cd pub/journal/DargonZine*

Quanta and Other Magazines

The science fiction and fantasy magazine *Quanta*, along with *InterText* and *Athene*. The newsletters *humus*, *purps*, and *m00se* are also available. The latter three are all described as "off-beat humor." My guess is that's rather modest.

Access via: *ftp quartz.rutgers.edu*; login *anonymous*; *cd pub/journals*

Science Fiction Reviews

The archive of mailing list discussions reviewing science fiction books. If you want to find what readers think about virtually any recent science fiction publication, this is where to look!

Access via: *ftp brolga.cc.uq.oz.au*; login *anonymous*; *cd pub*; *get sfguide6.tar.Z*
WAIS *Science-Fiction-Series-Guide.src*

Information:
E-mail: *farrell@coral.cs.jcu.edu.au*

Science Fiction News Group Archive

The archives of *rec.arts.sf.reviews*. The archives are available in "raw form," through anonymous FTP. The README file explains how the archive is organized. You can also search the archive through WAIS. This is another great place to look for spontaneous reviews or discussions of science fiction.

Access via: *ftp turbo.bio.net*; login *anonymous*; *cd sf-reviews*
WAIS *sf-reviews.src*

Star Trek Archive

You want Star Trek info? It's here! Everything from background bitmaps for X window systems to parodies and trivia, on the "original series," the "next generation," and the movies. This FTP site also has collections about other television shows and movies.

Access via: *ftp coe.montana.edu*; login *anonymous*; *cd pub/STARTREK*

SCIENCE

News Groups: *sci.[aeronautics, anthropology, archaeology, astro.hubble, astro, bio.technology, bio, chem, classics, comp-aided, crypt, econ, edu, electronics, energy, engr.biomed, engr.chem, engr, environment, geo.fluids, geo.geology, geo.meteorology, lang, logic, materials, math.num-analysis, math.research, math.stat, math.symbolic, math, med.aids, med.physics, med, military, misc, nanotech, optics, philosophy.meta, philosophy.tech, physics.fusion, physics, psychology.digest, psychology, research, skeptic, space.news, space.shuttle, space, systems, virtual-worlds]*

History of Science Server

An attempt to collect and catalog the writings and papers of respected scientists in a single place.

Access via: *ftp fatman.hs.jhu.edu*; login *anonymous*

Johns Hopkins University — History of Science and Medicine gopher server

Scientific Database Bulletin Board

This bulletin board exists to foster communication between natural and social scientists. There are discussion groups on astronomy, biology, chemistry, database technology, earth sciences, and many other topics. It also contains "chat" facilities and some e-mail facilities. It is made available by Argonne National Laboratory.

Access via: *telnet scid3b.eid.anl.gov*; login *cocotext*; password *WISDM*
Note: You will need to create a login name on initial contact.

SOCIETY & CULTURE

Electronic Frontier Foundation

The EFF exists to promote existing academic and personal freedoms in the new worldwide computer society. It fights against things like network censorship and for things like freely available information. Included on this server is information about the foundation (in the EFF directory), the Computer and Academic Freedom Archives, and many electronic journals and magazines, like Effector, Athene, and DragonZine.

Access via: *ftp ftp.eff.org*; login *anonymous*; *cd pub*
Note: Interesting things in various subdirectories.
WAIS eff-documents.src
E-mail: *ftphelp@eff.org*

Israel

Lots of documents about the state of Israel and the middle east. Includes the Israeli "Declaration of Independence," many articles about the PLO, and the tangled political relations in the area. Undoubtedly useful to anyone with an interest in this region.

Access via: *ftp pit-manager@mit.edu*; login *anonymous*; *cd pub/israel*

Pigkuli

A collection of news analysis, press reviews, and humor from or about Poland and the Polish community abroad.

Access via: *ftp mthvax.cs.miami.edu*; login *anonymous*; *cd pub/poland*
Note: If you're interested in Polish studies, also check out *Louisiana Tech Gopher/Electronic Media/ISSN Serials/Donosy*. The journal is in Polish.

Television Shows Archive

Guides to many different (current and past) television series, mostly sit-coms. Cast summaries, episode summaries, etc. In addition to current or recent programs, there's a fair amount of information about "historical" shows, like "The Prisoner" and "Lost In Space."

Access via: *ftp coe.montana.edu*; login *anonymous*; *cd pub/TV*

Excerpt from **Television Shows Archive**, *8/21/92:*

```
The Prisoner

Episode Guide 1967-68

An ITC production by Everyman Films Ltd.

Executive Producer: Patrick McGoohan
Script Editor: George Markstein

Made on location in the grounds of the Ho-
tel Portmerion, Penrhyndeudraeth, North
Wales by courtesy of Sir Clough Williams-
Ellis and at MGM Studios, Borehamwood, Eng-
land 1966/67

Director of Photography: Brenden J. Staf-
ford BSC
Art Director: Jack Shampan
Theme by Ron Grainer
Casting Director: Rose Tobias
Produced by David Tomblin

10/1/67 Arrival

Director: Don Chaffey
Writer:   George Markstein/ David Tomblin
Guy Doleman as No. 2
George Baker as the new No. 2
Angelo Muscat as The Butler.
```

Queer Resources Directory

A good resource for the gay, lesbian, and bisexual community. Has sections concerned with AIDS, facts and treatments; contact information for various support and activist groups; bibliography of publications of interest to the community; civil rights; and domestic partnerships. Also, has portions of the GLAAD Newsletter online.

Access via: *ftp nifty.andrew.cmu.edu;* login *anonymous; cd pub/QRD/qrd*

Information:
E-mail: *buckmr@rpi.edu*

Soviet Archives

The Library of Congress has an exhibit of materials from the newly opened Soviet archives. There is information about life under the Soviet system, Cherynobyl, the Cold War, and Cuban missile crisis, and many other top-

ics. Anyone interested in understanding recent history should know about this archive.

Access via: *ftp seq1.loc.gov;* login *anonymous; cd pub/soviet.archive*

Wedding Planner

Weddings are complicated affairs, particularly if you want to observe all the proper protocols. This resource may help you: it's a shareware Wedding Planner program for a personal computer.

Access via: *ftp wuarchive.wustl.edu;* login *anonymous; cd mirrors/msdos/database*

STANDARDS

Automated Data Server of the U.S. Naval Observatory

This resource gives you information about and access to the standard time services of the U.S. Naval Observatory. It also provides general information about the Observatory.

Access via: *telnet tycho.usno.navy.mil;* login *ads*

TRAVEL

News Groups: *rec.travel, rec.travel.air*

State Department Travel Advisories

See: Government, U.S. - State Department Travel Advisories

WEATHER, METEOROLOGY, & CLIMATOLOGY

News Group: *sci.geo.meteorology*

Minnesota Climatology Working Group

The University of Minnesota Climatology Working Group exists to provide climatological information to public agencies in the State of Minnesota. Information such as insect degree days (an important piece of information for campers!), crop degree days, and almost any type of climatological information pertaining to Minnesota that you'd want to know.

Access via: *University of Minnesota Soils Science dept. Gopher/Minnesota Climatology Working Group/Climate Data*

NCAR Data Support Section Server

The National Center for Atmospheric Research has a wide variety of data and programs available to aid meteorological research. Some of these are available for free through this server. Some are offline, but can be "mounted" (i.e., placed online for temporary access) for a fee. And some are so big they can only be ordered on tape. All the info to use these facilities is here. Start with the README file.

Access via: *ftp ncardata.ucar.edu;* login *anonymous*

National Space Science Data Center

Although this is primarily a space science service, some of the data available is climatological.

See: Astronomy - National Space Science Data Center

Network Sources for Meteorology and Weather

A file describing a number of ways weather and meteorological data are available on the Internet. A great place to find sources for weather maps, weather reports, climatological studies. (Some good resources for geologists are hidden in here, too.)

Access via: *ftp vmc.cso.uiuc.edu;* login *anonymous; cd wx; get sources.doc*

Weather Maps

Many sites make various different collections of weather maps available. The data available and their formats vary, so you'll have to look carefully at what you find. It's important to look at any README files, or other descriptions, that are in these archives.

Access via: *ftp vmd.cso.uiuc.edu;* login *anonymous; cd wx*
Note: GOES-7 data; according to one source, updated hourly.

ftp unidata.ucar.edu; login *anonymous; cd images*
Note: Weather radar maps, GOES HUGO images.

ftp aurelie.soest.hawaii.edu; login *anonymous; cd pub/avhrr/images*
Note: Sea surface temperature data (Hawaii and vicinity).

Excerpt from **Weather Underground**, *7/8/92:*

```
UPDATED GREATER BRIDGEPORT/NEW
HAVEN AREA FORECAST
NATIONAL WEATHER SERVICE
BRIDGEPORT CT
610 AM EDT WED JUL 8 1992

TODAY...MOSTLY SUNNY THIS MORN-
ING THEN CLOUDING UP THIS AFTER-
NOON.  HIGH 75 TO 80.  WIND
BECOMING SOUTH 10 TO 15 MPH.
TONIGHT...CLOUDY WITH SHOWERS
DEVELOPING.  CHANCE OF THUNDER-
STORMS.  LOW IN THE MIDDLE 60S.
SOUTH WIND 10 TO 20 MPH.  CHANCE
OF RAIN 80 PERCENT.
THURSDAY...A 60 PERCENT CHANCE
OF SHOWERS EARLY...BECOMING
PARTLY SUNNY IN THE AFTERNOON.
HIGH 80 TO 85.
```

Weather Underground

What's the weather like in Butte, Montana? This is where to find out; it's one of the most interesting (and, if you're a skier, useful) services on the Internet. The Weather Underground provides a menu-driven server giving current weather information and forecasts for non-commercial use. The weather reports are taken from the National Weather Service; reports are available for the entire United States and Canada. As we said, ski conditions are available in the winter. Several weather advisories and earthquake reports are also available.

Access via: *telnet madlab.sprl.umich.edu* port *3000*

Concert gopher/Internet Information Servers/General Information Servers/University of Michigan Weather Underground

WAIS weather.src

WHITE PAGES

Congressional Contact Information

See: Political Activism - Congressional Contact Information

Finding College E-mail Addresses

An indexed help guide to finding out what is available and how to use white pages servers at various colleges and universities.

Access via: WAIS *college-email.src*

Knowbot Information Service

The Knowbot Information Service is a "white-pages" service that will search for a name through a large number of Internet databases. It's a great way to look up friends and acquaintences. It's not yet as convenient as it might be, but Knowbots are among the newest and most advanced services on the Internet; it's worth knowing about them.

Access via: *telnet sol.bucknell.edu 185*

telnet nri.weston.va.us 185

Knowbot Information Service Documentation

Documentation describing the philosophy and use of the Knowbot Information white pages service.

Access via: *ftp nri.reston.va.us;* login *anonymous; cd rdroms ;* for postscript version *get KIS-id.PS* or for text version *get KIS-id.txt*

List of Internet Whois Servers

A list of all of the know **whois**-style white pages servers on the Internet.

Access via: *ftp sipb.mit.edu;* login *anonymous; cd pub/whois; get whois-servers.list*

Information:
E-mail: *mhpower@athena.mit.edu*

Netfind

A very persistent program that searches a variety of databases to help you find someone. Not very easy to use, but it may be easier than looking through several different white pages servers to find someone.

Access via: *telnet bruno.cs.colorado.edu* login *netfind*
Note: Start with an h for help.

Information:
E-mail: *jam@ccv.nersc.gov*

Network Managers Phonebook

Contains a one-line entry for each person in the WHOIS database as of August 1990. There is a paper copy called the Network Managers' Phonebook, published by the NSF Network Service Center.

Access via: WAIS *internet-phonebook.src*

PSI White Pages Pilot Project: User's Handbook

Access via: *ftp uu.psi.com*; login *anonymous; cd wp/ps ; mget user-**
Note: Four postscript files named *user-1.ps*, *user-2.ps . . . .*

USENET Addresses

This contains a list of all people who have posted to USENET news groups passing through MIT. This is an excellent way to find out a reasonably up-to-date address for many users of the Net.

Access via: WAIS *usenet-addresses.src*

mail mail-server@pit-manager.mit.edu; place *help* in the message body

ftp pit-manager.mit.edu; login *anonymous; cd pub/usenet-addresses; get addresses*
Note: You don't really want the whole thing, it's more than 15 Mbytes.

ZYMURGY

News Group: *rec.crafts.brewing*

Homebrew

Have you ever wanted to make your own beer? Here's a good place to start. This library contains a good collection of beer recipes, and other information.

Access via: WAIS *homebrew.src*

Homebrew Digest

Lots of information for home brewers, including software, recipe books, and archives of the Homebrew mailing list.

Access via: *ftp mthvax.cs.miami.edu*; login *anonymous; cd HomebrewDigest*

Send subscription requests to *homebrew-request.*

GETTING CONNECTED
TO THE INTERNET

Different Grades of Service
Service Providers

No matter who you are, you get access to the Internet via a "Service Provider." Service providers sell several different kinds of service, each with its own advantages and disadvantages. As with buying a car, you have to decide what features you want; how much you're willing to pay; and then go comparison-shopping.

But before you even read the list of providers, there's one thing you should do. In Chapter 1, *What Is This Book About*, we said that many, many people have access to the Internet, and don't know it. Are you one of these? Find out. If your company or school is on the Internet, it almost certainly has better service than you can afford as an individual.

In other words, you may *already* have an Internet connection available to you. You don't need to go out and find a service provider, you don't need to pay any extra bills; you just need to use what you already have. If you're a student at a medium to large four-year college or university, you can almost assume that your school is on the Internet, and you can probably get access as a student. Go to your computer center or computer science department and ask around. Ask a number of places before giving up—many times the only people who are aware of Internet are those people who actually use it. If you're no longer part of academia, the problem is a little more difficult.

How do you find out if your company has Internet access? Anyone who is responsible for managing computer systems or taking care of your corporate network should be able to tell you. If most of your computer systems run UNIX, there's a good chance that you're on the Internet or at least can exchange e-mail and USENET with the Internet. For historical reasons, if your computers are mostly running DOS, you probably aren't connected to the Internet—but there's no reason you couldn't be. Don't hesitate to dig some; if you're in marketing or accounting, you may not be aware of the nice Internet connection that the research or engineering group has been keeping to itself. If your company has a connection, but it's not in your department, your job is to ask "why?" Write a proposal and get it into next year's budget. Do whatever's necessary. If the resource already exists, it won't cost your company much more to give it to you. And even if your company doesn't have a connection, they're still the best place to start. Find some other people who need Internet access, figure out how to justify it economically, and make a proposal.

If your company doesn't have a connection, and you're not a student, there are still two ways of coming by Internet access inexpensively. The first thing to do is check out the public library. Some libraries offer a service called a *Freenet*. It is a community-based information and e-mail system which allows Internet access. You can either use the Freenet from the library or dial up. Although only a few libraries provide this service at the moment, the number is growing. The Freenets we knew about when we compiled the catalog are listed under Freenet.

The second is to become a student. Find out whether or not your community college has an Internet connection. If it does, sign up for a course or two. At many community colleges it is cheaper to take a course than it would be to arrange Internet services with a service provider as an individual. Learn basketweaving, and you can have something to do when you go crazy because of the network. Once you are enrolled, ask for Internet access. There's a need for a public archive of significant basket designs—isn't there?

Different Grades of Service

Well, you're still reading. So you probably didn't find any "free" Internet access points. Or, perhaps, someone said, "Sounds like a good idea. Why don't you do some research about what it will cost?" As we said, there are many different ways of connecting to the Internet. So, before you start your research, here's a summary of some types of connections that are available.

Dedicated Internet Access

Corporations and large institutions that want Internet access should look into "dedicated" network access. This gives you complete access to all of the Internet's facilities. A service provider leases a dedicated telephone line at a speed of your choosing (the faster the line speed, the more it costs), and places a special routing computer at your location. That router is responsible for taking communications from your site destined for somewhere else and sending them on their way (and vice versa). This is all quite expensive, running at least $2000 initially and several thousand dollars a year in monthly fees. However, once you've set the connection up, you can let as many computers as you would like be a part of the Internet—perhaps one computer in every classroom in your high school. To do so, you only need to place all the computers on one local area network, along with the router.

Dedicated access offers the most flexible connection. Each computer is a full-fledged Internet member, capable of performing any network functions. If there is some really neat new application you want to try, you only need to load the software and give it a whirl. However, since a dedicated connection is costly, it is most appropriate for a group setting, and impractical for "home users."

Dedicated Internet access usually requires some support structure for your local network. The service provider will help you in the beginning, but once you get running, he is only responsible for the router and the phone line. What happens on your local network is your business. If you are responsible for the care and feeding of the LAN, this book won't be enough. The Nutshell Handbook *TCP/IP Network Administration*, by Craig Hunt, will help you to set up and run your local network. A class or two wouldn't hurt. And keep this book in mind; you may want to give it to users who keep bothering you with simple questions.

SLIP and PPP

In the past few years, some less expensive techniques for "almost-dedicated access" have appeared. These are called SLIP and PPP; they are versions of the Internet software that run over normal phone lines, using standard "high-speed" modems. You may have to buy the SLIP or PPP software and a more expensive modem, but you won't have the very high connection costs.* You don't even have to use a "dedicated phone line"; you can use SLIP or PPP to dial in to your network when you want access, leaving the phone line free for other use when you don't need it. The real advantage of SLIP or PPP is that they allow a full-fledged connection to the Internet. You're not using someone else's system as an "access point" to the Net; you're on the Net yourself.

SLIP and PPP are very appropriate for connecting a home computer to a larger local network, which is in turn connected to the Internet. For example, you might use SLIP to connect your home computer to your company or campus network; then your home computer will have full Internet access, just as if it were on your company's Ethernet. SLIP and PPP are also appropriate for connecting a home computer (or perhaps a very small local network) to a service provider, who can give you full Internet access. They aren't appropriate for connecting a medium-sized or large network to the Internet; they can't talk fast enough to support a lot of people at once. So if you have a medium or large network (or if you might have one in a few years), it's best to look into "real" dedicated access.

SLIP is a "moderate cost" option: it provides very good service, but isn't terribly expensive—but you'd wish it were cheaper. A service provider, like UUNET or PSI, would typically charge something like $250/month for unlimited SLIP or PPP service; alternately, there may be a lower monthly charge, with an additional hourly fee. You also have to worry about the telephone bill. Many service providers provide 800 numbers or local access numbers in major urban areas to minimize this cost.

Installing SLIP or PPP, configuring them, and getting them running are not covered in this book. See the Nutshell Handbook *TCP/IP Network Administration* for more information about them.

---

*By "high-speed" we mean at least 9600 baud, or bits per second. A V.32bis or V.42bis modem is ideal. You could probably make SLIP work with a cheaper 2400 baud modem, but it would be painful. In any case, your service provider will be able to make recommendations about what to buy. Some service providers even sell modems; that's a good way to avoid problems.

Dial-up Access

What if you can't afford dedicated access, and you don't want to experiment with SLIP or PPP? Is there any easy way to get network access? Yes—just get an account on some computer that already has dedicated access. Then use your home computer to log in to this "remote" system, and do your network work there. Dial-up access is almost as good (but not quite as good) as having your own connection, and it's considerably easier to set up. Your computer doesn't actually become part of the Internet; it's just accessing a service computer that's permanently connected to the network. Many organizations provide this kind of service. Since you are sharing the connection with others, the cost of these services is greatly reduced (typically around $20 to $40 per month—possibly with some additional per-hour access fee). The cheapest rates apply if you contract for "off peak" service only (i.e., nights and weekends). If you can find a Freenet in your area, it will be even more economical; as the name implies, the service will be "free."

This type of connection has its pros and cons. On the good side, you probably have all the hardware and software you need (i.e., a modem and a terminal emulation package). Even if you had to buy them, you could come by them for less than $200. On the bad side, you can only do what the service provider allows. You may not be able to use all the services that the Internet has. There is probably no way to load a random nifty software application and use it. You'd have to appeal to the provider to add that service. Some access providers may limit the amount of disk space you can use. And again, you're also responsible for phone bills, though (as we said above) some providers have 800 numbers or local access numbers.

By the way, it's worth mentioning one new kind of "dial-up" service. PSI (one of the major service providers) is distributing a free software package called PSIlink. It allows a PC running DOS to connect to their system and use the Internet's electronic mail, bulletin board, and file transfer services. They've managed to hide most of the problems that "dial-up" access entails from you; the files you want automatically get transferred to your home system, for example. The cost of this service is roughly $30/month. The drawback to this kind of service is that you're limited to what one service provider gives you. As you might expect, the software these companies give away won't work with their competitors. If this strikes you as a fair trade, look into it.

UUCP Access

We'll mention, in passing, a subclass of "dial-up" access. All UNIX systems support a set of services called UUCP, which transfer data over standard phone lines. If you find a cooperating service provider (like UUNET, an employer, or a friend), you can arrange to use UUCP to pick up Internet mail and USENET news. Your system uses UUCP to dial into a remote system, and then transfer news and mail back home at regular intervals. You can therefore read your mail on your own system, rather than someone else's. You can't do much more than read mail and news, since you're really not connected to the Internet at all. Your computer just dials up an Internet computer periodically and transfers files.

UUCP is common and (if you have UNIX and a modem) you won't need to spend anything on software or equipment. Any UNIX system has all the software you need. And it's easy to find someone to give you a UUCP connection for free, or at least cheap. If all you want is electronic mail on your home system, it will do the job. Setting up UUCP is not trivial, but not terribly difficult, either. See the Nutshell handbooks *Managing UUCP and USENET* and *Using UUCP and USENET* for more information.

Access Via Other Networks

Most networking services, like Bitnet and Compuserve, have set up "gateways" that allow you to exchange electronic mail with systems on the Internet. Some have set up gateways that let you read the Internet's bulletin boards (USENET news). And there are a few services scattered around that let you request a file via an electronic mail message; such services fetch the file and mail it to you automatically. This isn't as good as getting the file directly, but it works.

This may be all you need. But it's definitely not an Internet connection; you only have access to a few services. What you can do is fairly limited; there's a lot more out there waiting for you.

There is another way you might use other networks to get to the Internet. If you are trying to use one of the "UNIX to the masses" services, like the Well, to provide you with Internet dial-up services, you usually have to pay for your own long distance calls to the mainframe. It might be more economical to use other networks, like CompuServe, to get from your home to the Internet computer. Then, you can get to wherever on the Internet you like.

Telephone Connections

Whatever alternative you choose, you're going to have some kind of telephone connection—whether it's a very expensive T3 line or a standard "voice" line. Here's a summary of the most common service grades:

Table A-1: Telephone Line Options

Service grade	Speed	Notes
Standard voice line	0 to 19.2 kb	No extra cost; SLIP or dial-up connections
Leased line	56-64 kb	Small "dedicated" link to a service provider
T1	1.544 Mb	Dedicated link with heavy use
T2	6 Mb	not commonly used in networking
T3	45 Mb	Major networking artery for a large corporation or university

Service Providers

Internet service providers are participating in a competitive market. For any given kind of service, there are usually several providers available—and several different price structures. In the tables coming up, we've listed as many service providers as we could find. There are probably others. I can't tell you which ones are better than others; like the evolution of species, each has its own niche in the market. As you investigate, you'll certainly find different trade-offs you can make: quality of service versus price; initial cost versus monthly cost; and so on. However, I can give you some hints about where to start.

The providers are grouped into one of two groups, national (shown in Table 1) and regional (Table 2) providers. National providers market their services to anyone in their nation. Regional providers have staked out an area of their country and only market their services within that area. Of course, once you're connected to the Internet, you have access to the entire world. So the difference between national and regional providers depends on what you like. Regional providers would claim that they give better ("more personal" service), and that they can adapt more quickly to their clients' needs. (One regional provider helps its clients do teleconferencing, for example.) Nationwide providers would counter that claim by saying that they can bring more resources to bear to solve a particular client's problems.

International providers are more difficult to categorize. One would assume that the national providers are ones who do international connections, too. This is true, but a number of regionals also do this. Many U.S. regional providers got dragged into providing international connections early in the Internet game, before most of the national providers existed, and they still have them today. So, if you are looking to connect to another country, you need to look at both national and regional provider tables.

Who you call depends on how and where you want to connect. The how is taken care of by the size of your connection. If you are an individual or really small business, you will probably be looking for providers of dial-up or SLIP PPP services. Medium to large businesses should look to SLIP PPP or dedicated services. Here are a few guidelines to help you in looking for a provider:

- If you want to connect a single site in the U.S. to the Internet, or if you want to connect several sites in the same geographical area to the Internet, call either national or regional providers that offer suitable services. For example, if you want to connect several offices in New England to the Internet, you can contact either Northeast regional providers or national providers. Obviously, if you're only interested in connecting one site to the Internet, regional and national providers can serve you equally well; your choice will be based on price and the services that are available.

- If you want to connect several widely distributed sites in the U.S. to the Internet (e.g., offices in Washington D.C., Los Angles, and Chicago), talk to suitable national providers. If you try to do this with regional providers, you will probably end up dealing with multiple contracts, operations centers, etc. It's probably not worth the effort.

- If you want to connect sites in the U.S. and sites in other countries to the Internet (e.g., offices in Washington D.C. and London), talk to a national provider or a regional provider with international connections on the coast closest to where you want to reach. It may be very hard to deal with a foreign bureaucracy; an experienced provider who is currently serving the country in question is valuable.

- If you are a lone researcher outside of the U.S., would like an Internet connection for yourself or your institution, and don't know where to start, try contacting:

```
Robert D. Collet
Principal Investigator,
NSFnet International Connections Manager (ICM)
Program Manager, SprintLink
Sprint Communications Company
Government Systems Division -- Mail Stop: VAHRNA611
13221 Woodland Park Road
Herndon, Virginia, 22071  U.S.A.

Tel: +1-703-904-2230
FAX: +1-703-904-2119
Pager: +1-800-SKY-PAGE   PIN: 45469

e-mail:  rcollet@icm1.icp.net, rcollet@sprint.com, or
         PN=ROBERT.D.COLLET/O=US.SPRINT/ADMD=TELEMAIL/C=US/@sprint.com
```

He is the person responsible for international connections for the NSFnet portion of the Internet.

In Europe, you might also try:

```
RIPE NCC
Kruislaan 409
NL-1098 SJ Amsterdam
The Netherlands

Tel: +31 20 592 5065
E-mail: ncc@ripe.net
```

Table A-2: Nationwide and International Service Providers

Provider	Coverage	Services
AARNet		
AARNet Support GPO Box 1142 Canberra ACT 2601 Australia +61 6 249 3385 +61 6 249 1369 (FAX) aarnet@aarnet.edu.au	Australia	Dedicated (9.6kb - 2Mb) SLIP PPP
AlterNet		
See UUNET		
ANS (Advanced Networks and Services)		
2901 Hubbard Road Ann Arbor, MI 48105 (313) 663-7610 maloff@nis.ans.net	Worldwide	Dedicated (1.5Mb - 45Mb)
a2i Communications		
1211 Park Avenue #202 San Jose, CA 95132 info@rahul.net	Continental U.S.	Dial-up
CLASS (Cooperative Library Agency for Systems and Services)		
1415 Koll Circle Suite 101 San Jose, CA 95112-4698 (800) 488-4559 (408) 453-0444	National (member libraries only)	Dial-up
Demon Internet Services		
Demon System Ltd. 42 Hendon Lane London N3 1TT England +44 81 349 0063 internet@demon.co.uk	UK	Dial-up SLIP PPP

Table A.2: Nationwide and International Service Providers (continued)

Provider	Coverage	Services
EUnet		
EUnet Support +31 20 59 25 12 4 glenn@eu.net	Europe	
PACCOM		
University of Hawaii, ICS 2565 The Mall Honolulu, HI 96822 (808) 956-3499 torben@hawaii.edu	Pacific Rim countries Hawaii	Dedicated (64kb - 1.5kb)
PSI (Performance Systems International)		
1180 Sunrise Valley Drive Suite 1100 Reston, VA 22091 (703) 620-6651 (703) 629-4586 (FAX) info@psi.com	Worldwide	Dedicated (9.6kb - 1.5Mb) Dial-up SLIP PPP/UUCP PSILink
SprintLink		
Sprint International 13221 Woodland Park Drive Herndon, VA 22071 (703) 904-2156 mkiser@icm1.icp.net	Worldwide	Dedicated (9.6kb - 1.5Mb)
UKnet		
UKnet Support +44 227 475497 postmaster@uknet.ac.uk	UK countries	Dedicated Dial-up UUCP
UUNET		
Suite 570 3110 Fairview Park Drive Falls Church, VA 22042 (703) 204-8000 (800) 4UU-NET3 info@uunet.uu.net	Worldwide	Dial-up SLIP PPP UUCP Dedicated (9.6kb - 1.5Mb)

Table A.2: Nationwide and International Service Providers (continued)

Provider	Coverage	Services
The Well		
27 Gate Five Road Saulsalito, CA 94965 (415) 332-4335 info@well.sf.ca.us	Access through X.25 and direct dial	Dial-up
The World		
Software Tool and Die 1330 Beacon Street Brookline, MA 02146 (617) 739-0202	U.S.	Dial-up

Table A-3: Regional Service Providers

Provider	Coverage	Services
AccessNB*		
Computer Science Department University of New Brunswick Fredericton, NB Canada E3B5A4	New Brunswick, Canada	
ARnet*		
Walter Neilson (403) 450-5188	Alberta, Canada	
BARRNET		
William Yundt Pine Hall Room 115 Stanford, CA 94305-4122 (415) 723-3104 gd.why@forsythe.stanford.edu	San Francisco, CA area International-Far East	Dedicated Dial-up SLIP PPP

Table A.3: Regional Service Providers (continued)

Provider	Coverage	Services
BCnet		
BCnet Headquarters 419-6356 Agricultural Road Vancouver, BC Canada V6T 1Z2 (604) 822-3932 BCnet@ubc.ca	British Columbia	Dedicated (2400 - 1.5Mb)
CERFnet		
PO Box 85608 San Diego, CA 92186-9784 (800) 876-2373 (619) 455-3990 help@cerf.net	Southern CA International- (Korea, Mexico, Brazil)	Dedicated (14.4kb - 1.5Mb) Dial-up (local & 800) SLIP PPP
CICnet		
ITI Building 2901 Hubbard Drive, Pod G Ann Arbor, MI 48105 (313) 998-6103 info@cic.net	Midwest U.S. (IL IA MN WI MI OH IN)	Dedicated (56kb - 1.5Mb)
Colorado Supernet		
CSM Computer Center Colorado School of Mines 1500 Illinois Golden, CO 80401 (303) 273-3471 (303) 273-3475 (FAX) info@csn.org	Colorado	Dedicated (9.6kb - 1.5Mb) Dial-up SLIP PPP
CONCERT		
PO Box 12889 3021 Cornwallis Road Research Triangle Park, NC 27709 (919) 248-1404 jrr@concert.net	North Carolina	Dedicated (56kb - 1.5Mb) Dial-up SLIP PPP/UUCP

Table A.3: Regional Service Providers (continued)

Provider	Coverage	Services
JVNCnet		
Sergio Heker 6 von Neuman Hall Princeton University Princeton, NJ 08544 (609) 258-2400 market@jvnc.net	Northeastern U.S. International	Dedicated (19.2kb - 1.5Mb) Dial-up SLIP
Los Nettos		
Information Sciences Institute 4676 Admiralty Way Marina del Rey, CA 90292 (310) 822-1511 los-nettos-request@isi.edu	Los Angles, CA area	Dedicated (1.5Mb)
MBnet*		
Gerry Miller (204) 474-8230	Manitoba, Canada	
Merit		
2200 Bonisteel Boulevard Ann Arbor, MI 48109-2112 (313) 764-9430 jogden@merit.edu	Michigan	
MIDnet		
29 WESC University of Nebraska Lincoln, NE 68588 (402) 472-5032 dmf@westie.unl.edu	Plains States U.S. (NE OK AR SD IA KA MO)	Dedicated (56kb - 1.5Mb)
MRNet (Minnesota Regional Network)		
511 11th Avenue So, Box 212 Minneapolis, MN 55415 (612) 342-2570 (612) 344-1716 (FAX) info@mr.net	Minnesota	Dedicated (56kb - 1.5Mb)

Table A.3: Regional Service Providers (continued)

Provider	Coverage	Services
MSEN		
628 Brooks Street Ann Arbor, MI 48103 (313) 998-4562 info@msen.com	Michigan	Dedicated (9.6kb - 1.5Mb) Dial-up SLIP PPP
NEARnet		
BBN Systems and Technologies 10 Moulton Street Cambridge, MA 02138 (617) 873-8730 nearnet-join@nic.near.net	Northeastern U.S. (ME NH VT CT RI MA)	Dedicated (9.6kb - 10Mb) SLIP PPP
Netcom Online Communication Services		
4000 Moorepark Avenue #209 San Jose, CA 95117 (408) 554-8649 ruthann@netcom.com	California (6 locations in major cities)	Dial-up
netIllinois		
Joel Hartman Bradley University 1501 W. Bradley Avenue Peoria, IL 61625 (309) 677-3100 (309) 677-3092 (FAX) joel@bradley.edu	Illinois	Dedicated (9.6kb - 1.5Mb)
NevadaNet		
University of Nevada System Computing Services 4505 Maryland Parkway Las Vegas, NV 89154 (702) 739-3557	Nevada	Dedicated
NLnet*		
Wilf Bussey (709) 737-8329	Newfoundland Labrador	

Table A.3: Regional Service Providers (continued)

Provider	Coverage	Services
NorthWestNet		
2435 233rd Place NE Redmond, WA 98053 (206) 562-3000 ehood@nwnet.net	Northwestern U.S. (OR WA WY AK ID MT ND)	Dedicated (56kb - 1.5Mb)
NSTN*		
900 Windmill Road, Suite 107 Dartmouth, NS Canada B3B 137 (902) 468-NSTN parsons@hawk.nstn.ns.ca	Nova Scotia, Canada	Dedicated (9.6kb - 56kb) SLIP Dial-up
NYSERNet		
111 College Place Room 3-211 Syracuse, NY 13244 (315) 443-4120 luckett@nysernet.org	New York State	SLIP PPP Dial-up Dedicated (9.6kb - 1.5Mb)
OARnet		
Ohio Supercomputer Center 1224 Kinnear Road Columbus, OH 43085 (614) 292-9248 alison@osc.edu	Ohio	Dedicated SLIP PPP
Onet*		
4 Bancroft Avenue Rm 116 University of Toronto Toronto, Ontario M58 1A1 Canada (416) 978-5058 eugene@vm.utcs.utoronto.ca	Ontario, Canada	
PEINet*		
Jim Hancock (902) 566-0450	Prince Edward Island, Canada	

Table A.3: Regional Service Providers (continued)

Provider	Coverage	Services
Portal Communications		
20863 Stevens Creek Boulevard Suite #200 Cupertino, CA 95014 (408) 973-9111 voice info@portal.com	San Francisco Bay (World wide through Sprintnet)	Dialup SLIP PPP
PREPnet		
305 S. Craig, 2nd Floor Pittsburgh, PA 15213 (412) 268-7870 twb+@andrew.cmu.edu	Pennsylvania (Dial-in from outside PA accepted)	Dedicated (9.6kb - 1.5Mb) Dial-up SLIP PPP
PSCnet		
Pittsburgh Supercomputing Center 4400 5th Avenue Pittsburgh, PA 15213 (412) 268-4960 hastings@psc.edu	Eastern U.S.	Dedicated
RISQ*		
3744 Jean Brillant Bureau 500 Montreal, Quebec Canada H3T1P1 (514) 340-5700 turcotte@clouso.crim.ca	Quebec	
SASK#net*		
Dean C. Jones (306) 966-4860	Saskatchewan	
Sesquinet		
Office of Networking and Computing Rice University Houston, TX 77251-1892 (713) 527-4988 farrell@rice.edu	Texas Latin America	Dedicated (8.6kb - 1.5Mb) SLIP

Table A.3: Regional Service Providers (continued)

Provider	Coverage	Services
SURAnet		
1353 Computer Science Center 8400 Baltimore Boulevard College Park, MD 20740-2498 (301) 982-4600 info@sura.net	Southeastern U.S. Caribbean Islands	Dedicated (56kb - 45kb)
THEnet		
Texas Higher Education Network Information Center Austin, TC 78712 (512) 471-2444 info@nic.the.net	Texas Limited Mexico	Dedicated (1.5Mb) Dial-up SLIP
VERnet		
Academic Computing Center GIlmer Hall University of Virginia Charlottesville, VA 22903 jaj@virginia.edu (804) 924-0616	Virginia	Dedicated Dial-up SLIP PPP
Westnet		
601 S. Howes, 6th Floor South Colorado State University Fort Collins, CO 80523 (303) 491-7260 pburns@yuma.acns.colostate.edu	Western U.S. (AZ CO ID NM UT WY)	Dedicated
WiscNet		
1210 W. Dayton Street Madison, WI 53706 (608) 262-8874 dorl@macc.wisc.edu	Wisconsin	Dedicated (56kb - 1.5Mb) Limited Dial-up/SLIP PPP
WVnet*		
Harper Grimm (304) 293-5192 cc011041@wvnvm.wvnet.edu	West Virginia	Dedicated SLIP PPP

Note: The information for providers marked with a * was not verified by press time.

INTERNATIONAL NETWORK CONNECTIVITY

Summary of International Connectivity
Country Codes and Connectivity

Outside of the United States, the top-level domain used in an Internet address is usually a two-letter "country code." The table below shows the codes for all the countries that have some kind of network connectivity. They are not all "on the Internet"; some are connected with BITNET, UUCP, FIDONET, or some kind of OSI network. Remember that if they don't have an Internet connection, connectivity will probably be limited to electronic mail. It also shows the country codes for all countries (or regions) that aren't currently on the Net. As you might expect, new countries are added almost weekly. You never know when Albania is going to appear on the Net. Given recent events, it might not be too long.

We've modified the table slightly to account for network use. For example, we don't have an entry for Puerto Rico, even though it has its own country code (PR): network sites in Puerto Rico use the United States' top-level domains. We've also made a few "corrections": Great Britain uses the country code UK, rather than its assigned ISO code (GB). When they appear on the Net, will the Virgin Islands use their assigned country codes or the British and American top-level domains? We don't know, so we left the entries in.

International affairs being what they are, it's impossible to predict exactly what will happen in the future. The SU (Soviet Union) country code was recently deleted from the official list; we put it back in, because the SU country code is still used—with increasing frequency, in fact. But you'll see all of the former Soviet states listed, many of which have some kind of international network connectivity. And so on. But that's just one of the things that makes the network exciting.

The total number of entities with international network connectivity is 107. Figure B-1 shows how to interpret the connectivity table. Table B-1 breaks the connectivity down according to network.

Summary of International Connectivity

Table B-1: International Connectivity Summary

	Minimal	Widespread	Expected	Other
BITNET	19	28	1	
INTERNET*		40	5	
UUCP	46	44	11	
FIDONET	12	47		7†
OSI	9	16		

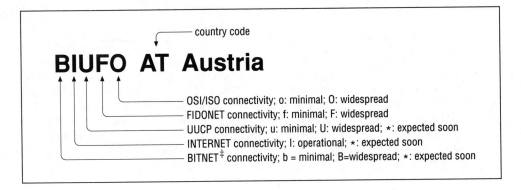

Figure B-1: Key to connectivity table

Country Codes and Connectivity

-----	AF	Afghanistan	-----	AW	Aruba
-----	AL	Albania	-IUF-	AU	Australia
-----	DZ	Algeria	BIUFO	AT	Austria
-----	AS	American Samoa	-----	AZ	Azerbaijan
-----	AD	Andorra	--*--	BS	Bahamas
-----	AO	Angola	-----	BH	Bahrain
-----	AI	Anguilla	-----	BD	Bangladesh
-*---	AQ	Antarctica	--*--	BB	Barbados
--*--	AG	Antigua and Barbuda	BIUFO	BE	Belgium
BIUF-	AR	Argentina	--*--	BZ	Belize
--u--	AM	Armenia	-----	BJ	Benin

---

*For the Internet, the "minimal" and "widespread" categories are merged into the single category, "operational."

†Link exists, but is not in public tables; contact **mike_jensen@p1.f26.n7101.z5.gnfido.fidonet.org**.

‡BITNET is used generically to refer to BITNET and similar networks, including EARN, NETNORTH, GULFNET, etc.

`-----`	BM	Bermuda		`---j-`	GH	Ghana
`-----`	BT	Bhutan		`-----`	GI	Gibraltar
`--u--`	BO	Bolivia		`BIUFo`	GR	Greece
`---f-`	BW	Botswana		`---f-`	GL	Greenland
`-----`	BV	Bouvet Island		`--u--`	GD	Grenada
`BIUFO`	BR	Brazil		`--u--`	GP	Guadeloupe
`-----`	BN	Brunei Darussalam		`--u--`	GT	Guatemala
`-*UF-`	BG	Bulgaria		`--u--`	GF	Guiana
`--u--`	BF	Burkina Faso		`-----`	GN	Guinea
`-----`	BI	Burundi		`-----`	GW	Guinea-Bissau
`--UF-`	BY	Byelorussian SSR		`-----`	GY	Guyana
`-----`	KH	Cambodia		`-----`	HT	Haiti
`--*--`	CM	Cameroon		`-----`	HM	Heard and McDonald
`BIUFO`	CA	Canada		`--u--`	HN	Honduras
`-----`	CV	Cape Verde		`BI-F-`	HK	Hong Kong
`-----`	KY	Cayman Islands		`bIUF-`	HU	Hungary
`-----`	CF	Central African Republic		`-IUf-`	IS	Iceland
`-----`	TD	Chad		`bIU--`	IN	India
`-----`	IO	Chagos Islands		`--u--`	ID	Indonesia
`BIUf-`	CL	Chile		`-----`	IR	Iran
`--u-O`	CN	China		`-----`	IQ	Iraq
`-----`	CX	Christmas Island		`BIUFo`	IE	Ireland
`--*--`	CI	Cote d'Ivoire		`BIUF-`	IL	Israel
`-----`	CC	Cocos (Keeling Islands)		`BIUFO`	IT	Italy
`b-u--`	CO	Colombia		`--u--`	JM	Jamaica
`-----`	KM	Comoros		`BIUF-`	JP	Japan
`--*--`	CG	Congo		`-----`	JO	Jordan
`-----`	CK	Cook Islands		`-----`	KK	Kazakhstan
`b*u--`	CR	Costa Rica		`---f-`	KE	Kenya
`b--fo`	??	Croatia		`-----`	KI	Kiribati
`--u--`	CU	Cuba		`-----`	KP	Korea
`b-U--`	CY	Cyprus		`BIUF-`	KR	Korea
`BIUF-`	CS	Czechoslovakia		`-----`	KW	Kuwait
`bIUFo`	DK	Denmark		`-----`	KG	Kyrgyzstan
`-----`	DJ	Djibouti		`-----`	LA	Laos
`--*--`	DM	Dominica		`--UF-`	LV	Latvia
`--u--`	DO	Dominican Republic		`-----`	LB	Lebanon
`-----`	TP	East Timor		`-----`	LS	Lesotho
`b-u--`	EC	Ecuador		`-----`	LR	Liberia
`b-uj-`	EG	Egypt		`-----`	LY	Libya
`-----`	SV	El Salvador		`-----`	LI	Liechtenstein
`-----`	GQ	Equatorial Guinea		`--uFo`	LT	Lithuania
`-*UF-`	EE	Estonia		`b-uFo`	LU	Luxembourg
`---f-`	ET	Ethiopia		`---F-`	MO	Macau
`-----`	FK	Falkland Islands		`-----`	MG	Madagascar
`-----`	FO	Faroe Islands		`-----`	MW	Malawi
`--u--`	FJ	Fiji		`b-uF-`	MY	Malaysia
`BIUFo`	FI	Finland		`-----`	MV	Maldives
`BIUFO`	FR	France		`--u--`	ML	Mali
`--u--`	PF	French Polynesia		`-----`	MT	Malta
`-----`	TF	French Southern Territories		`-----`	MH	Marshall Islands
`-----`	GA	Gabon		`--u--`	MQ	Martinique
`-----`	GM	Gambia		`-----`	MR	Mauritania
`-----`	GG	Georgia		`---j-`	MU	Mauritius
`BIUFO`	DE	Germany		`BIuf-`	MX	Mexico

-----	FM	Micronesia
---F-	MD	Moldova
-----	MC	Monaco
-----	MN	Mongolia
-----	MS	Montserrat
-----	MA	Morocco
-----	MZ	Mozambique
-----	MM	Myanmar
--u--	NA	Namibia
-----	NR	Nauru
-----	NP	Nepal
BIUFO	NL	Netherlands
-----	AN	Netherlands Antilles
-----	NT	Neutral Zone
--u--	NC	New Caledonia
-IuF-	NZ	New Zealand
--u--	NI	Nicaragua
--u--	NE	Niger
-----	NG	Nigeria
-----	NU	Niue Island
-----	NF	Norfolk Island
-----	MP	Northern Marianas
BIUFO	NO	Norway
-----	OM	Oman
--u--	PK	Pakistan
-----	PW	Palau
*----	PA	Panama
--u--	PG	Papua New Guinea
--u--	PY	Paraguay
--U--	PE	Peru
--uF-	PH	Philippines
-----	PN	Pitcairn Island
bIUF-	PL	Poland
bIUFO	PT	Portugal
-----	QA	Qatar
-----	RE	Re'union
--*--	RO	Romania
b-UF-	RU	Russia
-----	RW	Rwanda
-----	SH	Saint Helena
--*--	KN	Saint Kitts and Nevis
--*--	LC	Saint Lucia
-----	PM	Saint Pierre and Miquelon
-----	VC	Saint Vincent and the Grenadines
-----	SM	San Marino
-----	ST	Sao Tome and Principe
B----	SA	Saudi Arabia
--uj-	SN	Senegal
--u--	SC	Seychelles
-----	SL	Sierra Leone
bIuF-	SG	Singapore
b--FO	SI	Slovenia
-----	SB	Solomon Islands
-----	SO	Somalia
-IUFo	ZA	South Africa

b-UF	SU	Former Soviet Union
BIUFO	ES	Spain
--u--	LK	Sri Lanka
-----	SD	Sudan
--u--	SR	Suriname
-----	SJ	Svalbard and Jan Mayen
-----	SZ	Swaziland
BIUFo	SE	Sweden
BIUFO	CH	Switzerland
-----	SY	Syria
BIuF-	TW	Taiwan, Province of China
--u--	TJ	Tajikistan
---j-	TZ	Tanzania
---F-	TH	Thailand
--u--	TG	Togo
-----	TK	Tokelau Islands
-----	TO	Tonga
--u--	TT	Trinidad and Tobago
bIuj-	TN	Tunisia
B----	TR	Turkey
-----	TM	Turkmenistan
-----	TC	Turks and Caicos
-----	TV	Tuvalu
---j-	UG	Uganda
--UF-	UA	Ukraine
-----	AE	United Arab Emirates
bIUFO	UK	United Kingdom
BIUFO	US	United States
-----	UM	US Outlying islands
--Uf-	UY	Uruguay
--U--	UZ	Uzbekistan
--u--	VU	Vanuatu
-----	VA	Vatican City
-IU--	VE	Venezuela
-----	VN	Vietnam
-----	VG	Virgin Islands, British
-*---	VI	Virgin Islands, U.S.
-----	WF	Wallis and Futuna
-----	EH	Western Sahara
-----	WS	Western Samoa
-----	YE	Yemen
bIUf-	YU	Yugoslavia
-----	ZR	Zaire
---f-	ZM	Zambia
--uf-	ZW	Zimbabwe

ACCEPTABLE USE

This is the official "acceptable use" policy for the NSFNET, dated June 1992. As of publication, this is the most recent version of this policy. You can get an up-to-date version of the policy via anonymous FTP from **nic.merit.edu**, in the file */nsfnet/acceptable.use.policies/nsfnet.txt.*

Though the first paragraph of this policy sounds scary, don't be put off by it. As we said in Chapter 3, "support" of research and education is interpreted fairly loosely. And remember that the NSFNET is not the Internet. It's only a part of the Internet, and it has one of the strictest acceptable use policies. The network to which you connect may have a significantly different policy; some branches of the Internet actively encourage commercial use. Take up any questions with your service provider—your provider determines what's acceptable for your connection. If you want an Internet connection for strictly commercial or personal use, it's easy to find a provider who will serve you.

The NSFNET Backbone Services Acceptable Use Policy

General Principle:

- NSFNET Backbone services are provided to support open research and education in and among US research and instructional institutions, plus research arms of for-profit firms when engaged in open scholarly communication and research. Use for other purposes is not acceptable.

Specifically Acceptable Uses:

- Communication with foreign researchers and educators in connection with research or instruction, as long as any network that the foreign user employs for such communication provides reciprocal access to US researchers and educators.

- Communication and exchange for professional development, to maintain currency, or to debate issues in a field or subfield of knowledge.

- Use for disciplinary-society, university-association, government-advisory, or standards activities related to the user's research and instructional activities.

- Use in applying for or administering grants or contracts for research or instruction, but not for other fundraising or public relations activities.

- Any other administrative communications or activities in direct support of research and instruction.

- Announcements of new products or services for use in research or instruction, but not advertising of any kind.

- Any traffic originating from a network of another member agency of the Federal Networking Council if the traffic meets the acceptable use policy of that agency.

- Communication incidental to otherwise acceptable use, except for illegal or specifically unacceptable use.

Unacceptable Uses:

- Use for for-profit activities, unless covered by the General Principle or as a specifically acceptable use.

- Extensive use for private or personal business.

This statement applies to use of the NSFNET Backbone only. NSF expects that connecting networks will formulate their own use policies. The NSF Division of Networking and Communications Research and Infrastructure will resolve any questions about this Policy or its interpretation.

GLOSSARY

AFS

A set of protocols that allows you to use files on other network machines *as if* they were local. So, rather than using FTP to transfer a file to your local computer, you can read it, write it, or edit it on the remote computer—using the same commands that you'd use locally. Very similar in concept to NFS (q.v.), though it provides better performance. Not yet in widespread use, though a commercial version is currently available from a company called Transarc.

Application

(a) Software that performs a particular useful function for you. ("Do you have an electronic mail application installed on your computer?")

(b) The useful function itself (e.g., transferring files is a useful application of the Internet.)

Archie

A system for locating files that are publicly available by anonymous FTP. Archie is described in Chapter 9, *Finding Software*.

ARPAnet

An experimental network established in the 70's where the theories and software on which the Internet is based were tested. No longer in existence.

baud

When transmitting data, the number of times the medium's "state" changes per second. For example: a 2400 baud modem changes the signal it sends on the phone line 2400 times per second. Since each change in state can correspond to multiple bits of data, the actual bit rate of data transfer may exceed the baud rate. Also, see bits per second.

BIND

The UNIX implementation of DNS (q.v.). It stands for "Berkeley Internet Name Domain."

bits per second (bps)

The speed at which bits are transmitted over a communications medium.

BTW

Common abbreviation in mail and news, meaning "by the way."

CIX

Commercial Internet Exchange; an agreement among network providers that allows them to do accounting for commercial traffic. Although it has been discussed a lot in the press, it's primarily a concern for network providers.

client

A software application (q.v.) that works on your behalf to extract some service from a server somewhere on the network. Think of your telephone as a client and the telephone company as a server to get the idea.

datagram

A packet (q.v.) of information that is sent to the receiving computer without any prior warning. Conceptually, a "datagram" is somewhat like a telegram: it's a self-contained message that can arrive at any time, without notice. Datagraphs are usually used in applications where the amount of information transfer is occasional and small.

DDN

Defense Data Network; a portion of the Internet which connects to U.S. Military Bases and contractors; used for non-secure communications. MILNET is one of the DDN networks. It also runs "the NIC," where a lot of Internet information is archived.

DECnet

A set of proprietary networking protocols used by Digital Equipment Corporation operating systems, instead of TCP/IP. These protocols are not compatible with the Internet.

dedicated line

See "leased line."

DFS

For all practical purposes, another name for AFS. More specifically, DFS refers to the AFS implementation that's part of the OSF's DCE (Distributed Computing Environment). Enough letters for you?

dial-up

(a) To connect to a computer by calling it up on the telephone. Often, "dial-up" only refers to the kind of connection you make when using a terminal emulator and a regular modem. For the technoids: switched character-oriented asynchronous communication.

(b) A port (q.v.) that accepts dial-up connections. ("How many dial-up ports on your computer?")

DNS

The Domain Name System; a distributed database system for translating computer names (like **ruby.ora.com**) into numeric Internet addresses (like **194.56.78.2**), and vice-versa. DNS allows you to use the Internet without remembering long lists of numbers.

DoD

The (U.S.) Department of Defense, whose Advanced Research Projects Agency got the Internet started by creating the ARPAnet.

Ethernet

A kind of "local area network." It's pretty confusing because there are several different kinds of wiring, which support different communication speeds, ranging from 2 to 10 million bits per second. What makes an Ethernet an Ethernet is the way the computers on the network decide whose turn it is to talk. Computers using TCP/IP are frequently connected to the Internet over an Ethernet.

FAQ

Either a frequently-asked question, or a list of frequently asked questions and their answers. Many USENET news groups, and some non-USENET mailing lists, maintain FAQ lists (FAQs) so that participants won't spend lots of time answering the same set of questions.

Flame

A virulent and (often) largely personal attack against the author of a USENET posting. "Flames" are unfortunately common. People who frequently write flames are known as "flamers."

followup

A response to a USENET posting (q.v.).

Freenet

An organization to provide free Internet access to people in a certain area, usually through public libraries.

FTP

(a) The File Transfer Protocol; a protocol that defines how to transfer files from one computer to another.

(b) An application program which moves files using the File Transfer Protocol. FTP is described in detail in Chapter 6, *Moving Files: FTP*.

FYI

(a) A common abbreviation in mail and news, meaning "for your information."

(b) A series of informative papers about the Internet; they're similar to RFCs (q.v.), but don't define new standards.

gateway

A computer system that transfers data between normally incompatible applications or networks. It reformats the data so that it is acceptable for the new network (or application) before passing it on. A gateway may connect two dissimilar networks, like DECnet and the Internet; or it might allow two incompatible applications to communicate over the same network (like mail systems with different message formats). The term is often used interchangeably with "router" (q.v.), but this usage is incorrect.

Gopher

A menu-based system for exploring Internet resources. Gopher is described in detail in Chapter 11, *Tunneling Through the Internet: Gopher.*

IAB

The Internet Architecture Board; the "ruling council" that makes decisions about standards and other important issues.

IETF

The Internet Engineering Task Force; a volunteer group that investigates and solves technical problems, and makes recommendations to the IAB (q.v.).

IMHO

Common abbreviation in mail and news, meaning "in my humble opinion."

Internet

(a) Generally (not capitalized), any collection of distinct networks working together as one.

(b) Specifically (capitalized), the world-wide "network of networks" that are connected to each other, using the IP protocol and other similar protocols. The Internet provides file transfer, remote login, electronic mail, news, and other services.

IP

The Internet Protocol; the most important of the protocols on which the Internet is based. It allows a packet to traverse multiple networks on the way to its final destination.

ISO

The International Organization for Standardization; an organization that has defined a different set of network protocols, called the ISO/OSI protocols. In theory, the ISO/OSI protocols will eventually replace the Internet protocols. When and if this will actually happen is a hotly debated topic.

ISOC

The Internet Society: a membership organization whose members support a world-wide information network. It is also the governing body to which the IAB reports.

Knowbot

An experimental information-retrieval tool; a "robotic librarian." There isn't much to say about them yet, but they're something to watch for.

Leased line

A permanently-connected private telephone line between two locations. Leased lines are typically used to connect a moderate-sized local network to an Internet service provider.

mail reflector

A special mail address; electronic mail sent to this address is automatically forwarded to a set of other addresses. Typically, used to implement a mail discussion group.

MILNET

One of the DDN networks that make up the Internet; devoted to non-classified military (U.S.) communications. It was built using the same technology as the ARPAnet, and remained in production when the ARPAnet was decommissioned.

modem

A piece of equipment that connects a computer to a data transmission line (typically a telephone line of some sort). Normal people use modems that transfer data at speeds ranging from 1200 bits per second (bps) to 19.2 Kbps. There are also modems providing higher speeds and supporting other media. These are used for special purposes—for example, to connect a large local network to its network provider over a leased line.

NIC

(a) Network Information Center; any organization that's responsible for supplying information about any network.

(b) The DDN's NIC, which plays an important role in overall Internet coordination.

NFS

The Network File System; a set of protocols that allows you to use files on other network machines *as if* they were local. So, rather than using FTP to transfer a file to your local computer, you can read it, write it, or edit it on the remote computer—using the same commands that you'd use locally. NFS was originally developed by Sun Microsystems, Inc., and is currently in widespread use.

NOC

Network Operations Center; a group which is responsible for the day-to-day care and feeding of a network. Each service provider usually has a separate NOC, so you need to know which one to call when you have problems.

NREN

The National Research and Education Network; a U.S. effort to combine networks operated by different federal agencies into a single high-speed network. While this transition will be of significant technical and historical importance, it should have no effect on the typical Internet user.

NSFNET

The National Science Foundation Network; the NSFNET is *not* the Internet. It's just one of the networks that make up the Internet.

octet

Internet standards-monger's lingo for a set of 8 bits, i.e., a "byte."

OSI

Open Systems Interconnect; another set of network protocols. See "ISO."

packet

A bundle of data. On the Internet, data is broken up into small chunks, called "packets"; each packet traverses the network independently. Packet sizes can vary from roughly 40 to 32000 bytes, depending on network hardware and media, but packets are normally less than 1500 bytes long.

port

(a) A number that identifies a particular Internet application. When your computer sends a packet to another computer, that packet contains information about what protocol it's using (e.g., TCP or UDP), and what application it's trying to communicate with. The "port number" identifies the application.

(b) One of a computer's physical input/output channels (i.e., a plug on the back).

Unfortunately, these two meanings are completely unrelated. The first is more common when you're talking about the Internet (as in "**telnet** to port 1000"); the second is more common when you're talking about hardware ("connect your modem to the serial port on the back of your computer.")

posting

An individual article sent to a USENET (q.v.) news group; or the act of sending an article to a USENET news group.

PPP

Point to Point Protocol; a protocol that allows a computer to use the TCP/IP (Internet) protocols (and become a full-fledged Internet member) with a standard telephone line and a high-speed modem. PPP is a new standard for this which replaces SLIP (q.v.). Although PPP is less common than SLIP, it's quickly increasing in popularity.

protocol

A protocol is just a definition for how computers will act when talking to each other. Protocol definitions range from how bits are placed on a wire to the format of an electronic mail message. Standard protocols allow computers from different manufacturers to communicate; the computers can use completely different software, providing that the programs running on both ends agree on what the data means.

RFC

Request for Comments; a set of papers in which the Internet's standards, proposed standards and generally agreed-upon ideas are documented and published.

router

A system that transfers data between two networks that use the same protocols. The networks may differ in physical characteristics (e.g., a router may transfer data between an Ethernet and a leased telephone line).

RTFM

Common abbreviation in mail and news, meaning "read the (. . .) manual."

server

(a) Software that allows a computer to offer a service to another computer. Other computers contact the server program by means of matching client (q.v.) software.

(b) The computer on which the server software runs.

service provider

An organization that provides connections to a part of the Internet. If you want to connect your company's network, or even your personal computer, to the Internet, you have to talk to a "service provider."

shell

On a UNIX system, software that accepts and processes command lines from your terminal. UNIX has multiple shells available (e.g., C shell, Bourne shell, Korn shell), each with slightly different command formats and facilities.

signature

A file, typically five lines long or so, that people often insert at the end of electronic mail messages or USENET news articles. A signature contains, minimally, a name and an e-mail address. Signatures usually also contain postal addresses, and often contain silly quotes, pictures, and other things. Some are very elaborate, though signatures more than 5 or 6 lines long are in questionable taste.

SLIP

Serial Line IP; a protocol that allows a computer to use the Internet protocols (and become a full-fledged Internet member) with a standard telephone line and a high-speed modem. SLIP is being superseded by PPP (q.v.), but still in common use.

smiley

Smiling faces used in mail and news to indicate humor and irony. The most common smiley is :-). You'll also see :-(, meaning disappointment, and lots of other variations. Since the variations are so, er, "variant," it's not worth going into detail. You'll pick up their connotations with time.

SRI

A California-based research institute that runs the Network Information Systems Center (NISC). The SRI has played an important role in coordinating the Internet.

switched access

A network connection that can be created and destroyed as needed. Dialup connections are the simplest form of switched connections. SLIP or PPP also are commonly run over switched connections.

TCP

The Transmission Control Protocol. One of the protocols on which the Internet is based. For the technoids, TCP is a connection-oriented reliable protocol.

TELNET

(a) A "terminal emulation" protocol that allows you to log in to other computer systems on the Internet.

(b) An application program that allows you to log in to another computer system using the TELNET protocol. **telnet** is described in detail in Chapter 5, *Remote Login*.

time out

A "time out" is what happens when two computers are "talking" and one computer—for any reason—fails to respond. The other computer will keep on trying for a certain amount of time, but will eventually "give up."

tn3270

A special version of the **telnet** program that interacts properly with IBM mainframes.

Token Ring

A technology for creating a "local area network" that may then be connected to the Internet. Token Ring networks often use the TCP/IP protocols. See also "Ethernet."

UDP

The User Datagram Protocol. Another of the protocols on which the Internet is based. For the technoids, UDP is a connectionless unreliable protocol. If you're not a technoid, don't let the word "unreliable" worry you.

UNIX

A popular operating system that was very important in the development of the Internet. Contrary to rumor, though, you do NOT have to use UNIX to use the Internet. There are various flavors of UNIX. Two common ones are BSD and System V.

USENET

The USENET is an informal, rather anarchic, group of systems that exchange "news." News is essentially similar to "bulletin boards" on other networks. USENET actually predates the Internet, but these days, the Internet is used to transfer much of the USENET's traffic. USENET is described in detail in Chapter 8, *Network News*.

UUCP

UNIX-to-UNIX copy; a facility for copying files between UNIX systems, on which mail and USENET news services were built. While UUCP is still useful, the Internet provides a better way to do the same job.

WAIS

Wide-area information servers; a very powerful system for looking up information in databases (or libraries) across the Internet. WAIS is described in detail in Chapter 12, *Searching Indexed Databases: WAIS*.

White Pages

Lists of Internet users that are accessible through the Internet. There are several different kinds of white-pages servers and services, described in Chapter 10, *Finding Someone*.

World-Wide Web

A hypertext-based system for finding and accessing Internet resources. WWW is described in Chapter 13, *Hyertext Spanning the Internet: WWW*.

WWW

See World-Wide Web.

INDEX

B

C

THE WHOLE INTERNET

INTERNET

QUICK REFERENCE CARD

telnet: login to remote system — Chapter 5

Subcommands:

close	end a connection
help	print help information
open	start a connection
set echo	enable/disable local echoing
set escape	set current "escape" character. By default, CTRL-]
quit	exit telnet program
z	suspend telnet
RETURN	leave command mode
CTRL-]	enter command mode

ftp: transfer files — Chapter 6

Subcommands:

account	supply additional accounting info
ascii	transfer text files
binary	transfer binary files
cd	change remote working directory
close	end FTP session with current system
dir	full directory listing on remote system
get	get file from remote system
help	print help information
lcd	change "local" directory
ls	short directory listing on remote system
open	connect to new system
put	move file to remote system
pwd	print current remote directory

mail: send/receive email — Chapter 7

There are many mail programs, each with different ways for doing the same things. Check your documentation for the actual commands.

Converting Email Addresses

compuserve: 100,200 → 100.200@compuserve.com
bitnet: jane@host.bitnet → jane%host@cunyvm.cuny.edu
fidonet: john doe 1:2/3.4 →
    john.doe@p4.f3.n2.z1.fidonet.org
MCImail (numeric): 1234567 → 1234567@mcimail.com
MCImail (name): jane doe → jane_doe@mcimail.com
UUCP: uunet!host!joe → joe%host@uunet.uu.net
sprintmail: See Chapter 7

nn: read USENET news — Chapter 8

There are many news readers programs, each with different ways for doing the same things. Many are similar to nn. If you're not using nn, check your documentation for the actual commands.

Selection Mode Commands

a-z:	select article or group
SPACE:	move to next item
<	move back a page
>	move forward a page
K	kill or auto-select items
N	move to next newsgroup
Q	quit
U	unsubscribe or subscribe

Books That Help People Get More Out of Computers

Please send me the following:

☐ A free catalog of titles.

☐ A list of Bookstores in my area that carry your books (U.S. and Canada only).

☐ A list of book distributors outside the U.S. and Canada.

☐ Information about consulting services for documentation or programming.

☐ Information about bundling books with my product.

☐ On-line descriptions of your books.

Name

Address

City

State, ZIP

Country

Phone

Email Address
(Internet or Uunet)

nn: read USENET news *Chapter 8*

Reading Mode Commands

SPACE:	move to next page or next selected article
BACKSPACE:	move to previous page
=	go to selection mode
f	start follow-up posting
k	skip remainder of thread
K	kill or auto-select
p	move to previous article
r	reply to article via email
s	save article in file
U	subscribe/unsubscribe to current group
Q	quit

archie: find FTP archive *Chapter 9*

Public Archie Servers

telnet archie.rutgers.edu ; login as "archie"
telnet archie.sura.net ; login as "archie"
telnet archie.unl.edu ; login as "archie"
telnet archie.ans.net ; login as "archie"
telnet archie.mcgill.ca ; login as "archie"

Archie Commands

mail	mail result of last search back to you
prog	search for a file by name
quit	exit program
show search	show current search type
set search	change search type (to exact, regexp, case, or subcase)
whatis	search through descriptive index

Gopher: menu-based Internet searching utility *Chapter 11*

Public Servers:

telnet gopher.uiuc.edu ; login as "gopher"
telnet consultant.micro.umn.edu ; login as "gopher"

Subcommands:

<number>	select an item from the menu
q	quit from Gopher
u	return to previous item
m	mail an item to you
s	save an item in a file

WAIS: subject searches through selected archives *Chapter 12*

Public Servers:

telnet quake.think.com ; login as "wais"
telnet nnsc.nsf.net ; login as "wais"

WWW: World-Wide Web: hypertext searches *Chapter 13*

Public Servers:

telnet info.cern.ch

Subcommands:

<number>	select a link
find	search indexed database
help	go to introductory help page
home	return to home page
back	return to previous page
next	read next item in sequence
ret	return to a previous page
RETURN	go to next page of current document

COPYRIGHT © 1992, O'REILLY & ASSOCIATES, INC.

The Whole Internet User's Guide & Catalog

By Ed Krol

The Whole Internet User's Guide & Catalog is a comprehensive introduction to the international network of computer systems called the "Internet." The "Internet" is more than just one network; it's a network that's made up of virtually every computer network in the world. Whether you're a researcher, a student, or just someone who likes to send electronic mail to friends, the Internet is a resource of almost unimaginable wealth.

The Whole Internet User's Guide & Catalog covers the basic utilities that you use to access the network (telnet, ftp, mail and news readers). But it also does much more. The Guide pays close attention to several important "information servers" (Archie, Wais, Gopher) that are, essentially, "databases of databases": they help you find what you want among the millions of files and thousands of archives available. We've also included our own "database of databases": a resource index that covers a broad selection of several hundred important resources, ranging from the King James Bible to archives for USENET news.

400 pages, ISBN 1-56592-025-2

TCP/IP Network Administration

By Craig Hunt

TCP/IP Network Administration is a complete guide to setting up and running a TCP/IP network for practicing system administrators of networks of systems or lone home systems that access the Internet. It starts with the fundamentals: what the protocols do and how they work, how to request a network address and a name (the forms needed are included in an appendix), and how to set up your network.

After basic setup, the book discusses how to configure important network applications including sendmail, the r* commands, and some simple setups for NIS and NFS. There are also chapters on troubleshooting and security. In addition, this book covers several important packages that are available from the net (like gated).

Covers BSD and System V TCP/IP implementations.

502 pages, ISBN 0-937175-82-X

About the Author

Raised in the Chicago area, Ed Krol went to the University of Illinois, got a degree in Computer Science, and never left.

In 1985 Krol became part of a networking group at the University of Illinois where he became the network manager at the time the National Center for Supercomputer Applications was formed. It was there that he managed the installation of the original NSFnet. During the same period, he also wrote the "Hitchiker's Guide to the Internet" because he had so much trouble getting information and was sick of telling the same story to everyone.

In 1989 Krol opted to leave the fast lane and returned to pastoral life on campus where he remains to this day, Assistant Director for LAN Deployment, Computing and Communications Service Office, University of Illinois, Urbana.

He has a wife and daughter (who is in the hacker's dictionary as the toddler responsible for Mollyguards). In his spare time Krol is a pilot and plays hockey.

Colophon

Our look is the result of reader comments, our own experimentation, and distribution channels.

Distinctive covers complement our distinctive approach to technical topics, breathing personality and life into potentially dry subjects.

The image featured on the cover of *The Whole Internet* is an alchemist. Alchemy, the precursor of modern chemistry, first appeared around 100 AD in Alexandria, Egypt—a product of the fusion of Greek and Oriental culture. The goal of this philosophic science was to achieve the transmutation of base metals into gold, regarded as the most perfect of metals.

Alchemy was based on three key precepts. The first was Aristotle's teachings that the basis for all material objects could be found in four qualities: heat, cold, moisture, and dryness. These qualities combined to form the four elements: fire, water, air, and earth. By altering the proportion which the qualities were combined, elements could be changed into one another. The seco precept arose from the philosophic thought of the time: metals, like all other substances, co converted into one another. The third precept was taken from astrology: metals, like pla animals, could be born, nourished, and caused to grow through imperfect stages into a fect form.

Early alchemists were generally from the artisan classes. As alchemy gained adhere phers became more involved, and the cryptic language used by the early artisan- protect trade secrets became virtually its own language with symbols and fancif centuries, the language of alchemy became ever more complex, reaching its h Europe in the 14th and 15th centuries. Alchemy was superseded by the adve istry at the end of the 18th century.

Edie Freedman designed this cover and the UNIX bestiary that appears (Handbooks. The cover image is adapted from a 19th-century engravin Archive. Cover design was created in Quark XPress 3.1.

The inside formats were implemented in sqtroff by Lenny Muellne fonts are ITC Garamond Light and Garamond Book Italic. The ill are a combination of figures created by Chris Reilley, and woo Pictorial Archive and the Ron Yablon Graphic Archives, and Photoshop and Aldus Freehand.

System Performance Tuning

By Mike Loukides

System Performance Tuning answers one of the most fundamental questions you can ask about your computer: "How can I get it to do more work without buying more hardware?" Anyone who has ever used a computer has wished that the system was faster, particularly at times when it was under heavy load.

If your system gets sluggish when you start a big job, if it feels as if you spend hours waiting for remote file access to complete, if your system stops dead when several users are active at the same time, you need to read this book. Some performance problems do require you to buy a bigger or faster computer, but many can be solved simply by making better use of the resources you already have.

336 pages, ISBN 0-937175-60-9

Essential System Administration

By Æleen Frisch

Like any other multi-user system, UNIX requires some care and feeding. *Essential System Administration* tells you how. This book strips away the myth and confusion surrounding this important topic and provides a compact, manageable introduction to the tasks faced by anyone responsible for a UNIX system.

If you use a stand-alone UNIX system, whether it's a PC or a workstation, you know how much you need this book: on these systems the fine line between a user and an administrator has vanished. Either you're both or you're in trouble. If you routinely provide administrative support for a larger shared system or a network of workstations, you will find this book indispensable. Even if you aren't directly responsible for system administration, you will find that understanding basic administrative functions greatly increases your ability to use UNIX effectively.

466 pages
ISBN 0-937175-80-3

Practical UNIX Security

By Simson Garfinkel & Gene Spafford

If you are a UNIX system administrator or user who needs to deal with security, you need this book.

Practical UNIX Security describes the issues, approaches, and methods for implementing security measures—spelling out what the varying approaches cost and require in the way of equipment. After presenting UNIX security basics and network security, this guide goes on to suggest how to keep intruders out, how to tell if they've gotten in, how to clean up after them, and even how to prosecute them. Filled with practical scripts, tricks and warnings, *Practical UNIX Security* tells you what you need to know to make your UNIX system as secure as it can be.

"Worried about who's in your Unix system? Losing sleep because someone might be messing with your computer? Having headaches from obscure computer manuals? Then *Practical Unix Security* is for you. This handy book tells you where the holes are and how to cork'em up.

"Moreover, you'll learn about how Unix security really works. Spafford and Garfinkel show you how to tighten up your Unix system without pain. No secrets here—just solid computing advice.

"Buy this book and save on aspirin."—Cliff Stoll
512 pages, ISBN 0-937175-72-2

Computer Security Basics

By Deborah Russell & G.T. Gangemi Sr.

There's a lot more consciousness of security today, but not a lot of understanding of what it means and how far it should go. This handbook describes complicated concepts like trusted systems, encryption and mandatory access control in simple terms.

For example, most U.S. government equipment acquisitions now require "Orange Book" (Trusted Computer System Evaluation Criteria) certification. A lot of people have a vague feeling that they ought to know about the Orange Book, but few make the effort to track it down and read it. *Computer Security Basics* contains a more readable introduction to the Orange Book—why it exists, what it contains, and what the different security levels are all about—than any other book or government publication.

464 pages, ISBN 0-937175-71-4

COMPUTER
SECURITY
BASICS

Deborah Russell and G.T. Gangemi Sr.
O'Reilly & Associates, Inc.

Managing UUCP and Usenet

10th Edition
By Tim O'Reilly & Grace Todino

For all its widespread use, UUCP is one of the most difficult UNIX utilities to master. Poor documentation, cryptic messages, and differences between various implementations make setting up UUCP links a nightmare for many a system administrator.

This handbook is meant for system administrators who want to install and manage the UUCP and Usenet software. It covers HoneyDanBer UUCP as well as standard Version 2 UUCP, with special notes on Xenix. As one reader noted over the Net, "Don't even TRY to install UUCP without it!"

The Tenth Edition of this classic work has been revised and expanded to include descriptions of:

- How to use NNTP (Network News Transfer Protocol) to transfer Usenet news over TCP/IP and other high-speed networks
- How to get DOS versions of UUCP
- How to set up DOS-based laptop computers as travelling UUCP nodes
- How the UUCP 'g' protocol works

368 pages, ISBN 0-937175-93-5

Using UUCP and Usenet

By Grace Todino & Dale Dougherty

Using UUCP shows how to communicate with both UNIX and non-UNIX systems using UUCP and *cu* or *tip*. It also shows how to read news and post your own articles and mail to other Usenet members. This handbook assumes that UUCP and Usenet links to other computer systems have already been established by your system administrator.

While clear enough for a novice, this book is packed with information that even experienced users will find indispensable. Take the mystery out of questions such as why files sent via UUCP don't always end up where you want them, how to find out the status of your file transfer requests, and how to execute programs remotely with *uux*.

210 pages, ISBN 0-937175-10-2

Understanding DCE

By Ward Rosenberry, David Kenney,
and Gerry Fisher

Understanding DCE is a technical and conceptual overview of OSF's Distributed Computing Environment for programmers and technical managers, marketing and sales people. Unlike many O'Reilly & Associates books, *Understanding DCE* has no hands-on programming elements. Instead, the book focuses on how DCE can be used to accomplish typical programming tasks and provides explanations to help the reader understand all the parts of DCE.

266 pages, ISBN 1-56592-005-8

Guide to Writing DCE Applications

By John Shirley

A hands-on programming guide to OSF's Distributed Computing Environment (DCE) for first-time DCE application programmers. This book is designed to help new DCE users make the transition from conventional, nondistributed applications programming to distributed DCE programming. Covers the IDL and ACF files, essential RPC calls, binding methods and the name service, server initialization, memory management, and selected advanced topics. Includes practical programming examples.

282 pages, ISBN 1-56592-004-X

Learning GNU Emacs

By Deb Cameron & Bill Rosenblatt

GNU Emacs is the most popular and widespread of the Emacs family of editors. It is also the most powerful and flexible. (Unlike all other text editors, GNU Emacs is a complete working environment—you can stay within Emacs all day without leaving.) This book tells you how to get started with the GNU Emacs editor. It will also "grow" with you: as you become more proficient, this book will help you learn how to use Emacs more effectively. It will take you from basic Emacs usage (simple text editing) to moderately complicated customization and programming.

The book is aimed at new Emacs users, whether or not they are programmers. Also useful for readers switching from other Emacs implementations to GNU Emacs.

442 pages, ISBN 0-937175-84-6

Learning the vi Editor

5th Edition
By Linda Lamb

For many users, working in the UNIX environment means using *vi*, a full-screen text editor available on most UNIX systems. Even those who know *vi* often make use of only a small number of its features. This is the complete guide to text editing with *vi*. Early chapters cover the basics; later chapters explain more advanced editing tools, such as *ex* commands and global search and replacement.

192 pages, ISBN 0-937175-67-6

Learning the UNIX Operating System

2nd Edition
By Grace Todino & John Strang

If you are new to UNIX, this concise introduction will tell you just what you need to get started, and no more. Why wade through a 600-page book when you can begin working productively in a matter of minutes?

Topics covered include:

• Logging in and logging out
• Managing UNIX files and directories
• Sending and receiving mail
• Redirecting input/output
• Pipes and filters
• Background processing
• Customizing your account

"If you have someone on your site who has never worked on a UNIX system and who needs a quick how-to, Nutshell has the right booklet. *Learning the UNIX Operating System* can get a newcomer rolling in a single session."—;login

84 pages, ISBN 0-937175-16-1

MH & xmh: E-mail for Users and Programmers

By Jerry Peek

Customizing your e-mail environment can save you time and make communicating more enjoyable. *MH & xmh: E-mail for Users and Programmers* explains how to use, customize, and program with the MH electronic mail commands, available on virtually any UNIX system. The handbook also covers *xmh*, an X Window System client that runs MH programs.

The basics are easy. But MH lets you do much more than what most people expect an e-mail system to be able to do. This handbook is packed with explanations and useful examples of MH features, some of which the standard MH documentation only hints at.

728 pages, ISBN 1-56592-027-9

Guide to OSF/1: A Technical Synopsis

By O'Reilly & Associates Staff

OSF/1, Mach, POSIX, SVID, SVR4, X/Open, 4.4BSD, XPG, B-1 security, parallelization, threads, virtual file systems, shared libraries, streams, extensible loader, internationalization.... Need help sorting it all out? If so, then this technically competent introduction to the mysteries of the OSF/1 operating system is a book for you. In addition to its exposition of OSF/1, it offers a list of differences between OSF/1 and System V, Release 4 and a look ahead at what is coming in DCE.

This is not the usual O'Reilly how-to book. It will not lead you through detailed programming examples under OSF/1. Instead, it asks the prior question, What is the nature of the beast? It helps you figure out how to approach the programming task by giving you a comprehensive technical overview of the operating system's features and services, and by showing how they work together.

304 pages, ISBN 0-937175-78-1

POSIX Programmer's Guide

By Donald Lewine

Most UNIX systems today are POSIX-compliant because the Federal government requires it. Even OSF and UI agree on support for POSIX. However, given the manufacturer's documentation, it can be difficult to distinguish system-specific features from those features defined by POSIX.

The *POSIX Programmer's Guide*, intended as an explanation of the POSIX standard and as a reference for the POSIX.1 programming library, will help you write more portable programs. This guide is especially helpful if you are writing programs that must run on multiple UNIX platforms. This guide will also help you convert existing UNIX programs for POSIX-compliance.

640 pages
ISBN 0-937175-73-0

Managing NFS and NIS

By Hal Stern

A modern computer system that is not part of a network is an anomaly. But managing a network and getting it to perform well can be a problem. This book describes two tools that are absolutely essential to distributed computing environments: the Network Filesystem (NFS) and the Network Information System (formerly called the "yellow pages" or YP).

As popular as NFS is, it is a black box for most users and administrators. This book provides a comprehensive discussion of how to plan, set up, and debug an NFS network. It is the only book we're aware of that discusses NFS and network performance tuning. This book also covers the NFS automounter, network security issues, diskless workstations, and PC/NFS. It also tells you how to use NIS to manage your own database applications, ranging from a simple telephone list to controlling access to network services. If you are managing a network of UNIX systems, or are thinking of setting up a UNIX network, you can't afford to overlook this book.

436 pages, ISBN 0-937175-75-7

Power Programming with RPC

By John Bloomer

A distributed application is designed to access resources across a network. In a broad sense, these resources could be user input, a central database, configuration files, etc., that are distributed on various computers across the network rather than found on a single computer. RPC, or remote procedure calling, is the ability to distribute the execution of functions on remote computers outside of the application's current address space. This allows you to break large or complex programming problems into routines that can be executed independently of one another to take advantage of multiple computers. Thus, RPC makes it possible to attack a problem using a form of parallel or multi-processing.

Written from a programmer's perspective, this book shows what you can do with RPC and presents a framework for learning it.

494 pages, ISBN 0-937175-77-3

Help for UNIX System Administrators

Managing NFS and NIS

Hal Stern
O'Reilly & Associates, Inc.

UNIX Network Programming

Power Programming with RPC

John Bloomer
O'Reilly & Associates, Inc.

Practical C Programming

By Steve Oualline

There are lots of introductory C books, but this is the first one that has the no-nonsense, practical approach that has made Nutshell Handbooks famous. C programming is more than just getting the syntax right. Style and debugging also play a tremendous part in creating well-running programs.

Practical C Programming teaches you how to create programs that are easy to read, maintain and debug. Practical rules are stressed. For example, there are 15 precedence rules in C (&& comes before || comes before ?:). The practical programmer simplifies these down to two: 1) Multiply and divide come before addition and subtraction and 2) Put parentheses around everything else. Electronic Archaeology, the art of going through someone else's code, is also described.

Topics covered include:

- Good programming style
- C syntax: what to use and what not to use
- The programming environment, including *make*
- The total programming process
- Floating point limitations
- Tricks and surprises

Covers Turbo C (DOS) as well as the UNIX C compiler.
420 pages, ISBN 0-937175-65-X

Using C on the UNIX System

By Dave Curry

Using C on the UNIX System provides a thorough introduction to the UNIX system call libraries. It is aimed at programmers who already know C but who want to take full advantage of the UNIX programming environment. If you want to learn how to work with the operating system and if you want to write programs that can interact with directories, terminals and networks at the lowest level, you will find this book essential. It is impossible to write UNIX utilities of any sophistication without understanding the material in this book.
250 pages, ISBN 0-937175-23-4

Managing Projects with make

2nd Edition
By Steve Talbott and Andrew Oram

Make is one of UNIX's greatest contributions to software development, and this book is the clearest description of *make* ever written. Even the smallest software project typically involves a number of files that depend upon each other in various ways. If you modify one or more source files, you must relink the program after recompiling some, but not necessarily all, of the sources.

Make greatly simplifies this process. By recording the relationships between sets of files, *make* can automatically perform all the necessary updating. The 2nd Edition of this book describes all the basic features of *make* and provides guidelines on meeting the needs of large, modern projects.
152 pages, ISBN 0-937175-90-0

Checking C Programs with lint

By Ian F. Darwin

The *lint* program checker has proven itself time and again to be one of the best tools for finding portability problems and certain types of coding errors in C programs. *lint* verifies a program or program segments against standard libraries, checks the code for common portability errors, and tests the programming against some tried and true guidelines. *lint*ing your code is a necessary (though not sufficient) step in writing clean, portable, effective programs. This book introduces you to *lint*, guides you through running it on your programs and helps you to interpret *lint*'s output.

"Short, useful, and to the point. I recommend it for self-study to all involved with C in a UNIX environment."—Computing Reviews
84 pages, ISBN 0-937175-30-7

DNS and BIND

By Cricket Liu and Paul Albitz

DNS and BIND is a complete guide to the Internet's Domain Name System (DNS) and the Berkeley Internet Name Domain (BIND) software, which is the UNIX implementation of DNS. DNS is the system that translates hostnames (like "rock.ora.com") into Internet addresses (like 192.54.67.23) Until BIND was developed, name translation was based on a "host table"; if you were on the Internet, you got a table that listed all the systems connected to the network, and their address. As the Internet grew from hundreds to thousands and hundreds of thousands of systems, host tables became unworkable. DNS is a distributed database that solves the same problem effectively, allowing the network to grow without constraints. Rather than having a central table that gets distributed to every system on the net, it allows local administrators to assign their own hostnames and addresses, and install these names in a local database.

418 pages, ISBN 1-56592-010-4

sed & awk

By Dale Dougherty

For people who create and modify text files, sed and awk are power tools for editing. Most of the things that you can do with these programs can be done interactively with a text editor. However, using sed and awk can save many hours of repetitive work in achieving the same result.

This book contains a comprehensive treatment of sed and awk syntax. Plus, it emphasizes the kinds of practical problems that sed and awk can help users to solve, with many useful example scripts and programs.

"sed & awk is a must for UNIX system programmers and administrators, and even general UNIX readers will benefit. I have over a hundred UNIX and C books in my personal library at home, but only a dozen are duplicated on the shelf where I work. This one just became number twelve."
—Root Journal
414 pages, ISBN 0-937175-59-5

Programming Perl

By Larry Wall & Randal Schwartz

This is the authoritative guide to the hottest new UNIX utility in years, co-authored by the creator of that utility.

Perl is a language for easily manipulating text, files and processes. Perl provides a more concise and readable way to do many jobs that were formerly accomplished (with difficulty) by programming in the C language or one of the shells. Even though Perl is not yet a standard part of UNIX, it is likely to be available wherever you choose to work. And if it isn't, you can get it and install it easily and free of charge.
482 pages, ISBN 0-937175-64-1

UNIX for FORTRAN Programmers

By Mike Loukides

UNIX for FORTRAN Programmers provides the serious scientific programmer with an introduction to the UNIX operating system and its tools. The intent of the book is to minimize the UNIX entry barrier: to familiarize readers with the most important tools so they can be productive as quickly as possible. *UNIX for FORTRAN Programmers* shows readers how to do things that they're interested in: not just how to use a tool like *make* or *rcs*, but how it is used in program development and fits into the toolset as a whole.

"An excellent book describing the features of the UNIX FORTRAN compiler f77 and related software. This book is extremely well written."
—American Mathematical Monthly
264 pages, ISBN 0-937175-51-X

10.92